Praise for *Java EE and .I*

MW01102455

"It's a fact the .NET and Java p. touch points. Developers are very eager for information and examples on how the two environments can coexist. This book reflects our interoperability collaboration with Sun and provides best practices for using Web services to bridge .NET and Java applications."

—Dan'l Lewin
corporate vice-president,
Developer & Platform Evangelism, Microsoft Corp.

"This book is a developer handbook for implementing interoperable applications and services. It includes actionable strategies for developers and best practices from the field experience."

—Greg Papadopoulos
chief technology officer, Sun Microsystems

"A comprehensive, practical guide to developing applications that cross the Java EE .NET boundary."

—Bill Smith
director business alliances, Sun Microsystems

"Efficient, effective interoperability between Java EE and .NET is a crucial element in the IT architecture of large enterprises and is vital to running a successful business. This book takes interoperability to the next level, far beyond the cold coexistence of systems, by describing effective strategies that allow you to achieve true interoperability while reducing complexity in your applications and your data center. Additionally, it provides examples and practical advice on how to achieve this new level of interoperability and covers in depth all of the options available from bridging, to porting, to platform unification. The costs that this can save you, from management, maintenance and server consolidation are very significant."

—Yaacov Cohen
chief executive officer, Mainsoft

"A complete and up-to-date coverage of Java EE .NET security interoperability standards and related specifications."

—Hubert A. Le Van Gong
architect, Sun Microsystems, and the
coauthor of "Web SSO MEX Specification"

JAVA EE AND .NET INTEROPERABILITY

JAVA EE AND .NET INTEROPERABILITY

INTEROPERABILITY

Integration Strategies, Patterns, and Best Practices

Marina Fisher
Ray Lai
Sonu Sharma
Laurence Moroney

Sun Microsystems Press
A Prentice Hall Title

PRENTICE
HALL

Upper Saddle River, NJ • Boston • Indianapolis • San Francisco
New York • Toronto • Montreal • London • Munich • Paris • Madrid
Cape Town • Sydney • Tokyo • Singapore • Mexico City

The publisher offers excellent discounts on this book when ordered in quantity for bulk purchases or special sales, which may include electronic versions and/or custom covers and content particular to your business, training goals, marketing focus, and branding interests. For more information, please contact:

U. S. Corporate and Government Sales
(800) 382-3419
corpsales@pearsontechgroup.com

For sales outside the United States, please contact:
International Sales
international@pearsoned.com

The Safari® Enabled icon on the cover of your favorite technology book means the book is available through Safari Bookshelf. When you buy this book, you get free access to the online edition for 45 days. Safari Bookshelf is an electronic reference library that lets you easily search thousands of technical books, find code samples, download chapters, and access technical information whenever and wherever you need it.

To gain 45-day Safari Enabled access to this book:
• Go to http://www.awprofessional.com/safarienabled
• Complete the brief registration form
• Enter the coupon code 42NE-CTTL-BRFX-KHLA-1H7Y

If you have difficulty registering on Safari Bookshelf or accessing the online edition, please e-mail customer-service@safaribooksonline.com.

Visit us on the Web: www.prenhallprofessional.com

Copyright © 2006 Sun Microsystems, Inc.

All rights reserved. Printed in the United States of America. This publication is protected by copyright, and permission must be obtained from the publisher prior to any prohibited reproduction, storage in a retrieval system, or transmission in any form or by any means, electronic, mechanical, photocopying, recording, or likewise. For information regarding permissions, write to:
Pearson Education, Inc.
Rights and Contracts Department
One Lake Street
Upper Saddle River, NJ 07458
Fax: (201) 236-3290

ISBN 0-13-147223-2
Text printed in the United States on recycled paper at R.R. Donnelley in Crawfordsville, IN.
First printing, April 2006

Library of Congress Cataloging-in-Publication Data

Java EE and .NET interoperability : integration strategies, patterns, and best practices / Marina Fisher ... [et al.].
    p. cm.
  Includes bibliographical references and index.
  ISBN 0-13-147223-2 (pbk. : alk. paper) 1. Microsoft .NET. 2. Java (Computer program language) I. Fisher, Marina.

QA76.76.M52J23 2006
005.13'3—dc22
                        2006000235

To Edward, Tom, Sofya, Ilya, Alla, and George
For their love, support, and inspiration.
—Marina

To Angela and Johanan, thanks for your patience.
"Let us run with perseverance the race marked out for us."
(Hebrews 12:1)
—Ray

To Betu, the apple of my eyes, Kuttoos and Gypsy,
my two little angels,
Chikki, Moti, Mummy, Papa, Amma, and Appa
—Sonu

To Rebecca, Claudia, and Christopher
Thanks always, you are truly the greatest gift of all!
—Laurence

Contents

Chapter 4
Web Services for Synchronous Integration   *49*

Chapter 9
Messaging

Chapter 10
Resource Tier Asynchronous Integration

Chapter 13
Java EE .NET Security Interoperability 403

Chapter 15
Managing Java EE .NET Interoperability Applications　　509

Foreword

It is truly an exciting time for Sun and Microsoft. Since we announced our collaboration agreement in April 2004, we have made a lot of progress, especially in terms of Web single sign-on to Sun's Java Enterprise System and Microsoft's Windows Server. However, there is much more to interoperability than basic Web services integration. That's why Sun and Microsoft are working on ways for our partners and customers to streamline and automate business solutions developed in Java and .NET.

Our work together on single sign-on is essentially the resolution of what Sun has been doing with the Liberty Alliance and what Microsoft was trying to accomplish with Passport, and subsequently with WS-Federation. It makes it possible for a user to sign in once to either a Java service or a .NET service and—to the extent that identity agreements are in place between subsequent services—the user will not be asked to sign in again.

As a growing number of companies deploy Java and .NET applications in their mission-critical production environments, we will continue to look for ways to benefit our mutual customers by eliminating gratuitous incompatibility and addressing manageability across the two platforms.

This book is a developer handbook for implementing interoperable applications and services. It includes actionable strategies for developers and best practices from the field experience.

Thanks to Marina Fisher, Ray Lai, Sonu Sharma, and Laurence Moroney, you now hold in your hands an arsenal of integration solutions and strategies to address everyday Java .NET interoperability issues.

—Greg Papadopoulos, chief technology officer, Sun Microsystems

Acknowledgments

The authors would like to express our sincere appreciation for the support from all the reviewers and contributors who share with us their subject matter's advices, particularly, Gautam Tandon, Bhuvan Gupta, Abhishek Kumar, David A. Chappel (Sonic), Ross Altman, Akil Arora , Ruslan Belkin, Gerald Beuchelt, Hubert Le Van Gong , Mark Little, Guy Pardon, Sang Shin, Shanti Subramanyam, Jeremy Barkan, John Tollefsrud, and various unnamed reviewers.

We would like to thank Greg Papadopoulos for writing the Foreword for us and the industry experts—Dan'l Lewin (Microsoft), Bill Smith (Sun), Yaacov Cohen (Mainsoft), and Hubert Le Van Gong (Sun), who supplied their valuable endorsements. We would also like to express gratitude to our management—Samir Patel (Sun), George Drapeau (Sun), and Jenna Dobkin (Mainsoft), who supported us while we were writing after hours. Special thanks to our friends who open doors for us, including Ben Lenail (Sun), Mike Preradovic (Intrinsyc), numerous ISV partners, and unnamed hero/heroines who contribute to the contents in this book.

The authors would like to extend their thanks to the Prentice Hall publishing team, including Greg Doench, Mary Kate Murray, Christy Hackerd, and Jennifer Blackwell for the patience and guidance that has made this book project a success.

Marina Fisher

I would like to thank my family for endless support and inspiration, which they tirelessly carried through. I am incredibly thankful to my husband, Tom, who also encouraged me to keep the thread going, and my mother, Sofya, who took care of my dear son Edward through many weekends while I was writing the book.

Ray Lai

It has been quite a challenge to simultaneously work on two books, particularly when I began to have some health issues. It would be impossible for me to have completed this book project without physical and spiritual support from Angela and Johanan. Angela always listens when I need her. I would like to say thanks to Johanan because he will help me write (he wants to write a book on Java 4 when he grows up!). Our Bible study home group (too long to list all the names) always supports me with prayer. They keep me going with perseverance.

Thanks again for Hubert's valuable input to the security chapter and Shanti's to the RAS chapters. Not least of all, thanks for Samir's "ropes" (opportunities).

Last of all, I want to give my endless thanks to our coauthors who worked extremely hard toward the same goal.

Sonu Sharma

I would like to thank everyone who has helped bring this book to fruition. I would especially like to thank my coauthors, Marina, Ray, and Laurence, for their diligence and dedication to this book writing effort that sprang from a "Birds of a Feather" session at Java One 2003. I would also like to thank my husband, Sanga, for his support and encouragement and my son, Rohan, who brings so much joy and happiness to each day.

Laurence Moroney

I would like to thank my coauthors Marina Fisher, Ray Lai, and Sonu Sharma for inviting me to be a part of this fantastic work! I also want to thank Jenna Dobkin at Mainsoft for initially getting me involved in this process.

Finally, I want to thank my wife, Rebecca, and my children, Claudia and Christopher, for being patient with me when I am working hard and deep in the (anti-social) writing mode. Above all, I would like to thank God through whom all things are possible.

About the Authors

MARINA FISHER is a staff engineer at Sun Microsystems. As a Sun Certified Enterprise Architect for Java EE, she provides Sun's Fortune 500 customers with assistance in architecting, designing, implementing, and deploying large-scale enterprise applications. Her background spans across financial, retail, manufacturing, and other sectors, with emphasis on Service Oriented Architecture (SOA), interoperability, and application security.

RAY LAI, a principal engineer from Sun Microsystems Chief Technologist's Office, specializes in financial services and SOA solutions. He has developed and architected enterprise applications for leading multinational companies around the globe. He is also the author of the book, *J2EE Platform Web Services*, and coauthored *Core Security Patterns*. His current technology focus includes application security and JSF/AJAX-style prototyping.

SONU SHARMA is an engagement manager with Client Solutions Organization at Sun Microsystems Inc. Sonu specializes in managing, architecting, and implementing scalable, reliable, and high-performance business critical enterprise applications using Java EE and XML Web Service technologies for Sun's Fortune 500 customers. Prior to working at Sun, Sonu has worked on architecting, designing, and building enterprise solutions in the fields of e-commerce, banking, and insurance.

LAURENCE MORONEY is the director for technology evangelism for Mainsoft where he is responsible for sharing and shaping their unified .NET and Java EE architecture to enable and empower interoperability. Prior to Mainsoft he worked as a Senior Architect in the Reuters CTO office where he worked on research into Web Services Interoperability, Social Computing, and Trading Networks. Author of several books on Web Services and .NET, as well as dozens of technology articles, Laurence is based in Sammamish, Washington.

Introduction
Achieving Interoperability

Business Challenges

It is a common trait for business to have large and diverse systems and a rare one for them to have unified systems. Be it through acquisitions, mergers, staff and policy turnover, or a hundred other reasons the fact remains—they have systems built in different languages, running on different software platforms, and targeting different hardware. Add on top of this the need for businesses to be increasingly more nimble—fueling a requirement for integrated, interoperating systems that can aggressively respond to business requirements coherently and quickly—and you have a major challenge facing businesses today.

A few years ago the typical business data system was a simple, monolithic affair with business assets in a mainframe that were accessible via a tightly coupled user interface. Transfer of assets between domains was usually manual—for example the transfer of an order from a sales-facing system to a realization and delivery system was typically done by an operator keying in details of a printout from one system to the other. The operator herself was the interoperability layer.

Over time as systems evolved, technologies evolved to allow networking and to automatically integrate across protocols such as CORBA. These, however, proved to be very difficult and expensive to develop and maintain.

Today's landscape sees the data center split into two main deployment types. On one side is the Microsoft stack of products, covering everything except the hardware, from the operating system through the software platform to the application, with the Windows Server family and the .NET framework and runtime. Developers have a host of tools that allow them to develop and target this platform and can receive exceptional time to market and cost of development metrics. On the other side is the open family of Java

EE software frameworks, which can run on a variety of hardware platforms and that run applications written with the Java language. With this it has been shown that they offer exceptional *runtime* characteristics. Technologies such as Enterprise Java Beans (EJB) are designed with the characteristics of security, scalability, manageability, and performance in mind and are particularly useful in large-scale systems that serve large numbers of users.

However, getting an effective data center implementation of a product that utilizes these two sets of assets is a difficult process. Development management has often had to choose between the productivity of the .NET environment and the runtime characteristics of the Java EE platform. Having a "best of both worlds" solution was difficult given that there were few easy or cheap ways to get products running on these platforms to talk to each other effectively.

Consider the example of a company whose system is the result of several mergers and acquisitions and has an array of databases implemented on different technologies—diverse hardware for applications; different runtime platforms; and applications of varying architectures. Integrating this system would be a very challenging process indeed.

Enter Web services—abstract entities that encapsulate business processes and expose them via a standard interface. The underlying implementation doesn't matter! In the example just mentioned, each system's data retrieval layer can wrap itself in a Web service so that it exposes a standard interface. Then the development manager who wants to use his junior staff who are great at quickly putting together ASP.NET or JSP pages has an ideal opportunity to make the most of Web services technology and build a front end that can consume these Web services via proxies. It *should* be easy, but it isn't.

Why? Because while standards may be, well, *standard*—different implementers of software that uses these standards and allows you to build software that exposes these standards have done it in slightly different ways. These different ways mean that not everything that is wrapped with a Web service can talk cleanly to everything else that knows how to talk to a Web service. This *interoperability* is not as simple as it should be.

This, then, gives rise to a book such as this one in your hands. Armed with the knowledge that you'll gain from reading this book, you'll be able to go forth into your development team or data center and either solve interoperability problems you're having or, better still, design a system that doesn't suffer from interoperability problems.

Technology for Interoperability

There are several technology solutions for interoperability covered in this book. The first and most obvious one is Web services, whereby you can wrap your business entities in a standards-based layer so that their technology implementation is abstracted. Therefore, anything that interacts with this layer doesn't need to know about the technology that drives it and should interoperate cleanly. It's a powerful and compelling methodology, but it is not without its drawbacks. It is challenged in two main areas—diverse support for standards and performance. Strategies for handling these are used throughout the book.

A well-known and well-used methodology for integration and interoperability is the use of a **messaging platform**. This is where communication between layers is done through simple messages passed through managed queues. Technologies such as JMS, MQSeries, and MSMQ are examples of this. They can make for a very powerful and very performant interoperability layer, particularly where there are real-time requirements.

Another technology, **platform unification**, allows for clean interoperability between .NET and Java EE applications. With this concept the runtime layer is unified, and application developers for one language can deploy their applications to the runtime traditionally used by another. For example .NET developers can rehost their applications on Java EE. As such, the .NET and Java EE applications don't need to go through a separate layer to talk to each other—they are on the same platform and can talk cleanly. Interoperability doesn't just have to happen at the application layer; it can also take place on the resource tier. With new technologies allowing more and more business logic to be driven closer to the database, interoperability problems may also be solved. As the application layers get thinner, the easier it is for them to communicate with each other.

Structure of the Book

This book covers two main constituents of any Java EE–.NET integration. The first one pertains to the integration type such as synchronous or asynchronous, outlining how individual Java and .NET components can integrate using their diverse technology set. The second constituent relates to the quality of service requirements, such as security, reliability, and scalability, essential to meet a Service Level Agreement (SLA) across the heterogeneous enterprise environment. If you take a closer look at the book structure, you'll notice that the book represents a catalog of integration strategies that adheres to the following format:

- **Strategy Name**   The strategy has a unique name that reflects its objective.

- **Problem space**   Each strategy aims to address a specific Java EE–.NET interoperability problem. Asynchronous reliable integration is an example of such a problem.

- **Solution**   This part of the strategy details a strategy design and outlines technology choices.

- **Benefits and Limitations**   Any interoperability strategy has its pros and cons that are highlighted here. For example, ease of maintenance or scalability are common benefits of some of the strategies.

- **Related Patterns**   Industry patterns such as Core J2EE Patterns are used throughout this book to bring those that are familiar to you into the scope of Java EE–.NET integration. Are there similar resources in the .NET space?

- **Example**   Throughout the book, use cases from the WS-I Supply Chain Management Application (SCMA) are utilized to demonstrate how to implement a strategy. Most of the strategies have two sets of samples corresponding to the Java–.NET and .NET–Java communication.

The strategy catalog comprises the core of this book and can be used as a reference manual on Java EE–.NET interoperability. Before delving into the strategy discussion, it is helpful to review the fundamentals of the Java EE and .NET platforms. The emphasis in reviewing these platforms will focus on their interoperability characteristics. Both platforms expose APIs to develop component-based, loosely coupled integration points. The platform overview is followed by Part II, "Synchronous Integration Solutions," which discusses common business scenarios and reasons for synchronous integration. The de facto technology to integrate disparate applications is based on Web services. Chapter 4, "Web Services for Synchronous Integration," demonstrates how a .NET application can discover and access a Web service implemented in Java and vice versa. The synchronous integration discussion continues with the .NET Remoting technology that remains an alternative to Web services and is adopted by open source and various commercial solutions. The .NET Remoting is shipped as part of the Microsoft Indigo Services. Chapter 6, "Resource Tier Synchronous Integration," details database and legacy integration. It demonstrates a simple strategy to build a Data Access Layer to connect to heterogeneous RDMSs, such as MySql and SQL Server. All in all, synchronous integration strategies are useful if you have two systems with tight coupling or strong dependencies. The industry, however, is heavily leaning toward asynchronous application integration.

Asynchronous integrations between Java EE and .NET systems are easier to maintain, less brittle, and tend to be more scalable. Therefore, the majority of the strategies in this book fall under Part III, "Asynchronous Integration Solutions." The first two strategies, Automatic Callback and Response Polling, are based on Web services technologies. They fundamentally differ from the approach taken in the previous section. The main goal of these strategies is to factor out remote calls from the rest of the request processing. The response can be sent via the callback or polling technique. Chapter 9, "Messaging," unveils five distinct strategies that help to automate and streamline the Java EE and .NET system integration around MOM, SMTP, and Enterprise Service Bus technologies. Reliable message delivery is the key differentiator of these strategies. Similar to the previous section, Chapter 10, "Resource Tier Asynchronous Integration," shows how to asynchronously communicate with back-end resources.

Part IV of the book addresses "Quality of Services" for interoperability. It incorporates several chapters that discuss how to implement a secure, reliable, interoperable Java EE–.NET environment. This section encompasses distributed transactions and management of a heterogeneous environment, but most importantly it provides best practices on the enterprise architecture that mitigates security, manageability, availability, and reliability risks. The table here outlines strategies listed in this catalog.

Table 1-1
Strategies Catalog

Synchronous Integration Strategies	Asynchronous Integration Strategies	Quality of Services Strategies
Java Web Service Accessed by .NET	Automatic Callback	Transaction Management with Messaging
.NET Web Service Accessed by Java	Response Polling	Web Services Transactions
.NET Remoting: IIOP.NET, iHUB, J-Integra, Nbridge	Bridging	Secure Object Handler
Data Access Adapter	.NET Adapter	Secure Tracer
Legacy Integration	Web Services Messaging	Web Services Management
	Internet Email	Platform Unification
	Enterprise Service Bus Indirect Data Access Distributed Mediator Data Access Proxy	Management with CORBA, Bridging/.NET Remoting and Mono Interoperability

Aside from the integration and systemic quality strategies, this book discusses how to deploy a .NET application under a Java EE application server and how to manually port a .NET application to Java. These strategies are included in Chapter 16, "Migrating .NET Applications to Java." Each chapter of this book intends to give the reader an overview of the technologies and concepts used by individual strategies. Messaging, resource pooling, threading, and asynchronous programming models differ under the Java EE and .NET platforms. Understanding these programming models under each platform enables the reader to effectively apply strategy within a specific domain.

What the Book Is and Is Not

This book is a *collection of Java/.NET integration strategies* and *best practices*. It categorizes the interoperability technologies architecturally into synchronous integration, asynchronous integration, bridge, and Quality of Services.

Then different business scenarios (including WS-I interoperability scenarios) are used to put these interoperability technologies into context. Standards-based technology is explicitly introduced with examples of using different vendor products, thus enabling developers and architects to build vendor-agnostic interoperability solutions.

This book is *not about interoperability design patterns*. There are better and specialized design pattern books available that are related to integration and interoperability. This book uses a less formal language structure than design pattern when discussing Java/.NET interoperability, with the intent of making the contents easier to read.

This book is *not a programmer's cookbook*. A programmer's cookbook for Java/.NET interoperability usually includes a great deal of sample programs and intensive tutorial on the programmatic APIs to cover the full .NET and Java programming language features. The book does include, however, sample programs to illustrate how to craft a design strategy.

This book is *not a summary of interoperability standard specifications*. The goal was to keep the contents concise and short, so instead, URLs and references to interoperability literature and standards specification are included.

Who Should Read the Book

This book is targeted at *novice, practicing .NET and Java developers*. For novice developers, there are code samples for each integration and interoperability strategy, which are structured in the form of **Problem/Solution/Example**. This provides developers with a quick start for building interoperable solutions and allows for design reuse. For practicing developers, the "Best Practices and Pitfalls" sections highlight many "gotchas" from field experience. They can benefit from learning from the success or failure of others' past experience.

This book is also extremely useful to *architects and IT managers*. The text includes extensive discussion of emerging interoperability technologies and analysis of what they can or cannot do today. Architects and IT managers may get a brief overview of which interoperability technologies are relevant to their operating environments and can facilitate their architectural planning.

Benefits

This book is intended to provide added values to the readers with the following benefits:

- **Analysis, not plain summary, of the emerging interoperability technologies**   In particular, this book discusses what interoperability technologies work or cannot work and discusses the potential use of the technologies using different business scenarios.

- **Vendor-agnostic solutions**   This book discusses standards-based interoperability technologies and does not emphasize any vendor-specific design or implementation. Vendor neutrality allows better integration and increased interoperability.

- **Design reuse using integration/interoperability strategies and best practices**   This book uses a less formal language than design patterns when describing interoperability problems and their associated solutions.

Summary

Interoperability between Java EE and .NET applications is the "holy grail" in cross-platform integration. It is highly complex, time-consuming, and prone to implementation risks. Many integration and interoperability problems are not discovered until the interoperable solution is implemented. To manage interoperability, architects and developers need to identify the complex, technical issues for their interoperability technologies prior to implementation. It is often an exploratory experience with many trials and errors. This book intends to mitigate these risks by identifying the technology complexity and issues while using sample scenarios, describing best practices, and highlighting pitfalls.

With the availability of many new interoperability technologies such as Web services, you can see that standards-based integration and interoperability technologies become viable and increasingly important. Synchronous and asynchronous Web services have become a preferred choice of integration and interoperability technologies. When compared with earlier literature that emphasized vendor-specific technologies (such as .NET Remoting and bridge), those standards-based technologies provide more design options from which to choose.

Design reuse also becomes a priority to developers and architects. Many one-time integration efforts were made in the past to enable a .NET application interoperating with a Java application. In particular, when a proprietary technology or highly customized solution is used, developers cannot sustain the maintenance and ongoing support, thus this book puts considerable focus on reusable design strategies.

Finally, Quality of Services (QoS) for interoperable solutions denotes reliability, availability, scalability, security, and manageability. Traditionally, application development targets completion of coding and deployment. But, nowadays, with complex interoperable systems, the post-deployment phase and QoS are just as important. Very often, the QoS issues are deeply rooted in the application architecture design. Quality of Services is a key theme in this book.

Errata and Sample Codes Download

Readers can check updates, errata and sample codes from the Prentice Hall book Web site www.prenhallprofessional.com/title/0131472232 and https://javanetinterop.dev.java.net.

Selective sample codes, scripts, snippets, and additional release notes from chapters in the book will be available for download from the above URLs. They are provided for education and illustration purposes, and are not guaranteed to work on every operating system environment due to the changing software versions of the open source software components and any potential issues in the environment setup. The authors provide these sample codes as supporting materials.

Readers' Feedback

Readers can send their feedback to the authors via email:

Marina Fisher	j2eedotnet@marinafisher.com
Ray Lai	johananlai@yahoo.com
Sonu Sharma	sonu.sharma@sun.com
Laurence Moroney	ljpm@sportstalk-ny.com

The authors will try their best to consider readers' input for revision in the future reprints.

Java EE .NET Interoperability

Java EE Platform Interoperability Essentials

According to Tiobe Community research (www.tiobe.com/tpci.htm) as of March 2006, Java was the world's most popular programming language, used widely for Web-based application development in every arena, including finance, transportation, telecommunications, media, and retail industry. One reason Java technology is so popular is its multi-platform nature, which gives it the capability to write an application once and run it anywhere. It has also a variety of interoperability technologies that work with business applications and legacy systems running on other platforms as well as a large development/architecture community that has emerged thanks to open frameworks and democratic suggestions.

The Java EE Platform is capable of interoperating with applications built on the .NET framework. It has a variety of interoperability technologies to cater for messaging, distributed objects, and Web services. This chapter gives an overview of the architecture of the Java EE Platform and introduces the features of the interoperability technology.

Java EE Platform

Java is a programming language. The Java EE Platform provides a runtime environment (also known as JRE or Java Runtime Environment) as well as a development kit (also known as JDK or Java Development Kit) for building applications in Java. There are a few variants of the platform:

- **Java Platform, Standard Edition (Java SE)**   is the core of Java technology used mostly for application development. The runtime environment is widely used in Web browsers to run small applications known as applets. The development kit is used to compile and deploy Java applications or applets and is usually embedded in integrated development environment (IDE) tools.

- **Java Platform, Micro Edition (Java ME)** is a lightweight and trimmed down version of the Java SE. It is designed for mobile devices such as cellular phones.

- **Java Platform, Enterprise Edition (Java EE)**   builds on top of Java SE and adds many features that can build Web-based objects (such as servlets) and reliable enterprise applications (such as Enterprise Java Beans). Java EE is run on an application server. The next section contains many details on its architecture.

For example, you can create a simple Java program `MyInteropSample.java` using a text editor that prints out the simple message, "This is a simple Java application," as follows:

```
public class MyInteropSample {

    // define your variables here…

    public static void main(String args[]) {

        // you can insert your processing logic here…
        System.out.println
            ("Java EE .NET Interoperability Sample");
        ...
    }
}
```

This simple Java application has a structure

```
public class <program name> { ...}
```

followed by the variables and processing logic or methods used in the program. The `main()` method defines the processing logic when the program starts. In this example, the `main()` method prints out a text message.

For more information on getting started with Java, please refer to http://java.sun.com/docs/books/tutorial/index.html. The rest of this book assumes prior knowledge of Java.

To compile the Java program, use the command `javac` as follows:

```
%javac MyInteropSample.java
```

To run the Java application, use the command `java` as follows:

```
%java MyInteropSample
```

Java EE Architecture

The Java EE application program interface (API) consists of a suite of technology components and services that are used to build enterprise applications. It includes components that may be used to build presentation and business logic, APIs for managing business transactions, security and infrastructure tools to support the application operating environment, and tools for both internal and external integration. The following is a list of major technologies provided by Java EE. Refer to [J2EE15] pp 5-13 for more details (see also [J2EETutor] for additional information).

Enterprise Applications and Transactions

- **Components**   Servlet, JavaServer Pages (JSP), Java Server Faces (JSF), and EJB are server-side components that are used to define presentation logic and business logic.

- **HTTP**   The HTTP client-side API is provided by the java.net package, and the HTTP server-side API is defined using servlets and JSPs.

- **HTTPS**   The same HTTP protocol runs over the SSL protocol by the same client and server API.

- **JavaMail**   The mail API provides an application-level interface for application components to send Internet e-mails.

- **Java Transaction (JTA) API**   The JTA API is intended to demarcate transaction boundaries between the container and the application to implement distributed transactional applications.

- **Java Naming and Directory Interface (JNDI)**   JNDI API provides an application-level interface to access naming and directory services as well as a service provider interface to attach a provider of a naming and directory service.

- **JavaBeans Activation Framework (JAF)**   JAF provides a framework for handling data in different Multipurpose Internet Mail Extension (MIME) types, originating in different formats and locations.

Security Services

- **Java Authentication and Authorization Service (JAAS)**   Login context for authenticating and authorizing the serviced requester.

- **Java Authorization Service Provider Contract for Container** (JACC) Contract between a Java EE application server and an authorization service provider.

- **Java Secure Socket Extension (JSSE)**   API for Secure Socket Layer that provides session security for data confidentiality, data integrity and server authentication.

- **Java Cryptography Architecture (JCA)**   A basic framework for accessing and developing cryptographic functionality.

- **Java Crypto Services (JCE)** Cryptographic framework with advanced cryptographic functions to support multiple cryptographic service providers.

- **CertPath or Certification Path**   API for creating, building, and validating digital certification paths.

- **Java Generic Security Services Application Program Interface (JGSS)** API for uniform access to security services atop a variety of underlying security mechanisms, including Kerberos, which are building blocks for single sign-on and data encryption.

Integration and Interoperability

- **Java Message Service (JMS)**   JMS provides reliable messaging for both point to point and publish-subscribe messaging-oriented services

- **Remote Method Invocation over the Internet Inter-ORB Protocol (RMI-IIOP)**   The API allows remote Java calls using RMI over IIOP, which can access CORBA objects or services from a Java RMI application directly.

- **Java Interface Description Language (IDL)**   Java IDL allows a Java EE application to act as a CORBA client to invoke external CORBA objects using the IIOP protocol.

- **JDBC API**   JDBC API provides connectivity with the back-end database systems, which includes connections, connection pooling, and distributed database services.

- **Java EE Connector Architecture**   Connector Architecture is a service provider interface that allows resource adapters connected to Enterprise Information Systems (EIS) or legacy systems to be plugged in to any Java EE service components.

- **Web Services**   This includes API support for synchronous Web services (Java API for XML-based RPC, or JAX-RPC), asynchronous Web services (SOAP with Attachments API for Java, or SAAJ), and access to XML registry servers (Java API for XML Registries, or JAXR). JAXP provides a standard way to parse XML documents and to transform those using stylesheets. Java EE 5.0 adds simpler and broader support for Web services by introducing JAX-WS 2.0 (successor to JAX-RPC) and JAXB 2.0. Refer to [J2EE15Intro].

Management

- **Java Management Extensions (JMX)**   The JMX API captures application events and exceptions for application-level system management and diagnosis.

Figure 1-1 depicts the suite of Java EE technologies in a logical architecture diagram. Client applications can send service requests to the Web Container or EJB Container for accessing business transactions or services. The Web Container provides technologies for building Web-based applications and defining processing logic in the Web tier. The EJB Container provides technologies for building reliable business applications to manage reliable and scalable transactions. The security services are shared among the containers. The integration and interoperability technologies are used for both back-end system integration (such as legacy system and ERP system integration) and cross-platform interoperability (such as Java EE .NET interoperability).

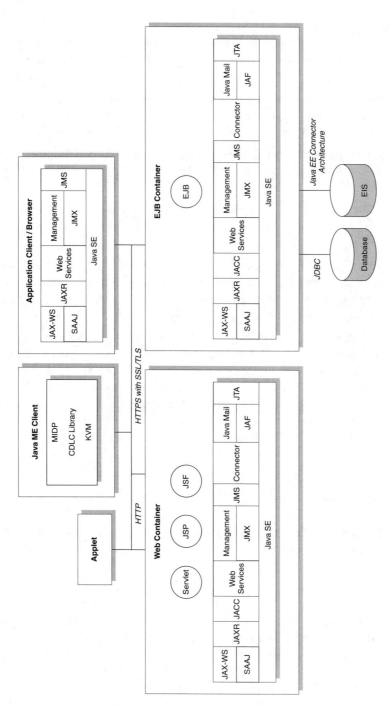

Figure 1-1
Java EE 5.0 architecture

Java EE technologies support a variety of clients, for example—Java EE: applet, Java ME client (or mobile devices), and application clients (browsers and rich clients). These clients can access different service components provided by the Java EE via HTTP protocol or secure HTTPS protocol using Secure Socket Layer (SSL) or Transport Layer Security (TLS). The Java EE consists of the Web Container (usually implemented as a Web server) and the Enterprise Java Bean (EJB) Container (usually implemented as an application server). A .NET client can also send service requests to the Web Container or the EJB Container via a variety of interoperability options such as Web services (which interoperate with JAX-RPC) and a bridge (which interoperates with RMI-IIOP).

Building Interoperable Components

Servlets, JSPs, EJBs and JSFs are programming language elements that can be used to build reusable components for interoperating with .NET or other platforms. Servlets and JSPs are usually categorized as Web components, as they are managed in a Web Container. For example, they can create Web services that can exchange business data synchronously or asynchronously with .NET applications. EJBs are categorized as EJB components, as they are managed in an EJB Container. For example, they can interoperate with a .NET application using an RMI-IIOP bridge. The underlying Java EE services are responsible to provide underlying system services and infrastructure functions for the Web tier (or Web Container) or business tier (or EJB Container) components while interoperating with a .NET application. For example, RMI/IIOP communication service is required when an RMI-IIOP bridge integration strategy is used.

The following provides a brief description of these programming language elements and the underlying Java EE services:

Servlets

Servlets are server-side Java programs that process business logic and handle HTTP requests and replies. A typical servlet is a Java class that extends `HttpServlet`. When the client submits a service request, a servlet receives an HTTP request (`HttpServletRequest`) and an HTTP response (`HttpServletResponse`) in the parameters using the `doGet` method. Data results or messages can be rendered as an HTML page by printing HTML tags of texts and data, for example, `out.println("<html><body> <p>Hello World, Java EE .NET Interoperability</p></body> </html>")`.

Servlets will be deployed to a "context" (a virtual name for the servlets deployed) on the local host, for example, `myContextRoot`, and can be invoked via the URL `http://localhost:8080/myContextRoot/myServlet` where `myServlet` is the name of the servlet. The file web.xml stores information about the servlet configuration, where the actual Java class will be referenced to a physical Java class name (in this example, `myServletClass`) and the URL pattern (for example, `/myContextRoot`). The `web.xml` file is a deployment file, stored in the `./WEB-INF` directory of the Web server or application server.

JSP

JSP is a Java scripting language that will be compiled dynamically into a servlet (and re-compiled again for any changes intelligently), and cached for better performance during execution. A typical JSP may consist of the following elements:

- **Static HTML Content**   This is a normal HTML document, where the JSP compiler does not need compilation.

- **Scripting Elements**   These are simple Java codes that are designed to handle presentation logic, rather than business logic.

- **JSP Directives**   These are instructions for the JSP compiler to process, for example, to import Java classes into the page or to provide special handling instructions for the page when invoked.

- **JSP Actions**   Actions are tags that control the runtime behavior of JSP and manage the responses returned to the client. Standard actions include `useBean` (instantiate and use the JavaBean in the JSP), `include` (include a file when the JSP is requested), `setProperty` (set the property of the JavaBean), `getProperty` (get the property of the JavaBean), `param` (provide the name and value of the parameter as additional information), `forward` (forward the requester to a new page), and `plugin` (generate client browser-specific HTML tags that result in invoking the Java Plug-in software codes).

- **JSP Taglibs**   Taglibs are XML-like custom tags with optional attributes and bodies for a JSP. They can be used to perform simple data transformation, filter certain data content, or to conceal the complexity of accessing data sources and other Java objects. Using taglibs can make the processing logic more structured and easier to maintain in a single JSP and can be included in a JSP by adding a JSP directive `<%@ taglib` `uri="/myTag" prefix="myPrefix" %>`. The prefix denotes a tag library descriptor (for example, `myTag.tld`). The actual Java class is referenced in the `web.xml` with the taglib name and the physical URI location.

JSF

JSF is a draft specification (http://java.sun.com/javaee/javaserverfaces) for new standardized user interface components that manage page state, application events, input validation, and page navigation and that support internationalization and accessibility. It augments JSP technology by providing an interface to the custom tag library within a JSP page. It is also a good tool supporting a Model-View-Controller architecture such as Struts.

EJB

EJBs are reusable components that encapsulate business logic. They make use of the container services that manage the life cycle of the business objects, operate the naming service, and provide transaction handling (for example, connecting to multiple data sources), security mechanisms (for example, identifying the principals and the users), and persistence mechanisms.

There are three types of EJBs:

- **Session Beans** Session beans denote a conversation between the client application and the remote service component. When a client requests a business service by invoking a remote service component, the session bean (the remote component) replies. A *stateful session bean* may determine to persist the session state of the interactions or invocations between the client and the remote service components. If the session state is retained, the stateful session bean can better manage the transaction integrity or resume after the session fails over. This is usually achieved by using the container services such as Java serialization and Java reflection. A *stateless session bean* does not persist the session state.

- **Entity Beans** Entity beans synchronize the state with a persistence data store using the container services. In other words, business data can be persisted to the back-end database reliably and securely using entity beans. If developers explicitly design and specify how business data should be persisted in the database, then the entity bean is said to be **bean-managed persistence**. If developers make use of the container tools, which are provided by the application server vendor, to manage the object-relational mapping from the entity bean to the underlying relational database, then the entity bean is said to be **container-managed persistence**.

- **Message Driven Beans (MDB)**   MDBs allow an EJB to receive a Java Message Service (JMS). In other words, an EJB can be the target of a JMS message. This can bring the benefits of providing reliable, asynchronous delivery of information from the client using JMS to the server using EJB—or vice versa. Besides, MDB can be easily interoperable with other Java EE components using messaging and EJB.

Java EE 5.0 introduces EJB 3.0, which uses annotation (@Stateless, @EJB) to simplify the development complexity and effort in building EJBs. Refer to [J2EE15Intro] for examples and details.

Supporting Services for Interoperability

Java EE containers provide common services that are shared by Java EE components. These system services provide functions for database connectivity, transaction management, naming service, communication and connectivity, and messaging.

- **Database connectivity service**   JDBC.
- **Transaction management service**   JTA.
- **Naming service**   JNDI.
- **Communication and connectivity services**   HTTP, HTTPS, SSL, RMI / IIOP.
- **Messaging service**   JMS, JavaMail.

Among these Java EE services, the communication and connectivity services are crucial to supporting Java EE .NET interoperability using the bridge technology (such as RMI/IIOP bridge). The Messaging service is often used for synchronous and asynchronous Web services integration strategy. For example, SAAJ requires JavaMail to handle document attachments.

Deploying Java EE Applications

Java EE applications are usually packaged and deployed in one or multiple units in EAR file format. An EAR file (depicted in the `META-INF/application.xml` file) consists of EJB components in JAR files (`META-INF/`

ejb-jar.xml), Web modules in WAR files (WEB-INF/web.xml), and Java modules in JAR files (META-INF/application-client.xml). Many application server implementations allow developers to deploy Java EE applications by any of the following mechanisms:

- Dropping the EAR file into an auto-deploy directory (for example, %AS_HOME%\domains\domain1\autodeploy in Sun Java System Application Server where %AS_HOME% is the directory where the application server binaries reside).
- Using an ANT script to deploy (for example, Sun Java System Application Server uses a customized ANT script called asant).
- Using a Web administration console to deploy.
- Using a command line interface (for example, asadmin deploy in Sun Java System Application Server).
- Using an IDE such as NetBeans to deploy.

Figure 1-2 shows the structure of Java EE deployment elements (that is, deployment descriptors and the contents such as EAR and WAR files). A Java EE application can be packaged and deployed in an EAR file, which in turn can consist of multiple JAR files (Java classes) and WAR files (for Web applications). A Java EE .NET interoperable application written in Java, whether it uses synchronous communication, asynchronous messaging, or bridge integration strategies, is also deployed using the same deployment mechanism (say, EAR or WAR file) here.

Management of access rights for security control is very important for application deployment. The security role is defined in the application.xml file, which is a declarative security feature of the Java EE architecture. An application deployment tool will copy all EAR files to the Java EE application server, generate any necessary implementation classes and help documentation, and deploy the application EAR files to the deployment directory of the Java EE application server. After that, architects and developers need to configure the application server-specific information, such as creating data sources and connection factories and administer JMS queue names.

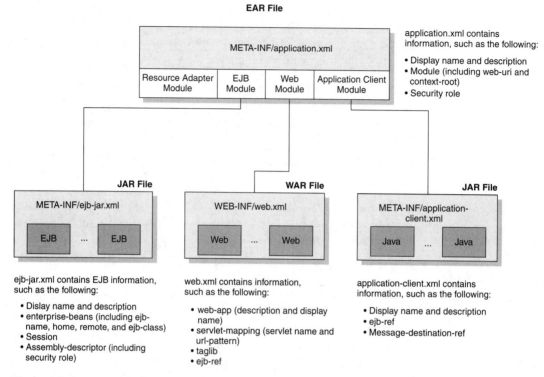

Figure 1-2
Java EE application deployment structure

Interoperability Capabilities

This section introduces major interoperability capabilities provided by Java EE Platform and discusses how these technologies can be applied to address Java EE .NET interoperability requirements.

Messaging

JMS provides a reliable asynchronous messaging between loosely coupled components with connection management and session management. For point-to-point messaging, a JMS producer issues a "send" command to transmit business data or service request in a pre-defined message format asynchronously to the JMS queue. The JMS consumer then issues a "receive" command to receive the message. However, JMS is an abstraction API, and it requires both ends (the producer and the consumer) to share the same underlying data transport and compatible physical implementation (such as the same middleware implementation).

Please note that Microsoft Message Queuing (MSMQ) does not use the same data transport or physical implementation as JMS products. Thus, it is not feasible for a .NET application to send a service request to the JMS queue via MSMQ and route to a Java application using JMS. For a .NET application to connect to a JMS queue, it is possible to wrap the JMS client (whether consumer or producer) with an ActiveX control. In such a way, the JMS client can act as an ActiveX control object that can send or return business data to a .NET application. Refer to Figure 1-3. [DotNetMQ] discusses an example of how WebSphere MQ uses an ActiveX control to interoperate with a .NET application.

Distributed Objects

RMI-IIOP with the Java Interface Description Language (IDL) provides a standard interface to discover and invoke distributed objects and CORBA services. The RMI-IIOP protocol and the Java IDL are means to invoke CORBA objects dynamically and remotely.

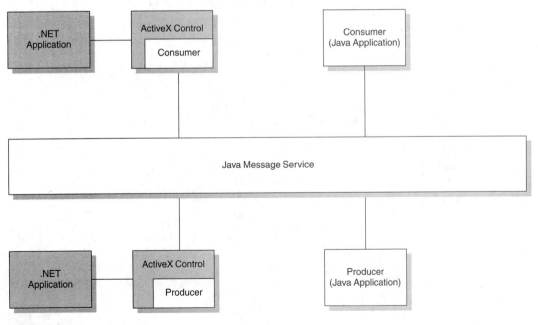

Figure 1-3
Interoperability capability for messaging using JMS

Java technology can also integrate and interoperate with the .NET plat-form. Java Native Interface (JNI) is a commonly used approach to integrate with C# programs. Developers can generate a JNI stub with a C header file, where JNI will communicate with C++ code, and the C++ code will invoke C# code. With this approach, Java clients initiate the remote C# applications. A COM bridge (Java SE 1.4.2) or a JavaBeans bridge for ActiveX (JRE 1.4.1) also can be used. The COM-ActiveX-OLE container will be able to capture application events fired by JavaBeans. JavaBeans can also act as a server for COM-ActiveX-OLE method invocation. Refer to [FisherSharma] for more details.

Web Services

Java APIs for XML-based Remote Procedure Call (JAX-RPC) enables a Java application to invoke a remote Web service synchronously using a remote procedure call mechanism. The client application can use a standard service definition (as defined in Web Services Definition Language or WSDL) to invoke remote business service or to reply with the data result. A JAX-RPC client stub maps the service request to data types specified in the WSDL file and invokes RPC calls via the service proxy. The server tie (service provider) receives the service request, maps the service request to the local data types, and processes the service request.

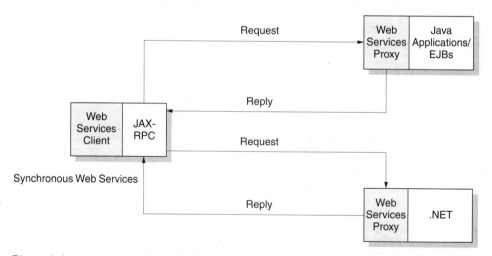

Figure 1-4

Interoperability using Web services—JAX-RPC

The example in Figure 1-4 depicts how a .NET application exchanges business data with another Java application using JAX-RPC synchronous Web services. In the Java EE .NET interoperability scenario, the client can be a JAX-RPC client issuing a service request to a .NET application. JAX-RPC decouples the business services from the underlying data transport, which simplifies the interoperability between the different underlying data transport in both platforms.

JAX-RPC version 1.1 provides the framework for exchanging SOAP messages. However, it does not handle SOAP messages with attachment, which includes large graphic objects or documents. Several mechanisms are used to encode the attachment (such as base64 binary encoding), but none of them is truly interoperable across platforms. SOAP with attachment has been problematic between Java and .NET platforms. Message Transmission Optimization Mechanism (SOAP MTOM) is a draft W3C specification that addresses SOAP with attachment. Java API for XML Web Services (JAX-WS) version 2.0 is a successor to JAX-RPC version 1.1 and is renamed from JAX-RPC to JAX-WS (refer to https://jax-rpc.dev.java.net/ for details). SAAJ provides a lightweight messaging capability for Web services components, including legacy systems. Unlike JMS, SAAJ does not have reliable messaging capabilities due to the nature of the underlying SOAP over HTTP protocol. However, it is more flexible to interoperate and work with a non-Java platform using asynchronous messaging.

Business Process Integration

Java Business Integration or JBI (www.jcp.org/en/jsr/detail?id=208), as specified in JSR 208, defines a framework to orchestrate different business processes. Sun releases early access versions of the reference implementation under http://java.sun.com/developer/earlyAccess/jbi/. Figure 1-5 depicts an example where JBI can connect a Java-based Web service to another .NET Web service. In this sample scenario, the middleware Enterprise Service Bus (also refer to Chapter 9, "Messaging," for details on Enterprise Service Bus) provides a multi-messaging protocol support for both the .NET client and the Java client.

The NET client may be using MSMQ or SOAP-based XML Web services to issue a service request. The Enterprise Service Bus acts as an intermediary and routes the service request to Business Service 1. The incoming service request ("IN") is processed in Business Service 1 and output ("OUT") to the Business Service 2. Business Service 2 processes the incoming service request (from the "OUT" of Business Service 1) and returns the result to the

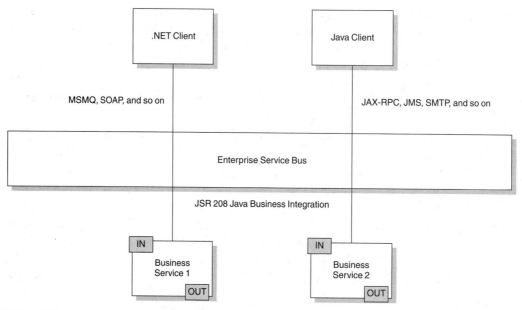

Figure 1-5
Interoperability using Java Business Integration

Enterprise Service Bus. Both Business Service 1 and Business Service 2 are using the protocol specification defined in JSR 208. Upon completion of both business services, the Enterprise Service Bus alerts the Java client to pick up the processing result using the client's preferred protocol (which can be JAX-RPC, JMS, SMTP, and others).

Enterprise Service Bus (ESB) is an overloaded term in the IT industry. IBM defines ESB as a "middleware that unifies and connects services, applications and resources within a business." (http://www-306.ibm.com/software/info1/websphere/index.jsp?tab=landings/esbbenefits). Gartner Research defines ESB as a core component in a Service-oriented Architecture and acts as a "shared messaging layer for connecting applications and other services throughout an enterprise computing infrastructure." (http://looselycoupled.com/glossary/ESB). Some vendors use the term ESB to refer to their current messaging infrastructure products, and some use the term to refer to their workflow products that are JBI-enabled. But in either case, ESB is a core technology that enables business process integration for Java EE .NET interoperability.

Integration with Non-Java Platforms

The integration capability using messaging, distributed objects, and Web services also allows business applications built in Java EE Platform to interact and integrate with non-Java platforms, including .NET and C++. The constraint is that non-Java platforms must support the same integration technology. For instance, there is a C++ implementation for JMS, CORBA, and Web services.

Others

Security and management are two other key interoperability technologies in Java EE Platform. Web services security defines the security framework for exchanging business data using Web services. WS-I Basic Security Profile defines the semantics of the SOAP messages using Web services security. Please refer to Chapter 13, "Java EE .NET Security Interoperability," for more details. WS-Management defines the framework for encapsulating service information in case of hardware fault or system failure. Please refer to Chapter 15, "Managing Java EE .NET Interoperability Applications," for more details.

Summary

This chapter has discussed extensible architecture and various architecture components in Java EE Platform. Java EE also provides a variety of interoperability technologies including

- JMS for reliable messaging
- RMI-IIOP for distributed objects
- JAX-RPC 1.1 and JAX-WS 2.0 for Web services
- JBI for loosely coupled business processes

Many mission-critical applications are built in Java. Datamonitor (http://theregister.com/content/53/31021.html) reported that about 44 percent of the European financial services institutions interviewed use the Java EE Platform as their primary development environment. eBay uses Java to implement their online bidding services and can support one billion hits per day [AlurJavaOne]. There is no doubt that the Java EE Platform has become a critical application platform for business applications, but because it isn't the only platform, it must be able to interoperate well with others. The good news is that Java is more than up to the interoperability challenge. The next few chapters discuss how the Java EE Platform and its APIs can be used to cleanly interoperate with systems running on Microsoft platforms as well as others such as legacy mainframes.

References

[AlurJavaOne] Deepak Alur, Rajmohan Krishnamurthy and Arnold Goldbert. "A Billion Hits a Day." Java One Conference 2003.
http://servlet.java.sun.com/javaone/resources/content/sf2003/conf/sessions/pdfs/3264.pdf

[DotNetMQ] Bill O'Brien Weblog. ".NET and MQSeries." March 16, 2005.
http://blogs.msdn.com/dotnetinterop/archive/2004/11/08/254113.aspx

[FisherSharma] Marina Fisher and Sonu Sharma. "Integration Strategies for Heterogeneous Enterprise Environments using J2EE and .NET." Java One Conference 2003.

[J2EE15] "Java 2 Platform Enterprise Edition Specification," version 5.0. Java Community Process, June 20, 2005.

[J2EETutor] Jennifer Ball, Debbie Bode Carson, Ian Evans, Kim Haase, and Eric Jendrock. "The Java EE 5 Tutorial." Sun Microsystems, February 17, 2006.

[J2EE15Intro] John Stearns, Roberto Chinnici, and Sahoo. "Introduction to Java EE 5 Platform." Sun Developer Network, February 2006.
http://java.sun.com/developer/technicalArticles/J2EE/intro_ee5

.NET Platform Interoperability Essentials

2

Emergence of the .NET Platform

The Microsoft .NET Framework was released in January 2002, shortly after the Common Language Infrastructure, a key component, was ratified by the European Computer Manufacturers Association (ECMA) standards body. A key part of it was a new language, C#, designed to be a simple, modern, object-oriented and type-safe language derived from C and C++. As a result, it bears many syntactic similarities to C++ and Java.

The framework was designed as a long-term replacement for the aging component technologies of COM and COM+, which had faced many challenges, particularly around management and interoperability. The up and coming XML Web services standards were identified as a major future trend by Microsoft and were placed front and center in the design, implementation, and marketing of the .NET framework. In addition to Web services, a number of technologies became key to the framework, such as .NET remoting, ASP.NET, ADO.NET and XML. In addition to this, .NET applications

21

were deployed to run on the Common Language Runtime (CLR), which is effectively a virtual machine that could be run on any platform. A benefit of this approach is that it allows for a multi-language development environment, where the code that runs on the CLR is an intermediate language compiled identically from C#, VB.NET, or other .NET languages. Therefore, an application might consist of code written in multiple languages. The CLR also implements a Just-In-Time (JIT) compiler that converts this intermediate language into native machine code for execution. At present, Microsoft has released the CLR for the various Windows platforms as well as an implementation called Rotor for FreeBSD.

An interesting offshoot of the .NET Framework is the independently developed and maintained Mono framework. This is a multi-platform, open-source implementation of many of the .NET Framework namespaces and tools that allows developers to build applications using C# and run them on a variety of platforms including MacOS and Linux. It is built upon the open ECMA standards that .NET is based on, and as such applications written for it are closely compatible with those written on the original .NET as far as interoperability is concerned.

This chapter provides a tour of the .NET Framework, looking at the underlying architecture and how it works. It includes a tour of the CLR as well as an overview of the programming framework, in particular the technologies for interoperability that it encompasses.

The Common Language Infrastructure and Runtime

The .NET Framework was designed to replace technologies such as COM (and its derivative ActiveX) and COM+. These technologies, while powerful, had many challenges, and with the emerging importance of the Internet, these challenges were proving too difficult to overcome. COM was a registry-intensive technology that only worked on Windows and that led to many configuration and installation problems. To use a COM component would require an installation, and the formation of several footprints within the Windows system registry that would allow the component to be referenced. It provided no sandbox for security after installation—so once a component was installed, it could literally do anything. As a result, it became inappropriate for many Web applications and wasn't trusted by system administrators.

The success of the Java Virtual Machine proved that a virtual machine at the desktop could have applications written to run on it, and these applications could be very easily distributed via a network or the Internet. As such, the architecture of a virtual platform is a natural method for running applications when the goal is easy and secure distribution.

Thus the CLR was born. In the .NET world, the compilers generate a language called Microsoft Intermediate Language (MSIL) which is roughly analogous to Java bytecode. Regardless of the originating language, be it C#, VB.NET or J#, the MSIL that is produced for an application is consistent. At runtime the CLR manages this code, providing memory management, thread management and remoting, as well as enforcing type checking and other forms of code accuracy. As such, code that targets the CLR is referred to as **managed code**.

The runtime can be hosted by other, unmanaged components whereby it is loaded into their processes to execute managed code. For example, the ASP.NET technology hosts the runtime to allow for a server-side technology that can provide managed server applications. This forms the core of the XML Web services technologies of the framework (discussed later).

The architecture of the .NET Framework, including the positioning of the CLR, is shown in Figure 2-1.

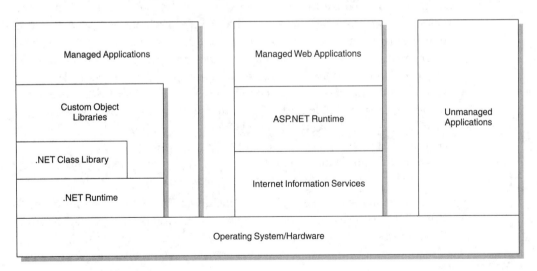

Figure 2-1
The .NET Framework architecture

With regard to security, components are awarded trust credentials based on several factors, such as their origin (Internet, trusted network, or local computer), so a managed component works within a sandbox and may be restricted from operations such as file or registry access, even if it is being used within an application that has different security characteristics. This is termed as Code Access Security (CAS) and requires code to have the requisite permission or credentials to access system resources or other code.

The .NET Framework Class Library

The .NET Framework class library defines a collection of reusable types that integrate with the CLR. It is object-oriented, providing types and classes from which a developer's code can derive functionality. For example, it defines a Web service class, `System.Web.Services.WebService`, from which a Web service can easily be created through derivation. Similarly, many common programming tasks and artifacts are implemented in the framework to improve productivity and ease the task of the developer.

The classes in the class library are divided logically into **namespaces**, which will look very familiar if one is used to using Java packages. These namespaces organize the many thousands of available classes into hierarchies that separate them according to their functionality. For example, if developing Windows applications, the classes are in the top level `System.Windows.Forms` namespace, and for Web applications they are organized under the `System.Web` namespace. For interoperability, Web services are at the heart of the .NET Framework, so a `System.XML` collection of namespaces is available and is separate from `System.Web.Services`—as Web services may be consumed by Windows applications. It is also logically separated as XML is decoupled from Web and Windows applications in that it is a useful data management technology that is separate and independent from Web or Windows applications that may use it.

A comprehensive overview of the .NET Framework namespaces is beyond the scope of this book, but there are many good references, including the Microsoft Developer Network (http://msdn.microsoft.com).

Integration Capabilities in the .NET Framework

COM Interoperability

The CLR can interoperate with *unmanaged* code such as COM components, ActiveX controls, and (unmanaged) DLLs via an interoperability layer. These components have an associated **type library** that defines their interfaces, and in the .NET Framework the tlbimp tool allows for the generation of this interoperability layer. It is important to note here that .NET assemblies are compiled into DLLs for many project types (class libraries, Web projects and so on), but these differ from COM DLLs in that they are managed code, run by the CLR and stored in the global assembly cache (GAC)—as opposed to unmanaged DLLs, which reside in specific application directories or are registered using the system registry. The latter type of DLL has led to the infamous "DLL hell" where different versions of the same DLL may be deployed to the same directory or may be registered over each other in the system registry, leading to system brittleness.

To interoperate with these unmanaged file types, this tool should be used, which converts the type definitions that are found within a COM type library into the equivalent definitions for a CLR assembly. The output is an assembly that contains runtime metadata for the types defined in the original library. Tools such as the MSIL disassembler (Ildasm.exe) may be used to inspect this file.

Using the type library importer is very straightforward. To generate an assembly that allows the developer to interoperate with a COM component whose type library is defined in myComponent.tlb, he or she would issue the following command:

```
Tlbimp myComponent.tlb /out:myComponent.dll
```

This generates a managed component called myComponent.dll that runs on the CLR but interoperates with the unmanaged COM component.

When using COM Interop, either side can call the other (Figure 2-2), and as such, COM can be a server to managed code applications or a client of them.

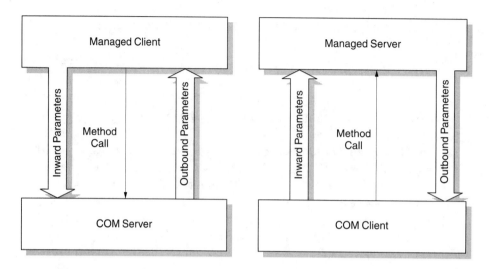

Figure 2-2
COM Interop is two-way.

Platform Invocation

Platform Invocation, commonly referred to as P/Invoke, enables managed code to call functions that are exported from an unmanaged library. It differs from COM Interoperability chiefly in that it doesn't allow unmanaged code to call back into managed code. It is achieved through `DLLImport` attributes within C# code like the following:

```
[DllImport("mycomponent.dll")]
static extern Boolean MyFunction(UInt32 nMyParameter);
```

This is all that is required for managed code to be able to call the unmanaged `MyFunction` API. To call it from the code is straightforward:

```
bool bReturn = MyFunction(0);
```

The `extern` keyword indicates to the compiler that the method is implemented by a function that is exported from a DLL, which is specified by the `DLLImport`. It then understands that a method body isn't expected.

An interesting aspect of this is in the data types and how they are marshaled. The code snippet just listed defines the return type as a `Boolean` (fully qualified as a `System.Boolean`) and the parameter being passed in as a `UInt32`. These data types do not exist within C or C++ with which an unmanaged component such as this one are developed. The respective data types are likely to be BOOL and UINT. The CLR manages the marshalling of these data types between the managed code and the unmanaged code. Note also that the managed code needs to have the data types defined as managed code data types—that is, BOOL in C# cannot be used.

Interoperability Using Synchronous Web Services

Web services are abstract entities that are defined by a document called a Web Services Description Language (WSDL), which is an XML document that defines the location and method signature for a Web service. With a WSDL, it is possible to generate or write code that can call these services based on their described characteristics. The call methodology is also standardized on a protocol called Simple Object Access Protocol (SOAP). The underlying technology used to create the Web service doesn't matter— the interface is standard. By definition, the client posts a SOAP document to the service to call the methods. This provides a number of interoperability benefits. One doesn't need to care about the technologies, simply about the services themselves. As the services are all defined based on commonly agreed-on standards, it should be simple to interoperate with them.

There are a number of drawbacks with this method—namely performance. As Web services are not real-time or close to it, the virtualization introduces a significant overhead. In addition to this, the implementation of the standards by different technology vendors isn't identical and can lead to problems passing data between services that have been implemented in different technologies. These are discussed throughout this book—and solutions are offered.

Web services (called XML Web Services by Microsoft) are front and center in the .NET Framework. They are considered a critical interoperability technology that allows for business connectivity.

One of the benefits of this attitude is that Microsoft has made it very simple to create Web services with their Visual Studio.NET IDE. It offers a Wizard that allows the user to create a simple `"Hello World"` Web service that configures ASP.NET and IIS to run it and automatically generates the

WSDL for that Web service at compile time. The source code for a simple Web service in C# looks like this:

```
public class Service1 : System.Web.Services.WebService
{
    [WebMethod]
    public string HelloWorld()
    {
        return "Hello World";
    }
}
```

To implement a Web service the developer would simply create a class that is derived from System.Web.Services.WebService. If he or she attributes methods of this class with the [WebMethod] attribute, the compiler generates the appropriate WSDL to define this method to external callers.

Creation of Web service clients is also very straightforward. The framework has a tool: wsdl.exe that takes the WSDL of the Web service and creates a proxy class (in either C# or VB.NET) that can be used to call the Web service.

Using it is very straightforward—to generate a C# proxy, one simply provides it with the URL of the WSDL document:

```
wsdl http://servername/serviceroot/service.asmx?WSDL
```

This proxy class can then be used within managed code to marshal communication with the Web service.

Interoperability Using Asynchronous Web Services

Proxies that are generated using the WSDL tool can be used to call Web services synchronously, where their thread is locked until the service returns the method call, or asynchronously, where after the call is made to the Web service, the client continues its operation until the Web service returns and calls a previously defined function as a callback.

To do this in code, the `AsyncCallback` class and `IAsyncResult` interface are used (refer to Listing 2-1).

Listing 2-1 *AsyncCallback and IAsyncResult* Interface

```
private void Button1_Click(object sender, System.EventArgs e)
{
localhost.Service1 myService = new localhost.Service1();
AsyncCallback cb = new AsyncCallback(WebServiceCallback);
myService.BeginHelloWorld(cb,myService);
}

public void WebServiceCallback(IAsyncResult ar)
{
localhost.Service1 myService =
            (localhost.Service1)ar.AsyncState;
string strTest = myService.EndHelloWorld(ar);
}
```

In this case the client, calling upon clicking Button1, defines an instance of the Web service proxy called `myService`. It generates an asynchronous callback called `cb` that defines its callback function as `ServiceCallback`. It then calls the `BeginHelloWorld` method, which has been generated by the proxy as an asynchronous caller to the `HelloWorld` method.

When the service completes, it does a callback to `ServiceCallback`, which pulls the state of the call from the `IAsyncResult` interface and gets from it the returned value from the Web service.

Interoperability Using .NET Remoting

.NET Remoting provides a framework to allow objects to interact with each other across application domains. It provides several services such as activation and support, as well as the important communication channels that transport messages to and from remote applications. It provides formatters that encode and decode the messages for transport on the channel.

There are different types of encoding such as **binary encoding**, which is primarily used for high–performance or text-based XML encoding where interoperability with other remoting frameworks are necessary. In a similar manner to Web services, XML encoding uses the SOAP protocol to encode the messages that are transported between application domains.

The .NET Remoting specification is based on an open standard, as ratified by the ECMA, so Java-based remoting technologies such as JNBridgePro are available.

An in-depth overview of .NET Remoting is beyond the scope of this book, but there are many resources available, including the Microsoft Developer Network site (msdn.microsoft.com) and the JNBridge site (www.jnbridge.com).

Interoperability Using Messaging Technologies

Asynchronous communication between business entities is achieved using messaging technologies such as Microsoft Message Queueing (MSMQ), WebSphere Message Queueing (WebSphere MQ), and the Java Messaging Service API (JMS).

The `System.Messaging` namespace in .NET allows for integration with MSMQ. It provides classes that allow individual queues to be accessed, messages to be composed and retrieved, and many other message queue functions. It also provides formatters to define the message format, and similar to .NET Remoting, provides a binary formatter and an XML formatter. Interoperability with MSMQ to Java clients may be achieved by using the .NET framework to build a Web service that wraps the `System.Messaging` functions and allows them to be called asynchronously as just shown, through SRMP (Soap Reliable Messaging Protocol), which provides an HTTP-based channel for MSMQ messages or using COM and a Java to COM bridge.

To access IBM WebSphere message queueing, IBM has released a .NET assembly that encapsulates the IBM.WMQ [IBM1] namespace that allows WebSphere message queues to be consumed in .NET. Should the Java-based applications run on WebSphere and require interoperability with .NET based clients, this provides an easy-to-use methodology.

Other Technologies for Interoperability

There are several other methods used in different scenarios that can be used easily to allow interoperability between Java and .NET applications.

Data Interoperability

The state and data around applications can be stashed in a database from which either application can read according to defined standards. For exam ple a Java-based application can write information to a database table, and a .NET-based application detecting an update to the table can read the values and establish its own state. It isn't a very efficient methodology but can be used where other methods fail or when the information needs to be stored anyway.

Presentation Layer Interoperability

In many cases, interoperability is a necessity when merging existing applications, as opposed to simply integrating them. In many cases, these applications may have had their presentation layers implemented using different technologies such as ASP.NET Web forms and JSP pages. There are few technology overlaps between the two that would allow for effective interoperability (for example page state or application state cannot be shared), but HTML/HTTP standards facilitate interoperability. For example, HTTP POST calls are standardized and handled in a standard way, so either can POST messages to each other and have them transparently managed.

Code Level Interoperability

A product called Visual MainWin for Java EE (VMW4JEE) from Mainsoft is an innovative solution for porting code that also allows unique levels of interoperability. It is covered in more detail in Chapter 16, "Migrating .NET Applications to Java." VMW4JEE is a plug-in for Visual Studio.NET that allows the developer to code and debug in C# or VB.NET and compile it to Java bytecode for deployment to a Java EE application server. It also allows for proxy generation to Java classes (in JAR files) or to Enterprise Java Beans (EJBs) so that they can be invoked directly from .NET, adding a whole new layer of interoperability. Functionality that is defined within a Java application running on Java EE now doesn't need to have an interface specifically developed to allow for interoperability, with the typical case being that it is wrapped by a Web service. Instead, the compiled Java classes can be imported to the C# project, VMW4JEE generates proxies for calling them, and the .NET coder can simply use them.

Interoperability Using Web Services Enhancements (WSE)

The granularity of releases of the .NET Framework is outpaced by the evolution of the various standards around Web services. To combat this, Microsoft has released periodic updates to the .NET Framework that allow developers to build Web services that can continue to interoperate with new or updated standards. WSE 3.0 contains updates for WS-Security, WS-Addressing, and others.

WSE 3.0 is not just a security extension of the .NET platform. It supersedes the previous releases by adding the following interoperability features:

- **Simplified Security**   Business data can be encrypted and digitally signed using Web services security via a "handler" defined in the policy file. Security policies, which support WS-Policy, are declarative and can be changed without rewriting the application codes.

- **Sending Large Amounts of Binary Data**   WSE 3.0 now supports the W3C SOAP Message Transmission Optimization Mechanism (MTOM) specification, which is basically a new specification to send SOAP attachments (such as video files or pictures) in a simpler and more effective manner. This provides the benefit of reducing the size of SOAP attachments over the wire. MTOM support is a key interoperability feature for Java EE applications using JAX-WS.

- **Support of WS-Trust, WS-SecureConversation, and WS-Addressing**   There are a few security enhancements that provide signature confirmation, opaque security tokens, and the ability to create encrypted tokens. It also supports re-establishing the secure session after the session has been lost or explicitly canceling a current secure session. This allows better interoperability with other service providers, including Java EE applications.

- **Interoperability with Windows Communication Foundation**   New .NET clients using Windows Communication Foundation can interoperate with WSE 3.0 using Web services and WS* (such as Web services security and WS-Trust) security features.

If the goal is to build a Java-based Web service or client that uses any standards that have been introduced in the last few years (such as the ones mentioned here) and it needs to interoperate with .NET, it is highly recommended to implement the application using the Web Service Enhancements.

Interoperability Using Windows Communication Foundation (WCF)

The Windows Communication Foundation (WCF), formerly known as Indigo, is the long-term solution from Microsoft for connected systems. It provides APIs that subsume Web services, remoting, messaging and all other connectivities. It is built around Web services architecture and is designed to provide secure, reliable, and transacted messaging along with interoperability—based on open standards. It is intended to span across multiple transports, security systems, messaging patterns, encodings, network topologies, and hosting models. It will be at the core of the upcoming Windows Vista (formerly Longhorn) series as well as have backward support for Windows XP and Windows Server 2003. Due for release in 2006, WCF is intended to interoperate cleanly with all systems (including Java EE systems), but as it evolves it is worth monitoring over time to prove out its adherence to standards before the decision is made to use or deploy it in a diverse system.

WCF is Microsoft's next generation "unified" programming platform as well as runtime environment that supersedes various technologies including ASP.NET Web services (ASMX) with WSE extensions, Microsoft Message Queue (MSMQ), the Enterprise Services / COM+ runtime environment and .NET Remoting. It addresses the limitation of RPC-based or synchronous Web services, where RPC-based Web services are invoked over HTTP/S (with limited support of transport protocol bindings) and is limited to the request-reply communication model (limited invocation mechanism).

To build a service in WCF, developers need to know the service address (for example, where the service is), the service binding (the data transport protocol such as SOAP over HTTP), and the service contract (for example, what kind of data should be passed). Developers can use an IDE (such as Visual Studio 2005) to build and test their application codes. In addition, they need to define the **services** (for example, type of services or service endpoints), **behaviors** (for example, how the service should interact under particular circumstances) and **bindings** (and binding types) in the file called `web.config` before the service can be created and deployed. Developers can also use `svcutil.exe`, an import and export tool for converting between service meta-data and application codes, to create proxy codes for the client.

WCF does not just add new programming APIs or new functionality. It provides different programming approaches to build services, but not necessarily Web services. (Refer to [PALLMANN] for details.)

- **Declarative Programming** In declarative programming, developers define specific attributes and interfaces, which are the key "data contract" between service requesters and service providers. In WCF, "service contracts" are used to specify session requirements and service operation direction using parameters.

- **Imperative Programming** Using data object models derived from the application programming interfaces provided by WCF, developers can use object-oriented programming to create and access services or extend existing services easily. In WCF, developers can also define "channels" to support a different transport or protocol. WCF channels connect the service model layer with the actual data on the wire. There are two different types of WCF channels: **transport channels** (responsible for sending and receiving data) and **protocol channels** (that implement specific message exchange protocols). This provides flexibility and extensibility for WCF applications to integrate and interoperate with different platforms (such as Java EE applications) that use different messaging protocols.

- **Configuration-Based Programming** Developers can specify part of an application's behavior (such as addresses, bindings, security details, or service behavior) in configuration files. This allows the runtime to make deploy-time decisions about services without rewriting the application codes.

WCF is fairly complex and is still evolving before the final release. It is much more powerful in its interoperability features than WSE or other .NET technologies. For example, WCF supports MTOM, Metadata Exchange or MEX (refer to Chapter 13, "Java EE .NET Security Interoperability," for details), and SAML 1.1. These are fairly significant interoperability features. From an interoperability perspective, it is important to understand that it provides flexible programming approaches to build services and interacts (and interoperates) with Web services implemented in different protocols and technologies. Table 2-1 summarizes the .NET interoperability capabilities of ASMX, WSE, and WCF (refer to [Chappell2005] and [msdn2005]).

Table 2-1
Interoperability Capabilities by .NET Technologies

Category	Protocol / Technology	ASMX 1.x	ASMX 2.0	WSE 2.0	WSE 3.0	WCF
Core	WSI Basic Profile 1.1	Yes	Yes	Yes	Yes	Yes
	SOAP 1.1	Yes	Yes	Yes	Yes	Yes
	SOAP 1.2		Yes		Yes	Yes
Opaque Data Transfer	WS-Addressing			Yes	Yes	Yes
	DIME			Yes		
	MTOM				Yes	Yes
Other Transports and Encodings	TCP			Yes	Yes	Yes
	UDP					
	HTTP	Yes	Yes	Yes	Yes	Yes
	MSMQ					Yes
	Named pipes					Yes
	Text-XML	Yes	Yes	Yes	Yes	Yes
	Binary-encoded XML					Yes
	Binary serialization			Yes*	Yes*	
Security	WS-Security 1.0			Yes	Yes	Yes
	WS-Security 1.1				Yes	Yes
	WS-SecureConversation			Yes	Yes	Yes
	WS-Trust			Yes	Yes	Yes
	WSI Basic Security Profile 1.0			Yes	Yes	Yes
	SAML1.1					Yes
Reliability Transactions	WS-ReliableMessaging					Yes
	WS-Coordination					Yes
	WS-AtomicTransaction					Yes
Metadata, Policy and	WS-MetadataExchange or MEX					Yes
	WSDL 1.1	Yes	Yes	Yes	Yes	Yes
	WS-Policy					Yes
	WS-PolicyAttachment					Yes
	WS-SecurityPolicy					Yes
	WS-ReliabilityPolicy					Yes

Custom WSE-specific serialization, not compatible with WCF.

Summary

This chapter provided a whirlwind tour of the .NET Framework offering from Microsoft. In particular it looked at the two major aspects of the framework—the Common Language Runtime (CLR) and the .NET Framework class library.

Technologies and methodologies to allow interoperability with native system components or components running on Java application servers were also discussed. These included

- COM interoperability
- P/Invoke
- Synchronous Web services
- Asynchronous Web services
- .NET Remoting
- Messaging technologies
- Database layer interoperability
- Presentation layer interoperability
- And code level interoperability

Products such as JNBridge, which allows Java components to interface with .NET services over remoting; Visual MainWin for Java EE, which allows .NET code to be compiled to run on Java platforms; and Java components directly called from within .NET were introduced.

At this point interoperability as a whole (Introduction), Java technologies (Chapter 1, "Java EE Platform Interoperability Essentials"), and .NET technologies (Chapter 2, ".NET Platform Interoperability Essentials") have all been introduced. The next section goes into much more depth and explores synchronous integration solutions.

References

[Chappell2005] David Chappell. "Introducing Indigo: An Early Look."
Microsoft, February 2005.
http://msdn.microsoft.com/webservices/indigo/default.aspx?pull=/library/
en-us/dnlong/html/introindigov1-0.asp

[IBM1] IBM API for accessing MQSeries in .NET.
ftp://ftp.software.ibm.com/software/integration/support/supportpacs/
individual/csqzav01.pdf

[msdn2005] Microsoft. "WSE 3.0 Security: Interoperability Considerations."
Microsoft MSDN, December 2005.
http://msdn.microsoft.com/library/default.asp?url=/library/enus/dnpag2/
html/wss_appx_interopcons_wse30.asp

[PALLMANN] The Indigo Programming Model.
http://msdn.microsoft.com/webservices/indigo/default.aspx?pull=/library/
en-us/dnlong/html/progindigoch3.asp

David Pallmann. "Programming Indigo: The Programming Model." Microsoft
MSDN, July 2005.

Synchronous Integration Solutions

Exploring Synchronous Integration

3

Introduction

There are as many reasons why systems need to integrate as there are methods for doing so. One thing is clear—for a competitive edge, businesses need to integrate internally as well as allow customers to integrate externally to their core business processes. It's a clear trend that companies that can leverage and coordinate their internal business processes to a single platform from a diverse chaotic one can gain a competitive edge. Systems tend to grow exponentially and are governed by factors such as mergers and acquisitions, diverse internal development groups, system purchases, and others. The typical application landscape in an enterprise is an unfocused one. Couple this with the increasing demand for customers to integrate business processes and the ensuing opportunity that this brings, and the need for easy integration is clear.

Consider Amazon.com, a company that has expanded its core database and sales engine to an affiliate network, allowing an extensive network of smaller sites to sell focused sets of products from the main Amazon.com site—with Amazon realizing the transactions. This benefits a new community of affiliated process consumers in widening the parent companies' market shares, boosting business for both, and increasing customer satisfaction—as customers' legwork, that is, fishing through the extensive product lines, is done for them by the affiliate.

The need for integration also operates within the enterprise. Consider another case where a large enterprise has, through acquisition, purchased several smaller companies, each with different processes for managing stock and inventory. For the overall enterprise to be successful, these inventories need to be physically and logically integrated onto a single system. A patchwork of glued code could be put together, having a single master application talk to the other applications on the user's behalf, but this is a poor substitute for a true, integrated process.

It is because of cases such as these that integration technologies have grown. Subsequent chapters of this book delve into these technologies and help provide understanding as well as an appreciation for how they can empower a company to maximize its assets and potentially open new areas for business.

There are two methodologies for integration that need to be explored, each with their relative advantages, but each carrying unique costs of their own.

The first, **synchronous integration**, is the focus of the next three chapters. This form of integration is when the systems enter a locking communication state for the life of the transaction on which they are integrating. A classic example of a synchronous integration occurs every time you visit a Web page—in this case your Web browser is effectively integrating your machine with the server for the purpose of retrieving information on-demand. The browser connects to the server, requests the page, and downloads the page, rendering it for view. It cannot do anything else while it is in this process—nor would you want it to.

The second, **asynchronous integration**, is the focus of Chapters 7 through 10. In this case, the systems do not enter a locking state when they are working on their transaction. One process calls the other and then goes off and does whatever it needs to do while the transaction is running. When it is ready, the callee calls it back and updates it with the results.

Using Synchronous Integration

On the surface it may appear that asynchronous integration is a better methodology, as it doesn't lock either process. This is not the case, however, given that there is really no "better" option. Each methodology has its advantages and its disadvantages relative to the other. The needs of the application should dictate which to use. So for example, there are a number of places where synchronous integration is a better option:

- Applications with a large user base is one. The best example of this is the Internet. You may have a public facing system that people from an enormous and anonymous user base can connect to and integrate with. As such, traffic is difficult to predict. Many times you may have one or two users connecting a day; other times you could have millions connecting an hour. In these cases, a synchronous integration strategy is the best option as it best handles peaks in traffic. An example of this can be seen with the traffic at the humorist site, www.jibjab.com. This site distributes flash animations lampooning political candidates, and their traffic can be seen to leap to five to six times their typical rate upon release of a new movie [JIBJAB].

- If it is urgent that the results of the process are available as quickly as possible to the constituents, then synchronous integration is a better strategy. It ensures, due to its nature, that a process is always "listening" for the others in the integration and can respond immediately to results. When using an asynchronous strategy, this is not always the case.

- A synchronous integration strategy is also necessary when up-to-date data is crucial. When following a synchronous strategy, many clients connecting to a server go through a queuing mechanism so that they get the response from the server upon the server finishing the transaction, and the data they receive is up to date. When following an asynchronous strategy, the data may change between the client receiving the callback and it being processed. As such, by the time the data is processed, it may be out of date. So in the example of time and sales information for stock trades, where for volatile stocks trades can occur many times per second, if calls to query the data are queued, they are ensured of always getting the "fresh" data returned through the session call. In the case of an asynchronous call, the fresh data is delivered, but the client application raises an event for the data to be processed. Having the application catch and process the event may lead to the data being "stale" by the time the application processes it.

There are several technologies that can be used for synchronous integration, which are explored in the following sections and in more detail in the following chapters.

Web Services for Synchronous Integration

A Web service is an abstract entity that defines a piece of functionality. It is particularly powerful due to this abstraction, as the business entity may be implemented with any technology. Commonly, Web services are seen as being built on .NET or Java EE, but there is nothing to stop someone building them in any technology, and there are toolkits available for other languages such as PHP and Perl.

When a Web service is deployed, it is defined using a WSDL (Web Services Description Language) document. This document, built in XML, is machine-readable and allows for processes to infer how to talk to a Web service and how to interpret the data that is returned. The typical scenario is that a developer uses a tool to generate a Web services *proxy* from the WSDL code and then implements functionality to talk to the Web service using this proxy. As such, integration is quick and simple. The consuming application calls this proxy, and the proxy is a standard, automatically generated class.

Unfortunately, this process isn't always as simple as it should be. Different software vendors have implemented how this WSDL should work in slightly different ways, which has led to the interoperability challenges that this book will help the reader surmount. In addition, the Web Services Interoperability (WSI) organization (www.ws-i.org) has been formed to define and scope out the interoperability challenges that implementers face. They define a sample application that branches multiple enterprises and multiple technologies, interoperating via Web services. This application, called **Supply Chain Management**, is used throughout this book to demonstrate the various interoperability technologies and techniques. By stepping through this application and its data requirements and by using both .NET and Java EE technologies, a good understanding can be gained—not only of the methodologies that may be used for system integration using Web services, but also how to build a system using these technologies.

Interoperability Using Web Services

Web services naturally allow for interoperability, but at this point in time they don't do it perfectly and face a number of problems and challenges, which are being defined and addressed by the Web Services Interoperability Organization (WS-I). The WS-I organization provides developers with a framework in the form of Profiles, interoperability guidelines, test assertions and testing tools to test conformance of their Web services. A brief description of each follows:

- **Profiles**   Profiles contain a list of named and versioned Web services specifications together with a set of implementation and interoperability guidelines recommending how the specifications should be used to develop interoperable Web services.

- **Interoperability Guidelines**   In addition to references to specifications or standards, a Profile contains interoperability guidelines that resolve ambiguities or specify how to achieve consistent usage. This in turn increases the potential for interoperability of the implementations of the specification.

- **Testing Tools**   Testing Tools are used to monitor and analyze interactions with a Web service to determine whether or not the messages exchanged conform to WS-I Profile guidelines.

  1. **Monitor**   A tool used to intercept and log interactions with a Web service. This tool generates a log that is later processed by the Analyzer to verify that the monitored interactions conform to a Profile.
  2. **Analyzer**   A tool used to process the logs generated by the Monitor to verify that the intercepted Web service interactions conform to the given Profile.

- **Sample Applications** Sample Applications demonstrate the implementation of applications that are built from Web services Usage Scenarios and Use Cases, and that conform to a given set of Profiles. Implementations of the same Sample Application on multiple platforms, using different languages and development tools, allow WS-I to demonstrate interoperability in action and to provide readily usable resources for the Web services practitioner.

.NET Remoting for Synchronous Integration

Microsoft offers as part of the .NET Framework a technology called **.NET Remoting**. This provides several services for application integration such as application activation, support, and channels for communication between these applications. It also provides formatters that may be used to manage the encoding/decoding of messages as they travel between the applications.

These are all very well if the application landscape is entirely based in .NET and remoting may be used throughout. However, to achieve interoperability with Java EE based systems, a bridging solution between .NET Remoting and Java is necessary.

Chapter 5, ".NET Remoting for Synchronous Integration," goes into several frameworks that enable this—namely

- IIOP.NET
- J-Integra
- IHub
- JNBridge

The chapter uses the aforementioned Supply Chain Management application and demonstrates remoting integration across application and technology domains using these frameworks. In 2006 Microsoft will release the Windows Communication Foundation (formerly Indigo), which supercedes remoting, Web services, messaging, and a number of other communication technologies into a single unified API. As this software is only in early access release at the writing of this book, and as this book covers available technologies only, the text concentrates on remoting and on the third-party technologies that implement it.

Resource Tier Synchronous Integration

Another place where business processes and assets may require integration is directly at the Resource tier. This is sometimes overlooked, but it is equally important to application-level integration. In some cases it can be straightforward—particularly if the Resource tiers of the applications are implanted using the same technologies, but in most it is generally a very complex but worthwhile integration. A successful Resource tier integration can lead to more harmonious applications that access these resources and thus ease integration and interoperability challenges at the application layer.

Chapter 6 looks at Resource tier synchronous integration, going into detail on the persistence layers that both .NET and Java EE offer as well as providing lots of hands-on experience in dealing with these to implement Resource tier access and integration for the Supply Chain Management scenario.

In addition to this, the chapter outlines methodologies for accessing non-database resources such as Enterprise Resource Planning (ERP) and other Enterprise Information System (EIS) entities.

Reference

[JIBJAB] Alexa Traffic Monitor for jibjab.com
www.alexa.com/data/details/traffic_details?q=&url=http://www.jibjab.com

Web Services for Synchronous Integration

4

Web Services Technology Overview

There are a number of ways to describe Web services, but for the purpose of using a standard definition this book uses the W3C definition of a Web service:

> A Web service is a software system designed to support interoperable machine-to-machine interaction over a network. It has an interface described in a machine-processable format (specifically WSDL, discussed later). Other systems interact with the Web service in a manner prescribed by its description using SOAP messages, typically conveyed using HTTP with an XML serialization in conjunction with other Web-related standards.

In a typical Web services scenario, a business application that could be a Web service uses SOAP message, usually over the HTTP transport protocol, to send a request to another service at a URL. The service receives the request, processes it, and returns a response. In a supply chain scenario, Web services and their consumers are typically businesses, making Web services predominantly business-to-business (B2B) transactions. An enterprise can be the Web service provider and also the consumer of other Web services. For example, a wholesale distributor of spices is in the consumer role when it uses a Web service to check on the availability of vanilla beans and in the provider role when it supplies prospective customers with prices for vanilla beans.

Problem

Integrating diverse business applications into a cohesive, reliable, and secure architecture is a common challenge that most enterprises have to address on a daily basis. In the previous example, depicted in Figure 4-1, a wholesale distributor may be a Java EE system, while a product manufacturer is a .NET or a legacy system.

As can be told from this diagram, the application-to-application interaction represents a traditional Remote Procedure Call (RPC), where two systems are integrated using a synchronous communication mechanism. A client receives information on the order placed based on the results received from the Product Manufacturer. Picking the right technology and determining the style of communication (synchronous versus asynchronous) are important success factors.

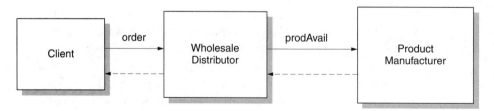

Figure 4-1
Sample scenario

Solution

Web services have become a de facto standard to effectively achieve interoperability across diverse sets of enterprise applications and offer a preferred technology choice for integration. Here is the reason why: Interoperability, simplicity, XML-based human readable format, and ease of use help streamline inter-application communication. Therefore, Web services are widely used for both B2B as well as corporate inter-application integration. Conceptually the Web service model involves the following elements:

- **Agents**   The agent is the concrete entity (a piece of software) that sends and receives messages.

- **Services**   A service is some well-defined operation or abstract functionality that is network-accessible by other systems using its service description.

- **Provider**   The provider is the owner of a service and could be a business or an individual.

- **Requester**   The requester entity is a business or individual that discovers or invokes the provider entity's Web service.

- **Service Description**   The service description is the interface for a Web service and describes the mechanics of message exchange. The description includes the message formats, data types, network location (that is, the URL), transport protocols, and transport serialization formats that should be used between the requester agent and the provider agent.

Web services often used to enable Service Oriented Architecture (SOA), with the primary goal of Web Services Architecture (WSA) being to promote interoperability. Web services provide a means of interoperability across heterogeneous systems, platforms, applications, and programming languages. As part of that, Web services present a useful mechanism for integration of Java EE applications with those built on the Microsoft .NET Framework. When using Web services for interoperability between Java EE and Microsoft .NET, you can gain a lot of architectural flexibility. Because they are XML-based, loosely coupled, and coarse grained—you can design a flexible adaptable SOA. However, Web services are not the "end all be all" of application integration approaches, and there are limitations in using them that need to be kept in mind. The benefits and limitations of Web services for interoperability are discussed in more detail toward the end of this chapter.

Web Service Technologies

Web services are fueled by XML, which, being a markup language, enables neutrality of platform, language, and vendor. XML is also the key to the loosely coupled nature of Web services. A Web service is an abstract entity defined by an XML-based interface, Web Services Description Language (WSDL), and communicated using an XML-based protocol (SOAP) or Representational State Transfer (REST). This is the essence of the Web services value proposition—the abstract nature of the Web service definition, discovery, and communication, the underlying implementation, be it .NET, Java EE, or something else is completely abstracted away from the consumer. Similarly, there is a flexibility of sending SOAP messages over HTTP/S, FTP, or SMTP transport protocols.

SOAP is the technology used for communicating with Web services. While very simple information transfer services can be implemented without SOAP, secure, reliable, multi-part, multi-party and/or multi-network applications are much easier to build if there is a standard way of packaging the messaging information in a protocol neutral way. This also allows the messaging infrastructure (which may be specialized hardware, SOAP intermediaries, or code libraries called by the ultimate recipient of a SOAP message) to provide authentication, encryption, access control, transaction processing, routing, and delivery confirmation services. SOAP envelope (and attachment) structure and header/processing models have proven to be a very robust and powerful framework within which to do this.

Interoperability across heterogeneous systems requires a mechanism to allow the precise structure and data types of the messages to be commonly understood by Web services producers and consumers. WSDL provides a precise description and is the basis of how Web services SOAP messages can be generated for exchange between the consumer and the service. In addition to describing the Web services application interface, WSDL also enables how a Web service is described in a business registry and from where it can be discovered. A business registry is somewhat like an electronic telephone directory, as it contains listings of services and how you can talk to them. Typically these registries are based upon the Universal Description, Discovery and Integration (UDDI), another XML-variant. Finally, the information that Web services interchange can be formatted according to a well-known public XML schema. Depending on the content, there are many schemas available such as Extensible Business Reporting Language (XBRL) and Market Data Definition Language (MDDL).

WSDL, SOAP, and UDDI act as the lowest common denominators for creating and consuming Web services, whereas the service implementing details are different in Java and .NET. The good news is that regardless of one's skill set, each of the platforms provides a means to develop and deploy interoperable services.

Java Web Services

On the Java side, several Java technologies work together to provide support for Web services. These technologies can be accessed via Java Web Services Developer Pack (JWSDP) toolkit or corresponding development tools that might be used to construct Web services. Please refer to [JWSDP] for details and download.

As a starting point, the Java API for XML-Based RPC (JAX-RPC) provides support for Web services using the SOAP over HTTP. JAX-RPC defines the mapping between Java classes and XML as used in SOAP RPC calls. Multiple examples in this book are implemented with JAX-RPC, demonstrating a diverse set of scenarios in which the developer can utilize this technology. With JAX-RPC and a WSDL, one can easily interoperate with clients and services running on Java-based or non-Java-based platforms such as Microsoft .NET. Figure 4-2 outlines key components of JAX-RPC.

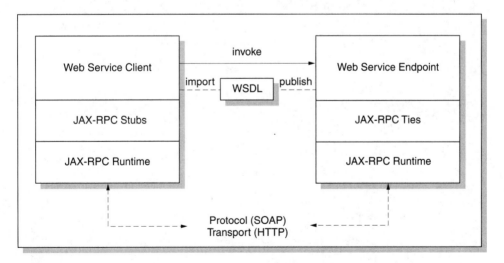

Figure 4-2
JAX-RPC overview

On the client side, there are stubs corresponding to Web services, while on the server side Web services are compiled into the corresponding ties. The underlying message and transport protocol should be the same to ensure interoperability between a client and a server. Please refer to [JAX-RPC] for more details. There are three modes in which a JAX-RPC client can interact with the server. The first one is a traditional synchronous request-response; the second one is a one-way RPC that allows a client not to block or wait for a response; and the third one is a non-blocking RPC where a client can continue execution within the same thread and later block for the receive or poll for the response. This chapter demonstrates how to develop the JAX-RPC request-response application using Java client and .NET server and vice versa.

Aside from JAX-RPC, Java Web Services include the SOAP with Attachments API for Java (SAAJ) [SAAJ]. This API is used to pass business documents (in binary format) by attaching them to the SOAP message. To ensure interoperability of the binary data attachments in the SOAP document, both Java Web Services (via JAX-WS) and .NET offer the SOAP Message Transmission Optimization Mechanism (MTOM), [MTOM].

DEVELOPER'S NOTE

Since the release of JAX-RPC 1.0, new specifications and new versions of the standards that it implements have been released. JAX-WS 2.0 [JAX-WS] is the successor to JAX-RPC and relates to the same specifications and standards, but adding significantly to it. It includes the following:

- JAXB
- SOAP 1.2
- WSDL 2.0
- WS-I Basic Profile 1.1
- Meta Data Annotation for Java (JSR 175)
- Web Services Metadata for Java (JSR 181)
- Enterprise Web Services (JSR 109)
- Web Services Security (JSR 183)

Additionally, it extends and improves support for document-based/message-based SOAs around:
- Asynchrony
- Non-HTTP transports
- Message access
- Session management

As part of the SOA, services are often published in the UDDI registry. The Java API for XML Registries [JAXR] provides client access to the XML registry. The Java API for XML Registries [JAXR] allows access to business and general-purpose registries over the Web. JAXR supports the ebXML Registry/Repository standards and the UDDI specifications.

The Java Web Service Developer Pack also includes APIs to bind XML schemas to Java classes, provided by the Java Architecture for XML Binding (JAXB) [JAXB]. The JAXB binding compiler can be used to automatically generate Java domain objects.

Document parsing and transformation often are necessary operations for Web services. For that you can use the Java API for XML Processing (JAXP) [JAXP] that supports processing of XML documents. JAXP can be used with Document Object Model (DOM), Simple API for XML Parsing (SAX), and XML Style sheet Language Transformation (XSLT).

Table 4-1 contains a summary of common APIs included in the Java Web Services Developer Pack:

Table 4-1
Java Web Services API Summary

JAX-RPC	Web Services implementation and invocation
JAX-WS	Java API for XML Web Services
JAXR	Service registry and lookup
JAXB	XML schema binding into Java object tree
JAXP	XML parsing and transformation
SAAJ	Document attachment

Perhaps the most important feature of the Java EE APIs for Web services and XML is that they all support industry standards, thus ensuring interoperability. Various network interoperability standards groups, such as the World Wide Web Consortium (W3C) and the Organization for the Advancement of Structured Information Standards (OASIS), have been defining Web services standards to allow disparate applications to seamlessly integrate with each other.

Web Services in Microsoft .NET Framework

Microsoft .NET provides two mechanisms for building Web services. The first and more widely used approach to implement Web services is to use the Microsoft .NET System.Web.Webservices namespace in the .NET Framework. A server application might have its methods defined as Web methods using the [WebMethod] attribute. This approach will be used to build a Microsoft .NET Web service for illustrating interoperability with a Java EE client later in this chapter, along with an explanation of the significance of various attributes and directives in WebMethods Framework.

Another technique is to write a custom HTTP handler class that plugs into the Microsoft .NET HTTP pipeline by implementing the IHTTPHandler interface. HTTP Handlers are objects that process requests for individual URLs or URLs with certain file extensions (such as .asmx or .aspx). Building custom handlers requires the use of System.Web APIs to process the incoming HTTP message along with the System.Xml APIs to process the SOAP envelope found in the HTTP body. Writing a custom handler also necessitates manually authoring the WSDL document that accurately describes the Web service implementation. It also requires a solid understanding of the XML, XSD, SOAP, and WSDL specifications. Microsoft ASP.NET ships with a special IHttpHandler class for .asmx endpoints (called WebServiceHandler), which provides the basic XML, XSD, SOAP, and WSDL functionality that developers need to build Web services.

The latter methodology allows for greater flexibility—particularly when there is the need to pre- or post-process the contents of the SOAP message, but for the sake of simplicity the former is used throughout this book.

On the client side, proxies are used to communicate with a Web service. These proxies are automatically generated by the wsdl.exe tool that is available within the .NET Framework or from Visual Studio.NET. These proxies, once included in a project and linked in when compiling code, manage communication with the Web methods that are exposed by the service. They are generated by parsing the WSDL file that describes the Web service.

XML Processing, which is central to Web services, is inherently part of the .NET Framework. For SOAP messages being passed in and out of a Web service, the XML processing is implicit, being performed by the runtime on the developer's behalf. So if a Web method is exposed (that expects a string to be passed into it) while the underlying communication from the client to the Web method is a SOAP message, the code simply receives the string passed in as if it were a local method call.

XML can, of course, be used directly, using the classes within the `System.Xml` namespace [MSXML] to create, load, parse, and edit XML documents, including SOAP examples.

The .NET Framework does not include UDDI functionality by default. If you want to publish or otherwise interact with UDDI servers, the platform UDDI software development kit (SDK) is necessary [MSUDDI]. This SDK implements a .NET assembly that may be used in applications, providing the Microsoft.Uddi namespace.

Following is an example of the UDDI SDK in action where the directory is being enquired for a particular service, and then the business services that match the enquiry are iterated:

```
UddiConnection myConn = new
    UddiConnection("http://test.uddi.myserver.com/inquire");
GetServiceDetail gs = new GetServiceDetail(strKey);
ServiceDetail servDetail = gs.Send(myConn);
foreach (BusinessService bs in servDetail.BusinessServices)
{
  ...
}
```

To handle attachments such as Direct Internet Message Encapsulation (DIME) or Message Transmission Optimization Mechanism (MTOM), Microsoft has a suite of libraries as an add-on to the .NET Framework called the **Web Services Enhancement packs**. These are updates to the .NET Framework that implement the latest WS-* standards in between large scale releases of the framework. More details on the WSE and how it can be used to implement MTOM attachment handling are provided later in this chapter.

For a complete guide on all things to do with Web services in the Microsoft and .NET world, the MSDN Web services developer portal is an excellent resource. [MSDNWSP]

The Microsoft philosophy for software is very much centered around building software as atomic service-oriented components. It is with this in mind that the next generation of Microsoft software development APIs includes a new Windows Communication Foundation, a single API for building software-as-a-service, which adds on to version 2.0 of the .NET Framework. This API, part of a family of foundation APIs (Windows

Workflow Foundation, Windows Presentation Foundation, and so on), will be the core API for building connected service-oriented systems. For more information, refer to the "Advanced Web Services" section in this chapter or the MSDN resource for WCF [MSDNWCF].

Building Synchronous Web Services with .NET and Java EE

The best primer in getting started with Web services in .NET, both from a server perspective (where the service is built in .NET and consumed by Java) and from a client perspective (where the service is built in Java and consumed by .NET) is by example.

The following sections discuss how to build and consume synchronous Web services using both technologies. The example used is a trivial one, passing a simple data type (string) between the services, but it provides the grounding necessary to understand how to build and deploy both the service and the client. Subsequent chapters look into how to handle much more complicated services and clients.

After exploring the Web services technologies provided by Java EE and Microsoft .NET platforms, it is important to talk about how Web services interoperability can be established between the two. This chapter looks into building synchronous Web services communication between Java and .NET applications. WS-I Supply Chain Management Application is used as a sample to implement the interoperability between Java and .NET.

Typically there could be two scenarios where integration is important:

- The service implementation is provided by Java EE, and the Microsoft .NET components need to access this functionality. In this case, a Microsoft .NET client is needed to access the service. In Web services terminology this implies having a Java EE-based Web service provider and a Microsoft .NET-based service requester that communicates with the service provider.

- The second scenario is where a Java EE system needs access to a Microsoft .NET Web service. This would require creating a Java EE Web service client that talks to the Microsoft .NET Web service.

There are dos and don'ts for ensuring Web services interoperability between Java EE and Microsoft .NET. It makes the most sense, however, to first focus on establishing simple interoperability between the two platforms using JAX-RPC and then discuss the best practices that will help ensure interoperability. In either of the scenarios just described, there are basic steps that need to be followed to integrate Java EE and Microsoft .NET-based systems using Web services. These are

- **Defining the schema for the Web service.**

- **Publishing the WSDL**   WSDL provides a mechanism to allow the precise structure and data types of the messages to be commonly understood by Web services producers and consumers.

- **Using WSDL to create Web service clients**   This can be done using tools provided by Java EE and Microsoft .NET frameworks for stub and tie generation. JAX-RPC provides a tool called `wscompile` that generates the artifacts that are required to link a JAX-RPC client application to a Web service. Similarly, the Microsoft .NET Framework provides a tool called `wsdl.exe` that generates the proxy classes that are the bridge between the client and the Web service. This book uses these tools for developing clients for Java EE and Microsoft .NET-based Web services.

.NET clients talk to Web services using proxies generated by `wsdl.exe` as just described. To consume and interoperate with a Java EE-based Web service, the following steps are used:

1. Build and expose Java EE services as Web service
2. Discover the Web services
3. Build proxy classes for communication with them from .NET
4. Develop a .NET client that uses the proxy classes
5. Execute the client

In the next section these steps are followed to build a Web service on Java EE and consume it using a .NET Framework-based application (see Figure 4-3). This application is based on the Retailer interaction in the WS-I Supply Chain Management use-case.

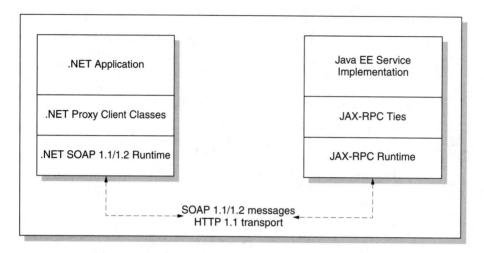

Figure 4-3
Java EE service implementation and .NET client

A Java-Based Web Service with a .NET-Based Client

Now that the basic steps for establishing Java EE .NET interoperability have been introduced, following is a look at a real-world example of how to create interoperable Web services with a Java EE-based service provider and a .NET-based service consumer. Figure 4-4 lists the high-level diagram outlining Retailer services:

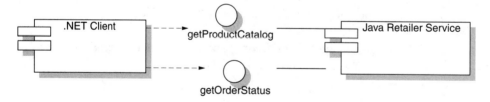

Figure 4-4
.NET client consuming Java Retailer service

Building the Java Retailer Service

Building this application is very straightforward. The following starts with a simple Java class that implements the Retailer.

First is to develop the interface that represents the store.

```
package javaretailer;

import java.rmi.RemoteException;import java.rmi.Remote;

public interface IRetailer extends Remote {
  String getProductCatalog () throws RemoteException;
}
```

The Java class that implements this interface to create the Retailer service is straightforward:

```
package javaretailer;

import java.rmi.RemoteException;
import java.rmi.Remote;

public class JavaRetailerService implements IRetailer {

  public String getProductCatalog() throws RemoteException {
    String strReturn = "We would build a list of items here";
    return strReturn;
  }
}
```

Typically these can be compiled using ant, a freely available tool that can be used to script compilation processes. The scripting is achieved using an XML configuration file called build.xml. A snippet of build.xml that compiles this Web service looks like

```
<target name="compile-javaservice" depends="prepare">
  <echo message="--- Compiling  application ---"/>
    <javac srcdir="${src.java}"
          includes="**/JavaRetailer*.java"
          destdir="${build.classes}" >
    <classpath refid = "compile.classpath"/>
```

```
    </javac>
  </target>
```

ant is invoked and instructed to build the service using the following command:

```
ant compile-javaservice
```

To deploy these as a Web service, the following configuration files are needed.

Config.xml—which specifies the names of the interface and its implementation. The wscompile tool reads this configuration to generate a WSDL for the Java Web service. It typically looks something like this:

```
<?xml version="1.0" encoding="UTF-8" ?>
<configuration xmlns="http://java.sun.com/xml/ns/jax-rpc/ri/config">
<!-- The wscompile reads the RMI interface to generate WSDL file. -->
  <service name="JavaRetailerService"
          targetNamespace="http://j2eedotnet.com/javaretailer/wsdl"
          typeNamespace="http://j2eedotnet.com/javaretailer/types"
          wsdl="http://j2eedotnet.com/javaretailer/WSDL"
          packageName="javaretailer">
    <interface name="javaretailer.IRetailer"
            servantName="javaretailer.JavaRetailerService">

  </service>
</configuration>
```

Web.xml is the standard deployment descriptor for Java servers. For the JavaRetailer service, it looks something like this:

```
<?xml version="1.0" encoding="UTF-8"?>
<!DOCTYPE web-app PUBLIC
        "-//Sun Microsystems, Inc.//DTD Web Application 2.3//EN"
        "http://java.sun.com/j2ee/dtds/web-app_2_3.dtd">
<web-app>
  <display-name>Java Retailer Web Application</display-name>
  <description>Java Retailer Web Service</description>
  <session-config>
    <session-timeout>60</session-timeout>
  </session-config>
```

```
</web-app>
```

Finally, `jaxrpc-ri.xml`, used by the `wsdeploy` tool to generate the WAR file that holds the Web service, looks like this:

```xml
<?xml version="1.0" encoding="UTF-8"?>
<webServices xmlns="http://java.sun.com/xml/ns/jax-rpc/ri/dd"
          version="1.0"
          targetNamespaceBase=
             "http://j2eedotnet.com/javaretailer/wsdl"
          typeNamespaceBase=
             "http://j2eedotnet.com/javaretailer/types"
          urlPatternBase="/javadotnet">

<!-- The <endpoint> element contains the Web Service's -->
<!-- interface and implementation classes -->
  <endpoint name="IRetailer"
          displayName="Retailer Service"
          description="Retailer service"
          wsdl="/WEB-INF/RetailerService.wsdl"
          interface="javaretailer.IRetailer "
          implementation=" javaretailer.JavaRetailerService"
          model="/WEB-INF/model.xml.gz"/>
  <endpointMapping endpointName="JavaRetailer"
                urlPattern="/JavaRetailer"/>
</webServices>
```

The service can now be built, put into a WAR file, and deployed to an applications server such as Tomcat.

Again, this can be achieved using ant. The scripts to build and deploy the application to Tomcat look like this:

```xml
<!-- Compiling classes -->
<target name="compile-javaservice" depends="prepare">
  <echo message="--- Compiling  application ---"/>
    <javac srcdir="${src.java}"
          includes="**/JavaRetailer*.java"
          destdir="${build.classes}" >
    <classpath refid = "compile.classpath"/>
    </javac>
  </target>
```

```
<path id="server.classpath">
    <path refid="compile.classpath"/>
    <pathelement location="${build.classes}"/>
</path>

<!-- Generate BookOrder Web Service components -->
<target name="generate-server" depends="compile-javaservice">
 <wscompile
    define="true"
    keep="true"
    base="${build.classes}"
    sourceBase="${build.src}"
    model="${build.model}/model.xml.gz"
    xPrintStackTrace="true"
    verbose="false"
    config="${etc.server}/config.xml">
    <classpath refid="server.classpath"/>
 </wscompile>
</target>

<!-- Archiving BookOrder components into BookOrder-raw.war -->
<target name="create-war" depends="generate-server">
  <war warfile="${build.home}/JavaRetailer-raw.war"
      webxml="${etc.server}/web.xml">
      <webinf dir="${build.classes}" includes="*.wsdl"/>
      <webinf dir="${etc.server}" includes="jaxrpc-ri.xml"
            defaultexcludes="no"/>
      <webinf dir="${build.model}" includes="model.xml.gz"
            defaultexcludes="no"/>
      <classes dir="${build.classes}" includes="**/*.class"
            defaultexcludes="no"/>
  </war>
</target>

<!-- Creating the final WAR file -->
<target name="build-war" depends="create-war">
  <echo message="--- Building war file ---"/>
  <wsdeploy
      keep="true"
      inWarFile="${build.home}/JavaRetailer-raw.war"
```

```
        outWarFile="${build.home}/JavaRetailer.war"
        verbose="false"
        tmpDir="${build.temp}">
        <classpath refid="server.classpath"/>
    </wsdeploy>
</target>


<!-- Deploying the BookOrder Web Service -->
<target name="deploy-javaservice" depends="build-war">
    <copy file="${build.home}/JavaRetailer.war"
todir="${tomcat.root}/webapps"/>
</target>
```

When using ant it can either be invoked without a parameter, in which case the entire file will be processed, or it can be passed a specific target such as ant compile-javaservice, in which case the commands specified at <target name="compile-javaservice"> are executed.

In the script just listed, the following targets are used:

- Compile-javaservice: Invokes the javac compiler to compile all the java classes needed to make the Web service.
- Generate-server: Invokes the wscompile tool that begins the packaging process for the Web service.
- Create-war: Creates the Web Archive (WAR) file that the Web service will reside in using the war tool.
- Build-war: Compiles the WAR file for the Web service using the wsdeploy tool.
- Deploy-javaservice: Copies the WAR file to the web applications directory on Tomcat.

Once deployed, the application can be run by hitting the context root that is specified in the configuration files. For example it can be run with the following URL if it is deployed to Tomcat (as in this ant script).

```
http://localhost:8080/JavaRetailer
```

To get the WSDL associated with this Web service, ?WSDL is simply applied to the end of the URL, like this:

```
http://localhost:8080/JavaRetailer?WSDL
```

Now that the Java Web Service is established, the next thing to do is to create a client in .NET that consumes this, which is a very straightforward matter.

The first thing to do is to generate a .NET proxy to the Web service using the .NET `wsdl` tool like this

```
wsdl.exe /out:Retailer.cs http://localhost:8080/JavaRetailer?WSDL
```

This generates a proxy module called Retailer.cs, based on the WSDL found at the specified URL. This proxy module can then be used in an application, as follows:

```
using System;
public class DotNetClient {
  public static void Main() {
    RetailerService srv = new RetailerService();
    String result = srv.getProductCatalog();
    Console.WriteLine(result);
  }
}
```

This gives a basic, synchronous .NET-based client that consumes a Java-based Web service.

A .NET-Based Web Service with a Java-Based Client

In this section the Retailer Web service is created using .NET technology and a Java client is built that synchronously consumes this service. The high-level diagram for this is shown in Figure 4-5.

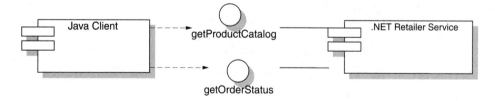

Figure 4-5
Java client consuming .NET Retailer service

The JAX-RPC reference implementation provides a number of tools that simplify building and deploying Java-based Web services. These include the `wscompile` and `wsdeploy` tools. These utilities can generate the Java code necessary to link both the client and server implementations to the underlying JAX-RPC infrastructure that ultimately creates or consumes SOAP messages. Application server vendors also provide similar tools.

Using the `wscompile` tool, it is possible to generate the client side stubs for a .NET-based Web service. These stubs can be used to write a JAX-RPC client for the Web service.

The Java EE model for Web service consumption in Figure 4-6 requires the following steps:

1. Develop and expose a .NET Web service
2. Discover the .NET Web service
3. Build the client side stubs for the Web service
4. Develop a JAX-RPC client using the stubs
5. Run the JAX-RPC client

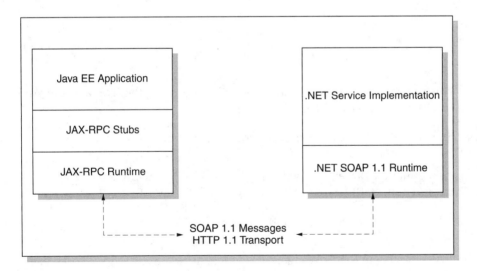

Figure 4-6
.NET service implementation and Java EE client

The easiest way to develop a Web service with .NET is to use the Visual Studio.NET tool from Microsoft. From here, File>New>Web Service is selected to generate a basic skeleton Web service. One called DotNetRetailer.asmx can be created.

Then underlying C# code for this Web service should then be changed to the following:

```
using System;
using System.Web.Services;

namespace dotnetretailer {

  public class DotNetRetailService : System.Web.Services.WebService {

    [WebMethod(Description = "BookOrder Web Service")]
    public string getProductCatalog() {
      string strReturn = "The Product Catalog would go here.";
      return strReturn;
    }
  }
}
```

This can then be compiled and deployed to IIS using the IDE, and the Web service can be accessed with this URL:

```
http://localhost/DotNetRetailer/DotNetRetailer.asmx
```

As mentioned earlier, the WSDL for the service is accessible using ?WSDL at the end of the URL, like this

```
http://localhost/DotNetRetailer/DotNetRetailer.asmx?WSDL
```

To create a client to this Web service in Java, the wscompile tool can be used. This requires a configuration file containing the settings that drive it to create Java stubs for a proxy to this service. The configuration file will look like this

```
<configuration xmlns="http://java.sun.com/xml/ns/jax-rpc/ri/config">
<wsdl
  location="http://localhost/DotNetRetailer/DotNetRetailer.asmx?WSDL"
  packageName="dotnetretailer"/>
</configuration>
```

Point `wsconfig` at this configuration file and it will generate the stubs for talking to this Web service in the package `dotnetretailer`. These stubs can then be used to talk to the .NET Web service in a Java client like this

```
package dotnetretailer;

import javax.xml.rpc.Stub;

public class JavaClient {

  public static void main (String[] args) {
  try {
     DotNetRetailService_Stub stub =
     (DotNetRetailServiceSoap_Stub)
     (new DotNetRetailService_Impl().getDotNetRetailService Soap());

      stub._setProperty(
         javax.xml.rpc.Stub.ENDPOINT_ADDRESS_PROPERTY,
         System.getProperty("endpoint"));

      System.out.println(stub.getProductCatalog());

  }
  catch (Exception ex) {
    ex.printStackTrace();
  }
 }
}
```

This client will now consume the .NET-based Retailer service.

Advanced Web Services Interoperability

The Web Services Interoperability Organization (WS-I)

In the preceding examples, a simple string was passed between the services running on different platforms. With interoperability being a major promise of Web services and with simple demonstrations such as this one showing how straightforward it is—one would think that Web services are the ultimate answer for disconnected, synchronous systems to interoperate with each other. In practice, this has proven to not be the case. Imperfect specification with levels of ambiguity being used to guide the different implementations by software vendors have led to incompatibilities. As such, unfortunately, it becomes the responsibility of the developer to identify problem areas that may lead to incompatibilities in implementation. Typically the interoperability problems arise with complex data types, but a solution of using simple data types to represent them (such as encoding a complex data type as a string, and passing that string as a simple data type) isn't always best.

In large, mixed-mode systems, root cause analysis for failures is an expensive and time-consuming effort. When data is passed on the wire between systems, the developers of each system may feel that they have done their jobs, and any problems are the cause of the infrastructure or of the other system in accepting their data. This is a bad habit that needs to be broken, for just as the mixed-mode systems are expected to work cleanly together, so are their developers. As such, teamwork around a core set of data types to be passed around is essential, and the "fire-and-forget" mentality that sometimes evolves around Web services development needs to be eradicated.

Additionally, the major software vendors have banded together to form the Web Services Interoperability Organization (WS-I) in February 2002. Its aim is to prevent interoperability problems by designing a typical complex scenario, implementing it in various technology bases, and testing interoperability between each thoroughly. Problems that arise are resolved and published in what is known as a **Profile**.

This body is intended to complement the W3C that drives Web services standards. It doesn't produce new specifications but instead provides guidance around existing ones. It has a number of working groups whose responsibility is to produce specific deliverables that assist interoperability challenges. These deliverables include profiles, scenarios, use cases, samples, and testing tools. It is highly recommended that all developers verse themselves in the WS-I deliverables before a large scale implementation of Web services, whether they have mixed mode systems or not. The WS-I information is freely available at www.ws-i.org.

The first profile produced by the WS-I is called the Basic Profile [WSIBAS] and was released in April 2004. It states that conforming Web services need to use SOAP, WSDL, and UDDI and provides guidance on using them properly. It also released the supply-chain management scenario that is used throughout this book as an example, and many software vendors provided their implementations that could be used as a basis for other applications that need to interoperate across mixed-mode implementations.

While it hasn't fully solved the problems of interoperability across mixed-mode systems, the Basic Profile and adherence to it has greatly eased them, and is a perfect starting point when designing systems that use Web services. It isn't intended as a guarantee of interoperability but a guideline of the pitfalls that have been discovered to date and how developers can get around them.

The Basic Profile does not take into account the WS-Security specifications, so applications using it cannot secure the message using XML-encryption or an XML-digital signature. However, the wire may be secured using HTTPS.

To solve this, the WS-I have a working draft of a Profile with security that extends upon the Basic Profile [WSISEC] to take into account security requirements whereby portions of the XML packets being passed between Web services may be encrypted and signed.

Additionally, a further area where interoperability within systems is challenged is when dealing with attachments in Web services. This is addressed in the finalized Attachments Profile from the WS-I [WSIATT].

Assuring Interoperability Using the Basic Profile

As part of their participation with the WS-I, vendors are updating their tools to allow developers to more easily build services that adhere and conform to the profile so that their chances of interoperability are improved.

For example, Microsoft has implemented Basic Profile conformance into ASP.NET 2.0, making it easy for developers to build services that conform. This can be done using the `ConformanceClaims` property on the `WebServiceBinding` attribute in this manner:

```
[WebServiceBinding(ConformanceClaims = WsiClaims.BP10)]
public class DotNetRetailer
{
}
```

Upon compilation and execution, the WSDL document for this service will contain an assertion that this service conforms to the Basic Profile. Should the developer do things in his or her code that breaks conformance with the Basic Profile, runtime exceptions will be raised because the runtime has built-in conformance validation. Finally, the 2.0 version of the `wsdl.exe` tool, which is used to generate Web service proxies, will flag exceptions within the WSDL that it is consuming where they violate the Basic Profile.

Web services may also be tested using WSI provided tools that check adherence to the Basic Profile. They intercept the SOAP messages traveling between the Web service and its client. They then analyze these messages along with the corresponding WSDL definition and UDDI entries and produce a report describing whether the service conforms or not.

Advanced Web Services Technologies

As Web services standards are constantly evolving and improving, the major releases of development APIs such as .NET and the JDK are also being updated and improved with add-ons to keep them up to date with the latest specifications and profiles.

Java EE Web Service APIs

For example, the primary Web services API for Java, JAX-RPC, has been updated and improved to JAX-WS 2.0 (Java API for XML Web Services version 2.0). This helps to limit confusion around JAX-RPC, which by name seems to suggest that it is an RPC API and not a Web services one. JAX-WS is up to date with conformance to the WS-I Basic Profile 1.1, the WS-I Attachments Profile 1.0, and the WS-I Simple SOAP Binding Profile 1.0. JAX-WS will also be the basis of Java-based interoperability with some of the newer Microsoft technologies such as the Windows Communication Framework (WCF, formerly known as Indigo) [SUNINTER]. New features introduced with JAX-WS include simplified development and deployment of a Web service, support for annotations such as listed in JSR 181 [JSR 181]. JAX-WS offers support for asynchronous client through traditional polling and callback mechanisms. Asynchronous Web services are further discussed in Chapter 8, "Asynchronous Web Services Integration," where JAX-RPC API is used to interoperate with .NET application using callback and polling-based strategies. Additionally, JAX-WS is aimed at the dynamic access of Web services via dynamic proxies. This helps to improve portability of an application.

As an example, with JAX-RPC, a traditional way to access a Web service is by creating an instance of a service and then obtaining a client stub:

```
// Obtain a copy of the Web service implementation class
RetailerService service = new RetailerService_Impl();

// Obtain a client stub
RetailerClient rc = (RetailerClient)service.getRetailerPort();

// Invoke the Web service
rc.getCatalog();
```

Implementing a similar routine using JAX-WS would allow your code to be portable, as there are no static client stub components that have to be generated. Instead, the service class is loaded at runtime.

Assuming the Retailer Web service is implemented with .NET, you can build an interoperable client by first generating Java source code corresponding to the Web service. You can achieve this via <wsimport> task:

```
<wsimport
    debug="${debug}"
    verbose="${verbose}"
    keep="${keep}"
    extension="${extension}"
    destdir="${build.classes.home}"
    wsdl="${server.wsdl}">
    <binding dir="${basedir}/etc" includes="${server.binding}"/>
</wsimport>
```

The <wsimport> Ant task is defined through the com.sun.toolsws.ant.WsImport class:

```
<taskdef name="wsimport"
classname="com.sun.tools.ws.ant.WsImport">
    <classpath refid="jaxws.classpath"/>
</taskdef>
```

You can then compile auto-generated source code and access the Web service in the following manner:

```
// Access the Web service port
RetailerSoap port =  new Retailer().getRetailerSoap();
```

```
// Invoke Web service
port.getCatalog();
```

With the JAX-RPC library, there is also a way to dynamically access a Web service. In the previous example of building the Java-based client to access a Web service, static client implementation was detailed out. There are two more types of clients that can be developed with JAX-RPC—Dynamic Proxy client and Dynamic Invocation Interface client. Figure 4-7 outlines all categories of clients that can be used with JAX-RPC.

The next two subsections demonstrate how to build the Dynamic Proxy Client and the Dynamic Invocation Interface (DII) client. You can learn more about building Web services with JAX-RPC and various client types at [JAX-RPC_Env].

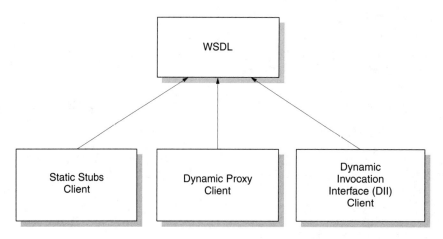

Figure 4-7
JAX-RPC WS client types

Dynamic Proxy Client

The RetailerDynamicProxyClient program constructs the dynamic proxy as follows:

1. Creates a service object named `retailerService`:

```
Service retailerService =
        serviceFactory.createService(retailerWsdlUrl,
            new QName(nameSpaceUri, serviceName));
```

A service object is a factory for proxies. To create the service object (`retailerService`), the program calls the `createService` method on another type of factory, a `ServiceFactory` object.

The `createService` method has two parameters, the URL of the WSDL file and a `QName` object. At runtime, the client gets information about the service by looking up its WSDL. In this example, the URL of the WSDL file points to the WSDL that was deployed with the .NET-based Retailer service:

```
http://localhost/retailerService/Retailer?WSDL
```

A `QName` object is a tuple that represents an XML qualified name. The tuple is composed of a namespace URI and the local part of the qualified name. In the `QName` parameter of the `createService` invocation, the local part is the service name, `retailerService`.

2. The program creates a proxy (`retailerProxy`) with a type of the service endpoint interface `RetailerSoap`):

```
    RetailerSoap retailerProxy =
    (RetailerSoap)retailerService.getPort(new
QName(nameSpaceUri, portName),
        RetailerSoap.class);
```

The `retailerService` object is a factory for dynamic proxies. To create `retailerService`, the program calls the `getPort` method of `retailerService`. This method has two parameters—a `QName` object that specifies the port name and a `java.lang.Class` object for the service endpoint interface (`RetailerSoap`). The `RetailerSoap` class is generated by `wscompile`. The port name (`RetailerSoap`) is specified by the WSDL file.

Dynamic Invocation Interface Client

The `RetailerDIIClient` program performs these steps:

1. Creates a Service object.

   ```
   Service service = factory.createService(new
           QName(qnameService));
   ```

   To get a service object, the program invokes the `createService` method of a `ServiceFactory` object. The parameter of the `createService` method is a `QName` object that represents the name of the service, `Retailer`. The WSDL file specifies this name as follows:

   ```
   <service name="Retailer">
   ```

2. From the service object, creates a `Call` object:

   ```
   QName port = new QName(qnamePort);
   Call call = service.createCall(port);
   ```

   A `Call` object supports the dynamic invocation of the remote procedures of a service. To get a `Call` object, the program invokes the Service object's `createCall` method. The parameter of `createCall` is a `QName` object that represents the service endpoint interface. In the WSDL file, the name of this interface is designated by the `portType` element:

   ```
   <portType name="RetailerSoap">
   ```

3. Sets the service endpoint address on the `Call` object:
   ```
   call.setTargetEndpointAddress(endpoint);
   ```

   In the WSDL file, this address is specified by the `<soap:address>` element.

4. Sets these properties on the `Call` object:

   ```
   SOAPACTION_USE_PROPERTY
   SOAPACTION_URI_PROPERTY
   ENCODING_STYLE_PROPERTY
   ```

   To learn more about these properties, refer to the SOAP and WSDL documents listed in the references section at the end of this chapter.

5. Specifies the method's return type, name, and parameter:

```
QName QNAME_TYPE_STRING = new QName(NS_XSD, "string");
call.setReturnType(QNAME_TYPE_STRING);
call.setOperationName(new QName(BODY_NAMESPACE_VALUE,
                    "getOrderStatus"));
call.addParameter("OrderNumber", QNAME_TYPE_INT,
                ParameterMode.IN);
```

To specify the return type, the program invokes the setReturnType method on the Call object. The parameter of setReturnType is a QName object that represents an XML string type.

The program designates the method name by invoking the setOperationName method with a QName object that represents getOrderStatus.

To indicate the method parameter, the program invokes the addParameter method on the Call object. The addParameter method has three arguments: a String for the parameter name (String_1), a QName object for the XML type, and a ParameterMode object to indicate the passing mode of the parameter (IN).

6. Invokes the remote method on the Call object:

```
Object[] params = new Object[]{new Integer(1)};
String result = (String)call.invoke(params);
System.out.println(result);
```

The program assigns the parameter value (order number) to an array (params) and then executes the invoke method with the object array as an argument.

Here is a complete listing of the source code for the Retailer DII client:

```
package j2eedotnet.chapter4.retailerservice.rpcstubs.client;

import javax.xml.rpc.Call;
import javax.xml.rpc.Service;
import javax.xml.rpc.JAXRPCException;
import javax.xml.namespace.QName;
import javax.xml.rpc.ServiceFactory;
import javax.xml.rpc.ParameterMode;
import java.net.URL;
```

```
/**
*Dynamic Invocation Interface Client for Retailer Service
*/
public class RetailerDIIClient {

        private static String qnameService = "Retailer";
        private static String qnamePort = "RetailerSoap";

        private static String BODY_NAMESPACE_VALUE =
                "http://tempuri.org/";
        private static String ENCODING_STYLE_PROPERTY =
                 "javax.xml.rpc.encodingstyle.namespace.uri";
        private static String NS_XSD =
                "http://www.w3.org/2001/XMLSchema";
        private static String URI_ENCODING =
                "http://schemas.xmlsoap.org/soap/encoding/";

        public static void main(String[] args) {

                System.out.println("Endpoint address = " + args[0]);
                String UrlString = args[0] + "?WSDL";

                try {
                        ServiceFactory factory =
                                ServiceFactory.newInstance();
                        URL retailerWsdlUrl = new URL(UrlString);
                        Service service = factory.createService(new
                                QName(BODY_NAMESPACE_VALUE,qnameService));

                        QName port =
                                new Name(BODY_NAMESPACE_VALUE,qnamePort);

                        Call call = service.createCall(port);
                        call.setTargetEndpointAddress(args[0]);

                        call.setProperty(Call.SOAPACTION_USE_PROPERTY,
                                new Boolean(true));
                        call.setProperty(Call.SOAPACTION_URI_PROPERTY,
                                 "http://tempuri.org/getOrderStatus");
                        call.setProperty(ENCODING_STYLE_PROPERTY, "");
```

```
QName QNAME_TYPE_STRING =
                     new QName(NS_XSD, "string");
call.setReturnType(QNAME_TYPE_STRING);
QName QNAME_TYPE_INT =
     new QName(NS_XSD, int");

call.setOperationName(
  new Name(BODY_NAMESPACE_VALUE,"getOrderStatus"));

call.addParameter("OrderNumber", QNAME_TYPE_INT,
     ParameterMode.IN);

Object[] params = new Object[]{new Integer(1)};

String result = (String)call.invoke(params);
System.out.println(result);

} catch (Exception ex) {
     ex.printStackTrace();
}
}


}
```

After having delved into a bit more detail on the JAX-RPC side, following is a closer look at .NET Web services APIs.

.NET Web Service APIs

Microsoft releases updates to the .NET Framework for Web services in the form of the Web Services Enhancements (WSE) packs. These are designed to simplify the development and deployment of Web services that comply with the published standards, particularly in the area of security. The latest version, WSE 3.0, an update to .NET 2.0, supports Kerberos tickets, X.509 certificates, and the most up-to-date WS-Security specifications. In addition to security, WSE 3.0 implements declarative behavior for security, where the security behavior of a service may be implemented using policy assertion files. These are then enforced in source code through use of attributes on the appropriate classes and methods [MSWSE3]. It also provides interoperability with the Windows Communication Foundation.

The Windows Communication Foundation, formerly known as Indigo, is the long-term strategy from Microsoft for connected systems, both synchronous and asynchronous. It is intended as a long term replacement for all technologies used for systems such as Web services, MSMQ, COM+, and .NET Remoting. It provides a single, consistent API for delivering software as a service that is secure, reliable, transactable, and conforms to the WSI Basic Profile. When developing for WCF, the developer mindset is to work with the **ABC** mnemonic:

- **A is for the Service Address**   Where is the service located?

- **B is for the Service Binding**   What methodology is used to communicate with it? Is it synchronous using SOAP or asynchronous using messaging?

- **C is for the Service Contract**   What does the service do? How do I invoke its methods? What do I pass in, and what do I get out?

To create a service, one has to first create the service contract, which is very similar to the initial step in creating a Java Web service as outlined previously, and then build an interface that is to be implemented later.

```
namespace IndigoRetailer
{
    using System;
    using System.ServiceModel;
    [ServiceContract()]
    public interface IRetailer
    {
        [OperationContract]
        string getProductCatalog();
    }
}
```

For the WCF to recognize this as a service, the service level interface is attributed with the `[ServiceContract()]` declaration, and the individual methods that are to be exposed as Web methods are attributed with `[OperationContract]`.

Next, the service class itself is implemented.

```
using System;
using System.ServiceModel;
```

```
namespace IndigoRetailer
{
    public class WCFRetailerService : IRetailer
    {
        public double getProductCatalog()
        {
            String dReturn = "Returned Values";
            return dReturn;
        }
    }
}
```

The Indigo classes are implemented in the `ServiceModel` namespace within `ServiceModel.dll`. To compile a WCF service, the following command is used:

```
Csc /r:System.ServiceModel.dll /out:WCFRetailerService.dll
    /t:library WCFRetailerService.cs
```

The service needs to be configured for the runtime to understand how to use it and how it should be conformed to any profiles, such as the WS-I Basic Profile.

This is achieved using web.config, where the `<system.serviceModel>` node configures how WCF uses this service.

```
<system.serviceModel>
  <services>
    <service behaviorConfiguration="RetailerBehavior"
        type="IndigoRetailer" >
        <endpoint address=""
          binding="wsHttpBinding"
          bindingConfiguration="Binding1"
          contract="IndigorRetailer.IRetailer" />
    </service>
  </services>
  <behaviors>
    <behavior configurationName="RetailerBehavior"
      returnUnknownExceptionsAsFaults="True">
    </behavior>
  </behaviors>
  <bindings>
```

```
<wsHttpBinding>
   <binding configurationName="Binding1" />
</wsHttpBinding>
  </bindings>
</system.serviceModel>
```

Within this configuration, the bindings behavior is set up, as well as the address endpoint of the service. The last thing that is needed is a service mapper—which is a simple text file (usually called service.svc). This file maps calls to the service to the appropriate class files and is placed within the IIS virtual directory in which the service resides and looks like this

```
<@Service language=c# Debug="true"
   class="IndigoRetaieler.RetailerService" %>
```

The WSDL for the service can now be accessed using the service mapper in this way:

```
http://localhost/servicedirectory/service.svc?wsdl
```

The WCF toolkit provides a tool, svcutil, which can be used to create proxies to this service and the necessary configuration files for clients to access them. It is used like this

```
svcutil /language:C# /config:app.config
http://localhost/servicedirectory/service.svd?wsdl
```

Extensions to the JAX-WS API from Sun will allow for future interoperability between Java and WCF applications. At the time of writing, these are not yet available [SUNINTER].

Best Practices and Pitfalls

When implementing Web services, particularly if it is already known that they are going to be used in a mixed-mode environment, there are a number of best practices that can be followed to ensure smooth interoperability. These include the following:

Data Type Definitions and Interoperability Testing

It is important to define the data types to be exchanged early on in the integration cycle. Knowing what data types work and what types don't in the early stages of integration mitigates risks and also helps define the integration architecture and design with greater consistency. It is also important to carry on interoperability testing at every stage of the integration life cycle especially if the integration encompasses multiple Java EE .NET applications.

Keep Types Simple—Avoid Advanced XML Schema Constructs

The XML Schema standard is very complex and difficult to implement. Moreover, XML Schema processing is quite time-consuming, so many frameworks sacrifice full XML Schema support for performance. Some advanced XML Schema constructs (for example, choice) are quite hard to express in a programming language, and few Web services frameworks support them. So the key success factor in Web services interoperability is to use basic data types, such as primitive data types, arrays, and structures. As a best practice, decompose the complex types in your interfaces into simple and clean interfaces with basic datatypes that are XSD-compliant. Also avoid using specific techniques (for example, INOUT parameter passing) that aren't widely supported.

Provide XML Schema Definitions for All Data Types

One common problem in today's frameworks is their limited ability to import multiple XML Schema and WSDL documents. It's always a good idea to provide complete XML Schema and WSDL definitions in one WSDL file rather than importing them from various locations. Specifically, the Microsoft .NET Framework is sensitive to XML Schema import functions.

Here is an example: If the need to include multiple WSDL and XML Schema files in a Microsoft .NET service is discovered, it is easier to pass the XML Schema definitions together with the WSDL definition to the command line MS Microsoft .NET WSDL compiler rather than trying to import the schemas into the WSDL file:

```
wsdl.exe /language:CS /protocol:SOAP MyService.wsdl MySchema.xsd
JavaCollections.xsd
```

WS-I Compliance

For better interoperability, it is recommended to adhere to the Web services interoperability guidelines in WS-I Basic Profile, discussed previously. Check the www.ws-i.org site for more details.

Multiple WSDL Bindings

Some frameworks generate multiple WSDL bindings that allow access to a Web service through multiple methods (that is, HTTP GET, HTTP POST, and SOAP). The client-side framework needs to know which binding to use, so specification of further parameters (usually the fully qualified name of the service and the name of the WSDL port) is needed when generating the programming language bindings from the WSDL document.

Default Document Style with Literal Encoding

Some Web services frameworks, including MS Microsoft.NET, generate, by default, a document style Web service, using literal encoding. Although the Web service uses document/literal, the Microsoft .NET Framework makes the service appear to be RPC style to Microsoft .NET clients. This isn't necessarily so for other Web service frameworks, and many users may find it difficult to access the Web service using an RPC style client. So if you're writing an RPC Web service, force your framework to generate the RPC style WSDL.

For example, use the `[SoapRpcService]` directive in your MS Microsoft .NET RPC Web service implementations, as shown here:

```
<%@ WebService Language="C#" Class="MSNetStockService" %>
using System.Web.Services;
using System.Web.Services.Protocols;
using System.Web.Services.Description;

[SoapRpcService]

public class MSNetStockService {

  [WebMethod]
  public double getQuote(string symbol) {
    if(symbol == "SUNW") {
      return 10;
```

```
  }
  if(symbol == "BEAS") {
    return 11;
  }
  if(symbol == "MSFT") {
    return 50;
  }
  return 0;
}

}
```

Use Unique SOAPActions for Your Methods

If you start your Web service development with a WSDL document definition, consider using unique SOAPAction attributes for all your methods in
the WSDL binding. Some frameworks rely on SOAPAction when routing
SOAP messages to the Web service implementation's methods.

For example, consider the following WSDL binding for a stock quote
service:

```
<binding name="MSNetStockServiceSoap"
        type="tns:MSNetStockServiceSoap">
  <soap:binding transport="http://schemas.xmlsoap.org/soap/http"
        style="rpc" />
  <operation name="getQuote">
    <soap:operation soapAction=http://tempuri.org/getQuote
          style="rpc" />
    <input>
      <soap:body use="encoded" namespace="http://tempuri.org/"
      encodingStyle="http://schemas.xmlsoap.org/soap/encoding/" />
    </input>
    <output>
      <soap:body use="encoded" namespace="http://tempuri.org/"
      encodingStyle="http://schemas.xmlsoap.org/soap/encoding/" />
    </output>
  </operation>
</binding>
```

Consider MTOM When Handling Attachments

There are many formats that have been bandied about to handle attachments in Web services. These include SOAP with Attachments (SwA), Direct Internet Message Encapsulation (DIME), and Message Transmission Optimization Mechanism (MTOM) [W3CMTOM]. The former, while power-ful, were unable to encapsulate the needs of security, being incompatible with WS-Security, the standard specification for using security within SOAP messages. MTOM, on the other hand, overcame this flaw and was moved into *recommended* status by the W3C. MTOM is supported in the Microsoft Web Services Enhancements (version 3.0).

Using MTOM in .NET Web services is very straightforward and is all configuration-driven—meaning that an existing Web service code does not need to be changed. Assuming WSE 3.0 is installed, the web.config file for the application is amended to enable MTOM. For example, if all incoming and outgoing SOAP messages are to be MTOM-encoded, the following sections will be in the web.config file:

```
<configuration>
  <configSections>
    <section name="microsoft.web.services3"

type="Microsoft.Web.Services3.Configuration.WebServicesConfiguration,
        Microsoft.Web.Services3, Version=3.0.0.0, Culture=neutral,
        PublicKeyToken=xxxxx" />
  </configSections>
  <system.web>
    <webServices>
      <soapServerProtocolFactory
        type="Microsoft.Web.Services3.WseProtocolFactory,
          Microsoft.Web.Services3, Version=3.0.0.0, Culture=neutral,
          PublicKeyToken=xxxxx" />
    </webServices>
  </system.web>
  <microsoft.web.services3>
    <messaging>
      <mtom serverMode="always" />
    </messaging>
  </microsoft.web.services3>
</configuration>
```

Once the web.config is configured for WSE 3.0 and MTOM, Web method can be built in the Web service that returns a binary file as an array of bytes with a Web method like this

```
[WebMethod]
public byte[] GetFileBinary(String fileName)
{
  StringBuilder filePath = new StringBuilder();
  filePath.Append(AppDomain.CurrentDomain.BaseDirectory);
  filePath.Append("App_Data\");
  filePath.Appent(filename);

  return File.ReadAllBytes(filePath.toString());

}
```

When using MTOM, the attachment appears within the body of the SOAP response. To call this from Java using JAX-WS, the GetFileBinary method is used.

```
ServiceFactory serviceFactory = ServiceFactory.newInstance();

Service service =
  (Service)serviceFactory.createService(
    new URL("http://localhost/binread/reader.asmx?WSDL"),
        Service.class);

ServiceSoap soap = service.getServiceSoap();

SOAPBinding binding =
(SOAPBinding)((BindingProvider)soap).getBinding();

binding.setMTOMEnabled(true);

byte[] fileData = soap.getFileBinary("Myfile.jpg");
FileOutputStream fStream =
  new FileOutputStream("C:\\MyFile.jpg");
fStream.write(fileData);
fStream.flush();
fStream.close();
```

The JAX-WS Soap binding object now supports a flag that allows MTOM to be enabled using the `setMTOMEnabled` flag. Once this is set, then it becomes a simple matter of calling the Web method and using a `FileOutputStream` to get the response.

Long Running B2B Transactions

Web services, while enormously useful, are not magic bullets that can tie all business processes together into a cohesive whole. There are a number of pitfalls that might be encountered when using them. One such pitfall is when there is a long running transaction, particularly one that requires maintenance of state during the transaction lifecycle. When using synchronous Web services, state isn't maintained—and as such these transactions become infeasible. Also many business transactions require asynchronicity—the callee returns to the caller at the end of the transaction once it is complete, which, depending on the transaction, can take milliseconds or can take years. For synchronous applications and Web services to wait for the completion of longer running services, resources would have to be used to maintain the long connections, which is infeasible, expensive, and prone to error.

Design Difficulties

In mixed-mode systems, there are interoperability challenges when passing complex data types between Web services implemented on .NET and those implemented using the various Java EE methodologies and application servers. One approach to ease this is to do contract-first design and implementation where the WSDL that describes the Web service is agreed upon by parties from both development teams and becomes the specification for developing the Web service and its clients. Coding from a WSDL-first approach can be difficult and tedious, as WSDL is intended to be a machine-readable, machine-producible format. Typically design tools such as Visual Studio.NET encourage the developer to build his or her logic in code such as C#, and it handles generation of the WSDL that describes this code when the service runs. However, following this easier approach (having the machine produce the WSDL) can lead to many interoperability challenges.

Debugging and Maintenance

Synchronous Web services pass messages to each other using XML encoded as SOAP. This is designed to be a machine-readable format containing service invocation via method calls and returned data in consistent packaging. When developing synchronous Web services, particularly ones in mixed-mode architectures containing .NET, Java EE, or other runtime operation platforms, the process of debugging and doing root cause analysis of failures is a difficult one. Consider the case where a .NET client calls a Java EE application server and there is a failure. There is no consistent application execution stack that the whole application can be debugged to. The caller can validate that he sent out a SOAP packet, and the receiver can validate that he received a SOAP packet, but when something goes wrong, the tendency is there to blame the other party, but it is difficult to verify exactly where the problem lies.

Performance and Stability

Web services give businesses tremendous flexibility in exposing their business assets in a machine-readable way that is easy to integrate. But this comes at a cost—performance. The overhead of exposing access to assets through a Web service stack involves the development of an application or layers of applications that access that information, encoding the response as XML/SOAP, and handling requests from incoming clients to get the information, encode it, and return it. This is problematic because first, it is slower than direct access to the asset (such as through a JDBC/ADO.NET connection to a database), and second, it doesn't take advantage of the automatic scaling or connection pooling provided by enterprise resource assets such as databases. Note that the Web service code itself can take advantage of these when accessing the Resource tier, but its external interface to the clients cannot unless it is explicitly coded to do so (further decreasing performance and increasing complexity) or it is configured to run on a system that provides these services.

Summary

This chapter introduced Web services—what they are, how they work, and what use they may be in enabling interoperability in applications or systems. Web services are an excellent approach to request/response interactions where state isn't maintained and due to their abstract, platform-independent nature are designed to facilitate cross platform execution. However, they suffer from some interoperability challenges due to different approaches to implementing the standards. In addition the chapter walked through an example of building a Web service using Java and how to consume it using .NET, and vice-versa.

Finally a number of best practices to ensure clean interoperability between Java and .NET-based Web services were presented, along with potential pitfalls that the developer or architect could face when using them.

References

[JWSDP] Java Web Services Developer Pack (Java WSDP). Sun Developer Network.
http://java.sun.com/webservices/jwsdp/index.jsp

[JAX-RPC] Java API for XML-Based RPC (JAX-RPC) Overview. Sun Developer Network.
http://java.sun.com/webservices/jaxrpc/overview.html

[JAX-RPC_Env] JAX-RPC SI Environment.
https://jax-rpc.dev.java.net/whitepaper/1.1/index-part2.html
Arun Gupta. "Understanding your JAX-RPC SI Environment, part 2." February 2004.

[JAX-WS] JAX-WS API for Java.
https://jax-ws.dev.java.net/

[JAXB] Java Architecture for XML Binding.
http://java.sun.com/webservices/jaxb/about.html
Scott Fordin. "Java Architecture for XML Binding (JAXB)." Sun Developer Network, October 2004.

[JAXP] JAXP for XML Processing.
http://java.sun.com/developer/technicalArticles/xml/jaxp1-3/
Neeraj Bajaj. Easy and Efficient XML Processing: Upgrade to JAXP 1.3. Sun Developer Network, October 11, 2005.

[JAXR] Java API for XML Registries (JAXR) Overview. Sun Developer Network.
http://java.sun.com/webservices/jaxr/overview.html

[JSR181] Web Services Metadata for the Java™ Platform.
http://jcp.org/en/jsr/detail?id=181

[MSDNWCF] Microsoft Windows Communication Foundation portal.
http://msdn.microsoft.com/webservices/indigo/default.aspx

[MSDNWSP] Microsoft Web services developer portal.
http://msdn.microsoft.com/webservices/

[MSUDDI] Microsoft UDDI Software Development Kit.
http://msdn.microsoft.com/library/default.asp?url=/library/en-us/uddi/uddi/
portal.asp

[MSWSE3] Microsoft Web Services Enhancements 3.0.
www.microsoft.com/downloads/details.aspx?familyid=018a09fd-3a74-43c5-8ec1-
8d789091255d&displaylang=en

[MSXML] Microsoft XML Classes in the System.Xml namespace.
http://msdn.microsoft.com/library/default.asp?url=/library/en-us/cpref/
html/frlrfsystemxml.asp

[MTOM] SOAP Message Transmission Optimization Mechanism. W3C W3C
Recommendation 25 January 2005.
www.w3.org/TR/soap12-mtom/

[SAAJ] SOAP with Attachments API for Java (SAAJ). Sun Developer Network.
http://java.sun.com/webservices/saaj/

[SUNINTER] Sun Facilitates Interoperability Between Java Technology and .NET
Via Open Source Web Services Implementations.
www.sun.com/smi/Press/sunflash/2005-11/sunflash.20051104.1.html

[W3CMTOM] SOAP Message Transmission Optimization Mechanism.
www.w3.org/TR/2005/REC-soap12-mtom-20050125/

[WSIATT] Attachments Profile Version 1.0.
www.ws-i.org/Profiles/AttachmentsProfile-1.0-2004-08-24.html

[WSIBAS] WSI Basic Profile 1.1.
www.ws-i.org/Profiles/BasicProfile-1.1-2004-08-24.html

[WSISEC] WSI Basic Security Profile 1.1.
www.ws-i.org/Profiles/BasicSecurityProfile-1.0.html

.NET Remoting for Synchronous Integration

5

Introduction

Microsoft .NET Remoting provides a framework that allows objects to interact with one another across application domains. The framework provides a number of services, including activation, lifetime support, and communication channels responsible for transporting messages to and from remote applications. Formatters are used for encoding and decoding the messages before they are transported by the channel. Applications can use binary encoding where performance is critical or XML encoding where interoperability with other frameworks that provide similar functionality is essential. One method of encoding is to use XML, which uses the SOAP protocol when transporting messages from one application domain to the other. It was designed with security in mind, and a number of hooks are provided that allow channel sinks to gain access to the messages and serialized stream before the stream is transported over the channel.

Attempting to manage the lifetime of remote objects without support from the underlying framework is often cumbersome, so .NET Remoting provides a number of activation models to choose from.

These models fall into two categories:

- Client-activated objects
- Server-activated objects

Client-activated objects are under the control of a lease-based lifetime manager that ensures the object is garbage collected when its lease expires. In the case of server-activated objects, developers have a choice of selecting either a "single call" or "singleton" model. The lifetime of singletons are also controlled by lease-based lifetime.

The Java EE .NET interoperability solutions described in this chapter use .NET Remoting for integration. The solutions described in this chapter include

- IIOP.NET
- J-Integra (formerly Ja.NET)
- JNBridge

IIOP.NET for Java EE .NET Integration

IIOP.NET is a technology that allows .NET, Java EE, and CORBA components to interoperate seamlessly using the CORBA-based Internet Inter-Orb Protocol (IIOP). This solution relies on the extensibility of the .NET Remoting architecture to offer transparent, object-level integration without incurring the performance overhead that gateways or SOAP-based products impose.

This technology is available to the software community under the LGPL license as an open-source project at http://iiop-net.sourceforge.net.

Scope

IIOP.NET is an interoperability solution for enterprise applications. It allows interoperation with other peers that understand the IIOP protocol, such as Java EE and CORBA-based objects.

It fully supports bi-directional interoperability, including callbacks, and using distributed objects allows a quasi-natural object-oriented programming style by making references to remote objects almost transparent. These remote objects can be both stateless or stateful.

The framework is also transparent to the applications that use it due to the fact that it is installed into the .NET Remoting infrastructure (which roughly corresponds to Java RMI)—objects can communicate with other remote objects without any knowledge of the underlying technology on which they are implemented.

Interoperation via IIOP is not a replacement for SOAP or Web services; the two approaches complement each other in a very natural way. SOAP is best suited for the integration of loosely-coupled services, which are typically stateless and relatively coarse-grained. CORBA objects and Enterprise Java Beans (EJBs) are usually finer-grained and more tightly-coupled than Web services; IIOP, which allows efficient, object-level interactions, is the optimal technology for such cases.

Solution

IIOP.NET takes advantage of the configurability aspects of the .NET Remoting infrastructure (refer to Figure 5-1). At its core is an IIOP Remoting channel that is plugged into the .NET Framework, exactly like the built-in binary and SOAP channels. Consisting of transport sink, formatter, and type-mapper, the remoting channel marshals method invocations and parameters between CORBA and .NET.

Besides these runtime components, the solution also includes the build tools that Java and .NET developers need to work with the CORBA interface definitions language (IDL) and the .NET common language specification (CLS):

- A compiler that parses the IDL description of Java or CORBA server classes and produces the corresponding CLS proxy classes needed by .NET clients.

- A generator that transforms the CLS metadata of the server classes into IDL that can be used to build Java or CORBA clients.

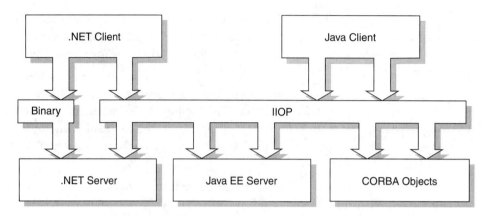

Figure 5-1
IIOP.NET opens the IIOP world to .NET.

IIOP.NET Channel

The IIOP.NET channel is a plug-in for the .NET Remoting infrastructure. It implements a formatter for marshaling the method invocations and a transport sink for handling the low-level networking details (in this case TCP/IP connections). Refer to Figure 5-2.

The major difference from the other built-in remoting components is that IIOP.NET allows interoperability with peers other than .NET.

To be part of a distributed object system, the .NET objects face one of two choices:

- Inherit from `MarshalByRefObject` to be accessible by reference from remote machines (corresponds to Java's Remote interface).

- Inherit from `ISerializable` or have the `Serializable` attribute to be cloned between remote machines (corresponds to Java's `Serializable` interface).

More details about .NET Remoting are beyond the scope of this text and can be found in the .NET Framework documentation.

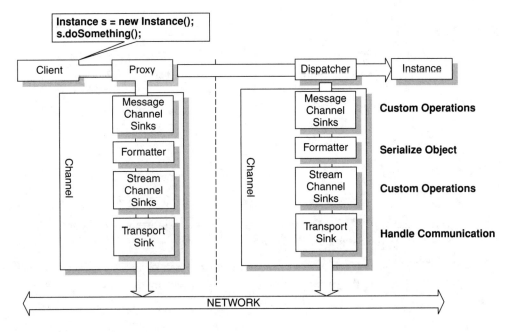

Figure 5-2
Overview of the .NET Remoting infrastructure

IIOP.NET Tools

IIOP.NET includes compilers to generate .NET proxies from CORBA IDL definitions and to generate IDL definitions from compiled .NET Assemblies.

The `IDLToCLSCompiler` takes one or more IDL definitions and generates a DLL containing the proxies for the defined types. Refer to Figure 5-3.

In Figure 5-4, the `CLSToIDLGenerator` creates the IDL definitions contained in one or more .NET assemblies. Both tools operate directly on the .NET assemblies to be completely language agnostic.

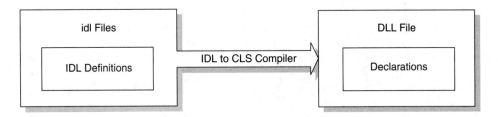

Figure 5-3
IDL to CLS compiler

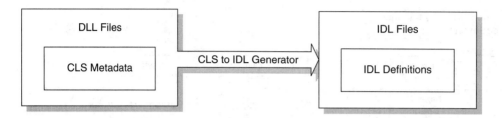

Figure 5-4
CLS to IDL compiler

Using IIOP.NET

Using IIOP.NET to implement client objects is relatively simple and can be done using four steps. Refer to Figure 5-5.

1. Generate the IDL description for your server objects
2. Generate the proxy classes from the IDL with `IDLToCLSCompiler`
3. Register the IIOP.NET channel
4. Use the proxy classes

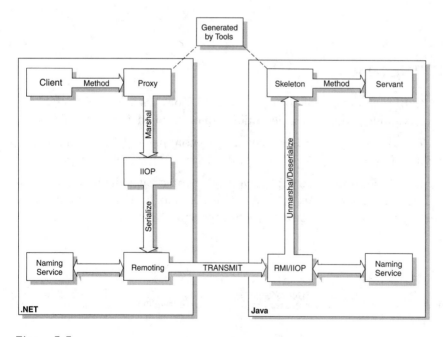

Figure 5-5
A distributed object system with IIOP.NET

Using .NET server objects from Java is as simple as:

1. Generating the IDL description for the server objects with `CLSToIDLGenerator`.
2. Generating the stubs from the IDL (rmic).

Benefits

IIOP.NET opens the CORBA world to .NET; CORBA defines a protocol that is used to support distributed object systems. This protocol is flexible enough to provide additional services, such as security and transactions, and has many widespread implementations.

Most of the architectural benefits are provided by the IIOP protocol.

- **Performance** IIOP is lighter and more efficient than SOAP; the IIOP remoting channel shares the same process as the objects it connects, and neither requires a separate gateway nor imposes an additional level of indirection.

- **Reliability** IIOP defines at-most-once call semantics to ensure that method invocations are processed only once.

- **Usability** IIOP.NET provides the flexible and powerful model of CORBA, integrated into the simple and intuitive .NET Remoting.

- **Scalability** The application must handle the scalability; IIOP.NET does not limit it.

Other benefits are

- **Tight Coupling** Tight coupling between distributed objects in .NET, CORBA, and Java EE; components on each platform can act in either client or server role.

- **Transparency** Existing servers can be used unmodified, without wrapping code or adapters; this provides a distinct advantage in both development cost and speed.

- **Extensive Coverage of CORBA/.NET Type Mappings** Most types are already implemented and more are on the way. Note that because of the underlying differences in CORBA and .NET, some types are simply not mappable; these cases are explicitly identified and documented.

- **Full Source Code is Available (in C#)** This allows users of the framework to configure it to their needs.

- **Native Integration in the .NET Framework**   Because it is directly based on the standard remoting infrastructure, it fits into most architectures and can be combined with other technologies and management systems.

- **Well Tested**   IIOP.NET has been tested with many peers, including Sun's SDK, JBoss, IBM Websphere, BEA Weblogic, Mico, TAO, and omniORB.

- **Custom Mappings**   Custom mappings can be defined for remoting classes with the same semantics but different implementation (that is, .NET and Java EE both define Hashtables, but they have different implementations).

Limitations

Architectural limitations are imposed by the model chosen and cannot be removed:

- **Data Typing**   .NET, Java, and CORBA types differ in some details like the exception types and the character set. IIOP.NET provides a mechanism for mapping custom types that may have a different implementations across the frameworks (for example, Hashtables), but this must be done by hand.

- **CORBA Valuetypes (Java Serializable objects)**   Their methods must be re-implemented in .NET, as the IDL doesn't carry code and Java classes cannot be used in .NET.

Examples

The Supply Chain Management reference application from the WS-I is used throughout this book for examples on interoperability. Here's a short example based on the Retailer part of the application. In Figure 5-6, Web services communicate between applications (like the client and the Retailer system), and a distributed object system implements the communication between the presentation and the Processing tier of the Retailer system.

The Retailer application consists in a Presentation tier, which provides the rest of the world with Web service access to the Retailer system and is implemented with .NET; the Processing tier consists of some Java-remotable components published through RMI/IIOP. Here stateful components are used and not EJBs because the same interface is already used for the Web access to the application.

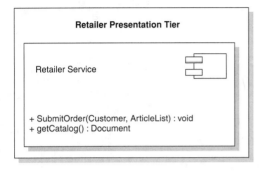

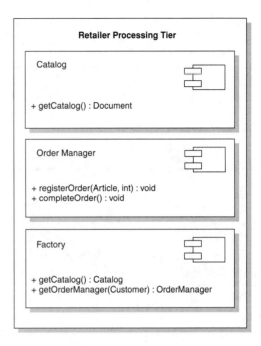

Figure 5-6
Logical architecture of Supply Chain Management application

The Presentation tier communicates with the Processing tier using IIOP.NET. The Processing tier defines three interfaces. Refer to Listing 5-1.

Listing 5-1
Catalog Interface

```
Public interface Catalog extends Remote{
   Public Document getCatalog() ;
}
public interface OrderManager extends Remote {
   public void registerOrder(Article article, int amount);
}
public interface Factory extends Remote {
   public Catalog getCatalog();
public OrderManager getOrderManager(Customer customer);
}
```

The Factory is a singleton object that creates instances of the other objects for remote use. Refer to Listing 5-2.

Listing 5-2
Three Interfaces Defined in the Processing Tier

```
// Create and register factory
Factory f = new FactoryImpl();
Context initialContext = new InitialContext();
InitialContext.rebind("factory", f);
```

The first step toward interoperability is to create the IDL description of the Catalog, OrderManager, and Factory interfaces:

```
rmic -classpath  . -iiop Catalog
rmic -classpath  . -iiop OrderManager
rmic -classpath  . -iiop Factory
```

Using these IDL files, the IDLToCLSCompiler generates the proxy classes for .NET:

```
IDLToCLSCompiler ProxyClasses Catalog.idl OrderManager.idl Factory.idl
```

This command generates ProxyClasses.dll, an assembly that contains the definitions for the types defined in the IDL files. Obviously it's important to have all files in the right directory, but all these commands also have options to use different directories for their work.

Now the .NET Web service is implemented, which must register the IIOP.NET channel, connect to the server, and access the remote objects.

The first thing to do is to configure the Web service by registering the channel and fetching a reference to the factory. Refer to Listing 5-3.

Second, the Web service implementation uses the objects in the Production tier. Note how the list of orders is processed by submitting each order singularly to the existing stateful interface. Refer to Listing 5-4.

Listing 5-3
Configuring .NET Web Service

```
public class Global : System.Web.HttpApplication {
    protected void Application_Start(Object sender, EventArgs e) {
        // register client channel, no callbacks
        IiopChannel ch = new IiopChannel();
        RemotingServices.RegisterChannel(ch);
        m_factory = GetFactory();

        // fetch reference to factory, store it into application
        // state access COS naming service
        CorbaInit init = CorbaInit.GetInit();
        NamingContext nameService = init.GetNameService(host, port);
        NameComponent[] name = new NameComponent[]{
            new NameComponent("Factory")};

        // get the reference to the factory
        Factory factory = (Factory)nameService.resolve(name);
        Application["Factory"] = factory;
    }
}
```

Listing 5-4
RetailerService

```
public class RetailerService: WebService {

    private Factory GetFactory() {
        return (Factory)Application["factory"];
    }

    [WebMethod]
    public void submitOrder(Customer customer, OrderList order) {
        OrderManager om = GetFactory().getOrderManager(customer);

        try {
            foreach (Part part in oders) {
                om.Order(part);
            }
        } finally {
            om.completeOrder() ;
        }
    }
}
```

Resources

The IIOP.NET project is hosted on sourceforge (http://iiop-net.source-forge.net/) and maintained by Dominic Ullmann and Patrik Reali and sponsored by ELCA Informatique SA.

The project includes many tutorials and code examples on how to interoperate with peers other than .NET, including the details for the various application servers and ORBs.

The documentation page (http://iiop-net.sourceforge.net/documentation.html) contains the overview of all documentation available. This page also links external tutorials and articles about IIOP.NET.

J-Integra for Java EE .NET Integration

Scope

While Web services provide a very powerful technology for enterprise application integration, they are not suitable for all applications and interoperability scenarios. Both the .NET Framework and Java offer implementations of Web services, with varying degrees of integration into the underlying platform. Because SOAP is text-based, Web service calls might be too slow for applications that require frequent, fast, and fine-grained communications.

Service-oriented interfaces such as Web services are also unsuited for conventional object-oriented models. Although a service can be thought of as a single, persistent server-activated object, client-activated objects such as ones that the new operator constructs and access requests to static methods are not generally supported.

Similarly, if an application needs to access a wide variety of objects and classes or link to a rich object-oriented set of Java APIs from the .NET Framework, Web services are probably not the solution. In addition to the preceding issues, Web services do not support callbacks in the same manner as local object-oriented architectures.

In such cases, an alternative solution is required that enables interoperability between .NET Framework applications and Java applications with .NET Remoting as the underlying connecting protocol. Developers familiar with Java EE technology may wish to view .NET Remoting as a .NET parallel to Remote Method Invocation (RMI) and Remote Method Invocation over Internet Inter-ORB Protocol (RMI-IIOP).

The problem is that .NET Remoting can normally only be used in a homogeneous (.NET) environment. To achieve interoperability using .NET Remoting, you can use J-Integra for .NET (also known as Ja.NET) that allows .NET applications to access existing Java/Java EE applications as though they were actually .NET. Ja.NET is part of Intrinsyc Software's J-Integra Interoperability Suite. It is a runtime bridging product that exposes Java objects and methods in a way that enables the user to address them with .NET Remoting and vice versa. Ja.NET differs from a number of other Java/.NET Remoting bridging products in that it is bi-directional. Thus, as well as enabling Java server side objects to be accessed from .NET clients, it can also be used to access .NET servers from Java.

Solution

Ja.NET provides a two-way implementation of the .NET Remoting stack for Java. It comprises a Java runtime component and a development toolset used to generate proxies and to configure the runtime.

Using Ja.NET, a set of C# proxies can be generated to access Java from .NET. Similarly because Ja.NET is a bi-directional bridge, Java proxies that expose or consume .NET Common Language Runtime (CLR) components using the .NET Remoting protocol can be generated.

The main components of Ja.NET are

- **Ja.NET Runtime** The Ja.NET runtime core is the main collection of Java classes that provides an implementation of the .NET Remoting stack for Java. It is the only Ja.NET component that is required at runtime. The runtime components are contained in the janet.jar file, and it uses a configuration file (by default janet.xml) that is generated during development by the Janetor tool. The Ja.NET runtime component also includes a Ja.NET TCP server that provides standalone hosting for Java classes through the Ja.NET runtime where the classes are not hosted on a Java EE/Web server and are accessed via a TCP channel.

- **Janetor** The Janetor tool allows viewing and modification of the Ja.NET runtime configuration settings. Janetor can also be used to generate Web Application Archive (WAR) files to assist with deploying the Ja.NET runtime onto a Web server.

- **GenNet** GenNet generates the .NET Framework proxies that access the Java classes through the Ja.NET runtime.

- **GenJava** GenJava generates Java proxies that access .NET Framework assemblies through the Ja.NET runtime.

- **GenService** The GenJava and GenNet tools use GenService to provide access to .NET Framework assemblies for proxy generation during development. GenService is only required for proxy generation and does not have to be installed in the production environment.

Accessing an EJB from .NET Framework

Accessing an EJB from a .NET client is achieved as follows:

- The GenNet tool is used to generate a .NET component containing proxies for the EJB classes. The generated .NET proxies use no custom code, just pure .NET Remoting. Refer to Figure 5-7.

- The Janetor tool is used to generate a WAR file containing all the files to be deployed in the Web server. Refer to Figure 5-8.

- The WAR file can then be deployed in any Web server that supports servlets. The CLR client (written in any supported .NET Framework language) can access the EJBs as if accessing local CLR components. Refer to Figure 5-9.

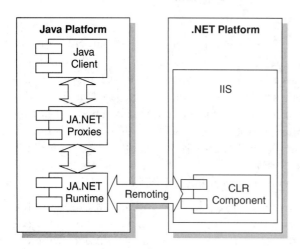

Figure 5-7
Generation of .NET proxies for EJB

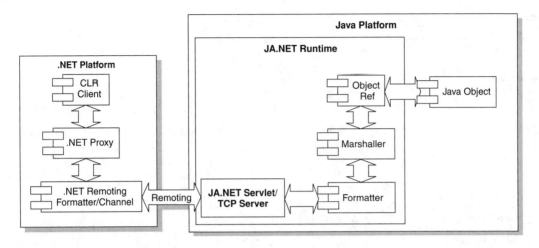

Figure 5-8
Generation of Web Application Archive

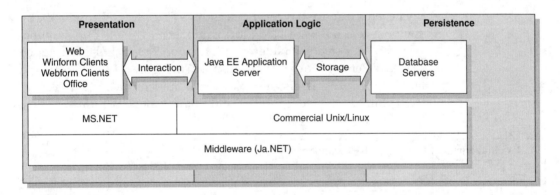

Figure 5-9
Deployment for accessing Java EJB from .NET CLR client

Accessing a .NET Component from Java

Ja.NET can also be used to enable Java clients to access .NET CLR components as follows:

- The GenJava tool is used to generate the Java proxies for the .NET component. Refer to Figure 5-10.

Figure 5-10
Generation of Java proxies for .NET CLR component

- The Janetor tool is used to configure the Ja.NET runtime. Details such as the URL of the CLR component can be specified here. Refer to Figure 5-11.

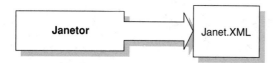

Figure 5-11
Configuration of Ja.NET runtime

- Java clients can use the generated proxies and access the remote CLR component as if it were a local Java component. The .NET CLR component can be hosted in an Internet Information Server (IIS) and accessed via .NET Remoting over HTTP (as shown in Figure 5-12). Alternatively, standalone .NET servers (such as a server implemented in Visual Basic .NET) can be accessed using TCP and a binary message format.

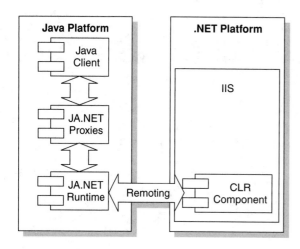

Figure 5-12
Deployment for accessing .NET CLR component hosted in IIS from Java

Channels and Formatters
(Messaging and Object Serialization)

The .NET Remoting Framework supports the use of interchangeable formatters and channels. **Channels** are used to transport messages to and from
remote objects. **Formatters** are used to serialize the data to be transmitted in a
particular format. Currently SOAP and binary formats are supported over
either HTTP or TCP channels. Using these channels and formats, Ja.NET is
wire-line compatible with the .NET Remoting Framework, which is why
there is no need to deploy any Ja.NET runtime components on the .NET side.

The HTTP channel is used when, as in the EJB case, the server-side component is accessed via a Java EE/Web server. Developers can choose to either
use the internal Web server that is shipped with Ja.NET to host their Java
server components or use a WAR file to deploy them in any other Java EE
application server/Web server that supports servlets. Alternatively, for
standalone hosting of Java classes, the TCP server that is part of the Ja.NET
runtime can be used to access them via a TCP channel.

The stream of messages flows when a .NET client invokes a method on a
Java server-side object, as illustrated in Figure 5-13. The .NET client invocation goes through the proxy object (generated by the GenNet tool) to the
.NET Remoting Framework, where it is serialized using the configured formatter (binary or SOAP) and sent to the configured URL using the specified
channel (HTTP or TCP).

On the Java side, the incoming message is received by the Ja.NET runtime (either via the Web server and Ja.NET servlet in the case of HTTP or via
the Ja.NET TCP server). The message is deserialized using the appropriate
Formatter (binary or SOAP) and dispatched by the marshaler to the appropriate Object Ref instance, which invokes the method on the actual Java
object. The response message flows back in the opposite direction for serialization and transmission to the .NET Framework. Refer to Figure 5-13.

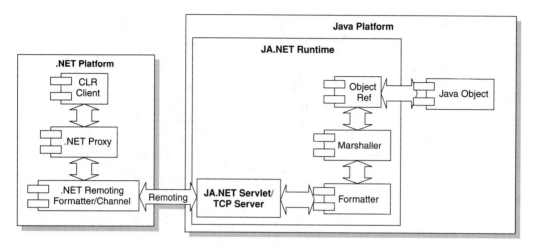

Figure 5-13
Message flow for invocation of Java component method from .NET CLR client

Object Lifetime Management

Knowing when to destroy an object that is referenced remotely is always a problem for distributed technologies. COM used reference counting to solve the distributed garbage collection problem. .NET Remoting uses leasing. With leasing, a remote object remains available for a configurable period of time before being destroyed. Leases may also be configured to be extended when the object is accessed, and additionally sponsors may be configured to be responsible for renewing leases before they expire.

Because Ja.NET adheres to the .NET Remoting standard, the Ja.NET runtime contains a Lease Manager for administering leases so that Java objects instantiated by .NET clients follow the same leasing mechanism.

Scalability

When using HTTP, Ja.NET is entirely compatible with the use of Web servers/Java EE application servers to achieve deployment scalability. For TCP-based deployments, Ja.NET gives developers and administrators the ability to manage resource usage through configuration of TCP server parameters, such as the thread pool size and the maximum request queue size. Ja.NET also provides a connection pooling mechanism to improve performance and optimize resource usage.

Security

Ja.NET leverages standard mechanisms for securing channels and authenticating clients. HTTPS may be used when accessing components via a Web server. Also the desired authentication method can be selected to specify how the client authenticates itself to a Web server when trying to access remote objects. HTTP Basic or Digest authentication methods may be used—or "Best," which causes the most secure method supported by the server to be automatically selected.

Ja.NET supports the `SecureRemoting` protocol and various standard encryption algorithms (3DES, DES, RC2, and Rijndael). TCP channels can be secured by configuring the Ja.NET runtime to use the desired encryption protocol and algorithm and deploying a .NET `SecureRemoting` channel provider to encrypt/decrypt the data on the .NET side.

Benefits

Web services is a technology that is specifically designed for businesses to provide services and exchange information over the Internet. While .NET Remoting is not an industry-wide standard, it does have the following advantages over Web services, which are especially relevant in an intranet environment:

- Multiple protocol support including high-speed binary over TCP—faster than SOAP over HTTP
- Support for activation and lifetime control of remote objects by the client
- Support for passing objects by reference and by value
- Support for callbacks
- Guaranteed interoperability
- Support for events
- Support for type system fidelity, which means that there is a one-to-one mapping between the class and type hierarchy. Web services and SOAP do not support such an object-oriented mechanism for accessing remote objects.

Because Ja.NET uses .NET Remoting, it also has these advantages over Web services.

Ja.NET is wire-line compatible with .NET Remoting and does not require any custom runtime components to be deployed on the .NET side. It supports standard Web server/.NET Remoting security mechanisms.

Interoperability between .NET and Java/Java EE is achieved without the need for developers to write any custom code on either the client or server sides. Ja.NET provides tools for auto-generation of the proxy classes that are used in deployment, and developers can access existing Java components from .NET as if they were accessing them as CLR components using the standard .NET Remoting protocol. Similarly, Ja.NET allows Java clients to access existing CLR server components as if they were local Java objects.

Limitations

Currently a single type of .NET Remoting exception is returned to the client, regardless of the specific type of the underlying exception that occurred. Future releases of Ja.NET will include support for returning specific system and custom exception types.

Examples

As an example, a financial services provider has used Ja.NET to integrate the components of an online trading system. Refer to Figure 5-14. The presentation layer runs on Windows Desktop devices and includes MS .NET GUI components that interact with other MS Office applications. These use Ja.NET to interoperate via .NET Remoting with business logic components that are hosted by Java EE application servers running on commercial Unix or Linux platforms. The application components in turn use JDBC/JMS to interact with database servers that provide persistent services.

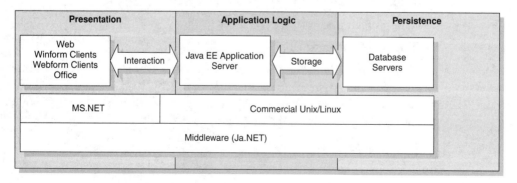

Figure 5-14
Online trading system (simplified architecture)

This deployment configuration is like the one shown previously for accessing EJB components from a .NET client.

The following sample code illustrates in more detail how a .NET client can access a Java server via .NET Remoting using Ja.NET. This example is based on a simplified scenario from the WS-I Supply Chain Management architecture, in which a client queries the server for a catalog of available products. The Java server comprises a `Catalog` class, which implements an `ICatalog` interface. This interface has a `getProducts` method, which returns an array of `Product` objects.

The `Catalog` class provides an example of a `PassByReference` object. Refer to Listing 5-5.

Listing 5-5
Sample "Pass by Object" Object

```
//-------------------------------------------------------------
// ICatalog.java
package java_server;

public interface ICatalog {
  Product[] getProducts();
}


//-------------------------------------------------------------
// Catalog.java. Example PassByReference class.
package java_server;

public class Catalog implements ICatalog {

  public Catalog() {
  }

  public Product[] getProducts() {
    // in a real implementation, this might involve a database query
    Product[] products = new Product[10];
    products[0] = new Product("TV", "Brand 1", 329.99);
    products[1] = new Product("TV", "Brand 2", 359.99);
    products[2] = new Product("TV", "Brand 3", 289.99);
    products[3] = new Product("TV", "Brand 4", 265.99);
    products[4] = new Product("DVD", "Brand 1", 128.99);
```

```
products[5] = new Product("DVD", "Brand 2", 156.99);
products[6] = new Product("DVD", "Brand 3", 145.99);
products[7] = new Product("video camera", "Brand 1", 425.99);
products[8] = new Product("video camera", "Brand 2", 476.99);
products[9] = new Product("video camera", "Brand 3", 520.99);
return products;
  }
}
```

The Product class provides an example of a PassByValue object. This class implements the Serializable interface. Refer to Listing 5-6.

Listing 5-6
Sample *PassbyValue* Object

```
//-----------------------------------------------------------------
// Product.java. Example PassByValue class.
package java_server;

import java.io.Serializable;

public class Product implements Serializable {

  public Product(String type, String manufacturer, double price) {
    this.type = type; this.manufacturer = manufacturer; this.price =
price;
  }

  public String type;
  public String manufacturer;
  public double price;
}
```

.NET proxies for these classes are generated using the Ja.NET GenNet tool. Upon examining the generated proxies, one should notice how the byvalue class contains all its fields, and the remote byreference class is only a shell that defines the class definitions. .NET needs these for compile definitions and then again at runtime for the .NET Remoting TransparentProxy class to mimic the remote server. If one attempts to create a local copy of this class, this generates an exception—only remote instances of this class are generated. The proxies use no custom code, just pure .NET Remoting managed code. Refer to Listing 5-7.

Listing 5-7
Sample .NET Proxy

```
//-----------------------------------------------------------------
/// <summary>
/// This file is a .NET proxy file auto-generated by JaNET, the
Java/.NET
/// integration product from Intrinsyc Software Inc.
/// </summary>
namespace java_server {
  using System;

  public class Catalog : System.MarshalByRefObject, java_server.ICatalog
{

    private String ProxyCalledExceptionMsg = "Configuration error:\nThis
exception is thrown by a Ja.NET-generated proxy file. \n" +
"This method should not be invoked; it is only used at compile
time.\nCheck the " +
"remoting.config file or remoting configuration.";

    public Catalog() {
      throw new System.Exception(ProxyCalledExceptionMsg);
    }

    public java_server.Product[] getProducts() {
      throw new System.Exception(ProxyCalledExceptionMsg);
    }
  }
}
```

Listing 5-7 (continued)

```
//----------------------------------------------------------------
/// <summary>
/// This file is a proxy file auto-generated by JaNET, the Java/.NET
/// integration product from Intrinsyc Software Inc.
/// </summary>
namespace java_server {
  using System;

  [Serializable()]
  public class Product {

    public string type;
    public string manufacturer;
    public System.Double price;

    public string getType() {
      return type;
    }

    public void setType(string param) {
      type = param;
    }

    public string getManufacturer() {
      return manufacturer;
    }

    public void setManufacturer(string param) {
      manufacturer = param;
    }

    public System.Double getPrice() {
      return price;
    }
    public void setPrice(System.Double param) {
      price = param;
    }
  }
}
```

The .NET CLR client application configures .NET Remoting in the standard way using the configuration file remoting.config. This file specifies the URL of the `java_server.Catalog` object and the channel and formatter types to be used. For example, if the Ja.NET TCP server is used to host the `java_server` on the same machine using port 7562, the configuration file would contain the following application entry:

```
<client>
    <wellknown url="tcp://localhost:7562"
    type="java_server.Catalog, JanetExample"/>
</client>
```

The client can then just instantiate and invoke methods on the Java server objects as if they were local CLR components. Refer to Listing 5-8.

Listing 5-8
Sample .NET Client to Access Product Catalog Java Server

```
// Example .NET client to access Product Catalog Java server
using System;
using System.Runtime.Remoting;
using java_server;

namespace csharp_client
{
  class Client
  {
    static void Main(string[] args)
    {
      // configure .NET Remoting
      RemotingConfiguration.Configure("remoting.config");

      // access the Product Catalog
      Catalog catalog = new Catalog();

      // call a method of the Catalog to get By-Value Product objects
      Product[] p = catalog.getProducts();

      Console.WriteLine("Products:");

      for (int i = 0; i < p.Length; i++)
```

Listing 5-8 (continued)

```
    Console.WriteLine(p[i].manufacturer + " "
        + p[i].type +  " $" + p[i].price);

    Console.WriteLine("Press any key to continue...");
    Console.ReadLine();
    }
  }
}
```

Resources

- More information on Intrinsyc's J-Integra Interoperability Suite, including a free trial version download, is available at http://j-integra.intrinsyc.com/.

- Ja.NET is also featured in Chapter 4 Part II of *Microsoft .NET and Java EE Interoperability Toolkit* by Simon Guest. Microsoft Press. ISBN 0-7356-1922-0.

- Some introductory technical articles on .NET Remoting are: http://msdn.microsoft.com/library/default.asp?url=/library/en-us/dndotnet/html/hawkremoting.asp and www.developer.com/net/cplus/article.php/1479761.

JNBridge for Java EE .NET Integration

Scope

Web services provide an excellent solution for allowing cross-platform components to interoperate. However, Web services are designed for loosely coupled interactions that are infrequent and coarse-grained; therefore, they are not appropriate for applications that require frequent and fine-grained calls between Java and .NET classes. In the scenarios where Web services fall short of the requirements, Java/.NET bridging solutions such as JNBridgePro are the answer. JNBridgePro, a leading Java/.NET interoperability bridging product, provides a bi-directional, easy to use, high-performance, fine-grained direct mapping between Java/Java EE and .NET languages.

JNBridgePro is appropriate to use when

- Exposing a rich interface for a large number of Java classes and objects is necessary.

- Client-activated objects need to be created using the standard constructor (new) mechanism.

- Speed is very important. JNBridgePro offers three communication methods: in-process shared-memory, a binary protocol over TCP, and HTTP/SOAP—whereas Web services uses only a text-based communication protocol.

- Reference semantics are needed for passing parameters or return values.

When using JNBridgePro to allow .NET code to call Java code, the .NET code calls proxy objects that were automatically generated using the JNBridgePro proxy generation tool. The proxies manage the communication; the calling .NET classes aren't even aware that they're ultimately calling Java classes. JNBridgePro provides bi-directional interoperability for a wide variety of architectures because the Java code and the .NET code can be on different machines, the Java code can run in a standalone JVM or in a Java EE application server, and the solution provides interoperability for any JDK version.

JNBridgePro Overview

JNBridgePro allows classes written in .NET languages like C#, C++, and Visual Basic to seamlessly and transparently access Java classes as though Java were itself a .NET language. JNBridgePro supports Java SE or Java EE and the leading Java EE application servers, allowing .NET code to access Java EE facilities including EJBs, JMS, and JNDI.

JNBridgePro is designed so that the .NET objects interact with the Java objects through an automatically generated set of proxies. The Java objects behind the proxies may be on the same machine as the invoking .NET objects or on a different machine on the local area network or across the Internet; communication between the .NET and the Java objects uses .NET's remoting mechanism. JNBridgePro provides Java/.NET interaction via three communication mechanisms: a very fast in-process "shared memory" channel, a fast TCP/binary communication channel, and an HTTP/SOAP communication channel. When the coarse-grained, high-overhead approach of Web services prevents their use, the JNBridgePro Java/.NET bridging solution is an excellent choice.

General Architectural Discussion of JNBridgePro

A system using JNBridgePro consists of components on both the Java side and the .NET side. Figure 5-15 shows the architecture for .NET calling Java. When going in the other direction, the architecture is symmetrical by using proxies that allow Java to call .NET code. On the .NET side are the classes of the driving .NET application, the assembly consisting of the generated proxies, and a runtime component containing a set of core proxies and classes to manage Java-.NET communication and references to Java objects. On the Java side are the Java classes (either as individual class files or JAR files) and a Java runtime component that manages communication, method dispatch, and object references on the Java side.

The Java side can run inside a standalone Java Virtual Machine (JVM) or in any application server that contains a Java EE servlet container. The .NET side can be a standalone application, an ASP.NET Web application, or a Web service. JNBridgePro supports communication between Java and .NET sides using an in-process shared-memory channel, a fast binary protocol based on .NET Remoting, or HTTP/SOAP. No change to the code is required to switch between communication protocols—only changes to configuration files.

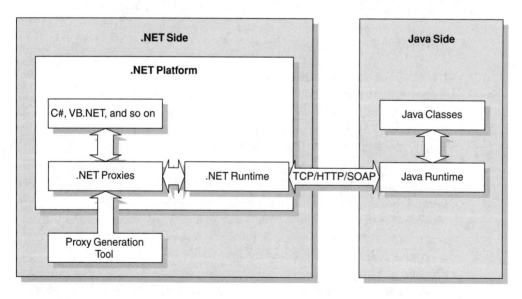

Figure 5-15
.NET calling Java architecture

Use Case Setup

Following is a quick sample scenario in the Supply Chain Management domain from the Web Services-Interoperability Organization's Supply Chain Management use case model at http://ws-i.org/documents.aspx. The goal of this use case is to show a consumer interacting with a GUI application that connects to a retailer's Java EE back-end system to purchase products.

There are three actors in this use case; the first is a human user, the second is a demo system (the GUI shopping application), and the third is a Retailer System (that fulfills the order). For simplicity's sake, preconditions will not be checked, but it will be verified that the order can be fulfilled. If the order cannot be fulfilled, an exception will be thrown. Here is a slightly modified main success path for Use Case 1 or UC1 from the WS-I use case model.

Table 5-1 depicts the main success path of the use case "purchase goods."

Table 5-1
Purchase Goods Main Success Path

Step	Actor	Description
1	Demo System	The Demo System presents a catalog of products.
2	Consumer	The Consumer enters the number of each product required (i.e. changes the number from zero to a required amount).
3	Consumer	When happy with the quantities, the Consumer submits the order to the Retailer System via the GUI interface.
4	Retailer System	Validates order. An exception is thrown if the order is not processed for any reason. If any errors were reported, the consumer is informed that the transaction failed.
5	Demo System	Demo system displays order confirmation information.
6		The use case ends.

Solution

For purposes of this example, it is assumed that for business reasons, the Demo System needs to be written in C#/.NET using Windows Forms while the Retailer System already exists and was built using a Java EE architecture. The main entry point to the order processing system is the method called `placeOrder` in the OrderProcessor Session EJB. Figure 5-16 shows the static UML model of the order processing subsystem. The `placeOrder` method of the `OrderProcessor` class throws an `InvalidOrderException`. The items returned by the `getItems` method are returned in an `ArrayList`.

Here is an outline of what will be shown in the following section. The Java code that will be used to get a list of items for sale and place orders is briefly discussed. The JNBridgePro proxy generation tool takes this code and generates .NET proxies to it in the form of an assembly (DLL). The text then looks at a high level at some of the C# code that calls the Java code through the proxies. Finally, a detailed view is given on how the actual cross-platform calls are made through a sequence diagram call to the `getItems` method. Refer to Figure 5-16.

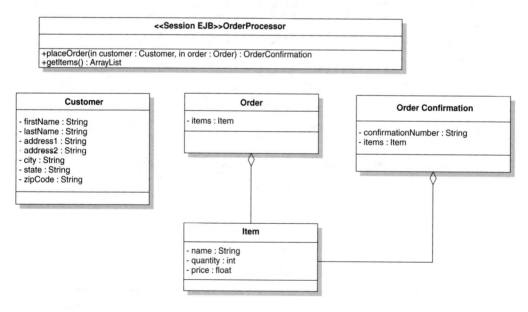

Figure 5-16
Entity relationship of the Java-side code

Java-Side Code

Listing 5-9 shows a snippet of the Java-side code.

Listing 5-9
Snippet of the Java-Side Code

```
package examples.ejb20.basic.statelessSession;

import javax.ejb.CreateException;
import javax.ejb.SessionBean;
import javax.ejb.SessionContext;
import javax.naming.InitialContext;
import javax.naming.NamingException;

/**
 * OrderProcessorBean is a stateless Session Bean.
 */
public class OrderProcessorBean implements SessionBean
{
  public OrderConfirmation placeOrder(Customer customer, Order order)
      throws InvalidOrderException
  {
    String confirmation = checkOrderAvailability(order);
    return new OrderConfirmation(confirmation, order);
  }
```

Generating Proxies

Each Java class that is to be accessible to .NET classes must have a corresponding .NET proxy class that manages communications with the Java class. The .NET classes interact with the proxy class as though it were the underlying Java class, and the actions are transparently communicated to the underlying Java class. JNBridgePro includes both a graphical and command line proxy generation tool. Proxies would only need to be generated for the methods of the OrderProcessor session bean and its supporting classes. Some additional proxies need to be generated to support EJBs (JNDI lookups and so on).

Generating proxies takes three steps:

- Describe the `classpath` and add classes to the environment to make them available for exploration and proxy generation.
- Select classes in the environment for which proxies are to be generated and add them to the exposed proxies list.
- Build the proxies into a .NET assembly. (Java-to-.NET calls—when creating a program that performs Java-to-.NET calls, the proxies are built into a Java JAR file.)

JNBProxy will, given one or more Java class names, generate .NET proxies for those classes and optionally all the supporting classes, including parameter and return value types, thrown exceptions, interfaces, and super classes, resulting in complete class closure. JNBProxy then generates a .NET assembly (a DLL file) that contains the implementation of the .NET proxy classes corresponding to the Java classes. Once this assembly has been generated, it can be used to access the corresponding Java classes.

Using Proxies

When writing the code for Listing 5-10, the assembly with the generated proxies for the `OrderProcessor` Session beans must be imported into the Visual Studio project. Once that is done, all of the Java proxies are called in the exact same way that one would call any other C# object. Even the code completion technology of Visual Studio .NET, Intellisense, functions properly when writing code using the proxies generated by JNBridgePro.

Listing 5-10 shows a small portion of the source code for the C# Windows Form portion of example code. As can be seen from Listing 5-10, the C# code for the Windows Form is strikingly similar to Java code. The `getInitialContext` and `getItems` methods have all the setup code expected to lookup an EJB including finding the initial context and getting the home and remote interface. Following is some of the source code along with a high-level explanation of what is happening between the C# and Java sides.

Listing 5-10
.NET-Side Code

```
using System;
using System.Collections;
```

```
using System.Windows.Forms;

// JNBridgePro Generated Proxies Contained in (OrderProcessor)
Assembly
using java.util;
using javax.naming;
using javax.rmi;
using com.jnbridge.examples.sunBook;

namespace OrderProcessorDemo
{
private void Form1_Load(object sender, System.EventArgs e)
{
        code to populate form removed
}

private Context getInitialContext()
{
  try
  {
   return new InitialContext();
  }
  catch( NamingException ne )
  {
   Console.WriteLine("We were unable to conntect to the App server");
   Console.WriteLine("Please make sure that the server is running.");
   throw ne;
  }
 }

private ArrayList getItems()
{
try
{
  InitialContext jndiContext = (InitialContext) getInitialContext();
   java.lang.Object objRef = jndiContext.lookup("theOrderProcessor");
   java.lang.Class orderProcessorClass =
java.lang.Class.forName("com.jnbridge.demo.sunBook.OrderProcessorHome";

  OrderProcessorHome home =
    (OrderProcessorHome)PortableRemoteObject.narrow(objRef,calcClass);
```

Listing 5-10 (continued)

```
OrderProcessor remote = home.create();

System.Collections.ArrayList items = remote.getItems().NativeImpl;
return items;
}

catch( java.lang.Exception ex )
{
  Console.WriteLine(ex.JavaExceptionClass);
  Console.WriteLine(ex.JavaExceptionMessage);
  Console.WriteLine(ex.JavaStackTrace);
        }
}
}
```

```
using javax.naming;
```

"imports" the proxies that were generated by JNBridgePro that are used to access the Java/JNDI code. These proxies are included in the `OrderProcessor` assembly that has been included in the Visual Studio .NET project. The `using` keyword actually imports the proxies generated by JNBridgePro.

```
new InitialContext();
```

creates a new object of type `javax.naming.InitialContext`. Because this is a proxy object, the new operator is actually creating a new object on the Java side and returning it as a C# object.

```
java.lang.Object objRef = jndiContext.lookup("theOrderProcessor");
```

simply makes a method call on the `jndiContext` object, though it is a bit more complicated. Of course, this lookup happens on the Java side, and the resulting Object is sent back to the C# side. One interesting note here is that the context lookup returns an anonymous class; therefore, the proxy for this object must be generated on the fly.

```
catch( java.lang.Exception ex )
```

catches any `java.lang.Exception` that is thrown by the code in the try/catch block. These exceptions are generated by the Java code and are automatically translated into exceptions that are compliant with the C# exception handling mechanisms.

Resulting System

The ordering screen, upon activation, makes a call to the `OrderProcessor` EJB method `getItems`. The `Item` objects returned are used to populate each of the four items seen on the ordering screen. When the user enters a non-zero quantity and clicks the OK button, the C# code then calls the `OrderProcessor` Session EJB method `placeOrder`. The return value from that call is used to populate the Order Confirmation screen. From this simple example, one can see how JNBridge makes the cross-platform method calls. Refer to Figures 5-17 and 5-18.

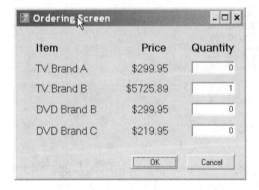

Figure 5-17
Running the Ordering Applications

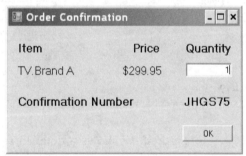

Figure 5-18
Windows form code

Detailed Architectural Discussion

Following is a detailed look at what happens when a .NET method makes a call to the Java side. For purposes of explanation, consider the following line of code:

```
System.Collections.ArrayList items = remote.getItems().NativeImpl;
```

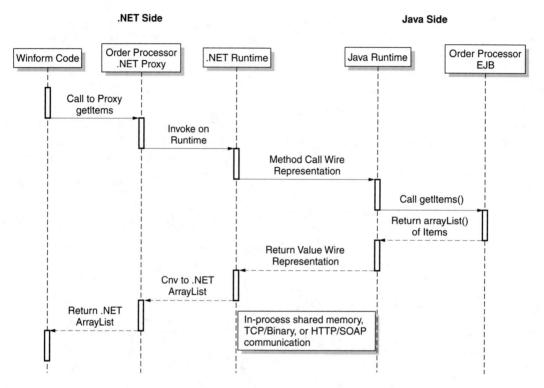

Figure 5-19
Sequence diagram for the .NET-to-Java integration example

Figure 5-19 shows a detailed sequence diagram for the preceding method call. To better understand the technology behind JNBridgePro, look at this line of code by walking through a sequence diagram of the resulting call path.

Object Lifelines

Table 5-2 summarizes the object lifelines discussed in this section.

Table 5-2

Summary of Object Lifeline

Lifeline Name	Lifeline Explanation
WinForm Code	The code written for the GUI front-end application to display a list of items to purchase.
Order Processor .NET-side Proxy	The proxy generated by the JNBridge proxy generation tool for the OrderProcessor EJB method named getItems.
.NET-side Runtime	The library (.DLL) included with JNBridgePro that is responsible for marshaling and un-marshaling .NET objects from the 'wire' representation that JNBridgePro uses.
Java-side Runtime	The library (Ja0) included with JNBridgePro that is responsible for marshaling and un-marshaling Java objects from the 'wire' representation. This library is also responsible for calling the Java-side objects and returning return values.
OrderProcessor EJB	The existing EJB that contains logic for return the available items for sale.

Message Calls

Table 5-3 summarizes the message calls discussed in this section.

Table 5-3

Summary of Message Calls

Message Call Name	Message Call Explanation
Call to .NET-side getItems	Calls the proxy generated by JNBridgePro.
Message2	Passes call information to .NET-side runtime.
Method Call 'Wire' Representation	Takes the method call, marshals it, and forwards it to the Java-side runtime. A binary representation is used for all three methods. For the HTTP/SOAP communication channel, a binary representation is contained in the SOAP message body.

continues

Table 5-3
Summary of Message Calls (*continued*)

Message Call Name	Message Call Explanation
Call getItems	The Java-side runtime unmarshals the message pay-load and finds the proper object and method to call.
Return Array List of Items	The EJB returns the ArrayList, which is passed to the Java-side runtime.
Return Value 'Wire' Representation	The ArrayList is converted into the binary 'Wire' representation and passed back to the .NET-side runtime. Because the user selected the java.util.ArrayList as directly mapped, the objects contained in the ArrayList are copied.
Convert to .NET System.Collections .ArrayList	The .NET-side runtime unmarshals the java.util.ArrayList. Because the user selected the java.util.ArrayList class to be directly mapped, the wire representation is unmarshaled into a System.Collections.ArrayList. (This is a by-value mapping so each object in the ArrayList is also copied.)
Return .NET ArrayList	The ArrayList of items is now available to be used in the WinForms code.

Benefits

As is apparent from the preceding example, using the JNBridgePro Java/.NET interoperability solution is quite easy.

- It can be built into a build process to automatically change proxies during development cycle.
- No Web service interoperability issues—this solution is guaranteed to work.

Reliability

JNBridgePro supports failover. In the "purchase goods" scenario given, it is possible that the Retailer System could be down. In most high-availability scenarios, a redundant failover server is available. Using JNBridgePro, a failover server can be specified. If the primary server fails for any reason, JNBridgePro can forward the request to the failover server. In this scenario, a `FailedServerException` is thrown so that the user knows that the primary server is not available and can then simply forward the request to the failover server. This is done semi-automatically because in many scenarios, an automatic rerouting of the order is sufficient.

Transactions

JNBridgePro provides support for the transaction mechanisms of the Java and .NET platforms. When dealing with messaging systems, Transactions are of the utmost importance where performance and reliability are concerned. For more information on interoperability with Transactions, see Chapter 12, "Managing Distributed Transactions."

Security

If one uses the in-process shared-memory channel, security is not a concern because the communication between the two applications is taking place in the same memory space. Using JNBridgePro's TCP/binary socket-based communication channel is normally done for applications running on the same intranet. JNBridgePro can also be used to interoperate between Java and .NET applications residing on any two Internet-connected machines.

Summary

This chapter looked at .NET Remoting for synchronous integration and in particular how this may be used for interoperability between .NET and Java EE. The discussion looked at several methodologies and products for how interoperability can be achieved, including:

- The IIOP Open Source Project
- JIntegra
- JNBridge

Each of these products was discussed along with their attributes with respect to interoperability.

Resource Tier Synchronous Integration

6

Introduction

The Resource tier often comprises a diverse set of enterprise applications such as databases, ERP, CRM, and legacy systems. It is common to develop point-to-point integration to each of these applications that in the end yields a convoluted system landscape. Adding the Java EE and .NET technology disparity increases the complexity of the integration task. Therefore, as a best practice, it is valuable to abstract out the back-end integration by building a so-called Integration tier. This Integration tier provides cohesive access to the corresponding Resource tier in a way that is transparent to the rest of the business logic. In the context of Java EE .NET integration, it is particularly important to factor out the integration logic to avoid a brittle architecture and allow individual services to interconnect using Service Oriented Architecture (SOA).

This chapter demonstrates how to achieve interoperability with back-end services using synchronous integration and how to overcome Java and .NET technology mismatches. The first strategy involves building an interoperable Data Access Layer that allows Java EE and .NET applications to access back-end applications. Additionally, the chapter discusses design techniques related to legacy integration that are present in most enterprise Resource tiers.

Those familiar with Java EE and .NET persistence layers, connection pooling techniques, and object-relational mapping mechanisms can jump straight to the "Data Access Adapter Strategy" section. Otherwise, it might be useful to learn the basics of Java and .NET database connectivity.

Java EE Persistence Mechanism

There are a few options available to Java developers to build database connectivity. Depending on the application requirements, they might select Plain Old Java Object (POJO) to connect to the back-end systems. Alternatively, if the system relies on Enterprise Java Beans (EJBs), there are two flavors of persistence mechanisms to choose from: Bean Managed Persistence (BMP), where database access is programmatically managed, or Container Managed Persistence (CMP) that relies on the underlying application server or third-party integrated CMP solutions to connect to the database and perform object-to-relational mapping. Both BMP and the POJO model directly leverage Java Database Connectivity (JDBC) and allow users to construct SLQ statements manually. With CMP as well as with Java Data Objects (JDO), which is another option available to assemble a persistence layer, developers do not have to manually construct SQL queries. With JDO, an XML mapping outlines how Java objects map with a relational database. XML mapping can be defined with tools that are available with commercial and open source JDO implementations. With EJB CMP, the `mapping-properties` element contains the object to relational database mapping. With both of these approaches, the Data Access Layer is transparent at development and configured at deployment.

JDBC APIs facilitate traditional database Create/Remove/Update/Delete (CRUD) operations and support embedded SQL statements that can be passed as method arguments. JDBC also supports stored procedures and prepared statements as well as SQL3 data types, scrollable result sets, and programmatic and batch updates. There are numerous providers for the JDBC drivers, see [JDBC_Drivers]. Depending on the database, the developer might have to choose one out of four different types of JDBC drivers:

- **Type 1** drivers provide the Java bridging technology to access a database driver. The JDBC-ODBC bridge is an example of such a driver.

- **Type 2** drivers are native API drivers that allow Java applications to make JNI calls to the corresponding low-level (for example, C/C++) methods for database access.

- **Type 3** drivers are based on the networking APIs and use sockets to communicate between the client application and middleware on the database server, which translates the client call to the corresponding database driver call.

- **Type 4** drivers are the most popular because they are pure Java drivers that use Java sockets to communicate to the database. This type of driver implements the JDBC specification in Java and is the simplest to configure.

The JDBC APIs are provided with the java.sql library and the optional package, javax.sql, which includes the JDBC 2.0 Standard Extension API.

From a programming standpoint, connecting to a database starts with a JNDI look up call, where the logical name assigned to the data source would be passed:

```
DataSource dataSource =
(DataSource)context.lookup("java:comp/env/jdbc/SupplyChainDB");
```

After obtaining a data source, the next step is to get the database connection that is either retrieved from a connection pool or newly created:

```
Connection conn = datasource.getConnection();
Statement stmt = conn.createStatement();
```

In cases where a JNDI context is not present, you can use `DriverManager` to obtain a connection:

```
DriverManager.getConnection()
```

The next step is to execute an SQL statement. The JDBC API supports regular SQL statements that can be embedded into Java applications in the following manner:

```
ResultSet rs = stmt.executeQuery("SELECT descr, qty FROM
ship_goods");
```

Updating database information can be achieved with the `executeUpdate()` operation:

```
String query1 =
    new String("INSERT INTO ship_goods VALUES ('847SWS',
                'SunFire V40z',3)");
stmt.executeUpdate(query1);
```

In addition to the embedded Java SQL statements, JDBC supports prepared statements using `PreparedStatement`, which allow passing parameters into a query at the time of statement execution:

```
PreparedStatement stmt =
    conn.prepareStatement("update ship_goods set qty = ?" );
```

The statement is invoked with the corresponding parameter passed at the time of invocation. The value of the parameter has to be bound to the corresponding data type, such as Integer:

```
stmt.setInt( 3, item.getQty() );
```

The prepared statement is now ready for execution:

```
stmt.execute();
stmt.closei();
```

Database stored procedures can be invoked via `CallableStatement`. In the example that follows, three parameters have to be passed to the `shipGoods()` stored procedure at the time of execution. This is shown in Listing 6-1.

Listing 6-1
JDBC Callable Statement

```
CallableStatement statement =
    connection.prepareCall("{call shipGoods[(?,?,?)]}");

stmt.setString(1, item.getId());
stmt.setString(2, item.getDescr());
stmt.setInt(3, itme.getQty());
stmt.execute();
```

It is important to note that an `insert`, `delete`, or `update` operation has to be enclosed within the scope of the transaction that either commits or rolls back, as shown in Listing 6-2.

Listing 6-2
Transaction Management

```
try{
    userTxn.begin();
    stmt.executeUpdate("update ...")";
    userTxn.commit();
}
catch (SQLException exc) {
    try {
        // In case of an error rollback the transaction
        userTxn.rollback()
    } catch (Exception e) {// process exception}
} finally {...}
```

JDBC ResultSet and RowSet

To retrieve and iterate over a result set, JDBC provides a `ResultSet` class that allows a parsing result of the executed query (Listing 6-3):

Listing 6-3
ResultSet Example

```
ResultSet rs = stmt.executeQuery("SELECT descr, qty FROM
ship_goods");
    while (rs.next())
        System.out.println(rs.getString("descr") + "        "
        + rs.getInt("qty"));
```

To preview information stored by the result set, JDBC APIs provide `ResultSetMetaData` and `RowSetMetaData` libraries. Previewing the number of records may be useful if a result set contains a large number of records to gradually process the result set. The `javax.sql.RowSet` is an extension to the `ResultSet` that complies with the JavaBean component model. Property manipulation and event notification are supported as part of that model. Another useful feature relates to the fact that `RowSet` can be serialized for remote processing. For a scrollable and updateable result set, `CachedRowSet`, which is is a JavaBean, should be considered.

CachedRowSet can be easily populated with database data and treated as a "disconnected" component from the data source. CachedRowSet can be sent to a remote client application for updates without maintaining an open database connection. This model is more scalable and offers a greater degree of flexibility. Aside from the CachedRowSet, the JDBC 3.0 API defines the JdbcRowSet interface that allows a ResultSet to be represented in the form of a JavaBean. A WebRowSet extends CachedRowSet with Web application functionalities. Specifically, a WebRowSet can read and write a RowSet object in a well formed XML format. A FilteredRowSet, as implied by its name, is used for filtering on inbound and outbound RowSet read and write operations. A JoinRowSet is another type of RowSet that acts as a container combining multiple RowSet objects. See [JavaSQLDescr] for more details on RowSet functionality.

JDBC also supports retrieval of the database metadata via DatabaseMetaData, ResultSetMetaData, and RowSetMetaData classes.

After data have been retrieved and corresponding database operations have been completed, it is time to close the database connection.

Closing Connections

When manipulating data using the JDBC API, it is important to close any database connections, statements, and result sets to prevent leaking resources. It is wise to close the database connection in the finally block to ensure that the closing logic is executed regardless of the program success or failure.

Listing 6-4
Closing JDBC Connection

```
finally {
    if (stmt != null)
        try {
            stmt.close();
        } catch (sqlexception sqlex) { }

    if (resultSet != null)
        try {
            resultSet.close();
        } catch (sqlexception sqlex) { }

    if (conn != null)
        try {
            conn.close();
        } catch (sqlexception sqlex) {}
}
```

The next sections look at database access functionality available under .NET.

Accessing Data via ADO.NET

On the .NET platform, ADO.NET is the main mechanism to access a database. Similar to JDBC drivers, ADO.NET providers enable access to the underlying data sources. There are three main types of .NET Framework providers. They are SQL Server, OLEDB, and ODBC providers, each having individual pros and cons, which will be discussed here.

The ADO.NET provider for SQL Server belongs to the class of *managed* providers that enable native connectivity to the underlying data source. Managed providers are executed within the CLR boundaries, which is to say, managed by the CLR. Managed providers are very appealing to .NET developers due to their inherit OOP support and optimal performance. The .NET Framework also allows connecting to a database via OLEDB and ODBC. .NET providers are commonly used to connect to legacy databases that do not have managed providers. The ODBC API is implemented in C, which makes it difficult to apply to the object-oriented .NET application model. Another drawback of the ODBC API is that it is strictly designed to work with relational databases, and therefore it is difficult to extend these APIs to connect to non-relational resources. Finally, OLEDB requires low-level programming that involves excessive complexity at development time. Both ODBC and OLEDB require corresponding .NET providers to facilitate application access to the underlying data sources. The ODBC .NET provider wraps the native ODBC driver. Similarly, the .NET OLEDB provider abstracts out the OLEDB data sources. Adding a layer of indirection between a driver and an application tends to degrade the overall application performance. Therefore, .NET managed providers, such as the SQL provider, help to overcome limitations of OLEDB and ODBC solutions. Figure 6-1 depicts the three main choices for .NET developers to connect to data sources.

Microsoft offers .NET managed providers for SQL Server and Oracle. In addition, managed providers for Oracle, SQL Server, DB2, and Sybase are available from DataDirect and OpenLink Software (see [DataDirect] and [OpenLink]). An example demonstrated later in the chapter uses the Microsoft SQL Server with an SQL managed provider and the Core Lab Software Development's MySql database managed provider.

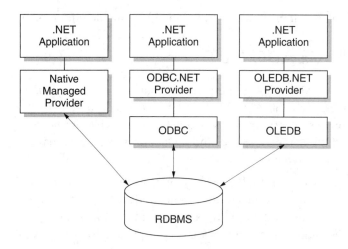

Figure 6-1
.NET Data source architecture

ADO.NET introduces managed object-oriented APIs compared to C-based unmanaged ADO APIs. The ADO.NET API is intended for Web applications development, supporting disconnected result sets and providing intrinsic XML support. A result set retrieved from the database can be easily represented in the XML format and transferred between applications for processing. ADO.NET inherits some of its logic from the ActiveX Data Objects (ADO) APIs, designed for COM applications, which simplifies ADO developers' transition to .NET development. Connecting to a database is fairly straightforward, as discussed next.

Connecting to a Data Source

The libraries that support ADO.NET are bundled within the System.Data.dll assembly. The API comprises five namespaces: Common, OleDb, SqlClient, SqlTypes, and Microsoft.Data.Odbc. The SQL Server System.Data.SqlClient namespace defines data provider classes to connect to the Microsoft SQL Server database. Third-party providers enable access to databases such as MySql [MySQL_DotNet], used by the sample application.

Figure 6-2 highlights how to establish a connection to the database.

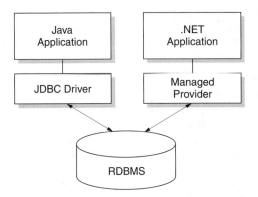

Figure 6-2
Database connectivity overview

A Connection object or in this case, the `MySqlConnection` and `SlqConnection`, provides connectivity to the underlying data source. A `DataAdapter` object uses the Connection to retrieve information by executing a corresponding command. The `Command` object, in this example `SqlCommand` and `MySqlCommand`, is used to execute standard CRUD operations.

The first step is to create a Connection object with the corresponding host, database name, and database user ID and password information that is passed in the form of a connection string:

```
string conString = "Data
Source=(local);uid=sa;pwd=admin;database=Warehouse_B";
SqlConnection conn = new SqlConnection(connString);
```

Next is to compose an SQL command that inserts some data into the `ship_goods` table:

```
string query =
    "INSERT INTO ship_goods (id, descry, qty)
    VALUES ('01JKY977Y','SunFire V40z',2)";
```

The `Command` object, created next, executes the previous SQL call:

```
SqlCommand command = new SqlCommand(query);
command.Connection = conn;
```

Next is to open the connection and execute the command:

```
con.Open();
command.ExecuteNonQuery();
```

ADO.NET allows using either a `Command` object directly to execute CRUD operations or use the `Command` in conjunction with a `DataAdapter` to retrieve data into a `DataSet` for disconnected processing. The code snippet that follows shows how to populate the `DataSet` object using `SqlDataAdapter`:

```
SqlDataAdapter adapter = new SqlDataAdapter(sql, conn);
DataSet dataset = new DataSet("ShipGoodsDescr");
adapter.Fill(dataset, "Descr");
```

The disconnected `DataSet` can then be passed to a remote client for display or further processing. As can be seen from the preceding example, `Connection`, `Command`, `DataReader`, and `DataAdapter` comprise core classes of the ADO.NET namespace. The `Command` object executes not only queries, but also stored procedures and returns `DataSet` or `DataReader` objects discussed hereafter.

Similar to the JDBC model, ADO.NET allows the execution of stored procedures. For that the command type needs to be set as follows:

```
Command.CommandType = CommandType.StoredProcedure;
```

The corresponding parameters can then be passed to the stored procedure. As a way to optimize the performance of stored procedures, Microsoft introduced a new component called Data Access Application Block (DAAB).

Data Access Application Block

The goal behind the DAAB component is similar to the JDBC objective, which is to develop code that is portable across multi-vendor databases such as SQL Server, Oracle, and DB2. DAAB introduces a layer of abstraction over database accesses, thus hiding database specifics from .NET developers. In terms of stored procedure optimization, DAAB defines the *ParameterCache* class that caches the necessary parameters associated with a stored procedure and avoids future look up calls to the database, in case subsequent stored procedure invocations are performed. Another nice feature of DAAB is abstraction over the database name. A logical name for a database, similar to the JNDI name, can be used by an application in lieu of hard-coded details of the underlying data source. Application configuration files store database specifics, which allows a developer to easily switch between databases without having to recompile the code. The *DatabaseFactory* object retrieves required configuration parameters at run time to access the corresponding database. See [DAAB] for additional information.

ADO.NET *DataReader* and *DataSet*

As part of the System.Data namespace, ADO.NET provides two main methodologies to fetch data—a connected model and a disconnected model. The **connected model** uses DataReader to fetch rows of data through an active connection to a data source and is somewhat similar to the JDBC ResultSet. The **disconnected model** uses the DataAdapter as a bridge between the database and a DataSet (which resembles the JDBC RowSet), offering disconnected, updateable, scrollable access to the data. DataSet can be used to pass information to a remote client application for processing. Because retrieved data often have to be preordered or filtered, the DataView object can be used to represent different views of the same dataset. A DataViewManager embraces a collection of views, which simplifies data management.

Listing 6-5 lists how to retrieve data from a database.

Listing 6-5
ADO.NET *DataReader* Example

```
string sqlSelect ="SELECT descr FROM ship_goods";
SqlExecuteReader reader = cmd.ExecuteReader();

while (reader.Read())
    Console.Write(reader.GetString(0).ToString());
```

DataReader is also useful in the situations where you need to execute multiple queries as a single batch job, as shown in Listing 6-6:

Listing 6-6
DataReader Batch Job

```
string query1 = "SELECT * FROM ship_goods";
string query2 = "SELECT * FROM purchase_order";
string query3 = "SELECT * FROM invoice";
SqlCommand command = new SqlCommand(query1, query2, query3);
    SqlExecuteReader reader = command.ExecuteReader();
```

From a best practices standpoint, `DataReader` should be used with `Command` object for rapid data access, as it only provides forward read-only functionality. `DataReader` does not allow modifying the fetched data. On the other hand, `DataAdapter` is used in conjunction with `DataSet` to enable modifications made to the retrieved data.

ADO.NET provides a rich set of data structures to store relational data in an object format. These objects include `DataTable`, `DataColumn Collection`, `DataColumn`, `DataRowCollection`, `DataRow`, `Constraint Collection`, and `Constraint`. ADO.NET also supports access to the underlying resource's metadata such as Data Column.

Closing ADO.NET Connection

After the data have been fetched, it's important not to forget to close the database connection:

```
reader.Close();
conn.Close();
```

See [ADO.NET_Examples], [ADO.NET_C#], and [DataAccess_Architecture Guide] for more details on best practices developing ADO.NET applications.

After having walked through Java and .NET database APIs, the next step is to explore the connection pooling functionality.

Connection Pooling with .NET and Java EE

Both Java and .NET support a connection-pooling mechanism that allows reusing database connections. The purpose behind a connection pool is to enhance application performance, reduce underlying resources utilization, and simplify the programming model.

In .NET you need to close or dispose the connection to ensure that the connection is returned back to the pool. Common parameters that can be set include initial pool size, connection lifetime, maximum pool size, and minimum pool size. See [ConnPooling_.NET] for more details on setting up a connection pool under .NET. Defining a connection pool in Java is similar. The connection pool can be established for both Java EE and Java applications. Former types of applications would leverage the pool of resources provided by Java EE application servers. See [ConnPooling_Java] for more details on setting up a connection pool in Java. Listing 6-7 defines a connection pool in Java.

Listing 6-7
Connection Pool in JDBC

```
Context ctx = new InitialContext();
ConnectionPoolDataSource datasource =
(ConnectionPoolDataSource)ctx.lookup("jdbc/Warehouse_A");
pooledConnection pcon = datasource.getPooledConnection("root",
"admin");
```

As has already been shown, the connection initialization starts with the JNDI look up call. The returned logical name of the connection pool is narrowed to a `javax.sqlConnectionPoolDataSource` type. A connection is then returned from the `getPooledConnection()` method.

Along with connection-pooling functionality, both Java and .NET applications leverage the persistence mechanism, which is explored next.

Object-Relational Mapping

Most enterprise applications use a mapping between the domain object model and the database relational model. There is often no direct correspondence that can be drawn easily between these two models, and application developers have to translate relational schema into an object-oriented class hierarchy.

To abridge the tedious translation routine between these two models, there are object-relational mapping (ORM) tools available for both Java and .NET platforms [.NET_ORM_Tools]. With the Java EE architecture developers can leverage Entity Beans with CMP or BMP to perform mapping between the object and relational layers. The complexity of the EJB persistence model resulted in the development of a simpler Java Data Object (JDO) specification and open source solutions such as Hibernate. Third-party products including Oracle, TopLink, SolarMetric, and Kodo offer tools that shield application developers from the underlying SQL calls.

Considering the importance of the persistence layer for any enterprise application and the complexity of EJBs, a new persistence model has been introduced in the EJB 3.0 specification, developed as part of JSR_220. This specification defines a persistence layer using Plain Old Java Objects (POJO), thus no longer requiring an EJB to implement the home interface. The idea behind this specification is to simplify and standardize Java persistence APIs. This new model leverages best practices from Java Data Objects (JDO) and Hibernate, both of which are commonly used in the industry to develop a persistence layer.

Common best practices such as Data Transfer Objects (DTO) and Service Locator patterns are used by the EJB 3.0 specification. Additionally, the specification uses annotations and the EJB QL query language. The EJB 3.0 specification intends to steer Java developers toward a cohesive persistence model and will be available as part of the Java EE 5.0 platform. See [JDO], [Hibernate], [JSR_220], [TopLink], and [Kodo] for more details.

Version 2.0 of the .NET Framework introduces ObjectSpaces that enable the O/R Mapping. Object to relational schema mapping with ObjectSpaces encompasses three parts: Relational Schema Definition (RSD), Object Schema Definition (OSD), and Mapping Schema that links the other two schemas. For initializing ObjectSpaces you can only pass the Mapping Schema that defines mapping rules, listed in Listing 6-8.

Listing 6-8
.NET Mapping Schema

```
<m:Mappings>
    <m:Map SourceVariable="ship_goods"
TargetSelect="Retailer.ShipGoods">
        <m:FieldMap SourceField="ID" TargetField="ID" />
        <m:FieldMap SourceField="QTY" TargetField="Quantity" />
        <m:FieldMap SourceField="DESCR" TargetField="Description" />
    </m:Map>
</m:Mappings>
```

More can be learned about ObjectSpaces in [ObjectSpaces] and download samples, documentations, and tools as part of the Win FX SDK, [WinFX_SDK].

If a persistence layer in Java or .NET is being built, there are numerous resources available to guide developers through the process and to determine the optimal O/R mapping tool. Interestingly, a popular open source Java O/RM tool, Hibernate, is being ported to .NET. See [NHibernate] for more details. Among commercial solutions, LLBLGen Pro and EntityBroker offer O/R Mapping solutions under .NET. See [LLBLGen_Pro] and [EntityBroker]. For an additional list of tools please refer to [ORM_Tools_Java] and [ORM_Tools_.NET].

After a lengthy introduction to various data access mechanisms, it is time to move on with this chapter's main objective—Resource tier interoperability. First is a brief discussion of the business scenario of the developed application, next is a review of a popular interoperability strategy, and finally a demonstration of the application.

Business Scenario Overview

The WS-I Supply Chain Management sample application continues to be the framework in these illustrations, and a Source Goods use case has been selected to demonstrate effective ways to connect to a back-end infrastructure. The Source Goods scenario is depicted in Figure 6-3:

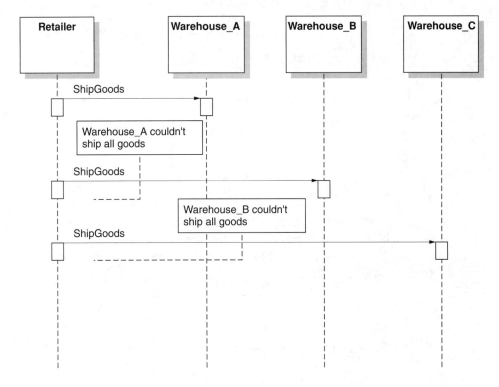

Figure 6-3
Business scenario sequence diagram

The main application processes a `ShipGoods` request, for which the application has to build integration points with multiple back-end warehousing systems. Depending on goods availability, the application submits requests to multiple warehouse systems until the order has been fulfilled. For the purpose of demonstrating how to connect to heterogeneous back-end environments, we will assume that Warehouse_A represents an RDBMS system such as Oracle or MySql, which is actually used for the code sample. Warehouse_B is represented with Microsoft SQL Server. Warehouse_C is a legacy system that has to be accessed in case the first two `ShipGoods` requests fail. Individual warehousing systems are accessed through the Data Access Layer (DAL) that will be developed in both the Java and .NET applications. First is a look at how to build the DAL from a retailer system implemented in Java and then how to build the same layer with .NET technologies.

Data Access Adapter Strategy

A role of the Adapter strategy is to enable Java or .NET components to transparently access heterogeneous data sources.

Scope

Enterprise applications often require connecting to a diverse set of underlying resources. Common proliferation of data access components across an enterprise application yields poor design. With time, the application expands with additional functionality and new integration points. Without a cohesive Integration tier, application maintenance and troubleshooting becomes quite expensive.

Solution

An Adapter component acts as a single gateway to the underlying resources and represents the core of the Data Access Layer. Depending on the type of systems accessed by the application and the underlying technologies such as Java or .NET, the Adapter component encapsulates corresponding data access functionality. An Adapter is also responsible for transactional context propagation as well as error handling. The example demonstrates how to build simple Adapter components in both Java and .NET. This component hides details of the underlying legacy system and enables access to the heterogeneous back-end environment. Figure 6-4 outlines the Integration Tier that is also referred to as the Data Access Layer:

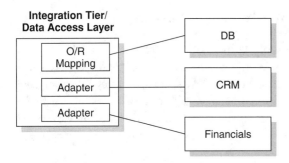

Figure 6-4
Data Access Layer

Benefits and Limitations

In both Java and .NET applications, this strategy can be applied easily to build a DAL. The main advantage of this strategy is the lack of tight dependencies between the underlying resources and the application logic. From a maintenance standpoint, the Adapter component consolidates logic to access an individual resource, which simplifies maintenance and the troubleshooting process.

One of the important aspects of the DAL is transactional and security support. Transactional boundaries are particularly critical when a single call spans across multiple resources. Being able to restore data to the original state in case of a failure has to be addressed during the design phase. Similarly, access to the individual back-end applications has to be authenticated and authorized. Building a common security mechanism to protect access to the Resource tier also has to be addressed at design time.

Related Patterns

The Data Access Object (DAO) pattern from the Core J2EE Patterns [CJ2EEP] defines an abstraction to encapsulate CRUD operations to the underlying RDBMS. The Adapter strategy can leverage DAO objects to connect to underlying databases. The Adapter strategy goes beyond basic database connectivity, as individual adapters have to connect to legacy systems.

The example that follows demonstrates how to implement an Adapter strategy in Java and .NET.

Example 1: .NET Data Access Adapter

Given that individual steps involved in creating a connection and executing an SQL statement have already been covered, now it is time to simply put it all together and illustrate how to build an Adapter that alternates between two different databases. In this case it is MySql and SQL Server. From the business logic, if the Warehouse_A, represented with MySql, is offline, an Adapter automatically connects to the Warehouse_B, represented with SQL Server.

To execute the .NET Data Access Adapter example, you need to download and place the CoreLab.MySql.dll managed provider for MySql into the corresponding chapter6\lib directory. See [CoreLab] to install the solution.

Listing 6-9 lists the C# code for the connectToMySql() method corresponding to the Warehouse_A, MySql connection for the .NET based Data Access Adapter:

Listing 6-9
C# Method Connecting to Warehouse_A, MySql Server

```
public static void connectToMySql(){
    Boolean connected = false;
    MySqlConnection mySqlConnection = new MySqlConnection();
    mySqlConnection.ConnectionString =
        "UserId=root;Database=Warehouse_A;Host=localhost;";

    string query =
      "INSERT INTO ship_goods
       VALUES('01JKY977Y','SunFire V40z',2)";

    MySqlCommand command = new MySqlCommand(query);
    command.Connection = mySqlConnection;

    try {
      Console.WriteLine("Opening connection");
      mySqlConnection.Open();
      Console.WriteLine("Connected to the MySql");
      connected = true;

      Console.WriteLine("Executing query");
      int recs = command.ExecuteNonQuery();
      if(recs!=0) Console.WriteLine("Query successfully
      executed.");
        else Console.WriteLine("Query failed.");

      Console.WriteLine("Closing MySql connection");
      mySqlConnection.Close();
```

```
    } catch (SqlException e) {
      Console.WriteLine(
        "Error connecting or communicating with MySql:"
        +e.ToString());
      connected = false;
    } finally{
    // Connecting to SqlServer
      if (!connected){
          Console.WriteLine(
            "Couldn't connect to the Warehouse_A,
            connecting to Warehouse_B");
      connectToSqlServer();
      }
    }
}
```

Similarly, the connectToSqlServer() method connects the Microsoft SQL Server. The C# implementation of this method is listed in Listing 6-10:

Listing 6-10
C# Method Connecting to Warehouse_B, Microsoft SQL Server

```
public static void connectToSqlServer(){
      string conString =
        "DataSource=(local);uid=sa;pwd=admin;database=Warehouse_B";
      string query =
          "INSERT INTO ship_goods
          VALUES('92M7Y6O','SunFire V40z',2)";

      SqlConnection con = new SqlConnection(conString);

      SqlCommand command = new SqlCommand(query);
      command.Connection = con;
      Console.WriteLine("Opening connection");
      con.Open();
      Console.WriteLine("Connected to Sql Server");

      Console.WriteLine("Executing query");
      command.ExecuteNonQuery();
      Console.WriteLine("Finished query execution");

      Console.WriteLine("Closing Sql Server connection");
      command.Connection.Close();
    }
```

Compiling and running the .NET application produces the following output, shown in Listing 6-11:

Listing 6-11
Connecting to the Database

```
Buildfile: build.xml

init:
    [echo] --- Building j2eedotnet.chapter9 ---

prepare:

compile-dotnet-retailer:
    [exec] Microsoft (R) Visual C# .NET Compiler version 7.10.6001.4
    [exec] for Microsoft (R) .NET Framework version 1.1.4322
    [exec] Copyright (C) Microsoft Corporation 2001-2002. All rights
           reserved.

run-dotnet-retailer:
    [echo] Running .NET Retailer
    [exec] Opening connection
    [exec] Connected to MySql
    [exec] Executing query
    [exec] Finished query execution
    [exec] Closing MySql connection

BUILD SUCCESSFUL
Total time: 1 second
```

Should you disable MySql database, you will see error messages that are followed up with a connection to the SQL Server. Listing 6-12 lists a snippet of the output:

Listing 6-12
.NET Data Access Adapter Application Output

```
run-dotnet-retailer:
    [echo] Running .NET Retailer
    [exec] Opening connection

    [exec] Unhandled Exception: Can't connect to MySql server on
           'localhost' (10061)
    [exec] Couldn't connect to the Warehouse_A, connecting to
           Warehouse_B
    [exec] Opening connection
    [exec] Connected to Sql Server
    [exec] Executing query
    [exec] Finished query execution
    [exec] Closing Sql Server connection
    [exec] Result: -532459699
```

The next sections look at the second example where the Data Access Adapter is implemented in Java.

Example 2: Java Data Access Adapter

The next task is to build the Java-based implementation of the Data Access Adapter. Notice that there are a fair amount of similarities between Java and .NET implementations. Before proceeding with development, the JDBC drivers for SQL Server and MySql need to be configured. To see the detailed configuration of Connector/J JDBC driver, see [MySql_Config]. To connect to the Microsoft SQL Server, the corresponding JDBC driver [SQLServer_JDBC] needs to be downloaded and installed. Add the following jars to the CLASSPATH:

```
install_dir/lib/msbase.jar
install_dir/lib/msutil.jar
install_dir/lib/mssqlserver.jar
```

The first step is to connect to the MySql database. Listing 6-13 shows Java code to connect to the Warehouse_A database, MySql server.

Listing 6-13
Java Method Connecting to Warehouse_A, MySql

```java
public static void main(String args[]) {
    Connection con = null;
    Statement stmt = null;
    ResultSet rs = null;

    try {
        // Since we are not using a connection pool,
        // we simply create a new connection
        Class.forName("com.mysql.jdbc.Driver").newInstance();
        con = DriverManager.getConnection(
            "jdbc:mysql:///Warehouse_A", "root", "");
```

Now establish a similar connection to SQL Server. To specify a connection string, the following information is needed:

```
jdbc:microsoft:sqlserver://hostname:port
    [;property=value...]
```

Where `property=value` is required for the database name and user account:

```
Class.forName("com.microsoft.jdbc.sqlserver.SQLServerDriver");
Connection conn = DriverManager.getConnection
("jdbc:microsoft:sqlserver://Warehouse_B:1433;User=sa;Password=admin
");
```

Listing 6-14 lists content of the Java main method that incorporates details of accessing the database.

Listing 6-14
Java Data Access Adapter Connecting to Warehouse_B, Microsoft SQL Server

```
stmt = con.createStatement();
   String query1 = new String(
       "INSERT INTO ship_goods
        VALUES('92558UYY60','SunFire V40z',2)");
   stmt.executeUpdate(query1);
   stmt.close();

   stmt = con.createStatement();
   String query2 = new String(
       "INSERT INTO ship_goods
        VALUES('83545HYT567Y','SunFire V20z',1)");

   stmt.executeUpdate(query2);
   stmt.close();

   System.out.println("Items              Quantity");
   stmt = con.createStatement();
   rs = stmt.executeQuery("SELECT desrc,qty FROM ship_goods");
   while (rs.next())
       System.out.println(rs.getString("desrc") + "        " +
           rs.getInt("qty"));
```

Executing the application produces the output listed in Listing 6-15:

Listing 6-15
Java Data Access Adapter Application Output, MySql Database

```
>ant run-java-retailer
Buildfile: build.xml

init:
     [echo] --- Building j2eedotnet.chapter9 ---
```

```
prepare:

compile-java-retailer:
    [echo] --- Compiling Java Retailer application ---
    [javac] Compiling 1 source file to
            C:\a_book\Chapter6_DBSync\chapter7\classes

run-java-retailer:
    [echo] --- Running Java Retailer application ---
    [java] Connection to Warehoues_A is established
    [java] Items           Quantity
    [java] SunFire V40z        2
    [java] SunFire V20z        1

BUILD SUCCESSFUL
Total time: 3 seconds
```

Should MySql be disabled, you will be automatically connecting to SQL Server representing Warehouse_B, as shown in Listing 6-16:

Listing 6-16
Java Data Access Adapter Application Output, SQL Server

```
init:
    [echo] --- Building j2eedotnet.chapter9 ---

prepare:

compile-java-retailer:
    [echo] --- Compiling Java Retailer application ---
    [javac] Compiling 1 source file to
            C:\a_book\Chapter6_DBSync\chapter7\classes

run-java-retailer:
    [echo] --- Running Java Retailer application ---
    [java] Cannot connect to Warehouse_A, connecting to Warehouse_B
    [java] Connection to Warehouse_B is established
    [java] Items           Quantity
    [java] SunFire V20z        1
    [java] SunFire V40z        2

BUILD SUCCESSFUL
```

What has been shown in the preceding code listings are implementations of an Adapter strategy. Java and .NET applications can share an adapter or use different adapters, depending on the Integration tier design.

Database connectivity is often accompanied by requirements to connect to legacy systems. Both synchronous and asynchronous integrations are used to connect to legacy applications depending on the scenario. A CRM system may incorporate user information pulled synchronously during use session, while an HR batch update typically happens asynchronously. The next section covers interoperability content related to the synchronous legacy integration. Asynchronous integration is discussed in detail in Chapter 10, "Resource Tier Asynchronous Integration."

Legacy Integration

The ability for an enterprise application to connect to a legacy system such as Enterprise Resource Planning (ERP) or other type of Enterprise Information System (EIS) is essential to nearly any business. Connectivity to ERP systems such as SAP, Siebel, and PeopleSoft support nonrelational databases such as Adabas, Teradata, and IMS, and finally access to 3GL or 4GL applications cannot be achieved with ADO.NET or JDBC APIs. Legacy integration entails support for transactional technologies such as BEA Tuxedo, IBM CICS, DB/MVS, IMS/TM, ebXML, and EDI protocols. Modern integration with mainframe and legacy systems evolves around Web services, which simplifies interoperability between Java or .NET integration with legacy systems. This section discusses common techniques available to Java and .NET developers to connect to legacy systems.

In Java, the Java Connector Architecture is a standard mechanism to access legacy systems. A JCA implementation is offered in the form of resource adapters, which can be deployed in two ways. If an adapter is deployed under an application server, it is deployed under a **managed environment**. If a resource adapter is tightly integrated with the client application, it is deployed under a **non-managed environment**.

To establish a connection to a legacy application using JCA, a client invokes a getConnection() method on the ConnectionFactory class, which is part of the javax.resource.cci.Connection APIs.

```
Connection con = (javax.resource.cci.Connection)
connectionManager.allocateConnection( managedFactory, info );
```

The first argument corresponds to the connection factory; the second parameter includes authentication and any other information that has to be passed along.

A connection pool is utilized for adapters deployed under an application server. JCA also defines support for distributed transactions where a transaction is defined as a group of operations spanned across multiple legacy systems. For this transaction to succeed, all of the operations have to pass. If any of the operations fail, the entire transaction fails. Similar to the JDBC standard interface, the JCA 1.5 specification defines a Common Client Interface (CCI) to allow consistent access to disparate back-end applications. With the Adapter strategy discussed in this chapter, CCI APIs would be used within the Data Access Layer to access legacy systems. In addition, the JCA specification defines lifecycle management, work management, message inflow, and transaction inflow. JCA resource adapters that integrate with messaging software enable asynchronous communication between Java EE applications and legacy systems. See [JCA] for an introduction to Java Connector Architecture.

Java EE application servers offer out of the box JCA implementation. Commercial vendors such as iWay Software and SeeBeyond (acquired by Sun Microsystems) ship JCA-compliant resource adapters. These commercial solutions also enable .NET application connectivity to EIS systems using common Microsoft technologies such as ODBC, OLE DB, and ADO.NET. On the .NET side, integration with an internal to the enterprise legacy system such as IBM mainframe, messaging, and data sources, can be achieved via Microsoft Host Integration Server, see [HIS].

A discussion around integration with ERP and other EIS systems often ties to the overall workflow management, where connectivity between individual Java EE, .NET, and legacy systems is executed as part of the business workflow. Therefore, vendors such as SeeBeyond offer workflow management to orchestrate a business conversation among heterogeneous applications. This orchestration simplifies Service Oriented Architecture where individual services are connected in a consistent way. Microsoft BizTalk server provides similar functionality. Please refer to [SeeBeyond], [iWay], [MS_WSLegacy], and [JCA_Legacy] resources for more details.

In essence, there are two ways to approach legacy integration. For a basic Java or .NET legacy integration, commercial solutions and adapters can be used to integrate with back-end systems. On a larger scale, for Java and .NET applications participating in a B2B transaction or internal business workflow, commercial integration servers that supply workflow management can be leveraged. This is shown in Figure 6-5:

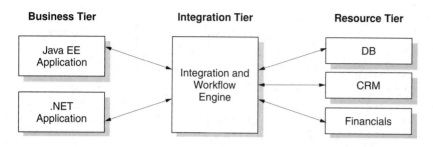

Figure 6-5
Legacy integration

Summary

This chapter has supplied sample strategies on how to develop Data Access Layer and perform legacy integration in a heterogeneous Java EE.NET environment. The purpose of this discussion is not only to enable developers with effective means to build interoperability at the Data Access Layer, but also to ensure that at the architecture level, presentation and business logic are separated from the underlying Resource tier integration. This approach simplifies manageability, security, and interoperability of the overall system.

While synchronous integration with back-end resources is useful, it might be decided that integrating with the Resource tier in an asynchronous manner is more efficient for the application throughput and the end user response time. Therefore, the discussion on the Resource tier integration continues in Chapter 10.

References

[ADO.NET_C#] Mahesh Chand. "A Programmer's Guide to ADO .NET in C#" ISBN: 1893115399. Apress; 1st edition (April 25, 2002)

[ADO.NET_Examples] William R. Vaughn, Peter Blackburn "ADO.NET Examples and Best Practices for C# Programmers." Apress. ISBN: 1590590120

[CJ2EEP] D. Alur, et al. "Core J2EE Patterns: Best Practices and Design Strategies," Pearson Education: 1st Edition. June 26, 2001.

[ConnPooling_Java] Sun Developer Network. Tutorials & Code Camps. Chapter 8 Continued: Connection Pooling.
http://java.sun.com/developer/onlineTraining/Programming/JDCBook/conpool.html

[ConnPooling_.NET] Connection Pooling for the .NET Framework Data Provider for SQL Server. .NET Framework Developer's Guide. Copyright © 2005 Microsoft Corporation.
http://msdn.microsoft.com/library/default.asp?url=/library/en-us/cpguide/html/cpconConnectionPoolingForSQLServerNETDataProvider.asp

[CoreLab] Core Lab Software Development, MySQLDirect .NET Data Provider.
http://crlab.com/mysqlnet/download.html

[DAAB] Enterprise Library. Data Access Application Block. Copyright © 2005 Microsoft Corporation.
http://msdn.microsoft.com/library/default.asp?url=/library/en-us/dnpag2/html/daab.asp

[DataAccess_ArchitectureGuide] Alex Mackman, et al. ".NET Data Access Architecture Guide" Microsoft patterns and practices for Application Architecture and Design. October 2001, Updated June 2003. Copyright © 2005 Microsoft Corporation.
http://msdn.microsoft.com/library/default.asp?url=/library/en-us/dnbda/html/daag.asp

[DataDirect] Data Direct Database Drivers
www.datadirect.com

[EntityBroker] EntityBroker.
www.thona-consulting.com/content/products/entitybroker.aspx

[Hibernate] Open Source project for object/relational persistence in Java.
www.hibernate.org/

[HIS] Microsoft Host Integration Server 2004. © 2005 Microsoft Corporation.
http://msdn.microsoft.com/library/default.asp?url=/library/en-us/his_2004main/htm/his_introduction_node_onij.asp

[iWay] iWay Software.
www.iwaysoftware.com/products

[JavaSQLDescr] Java 2 Platform SE 5.0 javax.sql.rowset package documentation.
http://java.sun.com/j2se/1.5.0/docs/api/index.html?javax/sql/rowset/package-summary.html

[JCA] Jennifer Rodoni, "What's New in the J2EE Connector Architecture 1.5," March 2003. Sun Developer Network. Copyright 1994-2005 Sun Microsystems, Inc.
http://java.sun.com/developer/technicalArticles/J2EE/connectorarch1_5/

[JCA_Legacy] Manish Verma. "Application Integration with Legacy Systems Using Java Connector Architecture." Sun Developer Network.
http://developers.sun.com/sw/building/codesamples/integration_jca.html

[JDBC_Drivers] Sun Developer Network, JDBC Drivers.
http://developers.sun.com/product/jdbc/drivers

[JDO] Java Data Objects.
http://java.sun.com/products/jdo/

[JSR_220] JSR 220: Enterprise JavaBeans™ 3.0.
http://jcp.org/en/jsr/detail?id=220

[Kodo] SolarMetric Kodo JDO.
www.solarmetric.com/Software/Kodo_JDO/

[LLBLGen_Pro] THE n-tier generator and O/R mapper.
www.llblgen.com/defaultgeneric.aspx

[MS_WSLegacy] Web Service Façade for Legacy Applications.
http://msdn.microsoft.com/library/default.asp?url=/library/en-us/dnpag/html/wsfaçadelegacyapp.asp

[MySQL_Config] Faisal Khan. Installing and Configuring MySQL Database and Connector/J JDBC Driver on Microsoft Windows. © 1999–2005. Stardeveloper.com.
www.stardeveloper.com/articles/display.html?article=2003090201&page=1

[MySQL_DotNet] Reggie Burnett. "Exploring MySQL in the Microsoft .NET Environment."
http://dev.mysql.com/tech-resources/articles/dotnet/#ADO.NET

[.NET_ORM_Tools] Object-relational mapping tool collection.
www.sharptoolbox.com/Pages/Category74089b0a-1105-4389-b1d-beedf27e20cfb.aspx

[NHibernate] What is NHibernate?
http://wiki.nhibernate.org/display/NH/Home

[ObjectSpaces] Dino Esposito. "A First Look at ObjectSpaces in Visual Studio 2005" February 2004. Copyright © 2005 Microsoft Corporation.
http://msdn.microsoft.com/library/default.asp?url=/library/en-us/dnadonet/html/objectspaces.asp

[OpenLink] ADO.NET Data Providers.
www.openlinksw.com/info/docs/uda51/mt/dnetarch.html

[ORM_Tools_Java] Object Relational Tools Comparison.
http://c2.com/cgi-bin/wiki?ObjectRelationalToolComparison

[ORM_Tools_.NET] Object-relational mapping tool collection.
www.sharptoolbox.com/Pages/Category74089b0a-1105-4389-b1db-
eedf27e20cfb.aspx

[SeeBeyond] SeeBeyond.
www.seebeyond.com/

[SQLServer_JDBC] SQL Server JDBC driver download.
www.microsoft.com/downloads/details.aspx?familyid=07287b11-0502-461a-b138-
2aa54bfdc03a&displaylang=en#filelist

[TopLink] Oracle TopLink. Java object-to-relational persistence tool.
www.oracle.com/technology/products/ias/toplink/index.html

[WinFX_SDK] WinFX Software Development Kit (SDK).
http://winfx.msdn.microsoft.com/library/

Asynchronous Integration Solutions

Exploring Asynchronous Integration

7

Overview

Asynchronous integration occurs when a number of processes integrate but do not lock for the time of the transaction on which they are integrated. In general, a caller makes a request of a server and then goes away and does its own thing. When the server finishes its part of the process, it sends the results back to the caller via a **callback**. This involves the caller and the server keeping information about each other in what is usually referred to as a **session**. It involves overhead on both sides, and as such, in large scale systems it requires careful design and usage.

In a typical scenario, asynchronous integration is appropriate where a request process takes a long period of time or if a client application can continue processing without waiting for a response. Asynchronous communication is often utilized for the Enterprise Application Integration (EAI). For example, processing an order fulfillment system often relies on asynchronous processing of incoming orders. Once the order is processed, a status confirmation is sent to the user or application that placed the order.

A classic example of an asynchronous service is when one orders a ticket for an airline. Typically the scenario starts with someone making a request, and then the system goes off and checks availability of the requested resource. When ordering an airplane seat, it assigns that seat to you and blocks it off for all other sessions.

The first asynchronous session occurs when the ticket query is made. In a typical browser session you get a 'waiting' screen, but what is happening here is that the HTTP session is being kept alive while the query for seats is being made. Once the query is complete, the server finishes the process, downloads the new data, and closes the HTTP session. (This isn't a perfect example because in a true asynchronous case, the user could go and browse other Web sites with the same browser and get redirected to the seat availability screen when the server is ready, but the HTTP protocol doesn't allow for this.)

At this point, the session is being maintained on the server, usually with an expiration time of two minutes. Should the user not complete the transaction in this timeframe, the session dies, and the resources are released. The next step of the session is that you confirm you want the seats and inform the server. In this case the session stays alive while the server finalizes the booking and blocks off the seats for you.

A third asynchronous session takes place for payment, with a call to another server to validate the given credit card information. This calls back to the booking server with a positive or a negative and based on those results the booking server calls back to the browser with the results of the successful booking or a request for an alternative payment.

In this manner two or more remote systems can interoperate in a more efficient way by hiding internal system complexity and only exposing high-level services forming an asynchronous Service Oriented Architecture (SOA).

Using Asynchronous Integration

Asynchronous integration, as seen in the given example, is generally used when transactions have a long lifetime or require resources that are shared between many users to be locked (like seats on an airplane) for the life of the transaction. Typical scenarios for asynchronous integration are

- In a peer to peer process (as opposed to a client server process). For example when making a stock trade, either selling or buying, an asynchronous implementation is necessary. Generally one requests a trade from the server, and the server then tries to find someone in the market that is requesting the resource that is being bought or sold. Negotiation may take place based on pricing rules (such as Bid/Ask automatic values based on lot size) and a price is met, the trade is executed and each party informed. This process can take several microseconds (in the case of a market trade) or years (in the case of a stop/limit trade).

- When notifications of the status of a transaction are required at fixed times or when based on certain external events occurring. A good example of this is an online auction. A fixed time update is required at the end of the auction; external events occur when others bid on the auction and you need to know what they are.

- When it takes a lot of time for a process to complete. For example if the call to a server requires a bulk update to a database that can take a long time. An asynchronous update informs the caller in this case when the transaction is complete. When using a synchronous transaction, the session would have to stay open for the lifetime of the process, or the caller would have to continually ping the server for the results.

There are several technologies that can be used to realize asynchronous integration, which are explored in more detail in the following chapters.

Asynchronous Web Services Integration

8

Introduction

While synchronous communication using Web services became the main means of integrating heterogeneous applications among the early adopters of Web services technology, the SOAP 1.2 specification highlights support for asynchronous Web services integration. Asynchronous application-to-application communication is rapidly gaining popularity in the industry. This chapter explores different means of building asynchronous interactions between Java and .NET.

Asynchronous Web Services Strategies

From the design standpoint, the focus is on two main strategies—**automatic callback** and **response polling**. There is, of course, a third scenario where a calling system does not expect anything back after submitting a request, which is fairly straightforward to implement. In starting to develop a Web services sample, it becomes obvious that in the simplest case the actual Web service does not have to change much and does not need to know that it is invoked asynchronously. As a matter of fact, with the response polling strategy, it is entirely up to the client to decide whether the invocation should be synchronous or asynchronous. In a more complicated scenario—that is, with an automatic callback strategy—there is some preparation involved on the service side to send a callback notification as soon as the request is processed. The Web service consumer has to listen for the incoming callback. The goal is to understand what underlying technologies are available to build asynchronous Java EE-.NET communications. The interoperability examples built reflect the Service Oriented Architecture (SOA) that encompasses coarse-grained Java EE and .NET Web services. These services are integrated in an asynchronous manner and address how to develop an automatic callback to a .NET Web service, automatic callback to a Java EE Web service, polling .NET Web service, and polling Java Web service.

Asynchronous Web Services Support in Java EE

Implementing asynchronous Web services in Java primarily revolves around document-oriented processing and Java messaging. A Web service consumer sends a request as an XML document. A Web service provider queues requests using a messaging system, processing them asynchronously. The messaging system, that is, a JMS-based system, acts as a middleman between the Web service endpoint, such as Servlet, listening to incoming requests on a well-known port and a business tier processing the request. Once the request has been processed, the response is either sent back to the client if the architecture is based on a callback strategy or a client periodically checks the status of a request in the case of a polling strategy. In the given example a document-oriented Web service is implemented. However, the use of messaging is avoided, and instead Java Proxy and .NET Façade techniques are explored. Messaging is discussed in the next chapter.

Asynchronous Web Services Support in .NET

The .NET Framework has built-in support for asynchronous development including asynchronous Web service communication. Two main strategies, **response polling** and **callback**, are supported out of the box by the .NET Framework. A WSDL of a published Web service is used to generate a proxy class for a Web service. This proxy, used by the Web service consumer, contains not only the Web service method, but also two extensions to that method such as a `begin` method and an `end` method. It is up to the Web service consumer to then invoke the Web service method asynchronously.

Achieving asynchrony outside of the Web services realm is based on the **Delegate** pattern. The Delegate component acts as a key enabler for asynchronous communication. A Delegate takes the same parameters as the method invoked asynchronously. The main trick with the Delegate is that the compiler extends the Delegate with two methods, `BeginInvoke` and `EndInvoke`. The purpose of the `BeginInvoke` method is to initiate the asynchronous call, whereas `EndInvoke` is called to obtain the result once the call processing is over. A thread pool is utilized behind the scene to process asynchronous calls on separate threads. So rather than invoking a method directly, a call is made on a Delegate's `BeginInvoke` method and at the end invoke `EndInvoke`.

This is a highlight of Java and .NET asynchronous Web service support. The two models have hardly anything in common. Nevertheless asynchronous Web service communication can be built successfully across the two platforms. The next generation of Web services will be able to leverage the SOAP 1.2 specification that simplifies asynchronous Web services communication.

Asynchronous Web Services with SOAP 1.2

SOAP messages are often transferred asynchronously using HTTP as the transport binding. It is important to notice that examples in this chapter are based on the HTTP binding in SOAP 1.1. Today, most asynchronous Web services are implemented by separating the request and response portions of an HTTP transaction as if they were two different transactions—in essence, making two synchronous request-response calls. In the first round, a client sends a request and gets back an acknowledgement along with an ID to be able to track the status of the response. Refer to Figure 8-1.

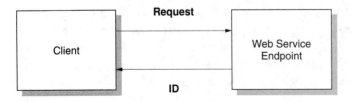

Figure 8-1
Client requesting an ID from a Web services endpoint

On the second round, the client receives the response as a callback and sends an acknowledgement back to the server. See Figure 8-2.

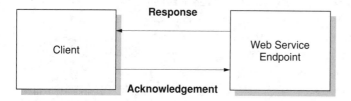

Figure 8-2
Response and acknowledgement in a Web service

SOAP 1.2 conveniently introduces new HTTP status codes. Specifically, status code 202 indicates that the HTTP response may optionally contain the SOAP response. Status code 204 indicates that the HTTP response does not contain the SOAP response. Once .NET and Java EE support SOAP 1.2, it will be possible to implement interoperable one-way messaging across Java EE and .NET using HTTP as the transport protocol.

As this chapter delves into the mechanics of implementing asynchronous Java EE and .NET integration and uses Sun's Web services Development Kit (WSDK), the Microsoft Visual Studio .NET, and the Microsoft .NET Framework.

Business Scenario Overview

The code demonstration for this chapter continues using the WS-I Sample Application defined as a sample Supply Chain Management application. The Replenish Stock use case of the WS-I Supply Chain application represents asynchronous communication between the Warehouse and the Manufacturer. In a nutshell, the Replenish Stock use case represents two main sub-systems—the Retailer and the Manufacturing systems. The scenario starts with the Warehouse component of the Retailer system initiating a call to the Manufacturing system by submitting a Purchase Order to process. The Manufacturing system then asynchronously processes the request. With the automatic callback strategy, the Manufacturing system submits the results once the processing is over, while with the polling strategy, the Warehouse component explicitly polls for a response.

Asynchronous Communication Techniques

To build asynchronous communication across Java and .NET, a layer of abstraction is needed to overcome incompatibilities of underlying platform support for asynchronous Web services communication. One can design this layer of indirection on either the .NET or Java side of the communication channel, depending on expertise level and overall system requirements. This chapter explores a few main techniques to build interoperable Web services. With the first technique the .NET Façade pattern is introduced, which hides complexity of asynchronous .NET processing. The façade is responsible for passing a request to be processed asynchronously and generating a callback or responding to the client polling requests. The second technique introduces the Asynchronous Java Proxy pattern and is a way to build a layer of abstraction on Java side. The asynchronous computation occurs between the proxy and its worker thread that initiates the Web service request. The actual Web service call is performed synchronously. The chapter also explores threading as a technique to asynchronous communication in Java and .NET. Benefits of the first technique encompass a fair degree of transparency on the Java side, whereas there is more work to be done on the .NET side. With the Asynchronous Java Proxy technique, extra work has to be done in the Java side but not in the .NET. As the chapter builds individual scenarios, complexity and workarounds of Java EE and .NET APIs are discussed, as asynchronous support on one platform does not guarantee interoperability with another platform. The chapter starts with building the Replenish Stock scenario with the .NET Façade pattern technique to implement the automatic callback strategy and .NET Façade.

Automatic Callback Strategy

The automatic callback strategy is fairly straightforward to understand but somewhat tricky to implement, taking into account two sets of technologies, as is seen later in this chapter. The UML diagram in Figure 8-3 highlights the Replenish Stock asynchronous communication scenario using the callback strategy.

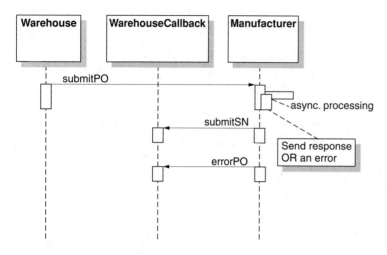

Figure 8-3
Replenish Stock sequence diagram

The Warehouse service submits a purchase order request to the Manufacturer. Once the purchase order request is received, the Manufacturer sends an acknowledgement back to the Warehouse service. The Manufacturer then asynchronously processes the purchase order request, and upon successful completion *automatically* sends the response, submitSN, to the Warehouse Callback service. In case of an error, the Manufacturer sends an errorPO message to the Warehouse Callback service. A callback is accompanied with an acknowledgement from the receiver.

At deployment, the Warehouse and the Warehouse Callback services are deployed as part of the Retailer system, while the Manufacturer service is defined in the scope of the Manufacturing System. Assuming the Retailer system is implemented using Java EE and the Manufacturing system is implemented in .NET, the deployment diagram in Figure 8-4 would look like the following.

As can be seen from the diagram, this callback to .NET Web service scenario is composed out of two synchronous calls. The first synchronous invocation is to the Manufacturer Web service and the second to the WarehouseCallback Web service. The following sections show what it takes to implement and deploy this scenario.

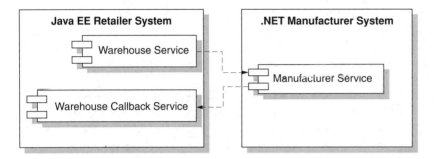

Figure 8-4
Replenish Stock deployment diagram

Implementing Replenish Stock Use Case

Practically speaking, there is no particular order of implementing the individual services given that any of the subsystems can always be stubbed out. The Replenish Stock scenario is started by the implementation of the Java `WarehouseCallback` Web service. Individual components of the entire system are depicted in the deployment diagram, Figure 8-4. Developing the .NET Manufacturer Web service follows the `WarehouseCallback` Service. The reason is that the .NET Web service has to asynchronously invoke the Java Callback Web service, which has to be up and running. Next is to construct the Java Warehouse client that initiates the .NET Manufacturing Web service call. Implementing this use case demonstrates how to perform asynchronous Web services integration between Java and .NET using the .NET Façade pattern callback strategy.

This scenario is a prime example of a Service Oriented Architecture, where the complexity of individual systems is transparent to the system interoperability. Only high-level services communicate across these systems. With the preceding example, one might question why Java EE was picked for the Retailer system and .NET for the Manufacturing system and what would be different if the two systems were swapped around. The reason for mapping the Retailer to Java EE and the Manufacturing system to .NET is because .NET actually integrates the asynchronous callback design, which is demonstrated later in the chapter.

Building Java *WarehouseCallback* Web Service

Creating Java *WarehouseCallback* Web Service

The callback service either receives a successful response or a fault response from the Manufacturer system. A fault response either indicates an application logic error or a time out on a given action. Therefore, there are two main Web methods defined in the callback interface, WarehouseCallback, submitSN and errorPO. Take a look at the interface in Listing 8-1

Listing 8-1
Retailer Example

```
package j2eedotnet.chapter8.retailer;

import java.rmi.RemoteException;
import java.rmi.Remote;

public interface WarehouseCallback extends Remote {
  public boolean submitSN(int invoiceNumber, String poStatus)
    throws RemoteException;
  public boolean errorPO(String errorType) throws RemoteException;
}
```

In case of a successful purchase order processing, the invoice number and the current status of an order are passed. The return type of a boolean acts as an acknowledgement for the method call. Similarly for the errorPO method, the error type is returned indicating the type of error. Now take a look at the implementation class, WarehouseCallbackImpl, as shown in Listing 8-2:

Listing 8-2
Retailer Callback Implementation

```
package j2eedotnet.chapter8.retailer;

import java.rmi.RemoteException;
import javax.xml.rpc.server.ServiceLifecycle;
import java.util.logging.Logger;
import java.util.logging.Level;
import java.util.logging.FileHandler;


public class WarehouseCallbackImpl
  implements WarehouseCallback, ServiceLifecycle {
```

```
Logger logger;
String className;
FileHandler file;
String methodName;
String logHome =
    "C:/j2eedotnet/bookcd/build/log/warehouseCallback.log";

public void init(Object context){
  logger = Logger.getLogger("j2eedotnet.chapter9.retailer");
  className = getClass().getName();
  methodName="init";

  try {
    file = new FileHandler(logHome);
    logger.addHandler(file);
    logger.setLevel(Level.ALL);
    //logger.fine("Initializing the logger");
  } catch (Exception exc) {
  logger.throwing(className, methodName, exc);
  logger.exiting(className, methodName);
  if (file !=null)
    file.close();
  }
}

public void destroy(){
  try {
    file.close();
  } catch (Exception ex){}
}
public boolean submitSN(int invoiceNumber, String poStatus)
    throws RemoteException {
  methodName="submitSN";
  String msgLog = "PurchaseOrder status ";
  String[] msgParam =
    {"Invoice: "+invoiceNumber, "Status: " + poStatus};
  logger.log(Level.FINE, msgLog, msgParam);
  return true;
}

public boolean errorPO(String errorType) throws RemoteException{
  logger.log(Level.WARNING, "PO Error", errorType);
  return true;
}
}
```

The core of the callback implementation class embraces the submitSN and errorPO methods that log corresponding PO processing statuses. To initialize the Java Logger, the code has leveraged the init() method of a Servlet, that allows the developer to perform any housekeeping routines at Servlet initialization time. The Servlet lifecycle methods are available to us via the `ServiceLifecycle` interface. The logger file remains open for as long as the Web service is running and is closed when the Servlet `destroy` method is invoked. It's important to stop the Web Server, such as Tomcat, to preview the content of the log file. Otherwise the log file lock prevents opening the log file. To simplify the Java Web services deployment process, an `ant` build has been leveraged and the Java `WarehouseCallback` service deployed. Individual `ant` tasks are described in the next section.

Deploying Java *WarehouseCallback* Web Service

To deploy the Java Web service, it's necessary to compile classes using the `javac` compiler, to generate corresponding server side components with the `wscompile` tool, to create the initial WAR file with the `war` utility, to create the final WAR file using `wsdeploy`, and to deploy the WAR file under Tomcat. Each of these steps is represented as an `ant` task as follows. If you want to skip individual `ant` tasks and simply test the deployment of the `JavaWarehouseCallback` service, simply invoke the build process in the following way:

```
> ant deploy-javacallback-service
```

You can then start Tomcat and test the callback service

```
http://localhost:8080/J2eeDotNet/Chapter8/Retailer/WarehouseCallback.
```

The Web service page displays the link to the WSDL and the model file. Refer to Figure 8-5.

Next is to perform the step-by-step deployment process, which encompasses quite a few operations. You might want to skip the remainder of this section and continue with the next section, Implementing .NET Manufacturing System, if you are not ready to deploy the solution or are deploying using an IDE.

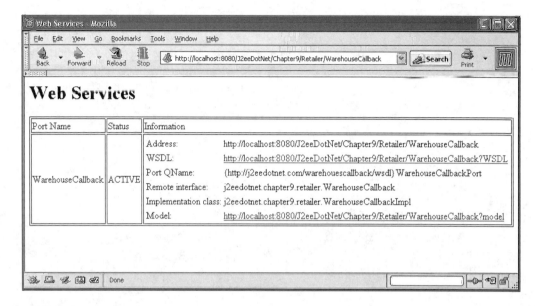

Figure 8-5
Deploying a Web service using a WSDL

Preparing Build Directories

The first step involves creating build directories specified in the `prepare` task, as in Listing 8-3.

Listing 8-3
Creating Build Directories

```
<target name="prepare" depends="init">
    <mkdir dir="${build.home}"/>
    <mkdir dir="${build.classes}"/>
    <mkdir dir="${build.src}"/>
    <mkdir dir="${build.model}"/>
    <mkdir dir="${build.temp}"/>
    <mkdir dir="${log.home}"/>
</target>
```

Each of the directories is defined by the `ant` properties.

Compiling a Web Service

After preparing build directories and implementing the interface and the implementation classes, the next task is to compile classes with the `javac` compiler. The `compile-server` task performs that function by referencing classpath to `compile.classpath` reference id. Refer to Listing 8-4.

Listing 8-4
Compiling a Web Service

```
<target name="compile-server" depends="prepare">
  <echo message="--- Compiling Warehouse application ---"/>
  <javac srcdir="${src.retailer}"
         includes="**/WarehouseCallback*.java"
         destdir="${build.classes}" >
    <classpath refid = "compile.classpath"/>
  </javac>
</target>
```

The `compile.classpath` incorporates all necessary JAR files, as in Listing 8-5.

Listing 8-5
compile.classpath

```
<path id="compile.classpath">
    <fileset dir="${jwsdp.home}" includes = "
     jaxrpc/lib/*.jar
     jwsdp-shared/lib/*.jar
     jaxp/**/*.jar
     jaxb/lib/*.jar
     saaj/lib/*.jar"/>
    <fileset dir="${lib.home}">
    <include name="*.jar"/>
    </fileset>
  </path>
```

Generating Server Components

Next is to employ the `wscompile` tool to create necessary server components, for which the Wscompile class is leveraged, available with the JWSDP toolkit, as in Listing 8-6.

Listing 8-6

wscompile to Create Server Components

```
<taskdef name="wscompile"
classname="com.sun.xml.rpc.tools.ant.Wscompile">
  <classpath refid="compile.classpath"/>
</taskdef>
```

Next is to use the `wscompile` task to create server ties, the WSDL file, the service model, and other pieces needed for the Java Web service. For that you specify various configuration parameters by passing the `config.xml` file. Refer to Listing 8-7.

Listing 8-7

config.xml

```
<target name="generate-server" depends="compile-server">
   <wscompile
      define="true"
      keep="true"
      base="${build.classes}"
      sourceBase="${build.src}"
      model="${build.model}/model.xml.gz"
      xPrintStackTrace="true"
      verbose="false"
      config="${etc.server}/config.xml">
      <classpath refid="server.classpath"/>
   </wscompile>
  </target>
```

From the classpath standpoint, in addition to the third-party libraries listed in `compile.classpath`, add the `WarehouseCallback` byte code generated by the `compile-server` task (refer to Listing 8-8):

Listing 8-8

compile-server Task

```
  <path id="server.classpath">
     <path refid="compile.classpath"/>
     <pathelement location="${build.classes}"/>
  </path>
```

For the `config.xml` interface and the implementation classes of the Web service, refer to Listing 8-9.

Listing 8-9
config.xml for the Interfaces and the Implementation

```xml
<?xml version="1.0" encoding="UTF-8" ?>
 <configuration xmlns="http://java.sun.com/xml/ns/jax-rpc/ri/
config">
<!-- The <service> element the RMI interface of the Web service -->
<!-- The wscopmile reads the RMI interface to generate WSDL -->
    <service name="WarehouseCallbackService"

        targetNamespace="http://j2eedotnet.com/warehousecallback/wsdl"
        typeNamespace="http://j2eedotnet.com/warehousecallback/types"
        wsdl="hhttp://j2eedotnet.com/warehousecallback/WSDL"
        packageName="j2eedotnet.chapter8.retailer">
<!-- Specify the name of the interface and implementation class -->
    <interface
        name="j2eedotnet.chapter8.retailer.WarehouseCallback"
        servantName="j2eedotnet.chapter8.retailer.WarehouseCall
        backImpl"/>
    </service>
</configuration>
```

Generating the Initial WAR File

Now it's time to generate the initial WAR file, `Warehouse-raw.war`, often referred to as a raw WAR. This Web archive file comprises components that have been prepared up until now, such as service model, build classes, and WSDL, and the deployment descriptor, that is, `jaxrpc-ri.xml`. Refer to Listing 8-10.

Listing 8-10
warehouse-raw.war

```xml
<target name="create-war" depends="generate-server">
    <war warfile="${build.home}/Warehouse-raw.war"
        webxml="${etc.server}/web.xml">
    <webinf dir="${build.classes}" includes="*.wsdl"/>
    <webinf dir="${etc.server}" includes="jaxrpc-ri.xml"
            defaultexcludes="no"/>
    <webinf dir="${build.model}" includes="model.xml.gz"
            defaultexcludes="no"/>
    <classes dir="${build.classes}" includes="**/*.class"
            defaultexcludes="no"/>
    </war>
  </target>
```

The content of the deployment descriptor, `jaxrpc-ri.xml`, provides information on Web service endpoints such as interface, model, and WSDL information as well as the endpoint URL mapping. Refer to Listing 8-11.

Listing 8-11

jaxrpc-ri.xml

```xml
<?xml version="1.0" encoding="UTF-8"?>

<!-- Defines Web services parameters. -->
<!-- The <webServices> elemenets contains <endpoint> elements -->

<webServices
    xmlns="http://java.sun.com/xml/ns/jax-rpc/ri/dd"
    version="1.0"
    targetNamespaceBase="http://j2eedotnet.com/warehousecallback
    /wsdl"
    typeNamespaceBase="http://j2eedotnet.com/warehousecallback/
    types"
    urlPatternBase="/asyncwebservices">

<!-- The <endpoint> element contains the Web service's -->
<!-- interface and implementation classes -->
    <endpoint
        name="WarehouseCallback"
        displayName="Warehouse Callback Service"
        description="Warehouse Callback service"
        wsdl="/WEB-INF/WarehouseCallbackService.wsdl"
        interface="j2eedotnet.chapter8.retailer.WarehouseCallback"

implementation="j2eedotnet.chapter8.retailer.WarehouseCallbackImpl"
        model="/WEB-INF/model.xml.gz"/>

<!-- The <endpointMapping> element associates it with a URL. -->
    <endpointMapping
        endpointName="WarehouseCallback"
        urlPattern="/Chapter8/Retailer/WarehouseCallback"/>
</webServices>
```

Creating the Final WAR File

Next is to use the `wsdeploy` tool to generate the final WAR file, `J2eeDotNet.war`. The `wsdeploy` reads the `Warehouse-raw.war` file and the `jaxrpc-ri.xml` file to produce the final `warehouse.war` file, which will be deployed under the Web server. Refer to Listing 8-12.

Listing 8-12
Using *wsdeploy* tool to generate the final WAR file

```
<target name="build-war" depends="create-war">
  <echo message="--- Building J2eeDotNet.war file ---"/>
  <wsdeploy
      keep="true"
      inWarFile="${build.home}/Warehouse-raw.war"
      outWarFile="${build.home}/J2eeDotNet.war"
      verbose="false"
      tmpDir="${build.temp}">
      <classpath refid="server.classpath"/>
  </wsdeploy>
</target>
```

Deploying the WAR File

The closing step involves deploying the WAR file under the Web server. This is achieved with the `deploy-javacallback-service` task. Refer to Listing 8-13.

Listing 8-13
deploy-javacallback-service Task

```
<target name="deploy-javacallback-service" depends="build-war">
  <copy file="${build.home}/J2eeDotNet.war"
      todir="${tomcat.root}/webapps"/>
</target>
```

This step results in the war file being deployed under Tomcat by placing the J2eeDotNet.war file under the tomcat-jwsdp-1.4/webapps directory.

DEVELOPER'S NOTE

It's important to point out that invoking this last step will automatically invoke the hierarchy of all dependent calls. Because each of the `ant` tasks has a specific dependent task, the sequence of individual calls is strictly defined in the `build.xml`.

Previewing Java Callback Web Service

Start the Tomcat server and then type in the WarehouseCallback URL: http://localhost:8080/J2eeDotNet/Chapter8/Retailer/WarehouseCallback.

You should see the same screen as shown earlier. If you want to see details of the Web service, follow the WDSL link.

DEVELOPER'S NOTE

It is useful to create a simple client to validate the correctness of the Web service. Because the next job involves the .NET Framework, it is worth writing a test suite to ensure correctness of the Java service.

Testing WarehouseCallback Web Service

To guarantee that the Web service works correctly, a simple client application can be created that makes a call to the WarehouseCallback Web service. Refer to Listing 8-14.

Listing 8-14
Client to Make a Call to *WarehouseCallback* Web service

```
public class CallbackTest {
  public static void main (String[] args) {
  try {
    WarehouseCallback port = (new
    WarehouseCallbackService_Impl()).getWarehouseCallbackPort();
    boolean result =port.submitSN(77777,"Processed 777");
    System.out.println("The result from the client is: "+result);
} catch (Exception e) {}
}// main

}
```

Build this test client and execute it. The final few lines will include the following message indicating the acknowledgement of receiving the request.

```
[echo] --- Running CallbackTest application ---
[java] The result from the client is: true
```

If the CallbackTest application runs successfully, there will be an entry in the Tomcat log file similar to this (refer to Listing 8-15):

Listing 8-15
Log file entry for *CallbackTest*

```
<record>
  <date>2004-10-14T12:14:04</date>
  <millis>1097741644640</millis>
  <sequence>51</sequence>
  <logger>j2eedotnet.chapter8.retailer</logger>
  <level>FINE</level>
  <class>j2eedotnet.chapter8.retailer.WarehouseCallbackImpl</class>
  <method>submitSN</method>
  <thread>12</thread>
  <message>PurchaseOrder status </message>
  <param>Invoice: 77777</param>
  <param>Status: Processed 777</param>
</record>
```

Having small unit testing performed at every step of a process helps to mini-mize the debugging effort. All that has been done so far is to create the Java `WarehouseCallback` service as part of the Warehouse system. At this point it is time to build the .NET Manufacturing system.

Implementing .NET Manufacturing System

The Manufacturing System performs core business logic of asynchronously processing the purchase order request. The .NET Framework enables asyn-chronous communication out of the box by implementing the .NET Asynchronous Design Pattern. Although in the example Java and .NET serv-ices communicate asynchronously, the Java application won't be able to asynchronously invoke the .NET service using this pattern, given that Java doesn't support the .NET asynchronous model, and vice versa. There are a couple of ways to overcome this limitation. In the simplest scenario, the Web services call can be submitted to the Manufacturing system, which later sends `POStatus` by calling the `WarehouseCallback` service. On the other side it's important to show a user how to develop asynchronous calls using .NET for which one would perform a Web service call to a Manufacturing system that asynchronously processes this call. To demonstrate the .NET asynchronous programming the Façade pattern, GoF Façade Pattern, is introduced. For the .NET audience this is the Service Interface pattern, and for those who are familiar with Core J2EE Patterns, this component can be interpreted as the Web services Broker. This Façade intercepts an incoming

Web services call and passes it further to the corresponding business component for asynchronous processing. The next section delves into various facets of the .NET Manufacturing system.

Manufacturing System Overview

The Manufacturing System needs to implement three main characteristics of the Replenish Stock use case. The first element of the Manufacturing system is processing the Java Warehouse client request. This component is implemented in the form of `ManufacturerFaçade`, which waits for a request and sends acknowledgement to the Java Warehousing system once the request has arrived. The `ManufacturerFaçade` follows a Façade GoF pattern and hides .NET semantics of processing the request. The façade invokes the next element of the Manufacturing system, `POValidator`, to actually perform asynchronous processing of the PO request. The `POValidator` class validates the purchase order, creates an invoice, and returns the `POStatus`. The third responsibility of the Manufacturing system is to submit the results of the asynchronous PO processing to the Java `WarehouseCallback` service, which is already deployed. Figure 8-6 highlights in gray the .NET Manufacturing system.

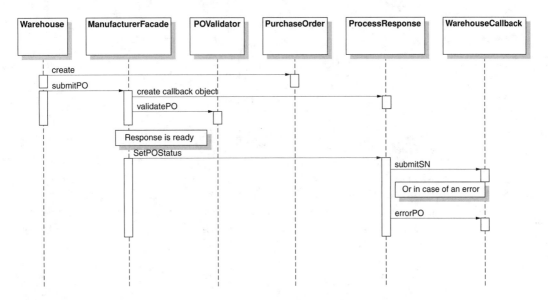

Figure 8-6
.NET Manufacturing system overview

As can be seen from the diagram, the validatePO method is invoked asynchronously. From the technical standpoint this call is implemented using the .NET Asynchronous Delegate strategy, as is described next.

The .NET Asynchronous Delegate

To implement asynchronous processing in .NET, this chooses to follow the Asynchronous Delegate strategy, for which there needs to be defined a Delegate component that has the same method signature as the method that will be invoked asynchronously. At runtime this Delegate will be extended by .NET CLR with BeginInvoke and EndInvoke methods. The BeginInvoke method is called first, while the EndInvoke method is automatically invoked upon request processing completion. While these wrapper methods are required for asynchronous processing, the actual method can be called synchronously. It is entirely up to the invoker to decide whether to call the method synchronously or asynchronously. In this case, the POValidator class contains the Delegate component:

```
public delegate void ManufacturerDelegate ( PurchaseOrder po, ref int
invoiceNumber, ref String poStatus);
```

Once again, the Delegate signature is identical to the method signature:

```
public void ValidatePO ( PurchaseOrder po,
                    ref int invoiceNumber,
                    ref String poStatus)
```

Implementing .NET *POValidator*

As the name implies, the POValidator checks the content of the purchase order and reports if it's valid or not. If the PO is valid it creates and returns an invoice; otherwise it throws an exception. The core method of this class is the ValidatePO method, which after purchase order validation sets values for the POStatus. Refer to Listing 8-16.

Listing 8-16
POValidator

```
namespace J2eeDotNet.Chapter8.Manufacturer {
 // Create an asynchronous delegate
 public delegate void ManufacturerDelegate ( PurchaseOrder po,
    ref int invoiceNumber, ref String poStatus);

 // Create a class that processes the purchase order
 public class POValidator {

 public void ValidatePO ( PurchaseOrder po,
    ref int invoiceNumber,ref String poStatus) {
  int poNumber = po.PONumber;
  if (( po != null || po.ProductQuantity.Length > 0 )){
  // generate invoice number and the PO status
    invoiceNumber = poNumber*10000;
    poStatus = "PO_"+poNumber+"_Validated";
  } else {
    throw new ProcessPOException("Invalid PO: +poNumber);
   }
  }
 }

 public class ProcessPOException : Exception {
   public ProcessPOException(string errorMsg): base(errorMsg){
    // Extra code can be added here...
   }
 }//class

} //namespace
```

In Listing 8-16, aside from the Delegate and the method definition, the POValidator file also includes an exception class, ProcessPOException, which is invoked in case the Purchase Order is invalid.

In continuing to implement the Manufacturing system, the next job is to build the ManufacturerFaçade that accesses the POValidator component.

Implementing *ManufacturerFaçade* Web Service

The next main step in creating the manufacturing system is to develop the ManufacturerFaçade class, which represents the Web service endpoint and encapsulates logic necessary for asynchronous processing of the purchase order request. The .NET asynchronous model is somewhat complex, so it's important to look into each segment of making this asynchronous call.

The `ManufacturerFaçade` class contains a single Web method, `SubmitPO`, which starts with initializing various parameters passed to the `BeginInvoke` method of the asynchronous Delegate.

Initializing Parameters

As discussed earlier, the `BeginInvoke` method takes the same parameters as the method invoked asynchronously:

```
public void ValidatePO ( PurchaseOrder po,
                ref int invoiceNumber,
                ref String poStatus)
```

Setting value for the PO status message is the next step in the process. Here the PO invoice value is also initialized.

```
int poNumber = order.PONumber;
String poStatus="PO_"+poNumber+"_Submitted";
int invoice=-1;
```

Next is to create an asynchronous Delegate, `ManufacturerDelegate`, by instantiating the `POValidate` class and passing the `ValidatePO` method to the delegate:

```
POValidator validator = new POValidator();
ManufacturerDelegate manufDelegate =
  new ManufacturerDelegate(validator.ValidatePO);
```

Prior to calling the `BeginInvoke` method of the `ManufacturerDelegate`, it is necessary to specify two more parameters—the asynchronous callback delegate class, `AsyncCallback`, and the state object. The `AsyncCallback` delegate class defines a callback method that is invoked once the PO validation is finished. As mentioned earlier, you cannot specify a Java class directly, instead implement a C# class called `ProcessResponse` that calls the `WarehouseCallback` to pass the PO status:

```
ProcessResponse resp = new ProcessResponse(poNumber);
```

The semantics of the `ProcessResponse` class is discussed as follows.

The asynchronous callback delegate, `AsyncCallback`, is initialized next by passing the callback method, `SetPOStatus`, of the `ProcessResponse` class.

```
AsyncCallback cb = new AsyncCallback(resp.SetPOStatus);
```

The .NET asynchronous model allows passing state, which is left empty for simplicity.

```
Object state = new Object();
```

This completes the initialization process.

Asynchronous Invocation

The next step is to call the `BeginInvoke` of the Asynchronous Delegate component. The `BeginInvoke` method initiates the asynchronous call and returns a value of type `IAsyncResult` interface. This interface links `BeginInvoke` and `EndInvoke` operations and provides the result of the `ValidatePO` method call. It is important to notice the order of arguments passed to the method as shown here. The method parameters are passed first, the callback delegate is always passed as the second to the last parameter, while state is passed last.

```
IAsyncResult ar = manufDelegate.BeginInvoke(
            order, ref invoice, ref poStatus,
            cb, state);
```

When the `BeginInvoke` method is invoked, the CLR invokes the `ValidatePO` method using a background thread from an internal thread pool, which is to say the .NET Framework relies on a thread pool to facilitate asynchronous processing.

ManufacturerFaçade

Listing 8-17 shows a listing of the `ManufacturerFaçade` class returning the PO status.

Listing 8-17

ManufacturerFaçade

```
public class ManufacturerFaçade : System.Web.Services.WebService
{
[WebMethod(Description = "Manufacturer WebService Façade")]
public string SubmitPO(PurchaseOrder order)
{
  int poNumber = order.PONumber;
  String poStatus="PO_"+poNumber+"_Submitted";
  int invoice=-1;
  POValidator validator = new POValidator();
  ManufacturerDelegate manufDelegate =
      new ManufacturerDelegate(validator.ValidatePO);
  // Specifying the callback class
  ProcessResponse resp = new ProcessResponse(poNumber);
  // Define the asynchronous callback delegate.
  AsyncCallback cb = new AsyncCallback(resp.SetPOStatus);

  // Define a state object
  Object state = new Object();

  // Asynchronously invoke the SubmitPO method
  IAsyncResult ar = manufDelegate.BeginInvoke(
    order, ref invoice, ref poStatus,
    cb, state);
  return poStatus;
  }
}
```

There are two classes referenced by the ManufacturerFaçade class that still need to be explored. They correspond to the ProcessResponse callback class and the PurchaseOrder class.

Implementing .NET Callback Class

Next up is implementing the .NET callback class that will be used to make a callback from the .NET Manufacturing system to the Java Warehouse system.

Once the PO processing is complete, the callback is invoked. This operation corresponds to the SetPOStatus method of the ProcessResponse class. This method is the OneWayAttribute method, which implies that it does not return any information.

```
[OneWayAttribute()]
public void SetPOStatus(IAsyncResult ar)
```

The `SetPOStatus` method is in control of invoking the `WarehouseCallback` Web service. Prior to calling the endpoint, the `ManufacturerDelegate` has to be obtained via the `IAsyncResult` interface. The way it works is somewhat convoluted. After the .NET Common Language Runtime completes the processing of the `SetPOStatus` method, the result is stored in the object of `AsyncResult`. The `AsyncResult` is used to retrieve its property called `AsyncDelegate`, which actually corresponds to the `ManufacturerDelegate` type. This is shown in the code below:

```
ManufacturerDelegate manufDelegate =
    (ManufacturerDelegate)((AsyncResult)ar).AsyncDelegate;
```

As already shown, the `IAsyncResult` interface connects the `BeginInvoke` call with the `EndInvoke` call, finishing the loop of executing by calling the `EndInvoke` method. By invoking `EndInvoke`, the output of asynchronous PO processing is retrieved.

```
manufDelegate.EndInvoke(ref invoiceNumber, ref poStatus, ar);
```

There are couple output parameters that are received—invoiceNumber and POStatus, which will further be passed to the Retailer system via a Web services call:

```
WarehouseCallbackService server = new WarehouseCallbackService();
bool callbackResult = server.submitSN(invoiceNumber, poStatus);
```

Listing 8-18 holds the content of the `ProcessResponse` class.

Listing 8-18
ProcessResponse Class

```
public class ProcessResponse
{
  int poNumber;
  public ProcessResponse(int poNum)
  {
    poNumber=poNum;
  }
  // This is a CallBack method with the one-way qualifier
  [OneWayAttribute()]
  public void SetPOStatus(IAsyncResult ar)
  {
    int invoiceNumber = -1;
    String poStatus    = "PO_Unknown";
```

continues

Listing 8-18 (continued)

```
    // Extract the delegate from the AsyncResult
    // (1) Need AsyncResult object to get delegate
    // AsyncResult asyncObj = (AsyncResult)ar;
    // (2) Get original delegate
    ManufacturerDelegate manufDelegate =
        (ManufacuturerDelegate)asyncObj.AsyncDelegate;

    // Obtain the result of the asynchronous call
    try
    {
        manufDelegate.EndInvoke(ref invoiceNumber, ref poStatus, ar);
    } catch (ProcessPOException e)
    {
        throw new SoapException ("Invalid Purchase Order: "+
poNumber,
            SoapException.ClientFaultCode);
        }

    // Execute callback on the WarehouseCallback Web service
    WarehouseCallbackService server = new
WarehouseCallbackService();
    bool callbackResult = server.submitSN(invoiceNumber, poStatus);
    // Log callbackResult...
    return;
    }
}
```

This class finishes the loop of asynchronous request processing. One piece of data that has not yet been discussed, however, is how to pass around the PurchaseOrder object, which is presented next.

Creating the Purchase Order

The Purchase Order class acts as a .NET Data Transfer object that encapsulates data that have to be passed to the remote system. While it is fairly easy to pass around common data types such as strings or arrays, passing objects through Web services requires XML serialization. In this example the PurchaseOrder encapsulates three pieces of information: the purchase order number, an array of product name, and an array of product quantity. Each of these datum has corresponding getter and setter methods. The PurchaseOrder class is implemented in .NET as in Listing 8-19.

Listing 8-19
PurchaseOrder.class

```
namespace J2eeDotNet.Chapter8.Manufacturer
{
    public class PurchaseOrder
    {
        int _orderNumber;
        string[] _productName;
        int[] _productQuantity;

        public int PONumber
        {
            get { return _orderNumber; }
            set { _orderNumber=value; }
        }
        public String[] ProductName
        {
            get { return _productName; }
            set { _productName=value; }
        }
        public int[] ProductQuantity
        {
            get { return _productQuantity; }
            set { _productQuantity=value; }
        }
    }
}
```

The PurchaseOrder object is serialized on the .NET side as part of the ManufacturerFaçade WSDL. The object is deserialized then on the Java side into the Java Web services stub, which is referenced by the Warehouse class. The chapter gets into the semantics of this after the Warehouse class is built. Listing 8-20 is an auto-generated XML representation of the PurchaseOrder.

Listing 8-20
XML snippet for *ManufacturerFaçade*

```
<s:complexType name="PurchaseOrder">
<s:sequence>
<s:element minOccurs="1" maxOccurs="1" name="PONumber"
type="s:int" />
<s:element minOccurs="0" maxOccurs="1" name="ProductName"
type="s0:ArrayOfString" />
<s:element minOccurs="0" maxOccurs="1" name="ProductQuantity"
type="s0:ArrayOfInt" />
</s:sequence>
```

continues

Listing 8-20 (continued)

```
</s:complexType>
<s:complexType name="ArrayOfString">
<s:sequence>
<s:element minOccurs="0" maxOccurs="unbounded" name="string"
nillable="true" type="s:string" />
</s:sequence>
</s:complexType>
<s:complexType name="ArrayOfInt">
<s:sequence>
<s:element minOccurs="0" maxOccurs="unbounded" name="int"
type="s:int" />
</s:sequence>
</s:complexType>
```

This XML snippet is part of the `ManufacturerFaçade` WSDL.

ARCHITECT'S NOTE

Ideally, the Purchase Order schema should be defined before the integration work starts. Defining a schema for any objects passed between Web services is a typical top-down approach, which is discussed later in the chapter. Examples of implementation of a top-down approach are provided later on in the book.

To summarize at this point, a number of classes and patterns have been implemented to comprise the .NET Manufacturing System. It may be useful now to go back to the original UML diagram in Figure 8-3, highlighting these components, to review relationships among them.

After implementing the .NET ManufacturerFaçade it is now time to deploy the Manufacturing system.

Deploying .NET Manufacturing System

The chapter continues building and deploying classes using an ant script. The build.xml file contains a single target to compile and deploy all .NET-related classes. This target is called deploy-dotnet-service. However, before starting to build these classes, it is important to ensure that the WarehouseCallback Web service is up and running. Check the http://localhost:8080/J2eeDotNet/Chapter8/Retailer/WarehouseCallback URL before starting the ant script. After validating that the WarehouseCallback is running, you can deploy the .NET Web service.

This command compiles and deploys all necessary constituents of the .NET Manufacturing system. You then can check for a running `ManufacturerFaçade` service by going to the URL, http://localhost/ J2eeDotNet/Chapter8/Manufacturer/ManufacturerFaçade.asmx.

The following screen (Figure 8-7) is displayed in the browser window.

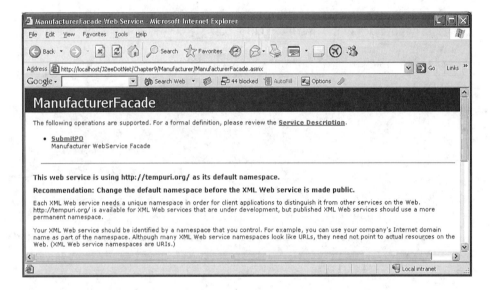

Figure 8-7
Output screen of *ManufacturerFaçade*

Following is a set of individual steps involved in the deployment process, so that you can build your own code in a similar manner.

Preparing Build Directories

The very first step involves creating build directories specified in the `prepare-dotnet` task. Refer to Listing 8-21.

Listing 8-21
prepare-dotnet task

```
<target name="prepare-dotnet">
  <mkdir dir="${iis.bin}"/>
  <mkdir dir="${iis.deployroot}/J2eeDotNet"/>
  <mkdir dir="${iis.deployroot}/J2eeDotNet/Chapter8"/>
  <mkdir
dir="${iis.deployroot}/J2eeDotNet/Chapter8/Eanufacturer"/>
  <mkdir dir="${build.src}/retailer"/>
</target>
```

The iis.bin property corresponds to the location of the Inetpub/wwwroot directory. The rest of the properties are relative to the iis.bin and are defined in the build.xml file.

Generating a *WarehouseCallback* Proxy Class

In the next step the WarehouseCallback Web service proxy class is prepared, by invoking the wsdl.exe and passing argument parameters—the name of an output class, .NET language, protocol, and location of the WSDL file corresponding to the WarehouseCallback endpoint. Refer to Listing 8-22.

Listing 8-22
WarehouseCallback.cs class

```
<!-- Creating the WarehouseCallback.cs class -->
<exec dir="${build.src}/retailer" executable="${wsdl.home}/wsdl.exe"
os="Windows XP">
<arg line="/out:WarehouseCallback.cs /language:CS /protocol:SOAP
${endpoint.warehousecallback}"/>
</exec>
```

This operation yields the auto-generated source code for the WarehouseCallback.cs class.

Generating *WarehouseCallback* Assembly

Now it is necessary to create an assembly DLL that will be referenced by the WarehouseCallback client application. This can be achieved by using the csc.exe compiler: csc.exe /target:library WarehouseCallback.cs or an equivalent ant operation, that looks like the following:

```
<!-- Creating the WarehouseCallback.dll library -->
<exec dir="${build.src}/retailer"
executable="${csc.home}/csc.exe" os="Windows XP">
<arg line="/target:library
/out:${iis.bin}/WarehouseCallback.dll WarehouseCallback.cs"/>
</exec>
```

This command produces a WarehouseCallback.dll.

DEVELOPER'S NOTE

At this point it is helpful to define a simple .NET client application to validate the deployment of the WarehouseCallback. This is a simple unit test, and yet it saves time and effort while troubleshooting distributed applications. Also remember to always display the SOAP message that you are sending over the wire. Previewing the SOAP call can typically help to reveal the details of the call, request, and response parameters.

Compiling .NET Classes

Having deployed the WarehouseCallback DLL, the next step is to compile the PurchaseOrder and POValidate classes that are accessed by the ManufacturerFaçade component. Once again the csc.exe compiler is used to create a single assembly, called PO.dll, as in Listing 8-23.

Listing 8-23
PO.dll

```
<!-- Compiling .NET classes -->
<exec dir="${src.manufacturer}" executable="${csc.home}/csc.exe"
os="Windows XP">
<arg line="/target:library /out:${iis.bin}/PO.dll PurchaseOrder.cs
POValidator.cs"/>
</exec>
```

Deploying .NET Assembly

This operation deploys the PO.dll under the Inetpub\wwwroot directory and will be referenced at runtime by the ManufacturerFaçade:

```
<!-- Deploying the .NET Manufacturer Web service -->
<copy file="${src.manufacturer}/ManufacturerFaçade.asmx"
todir="${iis.deploy}"/>
```

DEVELOPER'S NOTE

While this is relying on `ant` to generate the directory structure and deploy corresponding components, there is more than one deployment option. Depending on your skill set and preferences, you may choose to deploy your .NET application using XCOPY, VS.NET installer, or the Copy Project option in .NET The Visual Studio/IDE.

As a recap, the deployed application encompasses two constituents. The first one corresponds to the `ManufacturerFaçade.asmx` Web service represented with ASP.NET. It is deployed in the virtual directory, `wwwroot`. This Web service references the core business logic of the manufacturing system. It represents the second deployment constituent encapsulated into the `PO.dll` assembly. The callback, `ProcessResponse`, class invokes the `WarehouseCallback` Web service represented with `WarehouseCallback.dll`. These assembly files are located in the bin directory underneath the virtual directory. Listing 8-24 shows a sample deployment hierarchy:

Listing 8-24
Sample Deployment Hierarchy

```
Inetpub/wwwroot/
    |
    --- bin
            PO.dll
            WarehouseCallback.dll
    --- J2eeDotNet/Chapter8/Manufacturer
            ManufacturerFaçade.asmx
```

Previewing .NET *ManufacturerFaçade*

Once the Web service is deployed the deployed service and its WSDL can be explored. The same screen as was shown earlier is viewable at the corresponding URL, http://localhost/J2eeDotNet/Chapter8/Manufacturer/ManufacturerFaçade.asmx. Under the cover, the .asmx handler is automatically invoked to compile the application and deploy the assembly into the corresponding location. The .asmx handler also automatically creates WSDL. In this case, the client uses a GET request for the .asmx endpoint; therefore, the WSDL can be generated and previewed by appending "?WSDL" at the end of the URL, that is, http://localhost/J2eeDotNet/Chapter8/Manufacturer/ManufacturerFaçade.asmx?WSDL.

Before extending the code any further, look back and examine what has been built so far. The earliest component was `WarehouseCallback` that defined the `SubmitSN` method. This class is the last participant in the Replenish Stock flow and is invoked by the Manufacturing system, which was built next. The Manufacturing system embraces a number of components such as `ManufacturerFaçade`, `PurchaseOrder`, and `POValidator` that process the purchase order request. The `POValidator` class followed the Asynchronous Delegate .NET pattern, which is built into .NET but not into the Java programming language. In order to interoperate with the .NET Asynchronous Delegate model, a layer of abstraction has been created using the GoF Façade pattern. This abstraction is represented via the `ManufacturerFaçade` ASP.NET application. The `ManufacturerFaçade` is a Web service acting as a façade to the Retailer system.

By deploying the .NET Manufacturing system, most of the work required to develop the Replenish Stock use case has been accomplished. The only other class left to build is the Warehouse client that invokes the `ManufacturerFaçade` Web service endpoint. The Retailer system is implemented in Java, thus the Warehouse client is built in Java.

Implementing a Java Warehouse Client

The Warehouse client program is much simpler than any of the classes implemented so far. All the Warehouse client does is to create an instance of the purchase order and pass it to the Manufacturing system. Because the purchase order is processed asynchronously, keep in mind that the `ManufacturerFaçade` service only returns an acknowledgement.

Deploying a Java Warehouse Application

If you want to skip individual build steps and run the Warehouse client right away, you may do so by invoking the `ant` script with the `run-client` option. You will see a series of messages with the final few lines corresponding to the Warehouse output information. Refer to Listing 8-25.

Listing 8-25
ant Script to Deploy a Java Warehouse Application

```
$ ant run-client
Buildfile: build.xml

init:
    [echo] --- Building j2eedotnet.chapter9 ---
```

continues

Listing 8-25 (continued)

```
prepare:

generate-client:
    [echo] --- Generating Java stubs for the Manufacturer Web
service ---
[wscompile] Note: Some input files use unchecked or unsafe
operations.
[wscompile] Note: Recompile with -Xlint:unchecked for details.

compile-client:
    [echo] --- Compiling Warehouse application ---
    [javac] Compiling 1 source file to C:\bookcd\build\classes

run-client:
    [echo] --- Running Warehouse application ---
    [java] j2eedotnet.chapter8.retailer.Warehouse: In main...
    [java] After Impl
    [java] End point is:
http://localhost/J2eeDotNet/Chapter8/Manufacturer/Manu
facturerFaçade.asmx?WSDL
    [java] j2eedotnet.chapter8.retailer.Warehouse: The Purchase
Order Status is: PO_132_Submitted

BUILD SUCCESSFUL
Total time: 10 seconds
```

The preceding message only corresponds to the initial request submission, whereas the actual processing of the request occurs asynchronously. The actual result of the PurchaseOrder processing, listed in the log file, warehouseCallback.log, contains the invoice number and the status information. This log record is submitted by the WarehouseCallback application. Refer to Listing 8-26.

Listing 8-26
Log record for *WarehouseCallback*

```
<record>
  <date>2004-10-14T12:38:00</date>
  <millis>1097743080865</millis>
  <sequence>52</sequence>
  <logger>j2eedotnet.chapter8.retailer</logger>
  <level>FINE</level>
  <class>j2eedotnet.chapter8.retailer.WarehouseCallbackImpl</class>
  <method>submitSN</method>
  <thread>11</thread>
  <message>PurchaseOrder status </message>
  <param>Invoice: 1320000</param>
  <param>Status: PO_132_Validated</param>
</record>
```

As usual, the text examines each step of building the Warehouse application. Given that the Warehouse application has to access the .NET Manufacturing endpoint, the Warehouse application is started by generating corresponding client stubs.

Generating .NET *ManufacturerFaçade* Stubs and Other Components

The only operation performed by the Warehouse is accessing the .NET ManufacturerFaçade. For that, stubs, ties, WSDL, and other necessary components need to be prepared to interoperate between Java and .NET. These can be performed with the wscompile JAX-RPC command. The config.xml file is provided as an input to wscompile, specifying a Java package name for generated classes and the location of the ManufacturerFaçade WSDL file. The package name is used by wscompile when creating Java stubs. The config.xml file for the Warehouse is referenced in Listing 8-27.

Listing 8-27

config.xml for *ManufacturerFaçade*

```
<?xml version="1.0" encoding="UTF-8" ?>
 <configuration xmlns="http://java.sun.com/xml/ns/jax-rpc/ri/con-
fig">

<!--
     Warehouse client accesses the WSDL of the ManufacturerFaçade.
     The Warehouse client is part of the j2eedotnet.chapter8.retailer
package
-->
<wsdl
location="http://localhost/J2eeDotNet/Chapter8/Manufacturer/Manufact
urerFaçade.asmx?WSDL"
packageName="j2eedotnet.chapter8.retailer"/>

 </configuration>
```

The actual target invoking `wscompile` is called `generate-client`. Refer to Listing 8-28.

Listing 8-28

generate-client Task in the *ant* Script

```
<target name="generate-client" depends="prepare">
  <echo message="--- Generating Java stubs, WSDL,and other from the
Manufacturer Web service ---"/>
  <wscompile
       keep="true"
       client="true"
       base="${build.classes}"
       sourceBase="${build.src}"
       xPrintStackTrace="true"
       verbose="false"
       classpath="${compile.classpath}"
       config="${etc.client}/config.xml">
       <classpath>
          <path refid="compile.classpath"/>
       </classpath>
  </wscompile>
</target>
```

The `wscompile` command generates stub and interface classes. For interoperability, it is important to access the generated source code. In this case check the `PurchaseOrder.java` class to be able to create an instance of it, given the Warehouse application passes a `PurchaseOrder` object to the .NET system. The Java code that follows looks somewhat different from the one originally created with C#. For example, an array was translated into a new object, `ArrayOfString` and `ArrayOfInt`, which needs to be created to pass the `PurchaseOrder` object around. Refer to Listing 8-29.

Listing 8-29

Purchase Order Program

```
// This class was generated by the JAXRPC SI, do not edit.
// Contents subject to change without notice.
// JAX-RPC Standard Implementation (1.1.2, build R23)
// Generated source version: 1.1.2

package j2eedotnet.chapter8.retailer;
```

```
public class PurchaseOrder {
    protected int PONumber;
    protected j2eedotnet.chapter8.retailer.ArrayOfString
productName;
    protected j2eedotnet.chapter8.retailer.ArrayOfInt
productQuantity;

    public PurchaseOrder() {
    }

    public PurchaseOrder(int PONumber,
        j2eedotnet.chapter8.retailer.ArrayOfString productName,
        j2eedotnet.chapter8.retailer.ArrayOfInt productQuantity) {
        this.PONumber = PONumber;
        this.productName = productName;
        this.productQuantity = productQuantity;
    }

    public int getPONumber() {
        return PONumber;
    }

    public void setPONumber(int PONumber) {
        this.PONumber = PONumber;
    }

    public j2eedotnet.chapter8.retailer.ArrayOfString
getProductName() {
        return productName;
    }

    public voidsetProductName(
      j2eedotnet.chapter8.retailer.ArrayOfString productName) {
        this.productName = productName;
    }

    public j2eedotnet.chapter8.retailer.ArrayOfInt
getProductQuantity()
    {
        return productQuantity;
    }

    public void setProductQuantity(
      j2eedotnet.chapter8.retailer.ArrayOfInt productQuantity) {
        this.productQuantity = productQuantity;
    }
}
```

Writing the Warehouse Application

The Warehouse application obtains the `ManufacturerFaçade` Web service stub to access the .NET Web service.

```
ManufacturerFaçadeSoap_Stub stub = (ManufacturerFaçadeSoap_Stub) (new
ManufacturerFaçade_Impl().getManufacturerFaçadeSoap());
```

It then sets the service endpoint value, based on settings specified in the `build.xml` file:

```
stub._setProperty(
    javax.xml.rpc.Stub.ENDPOINT_ADDRESS_PROPERTY,
    System.getProperty("endpoint"));
```

The following step corresponds to initializing the `PurchaseOrder` object with all specifics of the generated `ManufacturerFaçade` stub classes:

```
int poNumber = 132;
String [] products = {"Table", "Chair", "Monitor"};
int[] qty = {2,3,4};
PurchaseOrder po =
    new PurchaseOrder(poNumber, new ArrayOfString(products), new
ArrayOfInt(qty) );
```

As a final step, the Warehouse accesses the stub to submit the `PurchaseOrder`:

```
String poStatus = stub.submitPO(po);
```

Listing 8-30 is the complete listing of the `Warehouse.java` class.

Listing 8-30
Warehouse.java Class

```
public class Warehouse
{
  public static void main(String[] args)
  {
  try
  {
    // Create service stub factory
    ManufacturerFaçadeSoap_Stub stub = (ManufacturerFaçadeSoap_Stub)
      (new ManufacturerFaçade_Impl().getManufacturerFaçadeSoap());
```

```
// Set the Web service Endpoint property,
stub._setProperty(
javax.xml.rpc.Stub.ENDPOINT_ADDRESS_PROPERTY,
System.getProperty("endpoint"));

// Preparing the PurchaseOrder
int poNumber = 132;
String [] products = {"Table", "Chair", "Monitor"};
int[] qty = {2,3,4};
PurchaseOrder po = new PurchaseOrder(poNumber,
    new ArrayOfString(products), new ArrayOfInt(qty) );

System.out.println("j2eedotnet.chapter8.retailer.Warehouse.main():
    Accessing endpoint "+System.getProperty("endpoint"));
String poStatus = stub.submitPO(po);

System.out.println("j2eedotnet.chapter8.retailer.Warehouse.main():
    The Purchase Order Status is: " + poStatus);
    }
    catch (Exception ex)
    {
        ex.printStackTrace();
    }
}// main
}
```

Compiling the Warehouse Java Application

Earlier the compilation of Java classes was described, and it is no different here. Refer to Listing 8-31.

Listing 8-31
compile-client Task in the *ant* Script

```
<target name="compile-client" depends="generate-client">
  <echo message="--- Compiling Warehouse application ---"/>
    <javac srcdir="${src.retailer}"
           includes="**/Warehouse.java"
           destdir="${build.classes}">
      <classpath refid="compile.classpath"/>
    </javac>
  </target>
```

Executing the Warehouse Java Client Application

The Warehouse program is executed in Listing 8-32.

Listing 8-32
run-client Task in the *ant* Script

```
<target name="run-client" depends="compile-client">
  <echo message="--- Running Warehouse application ---"/>
    <java classname="j2eedotnet.chapter8.retailer.Warehouse"
fork="true">
      <sysproperty key="endpoint" value="${endpoint.manufac-
turer}"/>
      <classpath refid="run.classpath"/>
    </java>
  </target>
```

Achieving Asynchronous Callback in Java

So far this chapter has explored how to embrace .NET solutions for the asynchronous callback strategy. Should one build the Manufacturing system in Java, it would require implementing asynchronous behavior in Java. From a Java EE .NET interoperability standpoint, nothing changes. Web services still remain the core technology for passing a `PurchaseOrder` request and sending the `status` callback between the Retailer and the Manufacturing system. What does change, though, is how requests are processed internally. While in the .NET Manufacturing system example, callback method was being passed to the asynchronous delegate; Java does not have a build in callback algorithm. The JDK1.5, also known as Java 5, introduces a new library, java.util.concurrent, to facilitate concurrency in Java applications as well as to address asynchronous processing. Primarily, the Executor framework of java.util.concurrent can be used to build asynchronous computations. Similar to the .NET example, the `POValidator` class is used to validate the PO and to return a `status` as a callback to `WarehouseCallback`. Instead, in this Java example a `status` class is created to encapsulate the PO id, invoice number, and status message. The `status` class implements the Serializable interface to be able to serialize the status into an XML document and send it via callback to the .NET Retailer system. Here is a prototype of the `status` class in Listing 8-33.

Listing 8-33
Implementation of the *Status* class

```
public class Status implements Serializble {
    PurchaseOrder po;
    String status;
    int invoice;

    public Status(PurchaseOrder po, int inv, String msg){
        order = po;
        invoice = inv;
        status = msg;
    }
    // setter and getter methods for each attributes
}
```

The preceding status class is first instantiated by the POValidator upon successful validation of the purchase order. The POValidator in Java is very similar to the one implemented in .NET. The only difference is that in Java a Runnable interface has been implemented to be able to invoke the validatePO method asynchronously in a separate thread.

```
class POValidator implements Runnable
```

The Runnable interfaces mandate implementation of the run() method, which in this case invokes the validatePO method. The validatePO() checks the PO, creates a Status, and invokes the ProcessResponse to make a Web service callback to the Retailer system, as in Listing 8-34.

Listing 8-34
validatePO

```
    private void validatePO () {
        // validate order
        // create an invoice or an error message
        int invoice = order.getNumber()*1000;

        // create status
        String statusMsg = "PO_"+order.getNumber()+"_Validated";
        Status status = new Status(order, invoice, statusMsg);

        // For a callback invoke ProcessResopnse class
        ProcessResponse response = new ProcessResponse();
        response.setPOStatus(status);
    }
```

Listing 8-35 shows a snippet of the POValidator class.

Listing 8-35
POValidator

```
class POValidator implements Runnable {
    private PurchaseOrder order;
    public POValidator(PurchaseOrder po) {
        order =po;
    }


    public void run(){
        validatePO();
    }

    private void validatePO () {
        // validate order
        // create an invoice or an error message
        int invoice = order.getNumber()*1000;

        // create status
        String statusMsg = "PO_"+order.getNumber()+"_Validated";
        Status status = new Status(order, invoice, statusMsg);

        // For a callback invoke ProcessResopnse class
        ProcessResponse response = new ProcessResponse();
        response.setPOStatus(status);
    }
}
```

The next big component to implement comprises the
ManufacturerFaçade, which is responsible for submitting the PO to
the POValidator. This class uses the new java.util.concurrent library. The
single important component of the ManufacturerFaçade corresponds to
the Executor class. Although the Java threading is detailed out later in the
chapter, here threads are used to achieve asynchronous invocation. The code
sample that follows exploits the ThreadPerTaskExecutor class, which is in
essence a flavor of an Executor that creates a new thread for each task, to
make an asynchronous call to the POValidator:

```
class ThreadPerTaskExecutor implements Executor {
    public void execute(Runnable r) {
        new Thread(r).start();
    }
}
```

In the real world it's much better to recycle threads via the thread pool.

There are multiple options for enabling threading in an application including thread pool creation, thread per task execution or a background thread for all tasks that have to be processed.

The `execute` method takes a parameter representing a task to be executed. The task is represented via the `Runnable` interface. The `Executor` starts a thread that performs a specific `Runnable` task, to allow the task to be executed asynchronously. Now it's time to demonstrate how to make an asynchronous invocation to validate the purchase order.

Asynchronous Invocation

The `ManufacturerFaçade` class starts with the `submitPO` method that follows, which initializes a new `Executor` thread:

```
ThreadPerTaskExecutor executor = new ThreadPerTaskExecutor();
```

Then an instance of the `POValidator` class is created, and the PO request is passed to the constructor:

```
POValidator validate = new POValidator(order);
```

The `POValidator` is the task to be passed to the `Executor`:

```
executor.execute(validate);
```

The `POValidator` implements the `Runnable` interface, whose `run()` method is invoked when the thread is started. This `run()` method calls `validatePO()` to validate the actual purchase order.

At the end of the `submitPO` method, it returns the corresponding Status to the Web service consumer:

```
String statusMsg = "PO_" order.getOrderNumber()+"_Submitted";
return statusMsg;
```

Listing 8-36 is the `ManufacturerFaçade` class.

Listing 8-36
ManufacturerFaçade Class

```
Public class ManufacturerFaçade {
   // A Web service method
   void String submitPO(PurchaseOrder order) {
```

continues

Listing 8-36 (continued)

```
ThreadPerTaskExecutor executor = new ThreadPerTaskExecutor();
POValidator validate = new POValidator(order);
executor.execute(validate);
// Create a response status message
String statusMsg = "PO_" order.getOrderNumber()+"_Submitted";

    return statusMsg;
  }
}
```

Processing the purchase order asynchronously in Java is not the end of the exercise. After the status of the order is ready, a callback needs to be made to the .NET `WarehouseCallback` system. As a best practice it's best to restrict responsibility of each class and keep the callback invocation within the scope of the `ProcessResponse` class. Assuming the .NET `WarehouseCallback` Web service stubs have been generated, the actual invocation of the Web service in Java can be performed as follows (refer to Listing 8-37).

Listing 8-37
ProcessResponse

```
public class ProcessResopnse {
    public void setPOStatus(Status status){


        // Create service stub factory, WarehouseCallbackSoap_Stub
        WarehouseCallbackSoap_Stub stub =
(WarehouseCallbackSoap_Stub) (new
WarehouseCallback_Impl().getWarehouseCallbackSoap());

        // Set the Web service Endpoint property
        stub._setProperty(
            javax.xml.rpc.Stub.ENDPOINT_ADDRESS_PROPERTY,
            System.getProperty("dotnetcallback.endpoint"));


        // Make a Web service call to .NET WarehouseCallback
        boolean ackn = stub.subnmitSN(status);
        // Log callbackResult...
    } catch (Exception ex) {
            ex.printStackTrace();
    }
```

All in all, implementing the Replenish Stock use case with the asynchronous callback strategy using an `Executor` is fairly simple. All that's needed is to create an `Executor` to execute a task and follow it up with a call to the .NET

`WarehouseCallback`. As a matter of fact, a similar approach with .NET could have been used. More about asynchronous processing in .NET is to come when the chapter talks about the response polling strategy.

SOAP Tools for Java and .NET Developers

With asynchronous Web service development, it is useful to use SOAP tools to take a closer look at the SOAP message sent as a request or response. Once your application has been deployed, the content of the message being sent must be found valid. There are a number of free and commercial tools to perform tasks such as reviewing the content of SOAP request and SOAP response. The .NET WebService Studio is a free tool that lets the user explore the SOAP message. There is a simple GUI tool from Apache, Mindreef's SOAPScope, as well as other tools available on the market.

Automatic Callback via Asynchronous Java Proxy

Creating the .NET `ManufacturerFaçade` and leveraging the .NET asynchronous model is one way to build interoperability across Java and .NET. The other technique mentioned earlier is Asynchronous Java Proxy. The proxy is a layer of indirection implemented on the Java Warehouse side, which employs threads to make a Web service call. The actual call to the .NET system occurs synchronously. The diagram in Figure 8-8 outlines the details of this technique, highlighting Java code in gray.

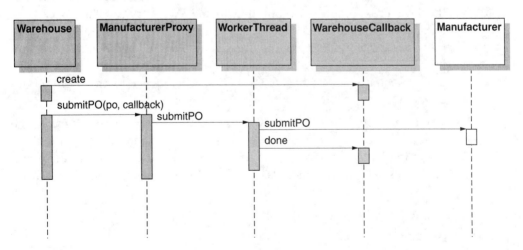

Figure 8-8
Asynchronous Java Proxy overview

The Warehouse client makes a call on the `ManufacturerProxy` to submit the purchase order request. The proxy uses a thread, which submits a request to the .NET system. The actual implementation involves opening the URL connection of the Web service and passing the `SoapRequest` over that connection. The thread blocks wait for a response and, once the response is available, pass it to the `WarehouseCallback`.

The Java Proxy technique has been published for a while and is documented under the Sun Developer Network: http://developers.sun.com/sw/building/tech_articles/async_paper.html, where the actual code can be downloaded and previewed. The preceding Java Proxy will be used to build the Replenish Stock use case. Keep in mind that the utility classes rely on Apache's Web services toolkits, xalan.jar and xerces.jar. But if you want to use these utility classes with Sun's WSDP, you will need to change the utilities import statement and recompile them. When you are ready to test out the sample, archive all utility classes into asyncproxy.jar and place it under the lib directory. You can always modify the sample code to fit your application needs.

Implementation Details

The key component of this asynchronous proxy implementation is the `wsdlCompiler` tool, represented as a `wsdlCompiler` class. It parses the Web service WSDL and creates all necessary classes to perform asynchronous communication. To be more precise, the `wsdlCompiler` tool auto-generates the Java Proxy class corresponding to the Web service. The proxy class encapsulates an asynchronous version of the Web method and a synchronous version of it. It is up to the client to invoke the Web method asynchronously. In this case, a new thread is created to execute the `executeWebMethod`, which passes a SOAP request to the Web service endpoint.

In addition to the proxy class, the `wsdlCompiler` creates the `IWebServiceCallback` interface. To make an asynchronous call, the client has to implement this interface and pass the callback instance to the proxy. The purpose of this callback class is to return the response back to the client.

ManufacturerService Web Service

To use `wsdlCompiler`, it is necessary to deploy the actual Web service. The `ManufacturerService` that follows is a very simple .NET Web service similar to the `ManufacturerFaçade` built previously. Refer to Listing 8-38.

Listing 8-38
ManufacturerService .NET Web Service

```
namespace J2eeDotNet.Chapter8.Manufacturer {

public class ManufacturerService : System.Web.Services.WebService {

[WebMethod(Description = "Manufacturer WebService")]
// The following demonstrates the Asynchronous Pattern using call-
back.
 public string SubmitPO(int order) {
   PurchaseOrder po = new PurchaseOrder();
   po.PONumber = order;
   int invoice=-1;
   String poStatus = "PO_"+order+"_Submitted";
   POValidator validator = new POValidator();
   validator.ValidatePO(po, ref invoice, ref poStatus);
   return poStatus;
   }
}
```

The preceding class invokes the `POValidator` component to validate the order, and the passing argument was simplified to take an integer rather than a complex type. The mapping between the XML schema and Java types can be extended to accommodate compound data types stored in the `WsdlCompilerDataTypes.xml` file that is accessed by the `wsdlCompiler` tool to generate the SOAP request and SOAPResponse XML documents.

To deploy the service, place the actual ASP.NET file under the same directory as the ManufacturerFaçade. Browse to the URL: http://localhost/J2eeDotNet/Chapter8/Manufacturer/ManufacturerService.asmx to ensure that the service is running correctly. Here is the WSDL of the Web service that is used next: http://localhost/J2eeDotNet/Chapter8/Manufacturer/ManufacturerService.asmx?WSDL.

Implementing *WarehouseCallback* Classes

After the Web service is deployed, it is possible to generate a Java Proxy. All that's needed then is to pass the WSDL location to the `wsdlCompiler`. The ant file can be previewed to see how to do that, but the focus right now are the artifacts of that operation. The `wsdlCompiler` created a `ManufacturerFaçadeProxy` and the `IWebServiceCallback` interface. The callback interface defines one method, `done`, that needs to be implemented. It is, however, up to the developer to modify the utility classes to generate a more sophisticated callback routine.

```
public interface IWebServiceCallback{
  public void done(InputStream in) ;
}
```

What is returned is the `InputStream` that essentially contains an XML SOAPResponse message.

The `WarehouseCallback` implements the callback interface by simply printing out the content sent to the `InputStream`. Refer to Listing 8-39.

Listing 8-39
WarehouseCallback Implementation

```
public class WarehouseCallback implements IWebServiceCallback
    {

    public void done(InputStream in)
    {
        try
        {
            int i= -1;
            System.out.println("Receiving the callback");
        String msg="";

            while((i = in.read()) > -1)
            {
                System.out.print((char)i);                      }
        }
        catch(IOException e)
        {
            e.printStackTrace();
        }
    }
}
```

Implementing Warehouse Classes

The `Warehouse` class is also very simple. It creates a callback instance to pass to the proxy and invokes the proxy to pass it the order id and the callback:

```
proxy.SubmitPOAsync(orderNumber, callback);
```

The proxy contains two methods for each Web service method—one corresponding to synchronous invocation and the other corresponding to asynchronous invocation. Invoking the `SubmitPOAsync` method implies asynchronous invocation of the `SubmitPO` Web method. Listing 8-40 is the entire `Warehouse` class.

Listing 8-40

Warehouse Class

```java
public class Warehouse {
  public static void main(String[] args) {
     ManufacturerServiceProxy proxy = new
ManufacturerServiceProxy();
     IWebServiceCallback callback = new WarehouseCallback();
     int orderNumber = 1244;

     System.out.println("Warehouse.main(): In main... ");
     proxy.SubmitPOAsync(orderNumber, callback);
     System.out.println("Warehouse.main(): Submitted
            PO,"+orderNumber+", to the Proxy...");
  }
}
```

Deploying Asynchronous Proxy Example

To simply run the asynchronous Proxy example, create the run-asyncproxy. This command invokes `wsdlCompile` to generate the proxy, compiles the Warehouse and the `WarehouseCallback` classes, and executes the Warehouse client. In the following output, Listing 8-41, the build and compile output is skipped:

Listing 8-41
ant Build Result

```
$ ant run-asyncproxy
Buildfile: build.xml

build-asyncproxy:
...
compile-asyncproxy:
...
run-asyncproxy:
    [echo] --- Running CallbackTest application ---
    [java] Warehouse.main(): In main...
    [java] Warehouse.main(): Submitted PO,1244, to the Proxy...
    [java] Receiving the callback
    [java] <?xml version="1.0" encoding="utf-8"?>
<soap:Envelope xmlns:soap="http://schemas.xmlsoap.org/soap/
envelope/" xmlns:xsi="http://www.w3.org/2001/XMLSchema-instance"
xmlns:xsd="http://www.w3.org/2001/XMLSchema">
<soap:Body>
 <SubmitPOResponse xmlns="http://tempuri.org/">
 <SubmitPOResult>PO_1244_Validated</SubmitPOResult>
 </SubmitPOResponse>
 </soap:Body>
</soap:Envelope>

BUILD SUCCESSFUL
Total time: 15 seconds
```

Build Asynchronous Proxy

There are ant tasks corresponding to the asynchronous Proxy example. To build the Java Proxy and auto generate the callback interface, the wsdlCompiler tool is used, as shown in Listing 8-42:

Listing 8-42
build-asyncproxy Task in the *ant* Script

```
<target name="build-asyncproxy">
    <echo message="--- Building async proxy ---"/>
    <java classname="asyncproxy.WsdlCompiler" fork="true">
        <arg line="${endpoint.manufService}
        j2eedotnet.chapter9.asyncproxy"/>
        <classpath refid="compile.classpath"/>
    </java>
    <move file ="ManufacturerServiceProxy.java"
          todir="${src.asyncproxy}"/>
    <move file ="IWebServiceCallback.java"
          todir="${src.asyncproxy}"/>
</target>
```

Compile Asynchronous Proxy Classes

The next step is to compile the classes. Refer to Listing 8-43.

Listing 8-43
compile-asyncproxy Task in the *ant* Script

```
<target name="compile-asyncproxy" depends="build-asyncproxy">
    <echo message="--- Compiling async proxy client ---"/>
    <javac srcdir="${src.asyncproxy}"
           destdir="${build.classes}">
      <classpath refid="run.classpath"/>
    </javac>
</target>
```

Run Asynchronous Proxy Example

To run the example, invoke the `run-asyncproxy` target, as shown in Listing 8-44.

Listing 8-44
run-asyncproxy Task in the *ant* Script

```
<target name="run-asyncproxy" depends="compile-asyncproxy">
    <echo message="--- Running CallbackTest application ---"/>
    <java classname="j2eedotnet.chapter8.asyncproxy.Warehouse"
          fork="true">
      <classpath refid="run1.classpath"/>
    </java>
</target>
```

Benefits and Limitations

The Asynchronous Java Proxy technique offers Java developers a way to achieve asynchronous processing without getting into the details of the .NET world. However, the biggest limitation of this technique, at least with the provided implementation, pertains to the fact that individual Java threads are going to keep the underlying HTTP connection open until the remote processing of the request is complete. It is also important to leverage a thread pool rather then create a new thread per individual task. This technique does not leverage the .NET asynchrony.

It is worth noting that this technique, just like .NET Façade, can be modi-fied to accommodate the response polling strategy in addition to automatic callback.

Using Java Proxy or .NET Façade?

Where you would use Java Proxy and where you would consider the .NET Façade depends on the developer's skill set and the status of the enterprise. For Java developers it may be much simpler to perform asynchronous Web services communication with Web services, while if the individual is a savvy .NET developer, the .NET Façade may be the way to go. By the status of the enterprise, the fact is that some of the systems are built in such a way that they are very difficult to extend or modify. Therefore, regardless of skill set, choice of options may be limited to accomplish asynchronous Web services across those systems.

You can learn additional techniques of developing a Java EE-based asynchronous callback strategy with JAX-RPC by referring to [Async ProcJAXRPC].

Asynchronous Callback Summary

By now the semantics of building the asynchronous callback may seem over-whelming and may even shadow the original objective of this chapter. What has been accomplished so far is the asynchronous Java EE-.NET processing that followed the course of the SOA. Design-wise it has started with the asynchronous callback strategy. As part of this effort, it has been demon-strated how to perform asynchronous callback in .NET as well as Java. The next objective is to understand the response polling strategy that is also use-ful to facilitate asynchronous Java EE .NET communication.

Response Polling Strategy

With the response polling strategy, a client application explicitly checks for completion of the remote processing. This approach is simpler to implement than the automatic callback strategy and involves less coding. Depending on the business scenario, the polling strategy may be quite useful. A good exam-ple where the polling strategy is often applicable includes client-side pro-cessing. For instance, a client application submits a request to the remote Java EE, .NET, and legacy back-end systems. Refer to Figure 8-9.

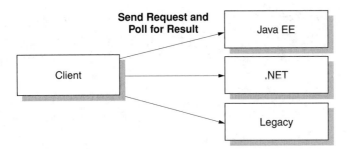

Figure 8-9
Client application submits a request to the remote Java EE, .NET, and legacy back-end systems.

To avoid having a user blocked, waiting for a result to come back, background threads can be leveraged to submit their requests and poll for results on individual systems, such as Java EE, .NET, and legacy. This strategy is appropriate in situations where a remote system may not be easily extended to perform a callback to the originator of a call or if the original caller may not be up and running at all times to receive a callback.

Implementing the Replenish Stock Use Case

Figure 8-10 depicts the Manufacturing System details of the Replenish Stock use case with the response polling strategy.

As can be seen in the diagram, it is up to the calling system to explicitly poll for results, which in this case is accomplished with the `getStatus` Web service call. It is also good practice to add a `terminateRequest()` method, in case a Web service consumer decides to cancel the call. From the design standpoint there are a number of ways to realize the response polling strategy.

As mentioned in the preceding example, a background thread can be leveraged to perform a status check. Details pertaining to threading are discussed subsequently.

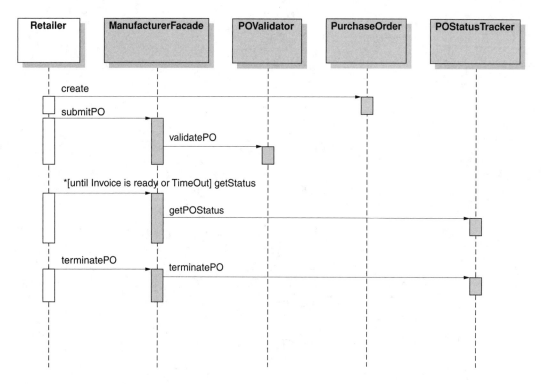

Figure 8-10
Response polling strategy sequence diagram

One of the common approaches often applied for asynchronous communication revolves around threading. The next sections look into Java and C# examples of implementing a threading model used for asynchronous communication. For Java examples, the java.util.concurrent library is used to perform the asynchronous request invocation and to poll for results.

Implementing Response Polling in Java

Once again, the Java concurrent library simplifies implementation of the response polling strategy. The purpose of the polling strategy is to query for the result of an asynchronous call. How to invoke a `Runnable POValidator` object in a separate thread with the asynchronous callback strategy has already been discussed. Here Java threads are used to implement the response polling strategy as well.

Building *PurchaseOrder* and *POValidator*

The present goal is to create a new thread using the `Callable` interface, introduced in JDK 1.5. The `Callable` interface allows the developer to return a result back, such as Status, as well as throw a checked exception. All that's needed to implement the `Callable` interface is to modify the `POValidator` class. The main method of the `Callable` interface is the `call()` method, which takes `PurchaseOrder` as a parameter, returns `Status` as a result, or if the PO is invalid throws `InvalidOrderException`. The actual processing occurs in the `validatePO` method, invoked by `call()`. Refer to Listing 8-45.

Listing 8-45
validatePO Method

```
private Status validatePO ( PurchaseOrder po) throws
   InvalidOrderException {
  int poNumber = po.getNumber();
  // validate PO
  // create an invoice:
  invoice = poNumber*10000;
  // create status message
  String statusMsg = "PO_"+poNumber+"_Validated";
  // create status
  Status status = (po, invoice, statusMsg);

  // if order is invalid
  //throw an InvalidOrderException

  return status;
}
```

Listing 8-46 shows an example of `POValidator` that implements `Callable` interface.

Listing 8-46
POValidator Implementation

```
public class POValidator implements Callable<Status>{

  public Status call(PurchaseOrder po) throws InvalidOrderException
    return validatePO(po);
  }

  private Status validatePO ( PurchaseOrder po)
    throws InvalidOrderException {
```

continues

Listing 8-46 (continued)

```
    int poNumber = po.getNumber();
    // validate PO
    // create an invoice:
    invoice = poNumber*10000;
    // create status message
    String statusMsg = "PO_"+poNumber+"_Validated";
    // create status
    Status status = (po, invoice, statusMsg);

    // if order is invalid
    //throw an InvalidOrderException

    return status;
    }
  }
// Don't forget to define the InvalidOrderException class
```

Building *POStatus Tracker*

To enable a Java EE .NET system poll for requests using Web services, there needs to be some sort of infrastructure in place to keep track of all submitted tasks to be able to obtain their status. In this case, a POStatusTracker class is created that is responsible for checking for the status of a given order. To enable the POStatusTracker to access the right task, one adds the FutureTask and the PO number of individual requests into a collection, such as a hash table:

```
    private HashMap<int,FutureTask<Status>> tasks = new
HashMap<int,FutureTask<Status>>();
```

The use of Generic types used by HashMap and FutureTask attributes might have been noticed. Generics were introduced in JDK1.5 and enrich the development environment with the ability to explicitly specify expected data types. It's already known that the key will be based on the PO id, which is an integer type, and the value stored by the HashMap is of type FutureTask. Hence, enforce type constraints are enforced at compile time rather than runtime.

For each PO number acting as a key, the FutureTask that provides us with a means of getting the status of the submitted task is stored. FutureTask is part of the same Java concurrent library that this chapter has been working with all along.

```
public void addTask(int poNumber, FutureTask<Status> result){
      tasks.put(poNumber,result);
      // Log a new task
}
```

The FutureTask acts as a handle to the executed task and makes it possible to check if the task is finished. The first task is to check if the result is ready, and if it is, get the Status of the submitted PurchaseOrder:

```
Public Status getPOStatus(int poNumber) {

   boolean ready = result.isDone();
```

A positive, that is, true, response indicates that either the result is ready, an exception occurred, or the task has been cancelled. If this method returns true, it's possible to check for a result:

```
Status status = (Status) result.get();
```

The get() method may throw an exception and therefore should always be invoked in the try-catch block.

To complete this example, the terminate task method is also added, which locates the task in the task list and attempts to terminate it. Refer to Listing 8-47.

Listing 8-47

terminateTask Method

```
public boolean terminateTask(int orderNumber){
   FutureTask<Status> result = (FutureTask<Status>)
   tasks.get(orderNumber);
   // terminate the task, pass true to cancel
   // the job even if it's running
   boolean cancelled = result.cancel(true);

   return cancelled;
}
```

Here is the POStatusTracker class. Refer to Listing 8-48.

Listing 8-48
POStatusTracker Implementation

```
public class POStatusTracker{
  private Status status =null;
  private HashMap<int,FutureTask<Status>> tasks = new
      HashMap<int,FutureTask<Status>>();

  public Status getPOStatus(int orderNumber) {
    FutureTask<Status> result = (FutureTask<Status>)
        tasks.get(orderNumber);
  if (result != null && result.isDone()){
  try {
    // Use FutureResult to retrieve status
    status = (Status) result.get();
  }catch (InterruptedException ex) { return; }
   catch (ExecutionException ex) { return; }

  tasks.remove(orderNumber);
  // Log completion of task
    }
  return status;
  }

 public void addTask(int orderNumber, FutureTask<Status>
futureResult){
    tasks.put(orderNumber, futureResult);
    }

 public boolean terminateTask(int orderNumber){
   FutureTask<Status> result = (FutureTask<Status>)
   tasks.get(orderNumber);
   // terminate the task, pass true to cancel
   // the job even if it's running
   boolean cancelled = result.cancel(true);

   return cancelled;
}
```

Building the *ManufacturerFaçade*

While the Web service semantics of the ManufacturerFaçade is quite clear, an emphasis is put on techniques of processing incoming PurchaseOrder requests and POStatus requests. First of all, it's important to ensure that the system is capable of performing and scaling to the necessary degree, thus a thread pool is leveraged to pass all incoming requests to a background thread to submit PO requests as well as perform the actual PO status check.

Processing PO Requests

The chapter has already discussed an `Executor` class from the asynchronous callback fragment. This time the `ExecutorService` is introduced, which extends `Executor` with the ability to manage tasks executed in the future. To obtain an `ExecutorService`, the `Executors`'s static method, `newCachedThreadPool`, is used, which creates a thread pool of a fixed size and recycles them throughout the application lifecycle:

```
ExecutorService executor =
Executors.newFixedThreadPoll(poolSize);
```

The `ExecutorService` extends `Executor`'s `execute()` method with a new method, `submit()`. This method returns a `Future` object, which enables the developer to check if the task has been completed or to terminate the task. Here is an example of creating a `POValidator` and passing the required task to the `ExecutorService`. For the original PO Validator request, invoke the following:

```
Callable<Status> task = new POValidator(order);
FutureTask<Status> result = executor.submit(task);
```

It's also necessary to be able to deal with response polling calls, which are performed on the `POStatusTracker` object.

```
private static POStatusTracker tracker = new POStatusTracker();
tracker.addTask(orderNumber, result);
```

Listing 8-49 shows the `submitPO` method that implements the response polling strategy:

Listing 8-49
submitPO Method

```
ExecutorService executor = Executors.newCachedThreadPool();

public String submitPO(PurchaseOrder order){
    Callable<Status> task = new POValidator(order);
    FutureTask<Status> result = executor.submit(task);
```

continues

Listing 8-49 (continued)

```
      tracker.addTask(result);
      String currentStatus="PO_"+order.getNumber()+"_Submitted";

      return currentStatus;
  }
```

DEVELOPER'S NOTE

As you saw, the `FutureTask` becomes quite handy for accomplishing the goal of obtaining a handle to the task executed asynchronously. Because the `FutureTask` class implements the `Runnable` interface, you can simplify the preceding code by passing `FutureTask` to an `Executor` directly. The code sets a new `Callable` task on `FutureTask` object:

```
FutureTask<Status> futureTask =
    executor.submit(new Callable()
    {
        public Status call()
        {
            return validator.validatePO(order);
        }
    });
```

The preceding code does not require the `POValidator` class to implement the `Runnable` or the `Callable` interface. Instead a `Callable` object is explicitly created, and the `call()` class is implemented.

ARCHITECT'S NOTE

It is suggested to factor out the task submission logic. Employing the Application Server pattern (see the Core Java EE Pattern Catalog) to manage the thread pool and facilitate access to the InvoiceTracker would simplify the `ManufacturerFaçade`, whose main job is to process incoming .NET requests.

POStatus Polling

Now it's time to implement the actual logic of processing requests. As a reminder, the Web service consumer will be making multiple calls to poll for a response. For each incoming request, the corresponding `FutureTask` needs to be located and its status checked. This task is accomplished by the `InvoiceTracker`. Refer to Listing 8-50.

Listing 8-50
getStatus Method

```
public Status getStatus(int orderNumber){
    Status status = tracker.getPOStatus(orderNumber);
    if(status ==null)
        return new Status(orderNumber, "NotReady", -1)

}
```

If `status` is null, the corresponding status message is set, and invoice value is set to `-1`.

Clean Up

At some point, the `ManufacturerFaçade` has to ensure that the `Executor` is shut down before the `ManufacturerFaçade` (or an Application Service) exits. So it is worth creating a cleanup method that waits for all threads to complete before exiting and shuts down the `Executor`. Refer to Listing 8-51.

Listing 8-51
Status Class

```
public Status cleanup(Executor executor){
  executor.shutdown();
  executor.awaitTermination();
}
```

While threading is a broad area for discussion, it's now time to switch gears and demonstrate how to implement the Response Pooling strategy under the .NET Framework.

All in all, submitPO, getStatus, and cleanup () are three main methods embodied by ManufacturerFaçade. These methods are the ones that are exposed as Web services, and these classes' signatures are placed into a Remote interface. Refer to Listing 8-52.

Listing 8-52

ManufacturerFaçade Implementation

```
public interface ManufacturerFaçade extends Remote {
    public String submitPO(PurchaseOrder) ) throws RemoteException;
    public Status getStatus(int orderNumber) throws RemoteException;
    public boolean  terminate(int orderNumber) throws RemoteException;
}
```

ARCHITECT'S NOTE

It is worth pointing out that you may leverage and FutureTask for realization of the callback strategy. It can be designed to effectively augment the Asynchronous Java Proxy technique. Additionally, you may design the communication between the worker thread and the callback via the event notification and listeners to those events. Overall, there are quite a few techniques that can be adopted when designing the asynchronous strategies.

It's now time to move on with the .NET implementation of the response polling strategy.

Implementing Response Polling Under .NET

Implementing the response polling strategy under .NET is somewhat similar to a callback. BeginInvoke and EndInvoke methods are invoked to pass an asynchronous call and poll for a response. In addition, the POStatusTracker component is adopted to store AsyncResults corresponding to individual PO number.

Part of this exercise illustrates how to use the WaitHandle component of .NET to wait for a response of an asynchronous call in addition to the .NET threading model.

ManufacturerFaçade

The ManufacturerFaçade looks slightly different from the one built for the callback strategy. Specifically, a callback and state parameters do not need to be specified in the BeginInvoke method. These parameters are set to null:

```
IAsyncResult asyncResult = manufDelegate.BeginInvoke(
          order, ref invoice, ref poStatus,
          null, null);
```

One thing to consider is to use the list of all tasks submitted to the Manufacturer by creating a POStatusTracker just like what was implemented in Java.

```
POStatusTracker tracker = new POStatusTracker();
Tracker.addTask(order.getNumber(), asyncResult);
```

Here is the ManufacturerDelegate used for response polling strategy. Listing 8-53 shows the listing of the ManufacturerFaçade class returning the POstatus.

Listing 8-53
ManufacturerFaçade Class

```
public class ManufacturerFaçade : System.Web.Services.WebService
{
[WebMethod(Description = "Manufacturer WebService Façade")]
        public string SubmitPO(PurchaseOrder order)
        {
                int poNumber = order.PONumber;
                String poStatus="PO_"+poNumber+"_Submitted";
                int invoice=-1;
                POValidator validator = new POValidator();
                ManufacturerDelegate manufDelegate = new
ManufacturerDelegate(validator.ValidatePO);

                // Asynchronously invoke the SubmitPO method
                IAsyncResult ar = manufDelegate.BeginInvoke(
                    order,
                        ref invoice,
                        ref poStatus,
                        null,
                        null);

        return poStatus;
    }
}
```

Later, when a polling request comes in, it can be passed to the
`POStatusTracker` to check whether the response, that is, `POstatus`, is
ready. The details of the status check are factored out of
`ManufacturerFaçade` and placed into the `POStatusTracker` class.

Implementing *POStatusTracker* Class

The `IAsyncResult` interface plays an important role in the response polling
strategy. This interface was already used when building Callback. In
`POStatusTracker`, `IAsyncResult` is used to obtain a reference to
`ManufacturerDelegate`:

```
AsyncResult result = (AsyncResult) tasks.Item(orderNumber);
ManufacturerDelegate manufDelegate =
        (ManufacturerDelegate)result.AsyncDelegate;
```

To check for a response, `IAsyncResult` is once again used, which provides
the `IsCompleted` attribute:

```
if (result != null && result.IsCompleted){
    // Obtain the return value
    Status status = manufDelegate.EndInvoke(result);
}
```

Listing 8-54 shows a snippet of the `POStatusTracker`:

Listing 8-54
POStatusTracker Pseudo-Code

```
public class POStatusTracker{
    private Status status =null;
    public static Hashtable tasks = new Hashtable();

    public Status getPOStatus(int orderNumber) {
      try {
        AsyncResult result = (AsyncResult)
                    tasks.Item(orderNumber);
        if (result != null && result.IsCompleted){

    // Retrieve status
    ManufacturerDelegate manufDelegate =
            (ManufacturerDelegate) result.AsyncDelegate;
    status = manufDelegate.EndInvoke(result);
    tasks.remove(orderNumber);
    // Log completion of task
      }
```

```
        return status;
    }
    ...
}
```

Response Polling with .NET WaitHandle

The `WaitHandle` technique in .NET asynchronous processing enriches the implementation of response polling. As was already discussed, response polling is useful in applications where a client application, in this case the .NET client, may have to make multiple Web service calls to remote systems. Later the client application has to aggregate the content to display to the user. The way the client application invokes these asynchronous calls may differ depending on requirements. In one case, the client may poll for a response. In another case, the client may have to wait for all responses to come back to be able to consolidate the content prior to displaying it to the user. For that type of scenario, .NET offers the `WaitHandle` component. From an implementation standpoint, the `ManufacturerFaçade` is very similar to the one that has already been built. Neither a callback nor a state object to the `BeginInvoke` method needs to be created:

```
IAsyncResult asyncResult = manufDelegate.BeginInvoke(
        order, ref invoice, ref poStatus,
        null, null);
```

The `IAsyncResult` interface, returned from the `BeginInvoke` method, provides the static property, `AsyncWaitHandle`. This wait handle has three methods that may potentially be invoked—`WaitOne`, `WaitAny`, and `WaitAll`. The first method allows waiting on a single handle. The other two take arrays of `WaitHandles` as parameters. The `WaitAny` method returns after any of the calls have completed; the `WaitAll` waits until all calls have completed. For details of `WaitOne`, `WaitAny`, and `WaitAll` methods, please refer to [WaitHandleAPI]. This example uses `WaitOne`, which waits for an asynchronous call to finish. Wait for 10 seconds and pass `false` to avoid reacquiring a synchronized context:

```
ar.AsyncWaitHandle.WaitOne(10000, false);
```

After the wait period simply check if the call has finished:

```
ar.IsCompleted
```

Listing 8-55 shows the complete definition of the getStatus method:

Listing 8-55
getStatus Method

```
public void getStatus() {
        IAsyncResult asyncResult = manufDelegate.BeginInvoke(
                order,
                ref invoice,
                ref poStatus,
                null,
                null);

        asyncResult.AsyncWaitHandle.WaitOne(10000, false);

        if (asyncResult.IsCompleted){
            // get Status information
        }
    }
```

ARCHITECT'S NOTE

Using AsyncWaitHandle blocks the thread of the current task execution until one or more tasks completes. Therefore, wait handles have to be used with caution.

Threading in .NET

The .NET asynchronous infrastructure already leverages multithreading when delegating an asynchronous call. In callback and response polling scenarios a delegate was defined corresponding to the method used to invoke asynchronously. The purpose of the delegate is to make the actual method call in a different thread, while the main application thread remains unblocked. There are, however, cases when the threading model can be leveraged to enhance application performance and scalability. In the Replenish Stock use case, the .NET Manufacturing system may leverage a pool of background threads, for example, to check status of the PO request. The .NET framework encloses a thread pool class, ThreadPool, which is part of the System.Threading library. There are a couple of methods that are useful to understand in that class. The first one is the QueueUserWorkItem, used to add a task to the thread pool. A task is executed when there is an available thread in the pool. The `QueueUserWorkItem` method does not take tasks directly; instead it takes a delegate parameter of type `WaitCallback`:

```
public delegate void WaitCallBack(Object stateObject);
```

This delegate wraps the actual method to be executed, which is passed as an input parameter, `stateObject`. To add a task to the queue, the following operation needs to be performed:

```
ThreadPool.QueueUserWorkItem(new WaitCallback(GetPOStatus));
```

The CLR executes the requested method once there is an available thread in the pool. Where would one use it? A thread pool may become useful to delegate execution of `GetPOStatus` requests.

In addition to adding work items, that is, tasks, to the queue, the .NET Framework also provides a mechanism of controlling these tasks by associating a wait handle to a work item. The wait handle can be set via the `RegisteredWaitForSingleObject` method. To check the pool status, methods such as GetAvailableThreads and GetMaxThreads of the .NET PoolThread class can be used.

Related Patterns

There are a few patterns to consider when designing asynchronous communication across Java EE and .NET.

Java EE Web Service Broker and .NET Service Interface Patterns

Problem Domain

It is often desired to separate business logic from the initial request processing. With SOA it is essential to define a Web service in a way that hides the complexity of the business processing and details of the request processing call chain. Instead, it is necessary to expose a coarse-grained, high-level interface to Web service consumers.

Solution

Both Java EE and .NET implement this idea through a pattern that differs in name depending on the technology referred to. The Java EE Core Pattern catalog lists this pattern under the Web services Broker, while under .NET this pattern is called the Service Interface. In both cases this component introduces a layer of abstraction between the Web service consumer and the service implementation details. In the Replenish Stock use case, this layer is realized with `ManufacturerFaçade` ASP.NET. The actual implementation class corresponds to the `POValidator`, while the Warehouse class acts as the WS consumer.

Asynchronous Request Assembler

Problem Domain

Initiating an asynchronous call to the remote Java EE or .NET system may require aggregating various properties as part of the request preparation routine. The Assembler is responsible for preparing the request in the corresponding format. There is also a need to look up a remote service and pass the request to the remote Java EE or .NET system. Finally, depending on business requirements, there may be a need to log an acknowledgement based on making an asynchronous call.

Solution

The Asynchronous Request Assembler ensures correct mapping from a schema or auto-generated stub classes into the corresponding domain object. It also provides a means of sending this request to the remote system and logging an acknowledgment or a fault.

Related Patterns

There are related patterns from the Core Java EE Pattern catalog that are similar to this one or can be used in conjunction with the Asynchronous Request Assembler. A Service Locator can be used, for example, to look up the remote .NET or Java EE Web service. A Business Delegate can be used to submit the actual request.

Asynchronous Request Handler

Problem Domain

To ensure reliability of asynchronous calls across distributed applications, there should be a component on each system that is responsible for tracking incoming calls.

Solution

While Java EE does not yet support the WS-Reliable Messaging, and .NET will be supporting it as part of the Indigo release, having custom components that trace incoming requests across distributed systems can be thought of as an option. In some cases architects may choose messaging as a communication mechanism rather than the asynchronous Web services to leverage full support of reliable messaging.

Compensating Asynchronous Request Handler

Problem Domain

Should reliability be enabled, it would be necessary to ensure that there is corresponding logic for rolling back any changes that have been submitted in case there is a failure.

Solution

The Asynchronous Request Handler is responsible for monitoring asynchronous calls for errors. If a call times out or if a problem occurs during the asynchronous request processing, this component has to issue a compensating transaction to rollback all changes that already have been submitted.

Orchestrate Asynchronous Calls

Problem Domain

Should multiple asynchronous calls span across multiple systems, it is worth considering an orchestration engine.

Solution

An orchestration engine component would coordinate Web services calls across different systems, such as Java EE and .NET. There is already an industry specification, WS Orchestration, and a set of products that can be used to avoid building this orchestration engine from scratch.

Best Practices and Pitfalls

This chapter next takes a look at various systemic qualities, such as manage-ability and scalability, which have to be addressed when building asynchro-nous Java EE .NET integration. Prior to that, the chapter discusses asynchronous communication support introduced in SOAP 1.2. Upcoming Java support of SOAP 1.2 and new features of Microsoft Indigo that simplify asynchronous programming are discussed, as well as the top-down develop-ment approach and industry standard compliance, which are discussed toward the end of the chapter.

Document-Oriented Approach

There are two main ways to submit a request to a Web service—either as a remote procedure call or as an XML document. A document-oriented approach is primarily intended for use with asynchronous Web services. A document, acting as a service request, is exchanged between a Web service client and the endpoint. In the Replenish Stock scenario, a Web service client, that is, Warehouse, asynchronously submits a Purchase Order document to the `ManufacturerFaçade` Web service. The Purchase Order is represented in XML format. The content of the document determines the processing steps required by the actual service, such as verifying validity of the request, sub-mitting the request further for replenish stock, generating an invoice, and sending invoice information back to the service consumer.

Soap Messages with Attachments

The document-oriented approach can be used in conjunction with the SOAP with Attachments (SwA) specification, which allows exchanging official doc-uments in binary format. Should an invoice for a purchase order be submit-ted along with an image of an item being shipped, SwA can be used. To consistently process attachments, the WS-I Basic Profile is extended with the WS-I Attachment Profile, which profiles SwA and WSDL MIME bindings in order to guarantee interoperability when sending documents as attachments. JAXRPC 1.1 implements these specifications, which provide Java and .NET developers with means of freely passing MIME types as an attachment to the SOAP message. This approach yields a smaller footprint SOAP message, which simplifies troubleshooting and minimizes the amount of memory required when processing the SOAP message.

Some limitations will likely be hit when using SwA between Java EE and .NET. Java supports MIME types, whereas Microsoft introduced the Direct Internet Message Encapsulation (DIME) type built into the .NET Framework. Specifically, Java-supported attachment types include images in .gif or .jpeg formats, plain text, XML document, and multipart type—all with the corresponding Java mapping. DIME basically supports the same types and provides mapping within the .NET Framework but does not interoperate with MIME. Thus having to agree on the transport binding using HTTP and a data format with a common schema does not indicate the end of interoperability concerns. The next problem resides in the packaging protocol: MIME versus DIME. There are third-party tools that can perform MIME to/from DIME translation. As an example, Smart421 offers a .NET extension to interoperate between MIME and DIME. The good news is that maturity and wide industry adoption of the MIME format caused Microsoft and other vendors to also support the MIME format. The Proposed Infoset Addendum to SOAP Messages with Attachments document [PASWA] discusses details of passing MIME formatted documents using Soap with Attachments, valid both for Java and .NET. Having a unified attachment format would allow developers to use SwA/MIME without having to solve yet another integration puzzle. MTOM, that was discussed in Chapter 4, "Web Services for Synchronous Integration," offers the interoperability of exchanging binary documents across Java EE and .NET Web services.

SOAP 1.2 Enhancements

SOAP 1.2 support for asynchronous communication has already been discussed. In addition to that, SOAP 1.2 abstracts out the transport bindings. While in SOAP 1.1 HTTP is the only supported binding, the new specification of SOAP 1.2 is designed to be fairly generic and support various transport protocols including SMTP, for example. A system may send an acknowledgment via e-mail, for which SMTP would be the necessary transport binding. Therefore, from an asynchronous Web services design standpoint, it is important to review supported bindings to identify the most suitable transport protocol prior to building the actual services. Additionally, SOAP 1.2 introduces a SOAP Response Message Exchange Pattern where a non-SOAP request can be followed by a SOAP response message, which may be important for designing asynchronous communication. Evaluating business requirements against new options in SOAP 1.2 can yield a simpler architecture.

Java Web Services Asynchronous Support

Both J2EE 1.4 and JWSDP 1.4 support JAX-RPC 1.1. The upcoming Java EE 1.5 will support JAX-RPC 2.0, which implements the SOAP 1.2 specification. With respect to asynchronous integration, JAX-RPC 2.0 will support the following new features:

- Non-Blocking RPC invocation, which allows an asynchronous Web services call not to have any return parameters.

- Automatic callback as part of the JAX-RPC 2.0 that would simplify asynchronous communication.

This book provides core Java samples using JAX-RCP APIs. The JAX-WS, unlike JAX-RPC, encompasses support for asynchronous Web services. Please refer to [JAX-WS_RI] for details. The JAX-WS reference implementation supports JAX-WS 2.0 specification, WS-I Basic Profile 1.1, WS-I Attachments Profile 1.0, and WS-I Simple SOAP Binding Profile 1.0. Following is the pseudocode for asynchronous Web services invocation. The actual Web service is implemented without knowledge of how it will be invoked. Because JAX-WS supports annotations, the Web service implementaion is quite simple:

```
@WebService(serviceName = "ManufacturerService", targetNamespace =
"http://tempuri.org")

public class ManufacturerImpl {

    public String submitPO(int prodID, int prodQty) {
        // String result ="receivedPO";
        // Process Purchase Order request
        // ...
      return result;
    }

}
```

A very similar definition of this service would be in .NET. Now look at the client application that asynchronously invokes this service via callback or response polling strategy. It was already described in Chapter 4 how to obtain a reference to a Web service using JAX-WS:

```
// Get instance of the Web service
   ServiceFactory serviceFactory = ServiceFactory.newInstance();
   ManufacturerService  service =
              (ManufacturerService)serviceFactory.createService(
              (java.net.URL)null, ManufacturerService.class);
   ManufacturerImpl port = service.getManufacturerImpl();
```

Here is a code snipped to access the service via response polling:

```
   Response<SubmitPOResponse> resp = port.submitPOAsync(122, 10);
   Thread.sleep(2000);
   SubmitPOResponse result = resp.get();
```

For the callback mechanism, a handler, *javax.xml.ws.AsyncHandler*, needs to be developed that will be invoked once the service finishes its execution. The response returned by the handler is type of javax.xml.ws.Response:

```
   public class SubmitPOCallbackHandler implements
AsyncHandler<SubmitPOResponse> {
       private SubmitPOResponse result;

       public void handleResponse(Response< SubmitPOResponse > res){
           try {
               result = res.get();
           } catch (ExecutionException exe) {
               exe.printStackTrace();
           } catch (InterruptedException exe) {
               exe.printStackTrace();
           }
       }

       SubmitPOResponse getResponse(){
           return result;
       }
   }
```

Next is to implement a callback client that uses the handler and the `java.util.concurrent.Future` API that should already be familiar:

```
SubmitPOCallbackHandler callbackHandler = new
SubmitPOCallbackHandler();
Future<String> response = port.submitPOAsync(122, 10, callbackHandler);
Thread.sleep(2000);
SubmitPOResponse result = callbackHandler.getResponse();
```

This example shows how JAX-WS can be leveraged to simplify implementation of the callback and response polling strategies.

Asynchronous Processing with Windows Communication Foundation

Microsoft is working on a new communication infrastructure called the Windows Communication Foundation (WCF, formerly known as Indigo) that modifies the programming models that Microsoft introduced in the past, such as support for asynchronous communication and bi-directional callback. The purpose of WCF is to realize SOA and provide developers with tools to build their business applications transparently to the underlying infrastructure. Along with WCF, Microsoft plans to release a new development environment called the Windows Presentation Foundation (WPF). WCF and WPF are aimed at simplifying the effort of building asynchronous Web services and adding security or reliability to the service. Once .NET and Java EE platforms support the same set of standards and specifications, for example WS-*, Java EE, and .NET, developers will be able to more easily build interoperable code.

While asynchronous processing simplifies remote system integration, it should be used with caution to ensure that requests processed asynchronously meet all required System Level Agreements (SLAs). Reliability is frequently a highlighted, necessary feature of asynchronous communication.

Reliability

The asynchronous callback strategy is a straightforward way of designing asynchronous communication. It is important, though, to ensure that a response eventually comes back to the original caller, which often is critical for the business flow. Having both Java EE and .NET support WS-Reliable Messaging would be ideal, but unfortunately this is not the case yet.

Therefore architects may consider persisting incoming requests to be able to track them down later and ensure that the request did not get lost. A certain degree of reliability can be realized by setting up a time out mechanism. A worker thread on the server side may iterate over persisted requests and check for whether or not they have been processed. Each request may stay in the queue for only so long. A worker thread can propagate an error to the client callback service once requests have reached their time out interval.

A client application may incorporate retry logic to resubmit the request if a response did not arrive within a certain timeframe. In this case the remote system has to be able to identify the incoming request to avoid duplicate processing. For example, creating two invoices for the same purchase order would violate the business logic.

Manageability

Distributed computing with Web services introduces a new challenge of effectively tracing calls across multiple remote systems. Asynchronous processing adds more complexity since not only the request and its acknowledgement have to be traced, but also the callback call. Some of the products today address manageability by offering solutions that track down the call chain. For example, AmberPoint Solutions ships products that are available for both Java and the .NET Framework. These tools allow troubleshooting distributed service infrastructure and later, once Web services are deployed, monitoring and measuring the performance of the call.

Security

Addressing security is as important with asynchronous communication as with synchronous communication—even more so with asynchronous processing, a server spends much more time dealing with each request, say a few hours or a few days. Thus it is imperative to prevent unauthorized requests from consuming server-side resources or causing a denial of service attack. Additionally, because it is likely that there will be two separate remote transactions for request and response, getting sensitive information transferred over a secure communication channel such as HTTPS is essential. In general, it is important to carefully analyze security requirements to address them early on during the design stage.

Scalability and Performance

It is often the case that the remote server should be able to process a high volume of asynchronous calls. For instance, an e-commerce site may redirect requests to a remote server for asynchronous processing. During the peak hours, the remote server would experience a high volume of requests that it would have to process. From a design standpoint it needs to be addressed that the remote server is capable of sustaining an increasing volume of requests. Additionally, assurance needs to be given that the volume of requests does not affect the response time, should it be a few seconds or a few hours. To ensure server scalability, it may be worth leveraging multi-threading. As a request comes in (in this chapter's example a `ManufacturerFaçade`), it may access a pool of worker threads to hand the request to an available thread in a pool. Java and .NET provide threading support that is explored later on.

Top-Down Approach in Web Service Development

The top-down approach to Web service development often is a good starting point to address developers' specific skill sets such as Java and .NET. As a best practice it is useful to start the Web services integration project with defining the Web Services Description Language (WSDL), based on the business and non-functional requirements. Defining actual service, request, and response parameters in XML can be the first step in defining the WSDL.

An XML document, understood well by both Java EE and .NET developers, can be easily understood and exchanged across development groups until everyone agrees on the semantics of a service. Sometimes a service provider group posts a WSDL corresponding to the existing service, and the service consumer group would only have to create a client compliant with the published WSDL.

With this top-down approach to Web services, Java EE and .NET developers can easily achieve a language and platform-independent level of interoperability. There are a number of tools available in the market to allow WSDL conversion into the corresponding language code and vice versa, to build the code as the next step in the development process. For example, the .NET Framework supplies a tool, `xsd.exe`, that can generate a Data Transfer object from the XML schema. On the Java side, the JAX-RPC tools follow the Java Architecture for XML Binding (JAXB), which defines open standard APIs for two-way mapping between XML documents and Java objects.

Implementing the Replenish Stock scenario may be involved if Java EE and .NET systems have an internal definition of the same business domain objects, such as Purchase Order and Invoice. This is a limitation that often has to be overcome within the scope of the integration project. In such a case, the Manufacturing system would have to convert the Purchase Order to map its internal representation. Likewise, the Retailer system would have to convert the Invoice into its internal representation. To achieve a higher degree of interoperability, it is suggested to create a schema of the Service being used in compliance with industry standards.

Universal Business Language (UBL) for Interoperability

UBL is one of the leading industry standards that identify multiple schemas to define a wide range of business domain objects. The Java Web services Development Pack, for example, extends Java binding with a sample application that demonstrates how to utilize the Universal Business Language (UBL) schemas in business applications. Most of the business applications require exchanging business related data, such as Order, Invoice, or Report. At the same time nearly all of the industry verticals have their own schemas specific to their industry. Individual companies extend those schemas with their business-specific domain objects. The interoperability between Java EE and .NET requires not only understanding of the integration technology, for example, Web services, but also the ability to interoperate across different heterogeneous domains. Therefore it is important to closely analyze the initial set of requirements to ensure interoperability at all levels.

Summary

This chapter explored how to get around the limitations of synchronous Web services by looking into the technologies and techniques that can bring a level of asynchronicity to applications. It looked in depth into the SOAP 1.2 specification and what it brings to allow for asynchronous Web service integration through some of the new HTTP status codes that it introduces, and it also explored how to implement these in .NET and Java.

Various techniques and design patterns were discussed, such as façades, for asynchronous communication between Web services running on mixed mode systems and how they can interoperate. These were demonstrated using the Supply Chain Management scenario from the Web Services Interoperability (WSI) organization.

Finally, a number of best practices and pitfalls associated with these approaches were discussed.

References

[AsyncProcJAXRPC] Patterns for Document-Based Web Services.
http://java.sun.com/developer/technicalArticles/xml/jaxrpcpatterns/index6.html

[JAX-WS_RI] JAX-WS Project. java.net.
https://jax-ws.dev.java.net/

[PASWA] Proposed Infoset Addendum to SOAP Messages with Attachments.
http://www.gotdotnet.com/team/mgudgin/paswa/paswa.pdf

[WaitHandleAPI] .NET Framework Class Library, WaitHandle Methods.
http://msdn.microsoft.com/library/default.asp?url=/library/en-us/cpref/html/frlrfSystemThreadingWaitHandleClassTopic.asp

Messaging

9

Introduction

Messaging has been adopted across the industry to achieve reliable asynchronous communication. If a company is already using some sort of Message Oriented Middleware (MOM), the messaging semantic and its benefits may be fairly familiar. A MOM decouples the sender from the receiver of the message and, at the same time, provides a robust data transport mechanism. The main interoperability constraint with various MOM solutions is that the messaging semantics of the middleware is tied to a specific format such as the Java Messaging Service, Microsoft Message Queue, or WS-Reliable Messaging. For instance, Java Message-Driven Beans enables the Java EE application to send and receive JMS-based messages. What happens if this Java EE application has to consume messages from MSMQ as a way to integrate with the .NET application domain? Message-driven beans cannot handle MSMQ messages out of the box. This is true for the opposite scenario—a .NET application handling JMS-based messages. This becomes a major limitation when building a reliable asynchronous environment.

To enable asynchronous message transfer across Java EE and .NET, the following five strategies can be employed:

1. **Bridging Strategy** for the application integration across MSMQ and a JMS provider
2. **.NET Adapter Strategy** to connect a Java application to MSMQ or a .NET application to a JMS provider, thus achieving interoperability with a single message queue
3. **Web Services Messaging Strategy** to send SOAP messages over a JMS or MSMQ messaging middleware
4. **Internet E-Mail Strategy** for exchanging SOAP messages over the SMTP protocol
5. **Enterprise Service Bus Strategy** to streamline asynchronous collaboration of heterogeneous applications

This chapter on the whole provides insight into determining an optimal messaging strategy for building Service Oriented Architecture (SOA) to asynchronously connect Java EE and .NET applications.

The sample code for individual strategies is based on the WS-I Supply Chain Management Replenish Stock use case, [SCMArchitecture], slightly modified to leverage messaging middleware. Figure 9-1 outlines the high-level components of this use case that includes Warehouse, WarehouseCallback, and Manufacturer applications. These applications are deployed as part of the Java EE Retailer and the .NET Manufacturing systems that are integrated by means of messaging middleware.

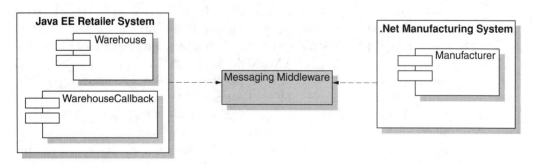

Figure 9-1
Replenish Stock use case deployment diagram

In the diagram, the Warehouse service sends a message in the form of an XML Purchase Order document to messaging middleware. The messaging middleware persists and sends a request to the `Manufacturer` service. Once the order is processed by the service, an Invoice message is sent to the messaging middleware to further send it to the `WarehouseCallback` service. Before delving further into the design and implementation of this use case, following is a brief discussion about messaging fundamentals. (If you are already familiar with implementation details of messaging under Java and .NET, you can skip this part to read about interoperability strategies.)

Messaging Fundamentals

When designing application integration with messaging, consider what type of integration best suits the company's needs. There are three main ways to arrange inter-application communication. These are discussed in the following sections.

Fire-and-Forget

When using this messaging pattern, a message is sent with no acknowledgement or guaranteed delivery requirements. It's pretty straightforward—the message is simply fired out and forgotten. This is not typically used when the system requires message integrity and delivery. It may be used for broadcasting messages where each individual message isn't necessarily important. An example of this might be a time and sales notification of trades in the stock market. Losing one or two individual messages isn't crucial to the overall consumer of the message—they're just interested in the general trend.

Publish-Subscribe

This mechanism is useful when an event has to be sent to multiple recipients. A sender tags each message with a topic name to be published. For example, the Replenish Order use case might require communication with multiple manufacturing systems. In this case, publish-subscribe would be an optimal solution. A Warehouse could publish a request on a topic, `StockOrder`, to multiple manufacturers, which asynchronously processes the request and responds back with individual Invoices. Each of the manufacturers would have to subscribe to the `StockOrder` topic to receive messages. Benefits of the publish-subscribe mechanics include loose coupling between producer(s) and consumer(s) of a message.

Point-to-Point

The main difference with the point-to-point as opposed to the publish-subscribe mechanism is that only one receiver can consume a message in the queue. A message queue, for example, `StockOrder`, is created to persist incoming messages before sending them to the receiver. In this case, a main detraction is needed for all senders to know about all receivers.

Regardless of whether one's experience is based on .NET or Java, it is useful to learn how to implement asynchronous integration with messaging under both platforms. Thus this discussion starts with an overview of messaging under Java and .NET as background for the following topic of integration strategies.

Implementing Messaging in Java and .NET

The discussion regarding messaging continues with defining messaging semantics under Java and .NET.

Messaging with Java

Java offers a mature standards-based approach to messaging via the Java Message Service (JMS) interface, [JMS]. Multiple industry vendors implement their messaging middleware in compliance with this standard to allow Java applications to asynchronously interact in a coherent manner. Any Java application, standalone or enterprise, can leverage a JMS-based infrastructure. For enterprise applications, Java EE developers may leverage the message-driven bean, EJB, introduced in the EJB 2.0 specification, [EJBSpec], which simplifies implementation of the messaging interaction by delegating some of the work to the underlying application server. Depending on the application design it might be best to select point-to-point application integration with javax.jms.Queue or the publish-subscribe integration with javax.jms.Topic libraries. Examples that follow highlight implementation details of building messaging with message-driven beans and a standalone Java application. In both cases implementation is based on JMS standards.

Using Java Message Service (JMS)

The series of three main steps that follow are outlined to show how to create a JMS-based application. This chapter demonstrates both publish-subscribe and point to-point integration that share the same way of creating a connection to the JMS destination and a session used to send and receive messages.

ConnectionFactory and Destination Look Up

The first step involves a Java Naming and Directory Interface (JNDI) API, [JNDI], call to look up the `ConnectionFactory` and `Destination`. A `javax.jms.TopicConnectionFactory` or `javax.jms.QueueConnectionFactory` is then used to create a connection to a message queue.

The first step is to create an initial context, `javax.naming.InitialContext`, object:

```
InitialContext context = new InitialContext();
```

A `NamingException` should be caught when creating the `InitialContext`. Next is to look up the queue connection factory and a JMS destination:

```
QueueConnectionFactory connectionFactory
   = (QueueConnectionFactory) context.lookup("QueueCF");
Queue destination = (Queue) context.lookup(destName);
```

For publish-subscribe, the topic connection `lookup` calls are similar:

```
TopicConnectionFactory connectionFactory
   = (TopicConnectionFactory) context.lookup("TopicCF");
Topic destination = (Topic) jndiContext.lookup(destName);
```

Typically, a `ServiceLocator` component is used to look up `ConnectionFactory` and get Topic or Queue.

Create a Connection and a Session

Now the connection factory is used to create a JMS connection to send and receive messages from a JMS provider:

```
QueueConnection connection =
    connectionFactory.createQueueConnection();
```

When creating a session, `false` should be passed as a parameter, indicating that session is not transacted. The session automatically acknowledges received messages by passing the `Session.AUTO_ACKNOWLEDGE` parameter:

```
QueueSession session =
  connection.createQueueSession(false,Session.AUTO_ACKNOWLEDGE);
```

Creating a connection and the JNDI context operations can throw exceptions, thus they have to be performed in a try catch block.

Asynchronously Sending and Receiving Messages

A `MessageProducer` is used to send multiple messages to a destination:

```
MessageProducer producer = session.createProducer(destination);
```

Now it's time to create a message, `javax.jmx.TextMessage`, and populate it with XML-based `PurchaseOrder` data to transfer an XML message to the destination:

```
message = session.createTextMessage();
message.setText(purchaseOrder));
producer.send(message);
```

For receiving a message, a `javax.jms.MessageConsumer` needs to be created:

```
MessageConsumer consumer = session.createConsumer(destination);
```

Also a message listener, `TextListener`, should be created for the `MessageConsumer`:

```
TextListener listener = new TextListener();
consumer.setMessageListener(listener);
```

Next is to start the connection to allow message delivery and to receive an answer message whenever asynchronous processing of the original request is over, as shown in Listing 9-1:

Listing 9-1
Answer to the Original Request

```
connection.start();

System.out.println("To end program, enter Q or q, then <return>");
inputStreamReader = new InputStreamReader(System.in);
while(!((answer == 'q') ||(answer == 'Q'))) {
    try {
        answer =(char) inputStreamReader.read();
    } catch(IOException e) {
        System.out.println("I/O exception: " + e.toString());
    }
}
```

The `TextListener` implements the `onMessage` method that transforms the incoming message into a `TextMessage`, as seen in Listing 9-2:

Listing 9-2
TextListener onMessage Method

```
public void onMessage(Message message) {
    TextMessage msg = null;

    try {
        if(message instanceof TextMessage) {
            msg =(TextMessage) message;
            System.out.println("Reading message: " +
                msg.getText());
        } else {
            . . .
        }
}
```

Clean Up

After the message has been sent/received, the JMS connection must be closed:

```
connection.close();
```

Closing a connection should be enclosed in a finally block to ensure that any runtime exceptions do not prevent the program from releasing resources. The session and `MessageConsumer` are closed automatically.

Deployment Descriptors

When deploying Java components, a deployment descriptor needs to be created, which is an XML file that specifies a connection factory and destination.

This chapter demonstrates via samples how to exchange SOAP messages over JMS.

Using Java EE Message-Driven Beans

A message-driven bean is a listener that allows reliable message consumption. With message-driven beans the underlying application server provides a listener service that monitors JMS destinations and passes incoming messages to message-driven beans. Each listener monitors a JMS queue or a JMS topic destination and when a message arrives it automatically fires an event to message listeners. A message-driven bean implements the `javax.jms.MessageListener`'s `onMessage()` method, which is invoked when the message arrives.

A Java EE application server transparently manages JMS listeners. This model contributes toward better application scalability. The underlying application server recycles these short-lived EJBs, thus reducing the processing cycle and pools these beans to allow concurrent message processing.

As an EJB, a message-driven bean needs to implement the `ejbCreate` and `ejbRemove` methods. In addition `setMessageDrivenContext` needs to be implemented to manage a transactional context. Either container-managed transactions or bean-managed transactions can be specified with message-driven beans. As already mentioned, the bean also has to implement the `onMessage` methods. The `onMessage` method is very similar to the one seen in the `TextListener` class, shown earlier. The only difference is that when an exception occurs, a message-driven bean calls the `MessageDrivenContext.setRollbackOnly` method to roll back the transaction. Listing 9-3 displays the `onMessage` method of the message-driven EJB:

Listing 9-3
Message-Driven Bean's *onMessage* Method

```
public void onMessage(Message msg) {
        TextMessage txtMsg = null;

        try {
            if(msg instanceof TextMessage) {
                txtMsg =(TextMessage) inMessage;
            } else {
                // continue with other type checking
            }
        } catch(JMSException exe1) {
            // Rollback transaction
        } catch(Throwable exe2) {
            // Manage runtime errors
        }
    }
```

Messaging Under .NET

Building asynchronous workflow under .NET in most cases relies on integration with MSMQ [MSMQReference]. The .NET Framework provides System.Messaging classes used to post messages to a queue for asynchronous processing. The following is a set of steps necessary to send or receive a message:

Specifying a Queue

There are several options to use under .NET to specify a queue. They include explicitly specifying a queue location path, specifying a Format Name that refers to the actual message queue, or using a label while the actual path is configured via the MSMQ admin interface. Here is an example of specifying a Format Name:

```
String queuePath = @".\Private$\ReplenishStockOrders";
```

Creating a Message Queue

In the second step an instance of the System.Messaging.MessageQueue is created:

```
MessageQueue msgQueue = new MessageQueue(queuePath);
```

All messages can also be marked as Recoverable to guarantee reliable messaging in case of a rollback:

```
msgQueue.DefaultPropertiesToSend.Recoverable = true;
```

Sending and Receiving a Message

To send a message, it is first converted into an XML format and then sent to the queue, as shown in Listing 9-4:

Listing 9-4
Sending a Message to MSMQ

```
// Convert PurchaseOrder to the XML format
String message = order.toXML();

// Send order to the message queue
msgQueue.Send(message);
```

On the receiving end the following operation can be performed to get the incoming message, as in Listing 9-5:

Listing 9-5
Receiving a Message from MSMQ

```
// Check if the queue exists
if( MessageQueue.Exists(msgQueue) {
try {
  // Receive the inventory check reques
  Message msg = msgQueue.Receive();
  String request =(String)msg.Body;
}
```

A status notification can then be sent back to the queue:

```
msgQueue.Send("Purchase Order received");
```

There are three message formatters available in .NET Framework, XMLMessageFormatter, BinaryMessageFormatter, and ActiveX MessageFormatter. The binary formatter is common to interchange images and large binary data, given that this formatter generates a serialization stream with a small footprint. The XML formatter is useful to serialize and deserialize objects using human readable XML format. The `ActiveXMessageFormatter` is used to interchange messages compatible with the MSMQ ActiveX Component.

To asynchronously receive messages, the `BeginReceive()` and `EndReceive()` methods of the `System.Messaging.MessageQueue` can be used. One needs to implement an event handler, `System.Messaging.receiveCompleteEventHandler`, to notify the program when the message retrieval is complete. This logic of asynchronous message retrieval is shown in Listing 9-6.

Listing 9-6
Asynchronous Message Retrieval with MSMQ

```
using System;
using System.Messaging;

public class AsyncMsgQueue{

MessageQueue msgQueu;

public void sendMsg(){
    string msgQueuePath = ".\\purchaseOrders";
    // Make sure to validate that the message queue exists
    // Connect to the queue
    msgQueue = MessageQueue(msgQueuePath);
    // Pass PurchaseOrder to the XML Formatter
    ((XmlMessageFormatter) msgQueue.Formatter).TargetTypeNames =
        new string []{"PurchaseOrder"};

    // Asynchronously receive messages
    msgQueue.ReceiveCompleted +=
        new ReceiveCompletedEventHandler( AsyncReceiveCompleted );

// Beginning of the asynchronous read
    msgQueue.BeginReceive();
}

// Once the read is complete the AsyncReceiveCompleted is invoked
void AsyncReceiveCompleted(Object src, ReceiveCompletedEventArgs
args) {
    try {
        PurchaseOrder po =
          (PurchaseOrder)msgQueue.EndReceive(args.AsyncResult).Body;

        // For a generic message:
        // Message msg = msgQueue.EndReceive( args.AsyncResult );
```

continues

Listing 9-6 (continued)

```
      // To restart the asynchronous read
      msgQueue.BeginReceive();
  } catch( MessageQueueException exe ) {
      // Handle exception
  }
}
```

Cleaning Up

Closing the message queue ensures that all system resources are released accordingly:

```
msgQueue.Close();
```

ARCHITECT'S NOTE

This section outlined details of sending and receiving asynchronous messages in both Java and .NET. It is important to note that for most enterprise applications, transactions are a big part of the inter-application workflow. Transactions ensure consistency of the data sent across applications. Both the Java and .NET platforms are quite flexible in their transactional support. Transactional semantics of Java EE and .NET and transactional interoperability are discussed in a separate chapter.

Addressing alternative integration flows with accurate error handling is another aspect of asynchronous integration with messaging. It is often the case that a message acknowledgement has to be timed out after a certain period of time or a submitted message has to be followed up with retry logic. These design aspects help to adequately address applications' non-functional requirements.

Bridging Strategy

Individual .NET and Java EE applications can transparently exchange messages by leveraging a bridging solution, which transforms messages into the corresponding format and moves them between MSMQ and the JMS message queues.

Scope

There are a number of companies invested into an architecture featuring the MSMQ messaging backbone to asynchronously connect various legacy applications. It is often the case that newer services are developed in Java and rely on a JMS based messaging solution. At some point in time, a growing number of businesses require seamless integration of these two sets of applications and the corresponding messaging solutions. Redesigning and reimplementing existing infrastructures may not be an option due to time and cost constraints. One of the ways to integrate existing message queues is by means of a bridge, which allows two heterogeneous sets of applications to remain unchanged and facilitates seamless integration across messaging backbones.

Solution

A bridging strategy enables communication between two message queues: in this case MSMQ and a JMS messaging infrastructure. It is typically used to integrate disparate solutions deployed over the Internet, but can also be used to achieve interoperability within a company network.

Figure 9-2 highlights a bridging solution to integrate a JMS provider with a MSMQ:

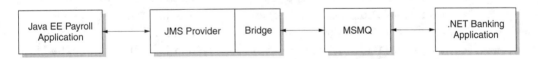

Figure 9-2
Bridging between a JMS provider and MSMQ

In the diagram, a Payroll application developed in Java EE has to interface with a MSMQ to pass information to a Banking system implemented in .NET. To address Java EE and .NET technology variances, a bridging strategy is applied. This bridging component assures reliable information transfer that is important for sensitive financial data. This architecture streamlines and automates the B2B payroll process that may have been accomplished manually in the past.

Bridging solutions do not restrict the data type exchanged between applications. JMS supported message types including Stream, Text, Bytes, and Objects can be freely sent out using a bridging solution. A bridge simply moves messages from one queue to another. Developers, however, have to ensure that messages are processed correctly between Java and .NET platforms. This can be done by either creating custom serializers or by sending SOAP messages that adhere to the agreed WSDL. Alternatively, applications may exchange XML messages that are consistent across Java EE and .NET application.

Commercial bridging solutions are available from various vendors such as SpiritSoft and Fiorano that offer integration between MSMQ and specific JMS providers. For details, please refer to [SpiritSoft] and [FioranoMQ-MSMQ]. Fiorano Bridge also offers integration with Tibco Rendezvous among other proprietary messaging infrastructures. The Microsoft Host Integration server ships with the MSMQ-MQ Series Bridge, [MSMQ-MQSeries]. IBM's proprietary WebSphere MQ ships with the .NET Assembly classes to allow Java EE-.NET interoperability, [WebSphereMQInterop]. The WebSphere MQ includes JMS support to allow a standards-based integration for Java EE applications.

Replenish Stock Use Case

To demonstrate how to implement asynchronous communication using a bridging solution, recall the Replenish Stock use case. Assume that a Retailer system that encompasses Warehouse and WarehouseCallback is implemented in Java, and the Manufacturer system is built in .NET. The UML diagram in Figure 9-3 outlines the sequence of calls for the Replenish Stock use case.

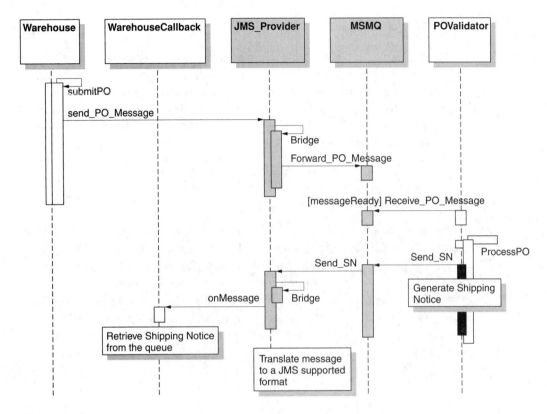

Figure 9-3
Replenish Stock sequence diagram

In the figure, the `Warehouse` service creates a Purchase Order (PO) request and sends the PO message using JMS APIs to a JMS provider. The message queue invokes the bridging solution to transform and forward the message to the MSMQ. `Manufacturer` then retrieves the document from the PO queue. Once the Purchase Order is received, the `POValidator` asynchronously processes it and generates the Shipping Notice (SN). The `ShippingNotice` is then sent to the MSMQ, which forwards the message to the bridging solution. The bridge translates the content of the SN document into a JMS-supported format. The bridging solution then passes the message to the Message queue. Upon the message's arrival to the Shipping Notice queue, an event notification is sent to the SN listener, i.e. `WarehouseCallback`, and the `onMessage` method is invoked. The `WarehouseCallback` can register with the queue and explicitly call the `receive` method to retrieve `ShippingNotice`.

Benefits

When selecting one messaging integration strategy over another, reliability is not the only factor to consider. It is also helpful to evaluate other systemic qualities such as manageability, security, and performance. These characteristics are discussed next to help making an optimal decision for your architecture. Most of the JMS providers offer a failover mechanism, dynamic routing, and clustering to ensure high availability and scalability of enterprise systems.

Manageability

Managing distributed transactions that travel across messaging hubs, particularly between MSMQ and JMS-based, is not trivial. Because a bridging solution is tightly integrated with a JMS provider, distributed messaging administration and configuration can be achieved with the JMS Provider administration tool. For instance the administration tool for Fiorano Bridge provides a way to manage messages sent to and from MSMQ, IBM MQSeries, or Tibco Rendezvous servers. Management with bridging is important particularly when transactions, session propagation, and multipart messaging are involved.

Security and Performance

Because MSMQ and JMS provider integration may involve firewalls and the Internet, secure communication is essential for bridging. Individual JMS vendors offer advanced security features, such as Access Control Lists (ACLs), encryption, and HTTPS as a transport protocol. To prevent a denial of service attack, Microsoft MSMQ can be configured with a quota on a size of message storage and exposure to unknown networks.

The bridging solution itself is fairly lightweight. It does not consume many resources and does not require a dedicated software or hardware container on which to be deployed.

To alleviate performance overhead associated with a large message size and to maximize the data throughput, leverage message compression. Various JMS providers support compression. On the MSMQ side, a custom message formatter that extends the IMessageFormatter interface can be used to implement compression. The custom build MSMQ data formatter can perform encryption and compression that is compliant with those offered on the JMS side to allow full interoperability.

Limitations

Along with benefits come limitations of this strategy. Because a bridging solution is the main mediator across heterogonous messaging servers, it may become a single point of failure. Therefore, failover should be considered when deploying this solution.

Interoperability

While a bridging solution offers interoperability with MSMQ, the actual bridge is not interoperable across different JMS providers. For instance, Microsoft Bridge only works with WebSphereMQ, while the Fiorano Bridge only works with the FioranoMQ. Therefore, a third-party bridging solution cannot be integrated practically with any JMS message queue.

Manageability

In terms of interoperability, a bridging solution has to be kept up to date with both JMS and non-JMS-based MQ solutions. Should a company upgrade MSMQ server with a new version offering new features, the Bridge has to be managed accordingly for developers to leverage new MSMQ features.

A bridge only transfers messages from a queue of one server to a queue on another server. It is important to notice that a bridge should be the only queue listener since messages are sent as a point-to-point mechanism. Technically, and by definition, the same cannot be provided for publish-subscribe topics. To handle this situation, JMS vendors like Fiorano provide repeaters that help replicate messages across two different messaging servers.

Performance and Scalability

It may already be clear that having two messaging infrastructures and a bridging solution on top of one of them does not produce the most optimal integration solution from a performance standpoint.

While commonly used XML messages exchanged between systems help to enhance interoperability between Java and .NET systems, XML processing significantly impacts overall performance. To address the performance overhead, in addition to the already discussed message compression, XML hardware accelerators can be deployed on both ends of the communication channel. In the financial sector, a high volume of transaction processing results in companies building custom data serializers. When developing data serializers, there should be compatibility between heterogeneous Java and .NET applications to allow a common data format to be transmitted over the wire. Custom serializers address performance but complicate manageability of the integrated environment. Any changes to the underlying data structures require changes of serializers on both .NET and Java EE ends.

Aside from the XML serialization, it is also important to take into account any data transformation requirements. In comparison to the bridging solution, discussed later, an Enterprise Service Bus solution typically supports an independent scalability model, where individual services can be scaled up to handle large volumes of XML data manipulation such as message transformation services.

Related Patterns and Best Practices

Gregor Hohpe and Bobby Woolf defined messaging best practices very well in their *Enterprise Integration Patterns* book, [EIP]. Both JMS and .NET implementations are provided for individual patterns such as Request-Reply. These patterns can be applied in this case as well. Depending on the application requirements, one's design may leverage patterns such as Aggregator, Splitter, Routing Slip, and Process Manager. As will be seen later in this chapter, these patterns become higher-level service abstractions that are implemented as part of an Enterprise Service Bus offering.

General best practices that were already used in the preceding example are to use the `ServiceLocator` and `ServiceLocatorException` to look up a message queue. Additionally, should any complex logic or processing occur within a component that directly accesses the message queue, this logic should be factored out of that class. Keeping the design simple helps troubleshooting and understanding heterogeneous integration environments.

When exchanging documents between Java and .NET systems, it is recommended to agree on a canonical message format. If XML documents are sent, the WSDL of that document should be defined and agreed on by both Java and .NET sides. This will allow a higher degree of interoperability.

Example

From an implementation standpoint, a bridging solution offers a transparent way to communicate messages across a JMS provider and MSMQ messaging systems. The beginning of the chapter walked through the step-by-step process of sending and receiving messages using both the JMS standard and the .NET-based APIs, which are already halfway through completing these undertakings. The only missing piece of the Replenish Stock scenario is definition of data structures in the form of a WSDL that will be passed across two messaging systems. The `PurchaseOrder` XML document will be sent from the `Warehouse` to the .NET *Manufacturer's* `POValidator`, while the `ShippingNotice`(SN) XML message will be sent to the Java `WarehouseCallback` component.

Building JMS-Based Warehouse System

First, a Purchase Order structure needs to be created that encapsulates a list of items, quantity, and has an order number. For simplicity and interoperability, XML is used to represent a Purchase Order. Both .NET and Java applications would share the Purchase Order XML Schema Definition File, i.e. `PurchaseOrder.xsd`. Listing 9-7 lists the Purchase Order XML file exchanged between Java and .NET applications:

Listing 9-7
Purchase Order XML Schema

```
<xs:schema xmlns:xs="http://www.w3.org/2001/XMLSchema"
targetNamespace="http://j2eedotnet.org/PurchaseOrder.xsd"
xmlns="http://j2eedotnet.org/po.xsd" elementFormDefault="quali-
fied">

    <xs:element name="purchaseOrder">
      <xs:complexType>
         <xs:sequence>
    <xs:element name="names" type="xs:string"
maxOccurs="unbounded"/>
    <xs:element name="quantity" type="xs:int"
maxOccurs="unbounded"/>
      </xs:sequence>
    <xs:attribute name="id" type="xs:string"/>
      </xs:complexType>
    </xs:element>
  </xs:schema>
```

Similarly, the `ShippingNotice` schema is created to allow both Java and .NET classes to exchange information that adheres to the same format. Once both XSD files are ready, one creates Java classes using JAXB tool, `jaxb.bat`, which is available with the Java Web Services Developer Pack. For more details on JAXB, refer to [JAXB]. Listing 9-8 shows the corresponding ant target to create Java classes from XML schema.

Listing 9-8
Purchase Order XML Schema

```
<!-- Create stub classes from XSD-->
<target name="createJavaClassesFromSchema">
  <echo message="--- creating java file of given schema---"/>
  <mkdir dir="${xsdclasses}"/>
  <exec executable="${wsdp.home}/jaxb/bin/xjc.bat">
    <arg value="-d"/>
    <arg value="${xsdclasses}"/>
    <arg value="${schema.dir}/PurchaseOrder.xsd"/>
    <arg value="${schema.dir}/ShippingNotice.xsd"/>
  </exec>
</target>
```

Before populating the Purchase Order and sending the message to the JMS Queue, it's necessary to initialize all needed JMS components. Service Locator pattern is used to look up the `ConnectionFactory` and JMS Topic name. Listing 9-9 lists components used throughout the `Warehouse` class:

Listing 9-9
Queue-Related Components

```
QueueConnectionFactory connectionFactory = null;
QueueConnection connection = null;
QueueSession session = null;
Queue queue = null;
QueueSender sender = null;
private static final String Queue_CONNECTION_FACTORY = "primaryQCF";
```

The next sample code, Listing 9-10, lists the `init` method of the `Warehouse` class, which creates queue-related components:

Listing 9-10
Initializing JMS Topic and *TopicSession*

```
public void init(String QueueName) {
    try {
        ServiceLocator servicelocator = new ServiceLocator();
        connectionFactory =
            servicelocator.getQueueConnectionFactory(
                        Queue_CONNECTION_FACTORY);
        connection = connectionFactory.createQueueConnection();
        session = connection.createQueueSession(false,
            Session.AUTO_ACKNOWLEDGE);
        try {
```

```
            queue = servicelocator.getQueue(QueueName);
        }
        catch(Exception e) {
            queue = session.createQueue(QueueName);
        }

        sender = session.createSender(queue);
    } catch(JMSException exe) {
        exe.printStackTrace();
    } catch(ServiceLocatorException e) {
        e.printStackTrace();
    }
}
```

This `init` method is fairly straightforward and is in line with JMS Queue initialization discussed at the beginning of the chapter.

Next an instance of the Purchase Order class needs to be created and populated with data, marshaled into the XML format, and passed to the message queue. Populating the `PO` object does not present any complexity, thus this only elaborates on how to marshal Java objects into XML. Listing 9-11 outlines the usage of the Java Architecture for XML Binding (JAXB) APIs for marshaling objects. These APIs, defined as part of the `javax.xml.bind` package, are used to manage XML/Java binding. The main marshaling operation, *marshal*, uses the `Marshaller` object, which is created from the `JAXBContext` context. The `JAXBContext` is an entry point to the JAXB APIs and in our case is used to obtain the `Marshaller` object, as shown in Listing 9-11:

Listing 9-11
Marshaling Purchase Order Object into XML Format

```
JAXBContext context = JAXBContext.newInstance("org.j2eedotnet.po");

// Marshal the PO object into outputStream
StringWriter writer = new StringWriter();
Marshaller marshaller = context.createMarshaller();
marshaller.marshal(pOrder, writer);
```

Listing 9-12 provides an example of the `getPO` method that creates the Purchase Order instance, populates it with data, and marshals the object into an output stream:

Listing 9-12
Warehouse *getPO()* Method

```java
private String getPO() throws javax.xml.bind.JAXBException {
  ObjectFactory factory = new ObjectFactory();
  PurchaseOrder pOrder = factory.createPurchaseOrder();
  pOrder.setId("1234");
  pOrder.getNames().add("GreenTea_847");
  pOrder.getNames().add("OolongTea_332");
  pOrder.getQuantity().add(new Integer(5));
  pOrder.getQuantity().add(new Integer(7));

  JAXBContext context =
JAXBContext.newInstance("org.j2eedotnet.po");

  // Marshal to outputStream
  StringWriter writer = new StringWriter();
  Marshaller marshaller = context.createMarshaller();
  marshaller.marshal(pOrder, writer);

  return writer.toString();
  }
```

The XML PO is now ready to be sent over to the JMS message queue. Listing 9-13 shows the submitPO method that takes the PO XML strings and returns a boolean status, indicating success or failure transmitting the PO message:

Listing 9-13
Publishing Purchase Order XML Message

```java
public boolean submitPO(String msg){
 System.out.println("Warehouse.submitPO(): Sending PO");
 boolean status = false;
 try {
   Message jmsMsg = session.createTextMessage(msg);
   sender.send(jmsMsg);
   System.out.println("Warehouse.submitPO(): PO sent");
   session.close();
   connection.close();
   status = true;
 } catch(Exception exe) {
 System.out.println("Warehouse: PO could not be submitted.");
 status=false;
 } finally {
   return status;
 }
}
```

The main() method of the Warehouse class invokes getPO and submitPO, discussed previously, to send the Purchase Order out.

The chapter continues examining the Java Retailer system by implementing the WarehouseCallback class. The WarehouseCallback receives the ShippingNotice message from the .NET Manufacturer system once Manufacturer validates the order. WarehouseCallback uses the JMS QueueReceiver to receive a message from the queue:

```
TextMessage shipNote = (TextMessage) receiver.receive();
```

Listing 9-14 shows the complete receiveSN() message that receives ShippingNotice from JMS. As can be seen from this snippet, the bridging solution pushes messages to and from JMS, and MSMQ message queues are completely transparent to the programmer.

Listing 9-14
Receiving Shipping Notice

```
public void receiveSN() {
  System.out.println("Ready to receive a Shiping Notice");
  String shippingNotice = null;

  try {
    TextMessage shipNote = (TextMessage) receiver.receive();

    shippingNotice = shipNote.getText();
    System.out.println("Received shipnotice:" + shippingNotice);

    session.close();
    connection.close();
  } catch(Exception exe) {
  System.out.println("Error receiving ShippingNotice " +
            exe.getMessage());
  }
  return shippingNotice;
}
```

After receiving ShippingNotice, JAXB APIs are once again leveraged to unmarshal the XML message into the Java object. The Warehouse Callback's getSN() method uses java.io.StringReader to read the XML ShippingNotice and then JAXB's Unmarshaller to unmarshal XML into the ShippingNotice object. This logic is shown in Listing 9-15:

Listing 9-15
Unmarshaling XML Shipping Notice

```
JAXBContext context =
JAXBContext.newInstance("org.j2eedotnet.sn.xsd");

Unmarshaller unmarshaller = context.createUnmarshaller();
ShippingNotice sNotice =(ShippingNotice) unmarshaller.unmarshal
    (new StreamSource(new StringReader(shipNotice)));
```

The `WarehouseCallback` can be implemented as a message-driven bean or as a `POJO` class, which is demonstrated in this example.

To run samples, the FioranoMQ-MSMQ Bridge must be running along with FioranoMQ and MSMQ servers. The bridge replicates messages from replenishstock queue of FioranoMQ to the ./privatequeue/replenishstock queue of MSMQ. Similarly, the bridge replicates messages from the ./private/shippingnotice queue of MSMQ to the shippingnotice queue of FioranoMQ. A sample configuration file, bridge.xml, is provided along with the code samples.

Additionally, it's important to make certain that the `build.property` file is defined in accordance with the environment.

Running the Retailer system requires executing the following ant command:

```
> ant retailer
```

This chapter is now going to switch to .NET content and look into implementation details of the `Manufacturer` system.

Building .NET-Based Manufacturer System

On the .NET side, the `POValidator` is the class that checks for availability of Purchase Order message in the queue and retrieves the message. Before looking at the message retrieval code, corresponding C# classes need to be prepared for `PurchaseOrder` and `ShippingNotice`. As was already shown on the Java side, both `Retailer` and `Manufacturer` systems share common XML schemas, i.e. `ShippingNotice.xsd` and `PurchaseOrder.xsd`. On the .NET side, C# classes are generated from XSD schemas. Listing 9-16 shows the `createC#classesFromSchema` target that invokes .NET Framework `xsd.exe` tool to generate corresponding classes.

Listing 9-16
ShippingNotice class in C#

```
<!-- Create stub C#classes from XSD-->
<target name="createC#ClassesFromSchema">
  <echo message="--- creating C# classes of given schema---"/>
  <mkdir dir="${build.classes}/schemaCsclasses"/>
  <exec executable="xsd.exe">
  <arg value="${schema.dir}/PurchaseOrder.xsd"/>
  <arg value="/classes"/>
  <arg value="/out:${build.classes}/schemaCsclasses"/>
  </exec>
  <exec executable="xsd.exe">
  <arg value="${schema.dir}/ShippingNotice.xsd"/>
  <arg value="/classes"/>
  <arg value="/out:${build.classes}/schemaCsclasses"/>
  </exec>
</target>
```

Receiving a `PurchaseOrder` message involves the following steps. First the queue needs to be initialized:

```
msgQueue = new MessageQueue(@".\private$\ReplenishStock");
```

Next, the `receivePO()` method retrieves a message from the MSMQ:

```
Message message = this.msgQueue.Receive();
message.Formatter = new ActiveXMessageFormatter();
string purchaseOrder = message.Body.ToString();
```

The `ActiveXMessageFormatter`, from .NET Framework `System.Messaging` library, is used to serialize or deserialize objects, such as `PurchaseOrder` or primitives, from a message compatible with an MSMQ ActiveX Component.

After the PO has been received, the `processesPO()` method is invoked to convert string `PO` into the object format. To accomplish this task `XmlSerializer` from .NET Framework `System.Xml.Serialization` library is used:

```
StringReader reader = new StringReader(receivedPO);
  XmlSerializer serializer = new XmlSerializer(typeof(purchaseOrder));
PO =(purchaseOrder)serializer.Deserialize(reader);
```

Assuming that the PO has been successfully validated, it's now possible to create a `ShippingNotice` and send it out to the MSMQ. This logic resides in the `sendShippingNotice()` method of the `Manufacturer` class:

```
this.shipNotice = new ShipNotice();
string SN = this.shipNotice.prepareShippingNotice(POID);
shipNotice.sendShippingNotice(SN);
```

The `prepareShippingNotice()` method, which takes the Purchase Order id as an input parameter and returns an XML string representation of the `ShippingNotice` object, is shown in Listing 9-17.

Listing 9-17
Populate and Serialize *ShippingNotice*

```
public string prepareShippingNotice(string POID) {
  // Create and populate ShippingNotice
  shippingNotice sNotice = new shippingNotice();
  sNotice.PONumber=111;
  sNotice.ShipmentID=222;
  sNotice.Description=POID;

  // Serialize ShippingNotice into XML format and
  // write it to a string
  XmlSerializer serializer = new
XmlSerializer(typeof(shippingNotice));
  StringWriter writer = new StringWriter();
  serializer.Serialize(writer,sNotice);
  string shipNoticeXMLMessage = writer.ToString();

  return shipNoticeXMLMessage;
}
```

The first part of this method populates `ShippingNotice`, and the second part is the actual XML serialization of the object. The `StringWriter` .NET Framework class is used to write XML `ShippingNotice` to a string. The `StringWriter` is available as part of the System.IO library. The string is returned by the method.

The next logical step in this sequence corresponds to submiting `ShippingNotice` to the MSMQ. The `ShippingNotice`'s `sendShippingNotice()` method performs this task. Because an XML string is being sent out, rather than an instance of the `System.Messaging`

`.Message`, it's necessary to specify the default property values for the message. The `System.Messaging.DefaultPropertiesToSend` is used for that purpose:

`this.msgQueue.DefaultPropertiesToSend.Recoverable = true;`

The Recoverable property is set to `true`, indicating that the `ShippingNotice` message is guaranteed to be delivered in case there is a network or other failure during the send operation. `ActiveXMessageFormatter`, which has already been shown, is in this case set as the message queue formatter:

`this.msgQueue.Formatter = new ActiveXMessageFormatter();`

This formatter is used to serialize the `ShippingNotice` into the body of a message that is written to the queue. After the formatter has been specified, it's time to send the `ShippingNotice` to the queue:

`this.msgQueue.Send(messageStr);`

Listing 9-18 lists the `sendShippingNotice()` method.

Listing 9-18
Sending Shipping Notice to MSMQ

```
public void sendShippingNotice(string messageStr) {

    this.msgQueue.DefaultPropertiesToSend.Recoverable = true;
    this.msgQueue.Formatter = new ActiveXMessageFormatter();

    try {
        this.msgQueue.Send(messageStr);
        Console.WriteLine("sent the message:"+messageStr);
    } catch(Exception ex) {
        Console.WriteLine(ex.Message);
    }
}
```

As might have already been noticed, the bridging strategy offers a flexibility of using Java and .NET components "as is" to achieve asynchronous integration via messaging. As is seen later, sending SOAP messages is also very straightforward. When exchanging SOAP messages, which are in essence XML, transactional and security context can be passed as part of the SOAP header. The bridging strategy allows leverage of Java and .NET skills that may already exist within your company, which contributes to rapid application delivery.

While a bridging strategy provides a means to integrate two heterogeneous messaging infrastructures, a .NET adapter strategy, discussed next, enables a Java application to communicate with .NET application using a JMS-based messaging infrastructure. There is no need to integrate a MSMQ as an intermediate solution. Additional resources on messaging with Java and .NET can be found in the "References" section.

Adapter Strategy

This section introduces an alternative to a bridging strategy, which is referred to as an **adapter strategy** and is designed with .NET Adapter and Java Adapter. The .NET Adapter strategy enables interoperability via custom .NET adapter libraries to access a JMS provider, and similarly Java Adapter libraries to access MSMQ.

Scope

It is often the case that in-house .NET expertise is used for building front-end applications, while the enterprise business logic and back-end integration rely on Java EE and JMS processing. Realizing the value of JMS as a standards-based solution, it may be advantageous to use a JMS provider to integrate a .NET client and a Java EE system. This would allow companies to preserve their .NET investment and leverage existing messaging infrastructure.

Aside from internal .NET and Java EE application integration, a common business scenario may require the following. A company's trading partners have to integrate business services using messaging. While a company's system may be based on .NET, their partners may favor Java EE. The .NET Adapter strategy offers an effective interoperability to Java and .NET.

A similar situation may require integration with MSMQ, in which case a Java Adapter strategy can be implemented to allow interoperability between Java and .NET MSMQ APIs.

Solution

The idea behind this strategy is to utilize .NET Runtime Libraries offered by commercial vendors or custom developed. A JMS-like messaging request can be initiated from within the .NET application. The .NET Runtime Libraries from vendors such as Sonic or Fiorano offer C#, C++, and C implementation of the JMS APIs. Please refer to [FioranoMQC#RTL], [SonicMQCom ClientGuide] and [SonicMQBridgesClients]. This solution allows .NET developers to leverage their skills in developing a seamless integration with the JMS message queue server.

Figure 9-4 shows how this strategy might fit in an architecture to realize a traditional Purchase Order scenario. In this case an ASP.NET Portal receives customer orders and submits them for processing to the Java EE-based Inventory system. The main means to exchange information between .NET and Java EE applications is via JMS Provider. The interoperability between .NET and JMS is resolved via the .NET Adapter Strategy that is realized via C# Runtime Libraries (RTLs).

Figure 9-4
.NET Adapter to the JMS provider

Using the .NET Adapter strategy the .NET client application can be seamlessly integrated with Java EE systems. To allow compliance with the JMS standard, all public C# APIs of the Sonic or Fiorano C# Runtime Libraries have similar signatures to the corresponding Java APIs defined by JMS. C# classes have a naming convention similar to JMS. Exception handling follows the same convention specified by JMS, with all APIs throwing a `CJMSException` with a specific error code and in some cases error description.

Alternatively, if a JMS provider does not supply its own .NET clients, .NET proxies can be created for JMS classes to access JMS provider using JNBBridgePro by JNBridge LLC or J-Integra for .NET by Intrinsyc Software products, see [JNBridgePro] and [JIntegraForDotNet].

Aside from commercial .NET Adapters, there is an open source project that has a free implementation of the ActiveX JMS client API, http://source-forge.net/projects/active-jms, [ActiveXJmsClient]. This is useful when a Windows-based client application needs to send and receive messages to and from a JMS queue.

To achieve similar interoperability with MSMQ, it's necessary to create a Java Adapter. This can be accomplished by generating .NET proxies for related MSMQ assemblies, using third-party libraries, such as Intrinsyc J-Integra.

Benefits and Limitations

The .NET Adapter strategy is one to consider if one wants to leverage existing JMS infrastructure to integrate a .NET application with the Java EE application. The reason for that may be a standards-based messaging solution or it may already have been deployed by an in-house JMS provider. This way, you don't have to depend on MSMQ for achieving interoperability.

Security

For the .NET Adapter, C# Runtime Libraries from Fiorano supports secure TCP and HTTP connections on the Win32 platform for both point-to-point and publish-subscribe models.

Manageability

Managing this environment may be a bit tricky—the .NET Adapter is either based on proprietary third-party runtime libraries or custom generated proxies. Any changes in the Runtime Library require an update to the code. Testing the integration flow is also involved.

Related Patterns

The main pattern that stands out here is the Adapter pattern defined in the GoF, [GoF], Design Patterns catalog. The .NET Adapter pattern is applied to adopt JMS interfaces in the .NET domain. Likewise, the Java Adapter is to adopt MSMQ APIs in the Java domain.

The .NET JMS Adapter

The purpose of this pattern is to use an adapter to implement JMS interfaces using .NET languages such as C#. This would enable the .NET application to send JMS messages to the JMS message queue. This .NET JMS Adapter resolves the incompatibility between Java and .NET in the scope of messaging. Figure 9-5 shows a simple class diagram of this pattern.

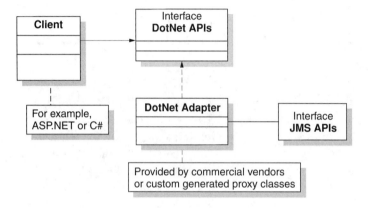

Figure 9-5
.NET JMS Adapter class diagram

The DotNetJmsAdapter represents a library of C# classes implementing JMS-like APIs. The .NET application uses the adapter to send and receive corresponding messages. This pattern should be very straightforward to use, given that the Adapter library can be available from your JMS message queue provider. Next is an example of how this strategy can be applied in development.

Example

In moving toward this example, there are no changes to be made on the Java Retailer system from the previous implementation. The .NET Manufacturer, however, uses the Fiorano C# Runtime Libraries to access the JMS message queue. To receive the message, this example explores the POValidator class that accesses the JMS provider to retrieve the incoming message. To initialize and access the message queue, one declares class variables including CsInitialContext, CsQueueConnectionFactory, CsQueue, CsQueuConnection, CsQueueSession, and CsQueueReceiver. As one can tell, those classes are quite similar to those in JMS. The constructor of POValidator class sets corresponding properties such as user name and password, initial context factory, and others, as shown in Listing 9-19:

Listing 9-19
Setting Queue Parameters

```
public POValidator() {
 m_qcfName = "primaryQCF";
 m_queueName = "ReplenishStock";
 m_usrName = "anonymous";
 m_usrPasswd = "anonymous";
 m_providerURL = "http://localhost:1856";
 m_initialContextFactory =
    "fiorano.jms.runtime.naming.FioranoInitialContextFactory";
}
```

A property file can be used to specify these sorts of parameters to avoid hard-coding them into a program.

Prior to the message retrieval, the `validatePO()` method initializes corresponding queue connection values by creating a queue connection factory, accessing a queue, and creating a queue session and a receiver. The initialization process is nearly adequate to ones performed in Java, which were already discussed when creating a JMS-based message queue. This is shown in Listing 9-20:

Listing 9-20
Using C# CRL to Initialize Message Queue

```
// creating the initial context
m_ic = new CsInitialContext(m_env);

// look up connection factory.
m_qcf =(CsQueueConnectionFactory)m_ic.Lookup(m_qcfName);

// Look up queue
m_queue =(CsQueue)m_ic.Lookup(m_queueName);

// Create the connection
m_qc = m_qcf.createQueueConnection();
m_qc.start();

//Create the session
m_qs = m_qc.createQueueSession(false, 1);
```

The `validatePO()` method is invoked to receive the actual PO message:

```
CsTextMessage textMessage = CsTextMessage)m_receiver.receive();
string txtMsg = textMessage.getText();
```

Listing 9-21 shows the entire `validatePO()` method that encapsulates core C# CRL-based logic to access the JMS message queue.

Listing 9-21
Using C# CRL to Retrieve a Message from JMS Provider

```
public string validatePO(){

    // Setting up environment for the Initial Context
    m_env = new CsHashTable();
    m_env.Put("SECURITY_PRINCIPAL", m_usrName);
    m_env.Put("SECURITY_CREDENTIALS", m_usrPasswd);
    m_env.Put("PROVIDER_URL", m_providerURL);
m_env.Put("INITIAL_CONTEXT_FACTORY",m_initialContextFactory);

    // creating the initial context
    m_ic = new CsInitialContext(m_env);

    // look up connection factory.
    m_qcf =(CsQueueConnectionFactory)m_ic.Lookup(m_qcfName);

    // Look up queue
    m_queue =(CsQueue)m_ic.Lookup(m_queueName);

    // Create the connection
    m_qc = m_qcf.createQueueConnection();
    m_qc.start();

    //Create the session
    m_qs = m_qc.createQueueSession(false, 1);

    // Receiving a message
    m_receiver = m_qs.createReceiver(m_queue);
    CsTextMessage textMessage
=(CsTextMessage)m_receiver.receive();
    string txtMsg = textMessage.getText();

    return txtMsg;
}
```

Sending out a message from a .NET application to the JMS provider is very similar. The `ShipNotice.cs` class shows how to accomplish this task. The process starts with initialization of the `InitialContext` environment shown in the previous diagram. To send a message, the following should be invoked:

```
CsTextMessage textMessage = m_qs.createTextMessage();
    textMessage.setText(messageStr);
m_sender.send(textMessage);
```

Web Services Messaging Strategy

Expertise with Web services and SOA can be applied in the messaging domain. What is exciting about this strategy is that a developer can build a generic architecture agnostic to a specific JMS provider to successfully link Java and .NET applications. Similarly, one can apply this strategy to achieve interoperability between Java applications and MSMQ. Demonstration on how to send SOAP messages over a messaging infrastructure is provided in the following sections.

Scope

There can exist an integration problem of asynchronously and reliably connecting Java and .NET applications. Deployed in-house messaging solutions can help to address asynchronous, reliable inter-application communication. Web services and the basic messaging infrastructure are sufficient to connect Java EE and .NET environments, which is discussed in the next sections.

Solution

The key interoperability component in this strategy is a MQFaçade that abstracts out a message queue server. For instance, from the Java application the .NET MQFaçade directly accesses an MSMQ, while from a .NET application the Java MQFaçade accesses a JMS message queue. This Façade interfaces with a message queue, MSMQ or JMS provider, using Web Services technology such as SOAP over JMS [SoapMsmqWSE]. To integrate with MQFaçade, a developer has the option of either using Web Services or proxy classes, which are based on Java implementations of .NET Remoting APIs. The main advantage of the Web Services based integration with the MQFaçade includes loose coupling between Java and .NET components. Proxy classes yield tighter coupling between Java and .NET constituents as opposed to Web Services integration. Additionally, proxy classes are generated using third-party libraries, such as Ja.NET or JNBridge.

The main idea of this design is abstracting out the message queue. Figure 9-6 outlines the architecture of the high-level components of this design.

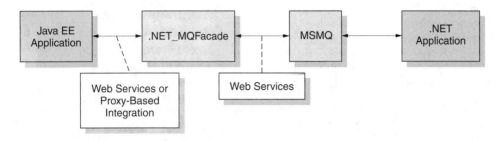

Figure 9-6
.NET MQ Façade Architecture

In the diagram, the .NET MQFaçade acts as a frontier to the MSMQ server. A Java application can invoke the .NET MQFaçade as a Java-based RPC call using proxy classes or as a JAX-RPC call using Java Web Services APIs. The .NET MQFaçade then creates a SOAP message out of this PO information and sends the request to the MSMQ server.

Should the messaging server be JMS-compliant, the design will look very similar, as in Figure 9-7:

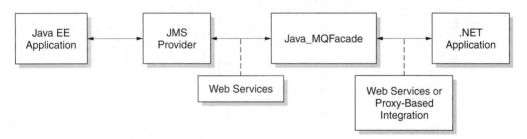

Figure 9-7
.NET MQFaçade sending a request to the MSMQ server

Here the .NET application is faced with interoperability constraints. To overcome those constraints, Java MQFaçade is accessed to exchange messages with a JMS provider.

Some of the commercial solutions offer implicit support for SOAP over HTTP, thus simplifying design of the Java EE .NET interoperable solution. For instance, SonicMQ and SonicESB have direct support for inbound and outbound SOAP calls using a feature known as "HTTP Direct." With HTTP Direct, the message server itself can act as an HTTP listener or issue an HTTP request. Therefore a Java EE application can send a JMS message with a payload that is a SOAP-formatted XML message. The message server (broker) delivers this message to its destination as a SOAP message over HTTP protocol. Likewise, a message server can listen for HTTP requests and automatically place an incoming SOAP message onto a JMS queue or topic. Out-of-the-box MQ SOAP/HTTP support eliminates need for an extra layer known as an MQ Façade.

Next, the chapter looks into the design details of the Message Queue with Web services-based interoperability scenario.

Replenish Stock Use Case

Applying this strategy to the Replenish Stock scenario yields the following interaction among Java, .NET and a message queue server. Refer to Figure 9-8.

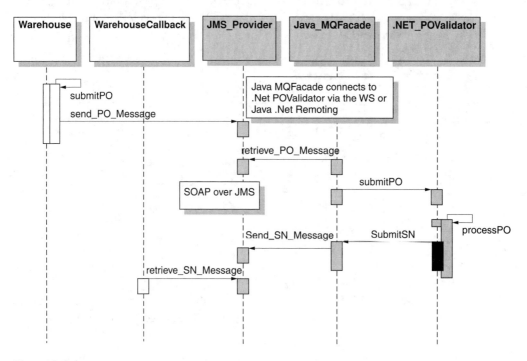

Figure 9-8
Sequence diagram for Java MQFaçade

The key component of this diagram is the Java MQFaçade, which integrates a .NET POValidator component with a JMS message queue.

If an integration infrastructure revolves around the MSMQ server, an analogous architecture can be constructed by creating a proxy that interfaces with the Java application. Figure 9-9 is a sequence diagram, similar to the previous one, with emphasis on MSMQ integration.

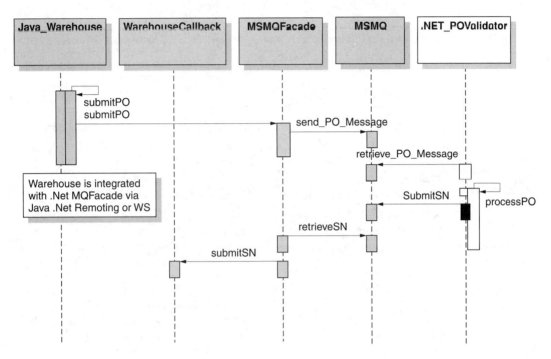

Figure 9-9
.NET MSMQFaçade integrates a Java *Warehouse* with MSMQ

This diagram highlights a .NET MQFaçade that integrates a Java `Warehouse` with the MSMQ system.

Should a SOAP message include session information, such as session id, user, and password, these data can be passed as part of the SOAP header. Commercial JMS solutions also provide a means to manage sessions.

Benefits

The advantage of this design entails flexibility of using Web services and a message queue to achieve interoperability. There is no proprietary and custom off-the-shelf solution involved to achieve the Java-.NET application interoperability. From a cost standpoint, this strategy is the one to consider. For example, Sun Java System Message Queue [SunJSMQ], Platform Edition is a free, commercial-grade Java Message Service (JMS) implementation. There are open source implementations of JMS standards available as well.

Manageability

Web services provide an ideal way to expose business functionality as easily reusable interfaces. Web services help leverage existing software investments by allowing a business process wrapped in a Web service interface to be replaced without impacting the consumers of the service.

Performance and Scalability

An additional benefit of this strategy is the ability to exchange rich documents and complex data types with negligible overhead, as most commercial messaging servers feature a high degree of scalability. Thus this strategy has a clear advantage over RPC-style Web services integration, which facilitates a remote method call execution. Similar to the RPC-style, agreeing on a WSDL for data structures exchanged between Java EE and .NET applications helps to provide a consistent message interchange.

Limitations

There are a few drawbacks to this design. One pertains to the fact that integration with messaging is not as transparent as it is using the bridging strategy. Developers have to manually create initial integration points.

Reliability

Because the main application does not exchange messages with a message queue server directly, the reliability of the entire message flow has vulnerability at the MQFaçade point. It is not a problem with proxy classes, that is, the .NET Remoting Proxy, because integration between an MQFaçade and the main application is tightly coupled, and an RPC call will not succeed if one of the building blocks is down or if there is a network failure. With Web services on the other hand, SOAP over HTTP does not guarantee reliable message delivery. Therefore, it is important to leverage a call back mechanism or use other means to achieve reliability across the entire component chain.

Performance and Scalability

The MQFaçade may become a bottleneck when there are multiple messages in the queue to process. For high-volume transactions, the MQFaçade should be designed as a multi-threaded component to alleviate the scalability problem. The MQFaçade may also turn into a single point of failure, thus its availability is critical to successful message processing.

Having the SOAP support built into the message brokers, the SonicMQ solution mitigates this risk. Performance and scalability can be achieved through the clustering capabilities that are built into the message broker.

Manageability

One of the challenges with this approach is maintaining two environments, Java and .NET, to maintain the interoperability logic. In this respect, this approach is more demanding compared to the bridging strategy.

Related Patterns

Both Java MQFaçade and .NET MQFaçade patterns are instances of the Façade pattern. They represent the Façade pattern applied in the specific context of Java EE-.NET integration. Actually in this example it is applied in the context of Java-.NET integration, although an enterprise application may easily employ message-driven beans.

Java MQFaçade and .NET MQFaçade

Both of these patterns naturally augment the Java EE-.NET asynchronous integration with messaging. They provide a layer of abstraction to the diverse messaging infrastructures and encapsulate intricacy of the technology interoperability. Depending on the actual implementation of these patterns, one can apply best practices from Web services or .NET Remoting technologies.

For the Web services strategy, two sets of code samples are demonstrated. The first example deploys a JMS provider, in our case FioranoMQ, and integrates a .NET application using the Java MQFaçade component. The second example deploys the MSMQ solution and interoperates with a Java application via the MQFaçade component. Each of the examples comes with the Readme.doc file that outlines individual classes and instructions on how to run the code.

Example 1: JMS MQFaçade Accesses JMS Provider and .NET Web Services

In the first example, the `Warehouse` and `WarehouseCallback` classes access the JMS provider with a traditional way of using JMS APIs. You can take a look at those classes and gain comfort with their pure Java implementation.

Therefore we skip the Java EE `Retailer` System discussion and move on with the `Manufacturer` system implementation.

Building Manufacturer System

Interoperability challenges occur after the message crossed the JMS message queue boundaries, specifically these challenges are embraced in the Java `MQFaçade` and `POValidator` classes that are focused on. For receiving the Purchase Order, `MQFaçade` invokes Java `POValidator` object to access the queue, retrieve the `PurchaseOrder` message, and then post the message to the .NET Web service. These series of events are shown in the `receivePO()` method of `MQFaçade` class, see Listing 9-22:

Listing 9-22
Receiving JMS Message

```
    private InputStream receivePO(String poQName) {
        InputStream inputStream = null;
        try {
            validator = new POValidator();
            validator.init(poQName);
            String receivedPO = validator.receivePO();
            inputStream = validator.postPOToWebService(receivedPO);
        } catch(Exception e) {
            e.printStackTrace();
        }

        return inputStream;
    }
```

As can be seen here, the logic of accessing the message queue and retrieving the message is hidden in the `POValidator` class, which is explored next. This class initializes the message queue components and retrieves the message from the message queue. The `POValidator's recievePO()` method uses the JMS `QueueReceiver` to receive the incoming message:

```
TextMessage pOrder =(TextMessage) receiver.receive();
```

A more interesting method of this class is the `postPOToWebSerivce()`, which generates SOAP Request and invokes the Web service endpoint—see Listing 9-23:

Listing 9-23
Posting SOAP Request to a Web Service

```
public InputStream postPOToWebService(String pOMessage) {
      byte[] soapRequest = getSoapRequest(pOMessage);
      String soapAction = "http://tempuri.org/ValidatePO";

      return executeWebMethod(soapRequest,soapAction);
}
```

The logic of creating a SOAP Request is encompassed in the `getSoapRequest()` method. Listing 9-24 lists the SOAP Request content that includes Purchase Order id along with necessary SOAP envelope attributes:

Listing 9-24
SOAP Request String

```
strSoapRequest = "<?xml version='1.0' encoding='UTF-8'?>
  <soap:Envelope  xmlns:xsi=\'http://www.w3.org/2001/XMLSchema-
    instance\' xmlns:xsd=\'http://www.w3.org/2001/XMLSchema\'
    xmlns:soap=\'http://schemas.xmlsoap.org/soap/envelope/\'>
        <soap:Body>
          <ValidatePO xmlns=\'http://tempuri.org/\'>
          <id>"+id+"</id>
          </ValidatePO>
        </soap:Body>
  </soap:Envelope>";
```

Marshaling and unmarshaling of the XML messages sent over the message queue have already been discussed. The `getSoapRequest` method, from the `POValidator` class, performs unmarshaling of the `PurchaseOrder` string retrieved from the queue and creates a SOAP Request, just shown. This SOAP request can easily be extended with the rest of the `PurchaseOrder` attributes. Listing 9-25 shows this method:

Listing 9-25
Get PurchaseOrder SOAP Request

```
private byte[] getSoapRequest(String POMessage) {
  String strSoapRequest=null;
  try {
    JAXBContext context =
        JAXBContext.newInstance("org.j2eedotnet.po");

    // unmarshal from ShippingNotice xml string coming
    Unmarshaller unmarshaller = context.createUnmarshaller();
    PurchaseOrder pOrder =
      (PurchaseOrder) unmarshaller.unmarshal(new StreamSource(new
        StringReader(POMessage)));

    String id = pOrder.getId();

    strSoapRequest = "<?xml version='1.0' encoding='UTF-8'?>
     <soap:Envelope
        xmlns:xsi=\"http://www.w3.org/2001/XMLSchema-instance\"
        xmlns:xsd=\"http://www.w3.org/2001/XMLSchema\"
        xmlns:soap=\"http://schemas.xmlsoap.org/soap/envelope/\">
     <soap:Body>
     <ValidatePO  xmlns=\"http://tempuri.org/\"><id>"+id+"</id>
     </ValidatePO>
     </soap:Body>
     </soap:Envelope>";
    } catch(Exception e) {
    System.out.println("Error reading XML:"+e.getMessage());
  }
  return strSoapRequest.getBytes();
}
```

The SOAP Request byte array and the SOAP Action, `ValidatePO`, are sent to the `POValidator`'s `executeWebMethod`:

```
String soapAction = "http://tempuri.org/ValidatePO";
return executeWebMethod(soapRequest,soapAction);
```

The `executeWebMethod()` is responsible for sending request to the `ValidatePO Web Method`. The `executeWebMethod` uses the Web service URL to open the URL connection:

```
URL endpoint = new URL(webServiceURL);
URLConnection con = endpoint.openConnection();
```

After setting up the URL connection parameters, such as `setDoInput` and `setDoOutput`, one can now write out the SOAP Request:

```
OutputStream out = con.getOutputStream();
out.write(soapRequest);
```

The return of `executeWebMethod` is an `InputStream` that reflects the `Web Method` return value. Listing 9-26 shows the entire `executeWebMethod()` content:

Listing 9-26
executeWebMethod

```
private InputStream executeWebMethod
    ( byte[] soapRequest, String soapAction) {
  InputStream inputStream = null;
  try {
    URL endpoint = new URL(webServiceURL);
    URLConnection con = endpoint.openConnection();
    con.setDoInput(true);
    con.setDoOutput(true);
    con.setUseCaches(false);
    con.setAllowUserInteraction(false);
    con.setRequestProperty("Content-Length",

    Integer.toString(soapRequest.length));
    con.setRequestProperty("Content-Type", "text/xml");
    con.setRequestProperty("SOAPAction", "\"" + soapAction + "\"");
    OutputStream out = con.getOutputStream();
    out.write(soapRequest);
    out.flush();
    out.close();
    inputStream = con.getInputStream();
  }
  catch(Exception e)
  {
    e.printStackTrace();
  }
  return inputStream;
}
```

The ASP.NET Web service, `DotNetWebApp.asmx`, deployed under IIS, offers a single Web method, `ValidatePO`, that takes input `string` as a parameter and returns this string back to keep things simple:

```
[WebMethod(Description = "POValidator Web Service")]
  public string  ValidatePO(string id)
  {
     return id;
}
```

This method can easily be tested by typing any string value in the `ValidatePO` text field, as shown in Figure 9-10:

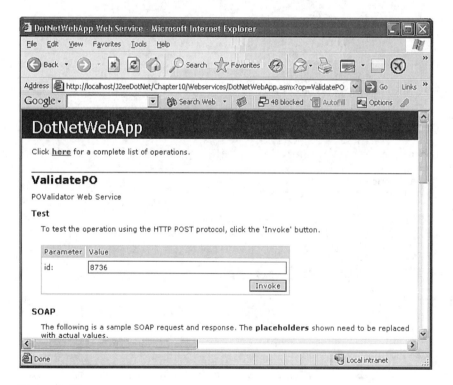

Figure 9-10
ValidatePO Web service

The result of this method is shown in Figure 9-11:

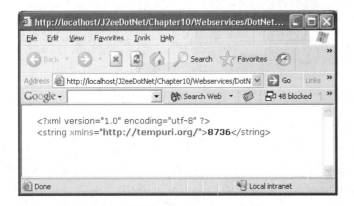

Figure 9-11
ValidatePO result

It's now time to test this Web service programmatically via a Java client represented with `POValidator`'s `executeWebMethod()`. Listing 9-27 lists the SOAP Response output, reformatted for ease of readability, from the `ValidatePO` method:

Listing 9-27
ValidatePO Web Service, SOAP Response

```
<?xml version="1.0" encoding="utf-8"?>
<soap:Envelope xmlns:soap="http
://schemas.xmlsoap.org/soap/envelope/"
xmlns:xsi="http://www.w3.org/2001/XMLSche
ma-instance" xmlns:xsd="http://www.w3.org/2001/XMLSchema">
   <soap:Body>
       <ValidatePOResponse xmlns="http://tempuri.org/">
           <ValidatePOResult>8736</ValidatePOResult>
       </ValidatePOResponse>
   </soap:Body>
</soap:Envelope>
```

As a quick recap, the Purchase Order ID submitted by `POValidator` to the Web service endpoint originated from the Java Retailer system. The `Warehouse` class, as part of Retailer system, submitted the Purchase Order request to the JMS message queue. The message was then received by the `POValidator` and sent to the `Web method`.

The next logical step is to generate a `ShippingNotice`. This might bring up the question of how the SOAP Response was received in the preceding example. This is actually part of the `ShipNotice.java` that reads results of the Web service, `ValidatePO` method, from the `InputStream` of the Web service URL connection. Here is the logic of the `readSNFromWebSrevice()` method:

```
int i = -1;
while((i = instream.read()) > -1)
  soapResponse +=((char) i);
```

The `ShipNotice` class parses the SOAP Response that it read from the `InputStream` and retrieves the PO id. To perform this task, the `javax.xml.parsers.DocumentBuilderFactory` class is used to obtain a parser in the form of `javax.xml.parsers.DocumentBuilder` and to generate a DOM object from an XML document. In this case the XML parser takes an `InputStream` corresponding to the `ValidatePO` Web service URL connection, as an input source (refer to Listing 9-28):

Listing 9-28
Parsing XML Document in Java

```
DocumentBuilderFactory docFactory =
         DocumentBuilderFactory.newInstance();
DocumentBuilder builder = docFactory.newDocumentBuilder();
Document document = builder.parse(strStream);
```

The original Web service can always be checked to determine the structure of the SOAP Response XML file to obtain the right element. In this case the structure is shown in Listing 9-29:

Listing 9-29
SOAP Response, XML Document

```
<?xml version="1.0" encoding="utf-8"?>
   <soap:Envelope xmlns:xsi="http://www.w3.org/2001/XMLSchema-
instance"
xmlns:xsd="http://www.w3.org/2001/XMLSchema"
xmlns:soap="http://schemas.xmlsoap.org/soap/envelope/">
  <soap:Body>
    <ValidatePOResponse xmlns="http://tempuri.org/">
      <ValidatePOResult>string</ValidatePOResult>
    </ValidatePOResponse>
  </soap:Body>
</soap:Envelope>
```

To obtain the `ValidatePOResults`, the XML tree needs to be traversed from `SoapEnvelope` to `ValidatePOResult`, that is, `SoapEnvelope-->SoapBody-->ValidatePOResponse-->ValidatePOResult`. This is shown in Listing 9-30:

Listing 9-30
Parsing SOAP Response XML Document

```
Node responseElem =
  document.getFirstChild().getFirstChild()
  .getFirstChild().getFirstChild();
String responseID = responseElem.getFirstChild().getNodeValue();
```

Purchase Order id, in this case a `responseId` variable, is set as part of the `ShippingNotice` XML document. The `ShipNotice` class populates the rest of the values as shown in Listing 9-31:

Listing 9-31
Creating *ShippingNotice* Object

```
ObjectFactory objFactory = new ObjectFactory();
ShippingNotice sNotice = objFactory.createShippingNotice();
sNotice.setPONumber(111);
sNotice.setShipmentID(222);
sNotice.setDescription(responseID);
```

After the data are populated, the next step is to marshal the `ShipNotice` into the `OutputStream` by using the already familiar JAXB APIs. This logic is shown in Listing 9-32:

Listing 9-32
Marshaling *ShippingNotice*

```
JAXBContext context =
JAXBContext.newInstance("org.j2eedotnet.sn.xsd");

Marshaller marshaller = context.createMarshaller();
marshaller.marshal(sNotice, writer);
```

Listing 9-33 is the complete listing of the getXMLShipNotice() method that has been discussed:

Listing 9-33

Preparing XML *ShippingNotice*

```java
private String getXMLShipNotice(String soapResponse) {
    StringWriter writer = new StringWriter();
    try {
        StringBufferInputStream strStream =
            new StringBufferInputStream(soapResponse);

        DocumentBuilderFactory docFactory =
            DocumentBuilderFactory.newInstance();
        DocumentBuilder builder = docFactory.newDocumentBuilder();
        Document document = builder.parse(strStream);

        //SoapEnvelope-->SoapBody-->ValidatePOResponse--
>ValidatePOResult
        Node responseElem = document.getFirstChild().getFirstChild().
                        getFirstChild().getFirstChild();
        String responseID =
responseElem.getFirstChild().getNodeValue();

        ObjectFactory objFactory = new ObjectFactory();
        ShippingNotice sNotice = objFactory.createShippingNotice();
        sNotice.setPONumber(111);
        sNotice.setShipmentID(222);
        sNotice.setDescription(responseID);

        JAXBContext context =
            JAXBContext.newInstance("org.j2eedotnet.sn.xsd");

        // marshal to outputStream
        Marshaller marshaller = context.createMarshaller();
        marshaller.marshal(sNotice, writer);
    } catch(Exception e) {
        System.out.println("Invalid SOAP Response:" + e.getMessage());
    }
    System.out.println(writer.toString());
    return writer.toString();
}
```

Listing 9-34 shows the output of the XML `ShippingNotice` that is created by the `getXMLShipNotice()` method of the `ShipNotice` class:

Listing 9-34
Shipping Notice XML Document

```
<?xml version="1.0" encoding="UTF-8" standalone="yes"?>
<shippingNotice xmlns="http://j2eedotnet.org/sn/xsd">
<PONumber>111</PONumber>
<ShipmentID>222</ShipmentID>
<Description>8736</Description>
</shippingNotice>
```

Finally, it's time to send the `ShippingNotice` to the JMS provider. The `ShipNotice`'s `sendSN()` method performs this task:

```
TextMessage jmsMsg = session.createTextMessage();
jmsMsg.setText(shipNoticeMessage);
sender.send(jmsMsg);
```

Coming back to the `Retailer` system, the `WarehouseCallback` retrieves the `ShippingNotices`.

In summary, this example integrates Java and .NET applications using a JMS message queue. To interoperate between JMS provider and .NET application, this example has developed an MQFaçade. MQFaçade communicates with the message queue using standard JMS APIs and communicates with the .NET application using java.net libraries to access a .NET Web service endpoint, as shown in Figure 9-12.

Figure 9-12
Java MQFaçade overview

All of the MQFaçade interoperability logic is embraced by the Manufacturer system and is implemented in Java. The interoperability is completely transparent to the Retailer system. As a reminder, it is important to explicitly ensure reliability between MQFaçade and the Web service.

The next adventure is to implement similar functionality with MSMQ and .NET-based MQFaçade.

Example 2: MSMQ Façade Accessing Web Services

In this example most of the focus is concentrated on investigating interoperability within the Retailer system, as Java-based Retailer system has to access the MSMQ message queue. The Manufacturer system remains the same as discussed in the bridging strategy.

Building Retailer System

As can be imagined, the `Warehouse` and the `WarehouseCallback` components cannot directly send messages to MSMQ, given incompatibility of APIs between Java and .NET. To address this challenge, ASP.NET Web service is implemented, acting as MSMQ MQFaçade to bring Java and .NET systems in harmony with each other. This MQFaçade is represented via the `DotNetWebAppFaçade.asmx` ASP.NET file. The MQFaçade Web service is similar to the Web service implemented in the preceding example, Example 1. The only additional functionality added to this service is access to MSMQ. The `ValidatePO` method starts with initializing two messages, `poValidator` queue for outgoing messages and `shippingNoticeQueue` for incoming messages. This is shown in Listing 9-35:

Listing 9-35
Initializing MSMQ Queues

```
MessageQueue ValidatePOQueue = new
MessageQueue(@"aseem\private$\replenishstock");
MessageQueue shippingNoticeQueue = new
MessageQueue(@"aseem\private$\shippingnotice");
```

Next is to set the Recoverable property of the `ValidatePOQueue` to `true` to ensure that a transaction rolls back in case of failure. The `ActiveXMessageFormatter` is also initialized to pass XML messages to MSMQ.

```
ValidatePOQueue.DefaultPropertiesToSend.Recoverable = true;
ValidatePOQueue.Formatter = new ActiveXMessageFormatter();
```

For simplicity, a string id is sent to MSMQ:

```
ValidatePOQueue.Send(id);
```

Once the Manufacturer system processes the request, a `ShippingNotice` is received back. Here for simplicity, once again a string ID is exchanged:

```
Message message = shippingNoticeQueue.Receive();
message.Formatter = new ActiveXMessageFormatter();
string sNotice = message.Body.ToString();
```

The next code snippet, Listing 9-36, lists the `DotNetWebApp.asmx` WebMethod, `ValidatePO()` that acts as an MSMQ Façade:

Listing 9-36
MSMQ MQFaçade Represented as .NET Web Service

```
[WebMethod(Description = "POValidator Web Service")]
   public string  ValidatePO(string id) {
      MessageQueue ValidatePOQueue = new
        MessageQueue(@"aseem\private$\replenishstock");
      MessageQueue shippingNoticeQueue = new
        MessageQueue(@"aseem\private$\shippingnotice");

      ValidatePOQueue.DefaultPropertiesToSend.Recoverable = true;
      ValidatePOQueue.Formatter = new ActiveXMessageFormatter();

      try {
   ValidatePOQueue.Send(id);
        Console.WriteLine("Sent the message");
      } catch(Exception ex) {
        Console.WriteLine(ex.Message);
   }

   Message message = shippingNoticeQueue.Receive();
   message.Formatter = new ActiveXMessageFormatter();
   string sNotice = message.Body.ToString();

   Console.WriteLine("Received shippingNotice");
   return sNotice;
}
```

When deploying the `DotNetWebServiceFaçade`, a familiar screen is revealed in Figure 9-13:

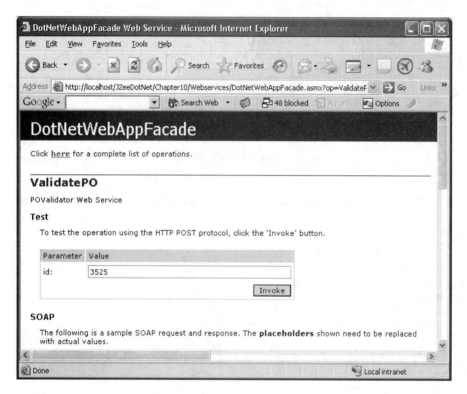

Figure 9-13
Deploying .NET WebService MQFaçade

The main Java application, `Java_EEApp.java`, initiates request to the MQFaçade by invoking the `sendPO()` method. The core logic of this method relies on the Warehouse's `postPOToWebService()` method:

```
poSender = new Warehouse();
String pOrder = poSender.getPO();
inputStream = poSender.postPOToWebService(pOrder);
```

Interestingly enough, a majority of the logic required for this sample is identical to the Web services Example 1 that was developed earlier in this section. It described `postPOToWebService` method, so it won't be scrutinized here again. The `InputStream` is returned from the *poSender*.post `POToWebService()` operation back to the `main()` method of `Java EEApp.java`.

On the receiving end, the `InputStream` received from `postPOToWebServer()` method is passed to the Java EEApp's `receiveShippingNotice()` method. This method creates an instance of the `WarehouseCallback` class to retrieve the `ShippinqNotice`:

```
snReceiver = new WarehouseCallback();
ShippingNotice sNotice =
    (ShippingNotice)snReceiver.getSNFromWebService(instream);
```

As has already been mentioned, C# classes including `Manufacturer`, `ShipNotice`, and `POValidator` remain nearly the same as ones implemented in the bridging strategy.

DEVELOPER'S NOTE

The Java EEApp synchronously invokes `Warehouse` and `WarehouseCallback` components. To implement asynchronous communication between .NET Web service and the Java program, you may leverage automatic callback strategy, demonstrated in Chapter 8, "Asynchronous Web Services Integration."

At a higher level, the .NET MQFaçade is integrated with Java and MSMQ using the following APIs, see Figure 9-14.

Figure 9-14
.NET Web Services MQFaçade overview

The last two examples explained how to implement interoperability using Web services and messaging. Web services is the weakest link in the integration chain from a reliable messaging standpoint; therefore, before making a decision on this strategy it's best to explore an alternative integration with proxy classes, which is examined next.

Example 3: Accessing MSMQ from Java Using Proxy Classes

From a messaging interoperability standpoint, the overall flow of the sample remains the same. The only difference is that instead of a Web services-based Façade, proxy classes are used. For more details on this, refer to Chapter 5, "NET Remoting for Synchronous Intregration." When it comes to Messaging integration with proxy, there are online resources available that demonstrate MSMQ access from Java using a third-party proxy library. For example, Intrinsyc's J-Integra solution, [JIntegraMSMQ], offers a bi-directional way to seamlessly access the MQMQ from Java. This solution utilizes Java proxy classes that are mapped from COM components API. To preview and run the example, refer to the following link, http://j-integra.intrinsyc.com/com/doc/other_examples/Java_from_MSMQ.htm.

In summary, depending on interoperability requirements and existing infrastructure, the MQFaçade strategy can become an effective solution to a Java-.NET interoperability problem.

Internet E-Mail for Asynchronous Messaging

Up until now the only strategies discussed have been related to the Message Oriented Middleware. To add a new flavor to the discussion, the next sections explore asynchronous integration of Java and .NET applications using Internet e-mail. Internet e-mail servers are used today to connect diverse sets of e-mail clients across different platforms. Desktop e-mail clients and Internet e-mail clients retrieve e-mails from an e-mail server. Most of the e-mail servers including Microsoft Exchange Server and Sun Java System Messaging Server support standard messaging protocols such as Simple Mail Transfer Protocol (SMTP), Post Office Protocol (POP), and Internet Message Access Protocol (IMAP). An important thing to remember with these protocols is the following: E-mail servers use the SMTP protocol to send messages, and e-mail client applications use POP and IMAP protocols to receive messages. Their latest versions are IMAP4 and POP3. Details on individual protocols can be found at [SMTP], [POP3], [IMAP], in the "References" section of this chapter.

Scope

Business requirements often employ message notification upon finishing request processing or as alert notification when an unexpected error or a failure occurs during request processing. For example, in the Replenish Stock scenario, upon order request validation a notification has to be sent to the WarehouseCallback system. For these types of requirements, developers may use an e-mail infrastructure to interchange messages between Java and .NET applications.

Solution

An SMTP/POP messaging server provides store and forward functionality on the incoming messages, thus guaranteeing message delivery. Both Java and .NET provide Mail APIs to send and receive e-mail messages and can be used to achieve interoperability between Java and .NET applications. Following are a couple examples of sending messages via standard mail APIs. On the .NET side, a System.Web.Mail.SmtpMail library is used to send a MailMessage:

```
MailMessage mail = new MailMessage();
// Set From, To, Subject, Body, and SmtpServer properties
SmtpMail.Send(mail);
```

On the Java side there are javax.mail libraries to achieve the same:

Listing 9-37
Sending E-mail from Java

```
Session session = Session.getDefaultInstance(props, null);
Message msg = new MimeMessage(session);
// Set From, To, Subject
Transport.send(msg);
```

Similarly, these Mail APIs can be used to retrieve messages from the server. A .NET or Java client application uses a POP3 protocol to send and access messages. A standard SMTP/POP messaging server receives and sends messages over SMTP transport layer. Figure 9-15 is a high-level diagram outlining the communication flow between the SMTP server and client applications.

Figure 9-15
SMTP/POP communication flow

As SOAP messages become the de facto data interchange format, achieving Java EE .NET interoperability with SOAP over SMTP communication is the strategy discussed in this section and is used to build an example. Using SOAP to represent the data contributes to a higher degree of flexibility and interoperability. This example shows how SOAP messages can be sent and received over the SMTP protocol layer with Java and .NET. For that, JAXMail Java APIs and Microsoft Web services Enhancements for Microsoft .NET(WSE) release 2 are used, which extends the .NET Framework and Visual Studio .NET with ability to send SOAP messages over different transport protocols such as TCP or SMTP. See [JaxMail], [JaxMailRI], and [WSE] for more information.

This example continues to use WS-I Replenish Stock use case, where a Java Retailer and the .NET Manufacturer system exchange Purchase Order and Shipping Notice information accordingly. The sequence diagram in Figure 9-16 outlines core classes that developed to implement this scenario:

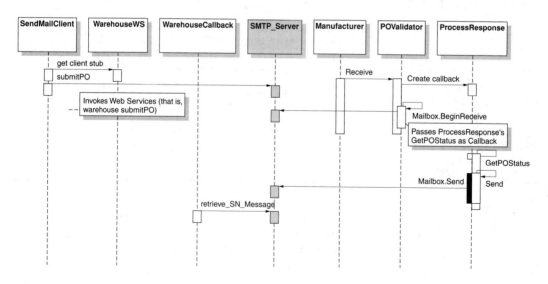

Figure 9-16
Exchanging SOAP over SMTP messages between Java and .NET applications

Benefits and Limitations

The main advantage of this design is that asynchronous integration between Java and .NET can be achieved without having to invest into a proprietary interoperability solution or having to build custom adapters. Instead, asynchronous integration can be achieved with a messaging infrastructure that most companies already deploy in-house. A client application can be fully offline and yet retrieve messages as needed. An SMTP server persists messages and guarantees their availability to the client.

Reliable Messaging

Compared to a MOM solution, this strategy does not fulfill a traditional requirement for reliable messaging. With e-mails there is typically no guarantee of delivery. The SMTP messaging infrastructure offers guaranteed delivery of messages via Delivery Status Notification (DSN) and Message Disposition Notification (MDN). But even with guaranteed message delivery, the once-and-only-once constituent of reliable communications may not be satisfied. Messages may get delivered more than once, which may not be an issue with the given application requirements.

Security

In this strategy, an e-mail message invokes a Web service. Considering security vulnerabilities with desktop applications such as Outlook or Internet Explorer, this scenario needs to be carefully reviewed prior to deploying in production. When using this strategy various security implications need be assessed to minimize potential security breaches.

Example

In the previous examples, the environment primarily consisted of a messaging server such as MSMQ or JMS provider and other components. This example uses an SMTP/POP server as the middleware infrastructure. See "References" for individual solutions and library downloads [SmtpWin2000].

Setting Up the Environment

To develop a Replenish Stock scenario with SMTP server, Apache Java Enterprise Mail Server (James) is used, [James]. It supports SMTP for sending and POP3 for receiving transport protocols. As mentioned earlier, the

JAXMail library is also used, which extends JAX-RPC with support for SMTP transport protocol. JAXMail architecture documentation outlines individual steps of setting up the environment, including James server. To begin the example, the James mail server needs to be started, and two users created, Retailer and Manufacturer. You can achieve this by using telnet to access the mail server's remote manager, and then executing the 'adduser' command,

```
telnet localhost 4555
adduser retailer java
adduser manufacturer dotnet
```

where the `retailer` is a user with the password `java` and the `manufac-turer` user has the password `dotnet`. E-mail messages can now be exchanged between Java Warehouse and .NET Manufacturer systems.

Because this example uses JaxMail extensions to JAX-RPC, the `${jwsdp.home}/jaxrpc/lib/jaxrpc-ri.jar` needs to be replaced with this one: `https://jaxmail.dev.java.net/jaxrpc-ri.jar`. This applies to both development environment of the Java Web services Development Pack and runtime environment of the Tomcat's JAX-RPC library. The sample application that comes with JaxMail needs to downloaded as this example references it throughout.

The IIS server also needs to be started. This is done by starting Computer Management and simply entering `compmgmt.msc` at the Start/Run text field and selecting Services and Applications. Right click the IIS Manager and select `Reconnect to localhost` or the `Refresh` option.

For building .NET SOAP over SMTP Manufacturer system, WSE 2.0 should first be downloaded and installed. Place the `Microsoft.Web.Services2.dll` under the mail/lib directory to be acces-sible to the `build.xml` file. In the .NET portion of the code, this example uses Steve Maine's sample of SMTP transport for WSE. Download and extract the Soap over SMTP sample code, [SteveMainSoapSmtp], under the src/manufacturer/SoapSmtp directory. As you may notice, this sample code references Pawel Lesnikowski's POP3 library `Mail.dll`, [PawelLesnikowskiMail], that is needed to build the code. Download and place the `Mail.dll` under mail/lib directory and also copy `Mail.dll` into the mail/ directory to be accessible by the final executable. All links for downloading individual libraries are listed in the "References" section.

Building the Retailer System

The implementation starts with a Retailer Web service that allows a client application to send SOAP messages over SMTP. Figure 9-17 outlines the high-level diagram of Retailer components:

Figure 9-17
Retailer System Integrated with SMTP Server

The Warehouse interface and the WarehouseImpl class implement the Web service endpoint, Retailer Web service. Listing 9-38 shows the code for Warehouse classes:

Listing 9-38
Warehouse Class

```
package j2eedotnet.chapter9.mail.retailer;

import java.rmi.Remote;
import java.rmi.RemoteException;

public interface Warehouse extends Remote {
    public String submitPO(String msg) throws RemoteException;
}
```

Basic implementation of this interface is listed in WarehouseImpl.java, Listing 9-39.

Listing 9-39
WarehouseImpl.java Class

```
package j2eedotnet.chapter9.mail.retailer;

public class WarehouseImpl implements Warehouse {
    public String submitPO(String msg) {
        String result ="Purchase Order: "+msg;
        return result;
    }
}
```

To deploy this Web service under Tomcat, the Web server should be started and the Web service needs to be deployed in a standard way.

The Web service then can be viewed by browsing to the following site, see Figure 9-18:

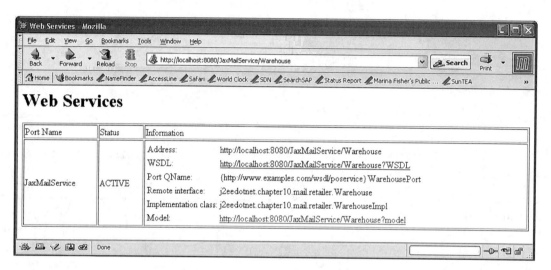

Figure 9-18
JaxMailWarehouse Web service

Client stubs can now be generated based on the deployed Web service.

Java Client Application

On the client side, the SendMailClient.java class accesses the send a SOAP message over SMTP. First the Web service stub, Warehouse_Stub, needs to be accessed:

```
JaxMailService_Impl service = new JaxMailService_Impl();
Warehouse_Stub wh =(Warehouse_Stub)service.getWarehousePort();
```

Using this stub sets corresponding properties such as user name, SMTP server parameters, and subject to send an e-mail message, Listing 9-40:

Listing 9-40
Setting JAX-Mail Properties

```
wh._setProperty(javax.xml.rpc.Stub.ENDPOINT_ADDRESS_PROPERTY,
    "manufacturer@localhost.");
wh._setProperty(javax.xml.rpc.Stub.USERNAME_PROPERTY ,
"retailer");
wh._setProperty(javax.xml.rpc.Stub.PASSWORD_PROPERTY , "java");
wh._setProperty("jaxrpc.transport","SMTP");
wh._setProperty("smtp.from", "retailer@localhost");
wh._setProperty("smtp.host", "127.0.0.1");
wh._setProperty("smtp.subject","/Warehouse");
```

For testing purposes, to preview the SOAP message, a `Client Handler.java` class has been created. The source code for the `ClientHandler` class can be found in the `j2eedotnet.chapter9. mail.handler` package. This class intercepts the SOAP message before it is sent to the e-mail server and displays the SOAP message on the console. Listing 9-41 shows `SendMailClient` code of handler registration with the Web service:

Listing 9-41
Registering *ClientHandler* class

```
QName portName =
  new QName("http://www.temp.com/wsdl/poservice",
"WarehousePort");
HandlerRegistry registry = service.getHandlerRegistry();
List handlerList = new ArrayList();
handlerList.add( new HandlerInfo(ClientHandler.class,null,null)
);
  registry.setHandlerChain( portName, handlerList );
```

Next step for the client application is to submit the `PurchaseOrder` request to the Web service. For that, the `SubmitPO` stub class is instantiated, which has been auto-generated based on the deployed service and has passed the po object to the Web services' `submtiPO()` method:

```
SubmitPO po = new SubmitPO("PurchaseOrder_123");
SubmitPOResponse response = wh.submitPO(po);
System.out.println("PO_123 Submitted");
```

WarehouseCallback

Before running the client code, this section takes a brief look at the Java `WarehouseCallback` class. The `WarehouseCallback` is responsible for retrieving messages from the SMTP server by polling the server for messages within a given interval. Once the .NET Manufacturing system, discussed next, asynchronously processes the `PurchaseOrder`, it sends back the `ShippingNotice`. This Shipping Notice is received by the `WarehouseCallback` component. To run the callback, there needs to be a set value for the corresponding user and SMTP server. These values are passed to JaxMail's `com.jaxmail.MailDownloader` class:

```
MailDownloader client = new
MailDownloader("retailer","java","localhost",30,"pop3");
```

The JaxMail sample application provides a class, `TestMailHandler`, to perform sample polling functionality, which we re-use in this code sample. To reuse the class, download and place the `TestMailHandler.java` file under the same directory as the `WarehouseCallback.java` file and modify the package name to `package j2eedotnet.chapter9.mail.client`. Here is the remaining logic of `WarehouseCallback`'s `main()` method:

```
client.setHandler(new TestMailHandler());
client.start();
```

The preceding logic includes setting the e-mail handler and starting to listen on the known port for incoming e-mail messages.

Running the *SendMailClient*

It is now time to compile and execute the client application. Running the client after the initial build produces the output shown in Listing 9-42:

Listing 9-42
Output of Submitting the Purchase Order by *SendMailClient* Class

```
>ant run-client-again
Buildfile: build.xml

run-client-again:
     [echo] Running the Client program....
     [java] --------------------
```

```
[java] OUTGOING MESSAGE:
[java] <env:Envelope
xmlns:env="http://schemas.xmlsoap.org/soap/envelope/"
xmlns:enc="http://schemas.xmlsoap.org/soap/encoding/"
xmlns:ns0="http://www.examples.com/types"
xmlns:xsd="http://www.w3.org/2001/XMLSchema"
xmlns:xsi="http://www.w3.org/2001/XMLSchema-instance">
  <env:Body>
    <ns0:submitPO>
       <String_1>PurchaseOrder_123</String_1>
    </ns0:submitPO>
  </env:Body>
</env:Envelope>

[java] PO_123 Submitted

BUILD SUCCESSFUL
   Total time: 2 seconds
```

To follow the business logic of the Replenish Stock use case, this example now shifts to the .NET programming and builds the Manufacturer system.

Building Manufacturer System

First of all it's important to ensure that the `soap.smtp` sample C# classes, listed under the "Environment Setup" section earlier, are available for build process. The main `Manufacturer.cs` class uploads the configuration file for the e-mail user and server configurations and invokes `POValidator` to asynchronously retrieve messages. Core logic of the `Main` method is shown in Listing 9-43:

Listing 9-43
Manufacturer Class

```
AppDomain.CurrentDomain.SetData(APP_CONFIG_FILE,"Manufacturer.con-
fig");
POValidator validator = new POValidator();
validator.receive();
```

The POValidator calls Mailbox's asynchronous BeginRecieve() method, passing the ProcessResponse's GetPOStatus() method for asynchronous callback (refer to Listing 9-44):

Listing 9-44
POValidator's Receive Method

```
public void Receive() {
  // Creating a SOAP URI
  Uri uri = SoapSmtpUri.UriFromAddress("manufacturer@localhost");
  Mailbox mailbox = new Mailbox(uri);
  if( mailbox.Listening )
    Console.WriteLine("Already Listening...");

    ProcessResponse resp = new ProcessResponse(mailbox);

    // Define the asynchronous callback delegate.
    AsyncCallback callback = new AsyncCallback(resp.GetPOStatus);

    Console.WriteLine("Invoking Mailbox.BeginRecieve()... ");
mailbox.BeginRecieve(callback);
    }
```

The ProcessResponse class has two important methods. The first one is GetPOStatus, which is passed as a callback to the mailbox.BeginReceive() method. GetPOStatus invokes Mailbox's EndReceive() method to retrieve the SOAP message from the SMTP server. Assuming that the message contains a valid PurchaseOrder request, the GetPOStatus calls the send() message, discussed hereafter. Listing 9-45 shows the GetPOStatus() method:

Listing 9-45
PurchaseOrder's GetPOStatus Method

```
    public void GetPOStatus(IAsyncResult ar) {
      writer.WriteLine("Received a PO Message");

      SoapEnvelope[] res =(SoapEnvelope[]) mailbox.EndReceive(ar);
      SoapEnvelope env =(SoapEnvelope)res[0];
      writer.WriteLine(env.Body.InnerXml);
      writer.WriteLine("\n");

      // Sending a Shipping Notice
      Send();
    }
```

In the preceding code, aside from the described logic, System .Diagnostics is used. TextWriterTraceListener is used as the writer variable that follows, to record e-mail retrieval to the console. The writer is initialized in the init() method:

```
writer = new TextWriterTraceListener(System.Console.Out);
Trace.Listeners.Add(writer);
```

The last line of the GetPOStatus() method calls a send() routine that prepares a ShippingNotice SOAP message and sends it to the retailer (see Listing 9-46):

Listing 9-46
ProcessResponse's Send Method

```
private void send(){
    Uri uri = SoapSmtpUri.UriFromAddress("manufacturer@local-
host");

    SoapEnvelope envelope = new SoapEnvelope();
    envelope.CreateBody();
    string xmlstr =
        @"<ShippingNotice>
            <PONumber>123</PONumber>
            <ShipmentID>222</ShipmentID>
            <Description>8833</Description>
        </ShippingNotice>";

    envelope.Body.InnerXml = xmlstr;
    writer.WriteLine("Sending Shipping Notice: ");
    writer.WriteLine(xmlstr);
    mailbox.Send(envelope, uri);
    CloseTrace();
}
```

Before compiling the .NET Manufacturer classes, corresponding parameters of the Mailbox.cs class need to be configured to ensure that messages between the retailer and the manufacturer users created earlier are exchanged. For that, in the Mailbox.cs file, application settings must be modified to match ones specified in the Manufacturer.config file. The configuration file is located under the same directory as the build.xml file—specifically, in the private void Receive() method, configure host, user name, and password as follows:

```
string server = ConfigurationSettings.AppSettings["MailServer"];
string username = ConfigurationSettings.AppSettings["UserFrom"];
string password = ConfigurationSettings.AppSettings["Password"];
```

In the same file, that is, `Mailbox.cd`, within the `MailClientAsyncResult` class definition section, for testing purposes comment out creation of the new thread pool for asynchronous invocation of the `Receive()` method. Instead the `Receive()` operation is explicitly invoked, passing an arbitrary state:

```
// ThreadPool.QueueUserWorkItem( new WaitCallback( this.Receive ));
this.Receive("state1");
```

Finally, in the `Send()` message of the `Mailbox` class, modify the target user information and a subject based on the configuration file parameters, as shown in Listing 9-47:

Listing 9-47
Outgoing Message Configuration

```
string smtpServer = ConfigurationSettings.AppSettings["MailServer"];
string to        = ConfigurationSettings.AppSettings["UserTo"];
string from      = this.Address;
string subject   = ConfigurationSettings.AppSettings["Subject"];
```

Running the Manufacturer Application

Ensure that all classes and libraries such as `Mail.dll` and `Microsoft.Web.Services2.dll` are available under lib directory. Compiling the Manufacturer application results in the `Manufacturer.exe` executable. Running the Manufacturer.exe produces an output corresponding to the Purchase Order SOAP received from the `Retailer` system and the `ShippingNotice` that it sends back to the `Retailer`. Listing 9-48 lists the output:

Listing 9-48
Running Manufacturer Application

```
>Manufacturer.exe
POValidator.receive(): Invoking Mailbox.BeginRecieve()...
ProcessResponse.GetPOStatus() Received a PO Message
<ns0:submitPO xmlns:ns0="http://www.examples.com/types">
```

```
    <String_1>PurchaseOrder_123</String_1>
</ns0:submitPO>


Sending Shipping Notice:
    <ShippingNotice>
        <PONumber>123</PONumber>
        <ShipmentID>222</ShipmentID>
        <Description>8833</Description>
    </ShippingNotice>
```

On the Retailer side, it's time to start the WarehouseCallback listener to receive the ShippingNotice. Listing 9-49 lists the output from the WarehouseCallback program:

Listing 9-49
Running *WarehouseCallback* Application

```
    [java] Receiving Message...
    [java] FROM: manufacturer@localhost
    [java] TO: retailer
    [java] SUBJECT: Shipping Notice
    [java] String body message
        <?xml version="1.0" encoding="utf-8"?>
        <soap:Envelope
xmlns:soap="http://schemas.xmlsoap.org/soap/envelope/">
        <soap:Body><ShippingNotice>
    [java]                <PONumber>123</PONumber>
    [java]                <ShipmentID>222</ShipmentID>
    [java]                <Description>8833</Description>
    [java]            </ShippingNotice></soap:Body></soap:Envelope>

    [java] ----------------------------
```

In summary, the example developed in this section discusses how to interoperate between Java and .NET using an SMTP server as the messaging middleware and exchange SOAP messages across two applications.

Enterprise Service Bus

Having come a long way, Web services considerably simplify integration of heterogeneous applications. However, Web services alone become insufficient to execute complex business processes due to the lack of inherent support for workflow orchestration and management of the distributed infrastructure. Also the messaging patterns mentioned earlier such as

Aggregator, Splitter, Routing Slip, and Process Manager, are built in as higher-level functionality implemented as part of an Enterprise Service Bus (ESB), offering, rather than requiring, low-level programming at the messaging layer. Please refer to [ESB] for details.

Scope

Today most companies invest in implementing Web services based on applications in Java or .NET. In most cases these new applications have to be co-dependent on legacy business systems. Building reliable integration across disparate applications can be achieved with Web services and messaging. However, for a successful business execution, enterprises require a platform that delivers a high degree of technology interoperability and offers support for business workflow orchestration, data transformation and routing, security, and process management. Management of a distributed Web services environment includes automated deployment and monitoring functionality.

Solution

The answer for these complex Java EE .NET and legacy integration requirements brings into light the value of the Enterprise Service Bus. In a nutshell, an ESB is an integration infrastructure that enables interoperability across heterogeneous applications including Java EE and .NET. For example, a Java EE Customer Sales, .NET Finance, and a legacy ERP system may have to communicate as part of the business flow. Each of those systems may expose different sets of APIs and do not seamlessly integrate with each other. An Enterprise Service Bus can be used to achieve interoperability across these systems. Modern ESB solutions offer support for Business Process Execution Language (BPEL) and WS-ReliableMessaging in addition to traditional Web services SOAP and WSDL support. Companies such as Sonic Software, Fiorano, Cape Clear, and SpiritSoft, among others, ship ESB solutions. Industry leading ESB vendors offer enhanced performance and security, support for multiple protocols, and adapters to integrate with legacy applications. An open source ESB solution is available from Mule, www.muleumo.org. Refer to [OASIS_WSBPEL], [WS-ReliableMessaging Spec], [SonicESB], [FioranoESB], [SpiritWaveESB], [CapeClearESB], and [MuleESB] for more information.

Figure 9-19 outlines the integration points of an enterprise Web services architecture where the business flow has to be orchestrated across multiple systems.

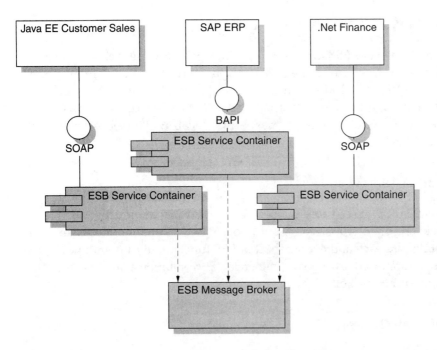

Figure 9-19
Integration points of an enterprise Web services architecture

Figure 9-19 depicts a typical ESB-distributed object broker infrastructure. The architecture is composed out of ESB service containers deployed along with a lightweight message queue. These containers are distributed at the individual application nodes, such as the Java EE application node and .NET application node, and leverage either Web services or custom, proprietary APIs. Specifically, this architecture comprises Java EE and .NET systems accessed via Web services APIs and a SAP legacy system accessed via proprietary SAP BAPI interfaces. The ESB facilitates the overall business process orchestration across Customer Sales, Finance, and ERP systems critical to successful business operations. One of the main benefits of an ESB solution is the ability to plug in existing applications to the integration environment with a minimal amount of work. Some implementations of the ESB solution offer communication between individual service container nodes in addition to the centralized hub provided by the ESB message broker. Most of the ESB vendors offer the capability of monitoring a distributed Web services environment to ensure successful execution of the business processes.

Data Routing

In the context of ESB, data routing is transparent to the Web services implementation. A service can be implemented in Java EE and .NET or embracing legacy ERP and CRM systems. This element of ESB allows individual services to be agnostic to the transport protocol, for example, HTTP or TCP. Data routing can utilize different transport protocols while Web services remain unchanged.

Benefits

An ESB offers a scaleable and secure middleware solution that operates as a backbone of enterprise communications. The remainder of this chapter does not discuss each and every aspect of ESB functionality, but outlines key features supported by most commercial ESB solutions, for example, from Fiorano or Sonic Software.

Management

One of the fundamental requirements of a distributed Web services architecture is the ability to monitor services deployed over the entire network, as well as offer versioning and configuration management of the Web services infrastructure. Administrative tools that are provided as part of the ESB infrastructure allow monitoring of the distributed services from any ESB node on the network. Event-based notification can be employed to notify the administrator of a critical error in the business flow. Developers can troubleshoot live data flows via break points on distributed message queues and dynamically change trace levels for debugging components and business processes.

Remote deployment and upgrades of services across the distributed application environment, which is supported by most ESB solutions, significantly simplifies the system management and accelerates an SOA development cycle. Web services versioning is one of the common issues encountered during SOA development. To address this, FioranoESB, for example, provides a GUI-based tool for managing multiple versions of Web services. Web services endpoints are being labeled accordingly based on development, QA, staging, or production version. These features address common development concerns when building SOA.

Scalability and Performance

The idea of ESB is to be able to leverage Web services technologies and additional functionality within a flexible and scalable architecture. This idea is realized by executing some of the activities nearer to the application itself to avoid bottleneck of a central hub. As was shown Figure 9-19, each of the applications has a component of an ESB deployed near that application to achieve a loosely coupled component-based architecture.

For instance, both Sonic and Fiorano's Enterprise Service Bus employ a brokered Point-to-Point (P2P) architecture that includes the following functionalities: data routing, business workflow processing, and data transformation. Each of these functionalities is performed at the individual network endpoints that interface specific applications. This distributed architecture improves scalability of the overall enterprise system. Centralized ESB servers are responsible for reliable messaging, event handling, security, and administration.

SonicESB supports independent scalability of remote services through a service container architecture. This service container model can provide selective scalability of intermediary services that facilitate the integration process itself. For example, an XSLT-based data transformation can be deployed as a separate service on the ESB. Using the scalability model of the ESB service container, multiple instances of an individual transformation service can be load-balanced across multiple machines to handle various kinds of processing loads, required by the individual data transformations. The ESB messaging servers can also be independently load-balanced and scaled across multiple machines to handle a high volume of message traffic. The independently scalable distributed container model and the independently scalable messaging layer, which work together to support one unified view of an abstract process model, are what make an ESB unique from other approaches to interoperability.

Orchestration

One of the main advantages of an ESB solution over a plain messaging infrastructure is the ability to perform content-based routing. Being able to determine a message destination based on its content to orchestrate business flow simplifies individual application design. With respect to intelligent routing, an ESB solution enables SOA across the enterprise and over the Internet. Otherwise, each and every application participating in a business flow has to have a built-in knowledge of the service endpoint, which results in hard-to-manage and costly integration.

Web Services Security with ESB

The wide acceptance of open-standards like HTTP, XML, SOAP, WSDL, and secure JMS yields an ideal foundation for Web services. When building a secure Web services environment, application assets can be protected using firewalls, SSL, and digital signatures. An XML digital signature is typically applied to only the sensitive portion of a SOAP message to ensure non-repudiation of the message and at the same time to reduce performance overhead. By selectively applying security techniques to a granular content, performance overhead of the application is minimized.

Using Access Control Lists, Java EE, and LDAP-compliant security features enables system administrators with a fine-grained security control across distributed Web service environments. Enhanced security offered by Sonic and Fiorano ESBs includes support for digital signatures, SSL, RSA and DSA encryption, and single sign-on capability.

Support for Standards

Standards-wise, Java and .NET interoperability is achieved by ESB solutions via Web services standards such as WSDL and SOAP. On the Java side ESBs support JMS and Java Connector Architecture (JCA) standards. As you may have already noticed, the business orchestration is one of the fundamental features of an ESB. As a part of the Java Community Process, leading industry vendors are collaborating on standardizing enterprise application integration (EAI) as part of JSR 208, Java Business Integration (JBI), [JSR208]. JBI will provide further standardization around the ESB container and will help drive the shape and definition of ESBs, much like the EJB specification drove the shape and definition of application servers.

The JBI initiative defines architecture and Java and Web services interfaces for plug-in components including document transformation and business process engines. Once JSR-208 becomes a standard, it will foster an ecosystem where integration architects will be able to pick and choose from best of breed integration enabling components that will plug together into an ESB using JBI-conformant SPIs. Examples of pluggable integration enabling components include a Business Process Execution Language (BPEL) engine, or a business rules engine.

JSR-208 will bring a standards-based technology to the industry, and it will be up to the individual ESB vendors to comply with the standards to achieve, Java, .NET, and legacy code integration. Sun Microsystems plans to implement an integration solution, known as Project Shasta, based on the Java Business Integration architecture. There's no doubt that ESB industry leaders such as Sonic Software will deliver commercial ESB solutions that adhere to upcoming JBI standards.

Limitations

Until Java Business Integration standards are adopted across the industry, ESB remains mostly a proprietary solution. Not all ESB vendors provide the independent scalability model of the ESB as outlined in this chapter, thus it is important to evaluate the ESB feature set required by an enterprise. Some integration broker vendors are adding Web services interfaces to their integration brokers and EAI broker products—and labeling it an ESB. Enhanced performance, clustering, failover, and other features are specific to the individual ESB provider and may vary drastically.

References

[ActiveXJmsClient] ActiveX JMS client API.
http://sourceforge.net/projects/active-jms

[CapeClearESB] Cape Clear Enterprise Service Bus.
www.capeclear.com

[EIP] Gregor Hohpe, Bobby Woolf. *Enterprise Integration Patterns: Designing, Building, and Deploying Messaging Solutions.* Boston: Addison-Wesley: 2004.

[EJBSpec] Enterprise JavaBeans™ 2.0 Specification.
http://java.sun.com/products/ejb/2.0.html

[ESB] Dave Chappell. *Enterprise Service Bus.* Sebastopol, CA: O'Reilly Media, 2004.
[FioranoESB] Fiorano ESB.
www.fiorano.com/products/fesb/fioranoesb.htm

[FioranoMQ-MSMQ] FioranoMQ-MSMQ Bridge.
www.fiorano.com/products/fmq/overview.htm#bridges

[FioranoMQC#RTL] FioranoMQ Native C# RTL Guide, version 8.0.
www.fiorano.com/downloads/fmq/fmqcsrtlguide.pdf

[GoF] Erich Gamma, et al. *Design Patterns*. Boston: Addison-Wesley, 2004.

[IMAP] "INTERNET MESSAGE ACCESS PROTOCOL - VERSION 4rev1. RFC 2060." The Internet Engineering Task Force. www.ietf.org December 1996. www.faqs.org/rfcs/rfc2060.html

[James] JAMES Apache Mail Server.
http://james.apache.org/

[JAXB] Java Architecture for XML Binding (JAXB) .
http://java.sun.com/xml/jaxb/

[JaxMail] Sameer Tyagi. JAX Mail - SMTP/POP bindings for JAX-RPC. November 2003.
https://jaxmail.dev.java.net/

[JaxMailRI] JAX Mail JAX-RPC Reference Implementation .
https://jaxmail.dev.java.net/jaxrpc-ri.jar

[JIntegraForDotNet] J-Integra for .NET Intrynsic Software Inc.
http://j-integra.intrinsyc.com/net/info/

[JIntegraMSMQ] Accessing Java from MSMQ .
http://j-integra.intrinsyc.com/com/doc/other_examples/Java_from_MSMQ.htm

[JMS] Java Message Service (JMS).
http://java.sun.com/products/jms/

[JNBridgePro] JNBridgePro by JNBridge LLC.
www.jnbridge.com/jnbpropg.htm

[JNDI] Java Naming and Directory Interface (JNDI).
http://java.sun.com/products/jndi/

[JSR208] JSR 208: Java Business Integration.
http://jcp.org/en/jsr/detail?id=208

[MSMQReference] Microsoft Message Queuing Reference.
http://msdn.microsoft.com/library/default.asp?url=/library/en-us/msmq/msmq_ref_functions_6751.asp

[MSMQ-MQSeries] Microsoft MSMQ-MQSeries Bridge.
www.microsoft.com/resources/documentation/host/2000/all/proddocs/en-us/appint/mqb_msmq_mqseries_bridge.mspx

[MuleESB] Mule Open Source ESB.
http://wiki.muleumo.org/display/MULEPROJ/Home

[OASIS_WSBPEL] OASIS Web Services Business Process Execution Language (WSBPEL).

www.oasis-open.org/committees/tc_home.php?wg_abbrev=wsbpel

[PawelLesnikowskiMail] Pawel Lesnikowski. POP3 library. February 16, 2005.

http://lesnikowski.fm.interia.pl/Mail/mail.html

http://lesnikowski.fm.interia.pl/Mail/Mail.zip

[POP3] J. Myers, et al. "Post Office Protocol - Version 3. RFC 1939." *The Internet Engineering Task Force*, www.ietf.org, May 1996.

www.ietf.org/rfc/rfc1939.txt

[SCMArchitecture] WS-I Supply Chain Management Sample Application Architecture.

www.ws-i.org/SampleApplications/SupplyChainManagement/2003-12/SCMArchitecture1.01.pdf

[SMTP] Jonathan B. Postel "Simple Mail Transfer Protocol." RFC 821.*The Internet Engineering Task Force*, www.ietf.org, August 1982.

www.ietf.org/rfc/rfc0821.txt

[SmtpWin2000] Configure SMTP Virtual Server in Win 2000.

http://support.microsoft.com/default.aspx?scid=kb;en-us;308161

[SoapMsmqWSE] Roman Kiss "SOAP over MSMQ Transport with Microsoft's WSE Custom Transporter." 2004.

www.codeproject.com/useritems/SoapMSMQ.asp

[SonicESB] Sonic ESB.

www.sonicsoftware.com/products/sonic_esb/index.ssp

[SonicMQBridgesClients] SonicMQ Bridges & Clients.

www.sonicsoftware.com/products/sonicmq/bridges_clients/index.ssp

[SonicMQComClientGuide] "SonicMQ COM Client Guide." April 2004.

www.sonicsoftware.com/products/documentation/docs/sonicmq_com_v60.pdf

[SpiritSoft] SpiritWave Message Queue to MSMQ Bridge.

www.spirit-soft.com/index.do?id=13

[SpiritWaveESB] SpiritSoft ESB.

www.spirit-soft.com/index.do?id=62

[SteveMainSoapSmtp] Steve Maine. SOAP over SMTP code sample with WSE 2.0.

http://hyperthink.net/blog/CommentView,guid,d337a6f5-a0c8-45b8-920e-132391eedc31.aspx

[SunJSMQ] Sun Java System Message Queue - Java Message Service.
www.sun.com/software/products/message_queue/index.xml

[WebSphereMQInterop] Saida Davies, et al. *WebSphere MQ Solutions in a Microsoft .NET Envirnonment*. IBM: January, 2004.
www.redbooks.ibm.com/redbooks/pdfs/sg247012.pdf

[WSE] Web Services Enhancement(WSE).
http://msdn.microsoft.com/webservices/building/wse/default.aspx

[WS-ReliableMessagingSpec] Ruslan Bilorusets, et al. "Web Services Reliable Messaging Protocol (WS-ReliableMessaging)." February 2005.
http://specs.xmlsoap.org/ws/2005/02/rm/ws-reliablemessaging.pdf

Resource Tier Asynchronous Integration

Introduction

Modern large-scale enterprise applications encompass a multitude of services that have to remain secure, highly available, and scalable to an increasing volume of Internet transactions. In a traditional common e-commerce application, a purchase order request has to be submitted across multiple systems. These can include a warehousing system that tracks goods, an order fulfillment service that manages individual orders, and a CRM system that maps orders to corresponding customer records. The list can vary depending on the business workflow and complexity of the Service Oriented Architecture (SOA). Individual transactions may take minutes, hours, or days to complete; therefore, in most cases the business workflow is executed as part of a long-running asynchronous process. In the context of Java EE and .NET, Figure 10-1 shows asynchronous interactions between components of the Business tier and the back-end resources such as CRM, HR, and other applications.

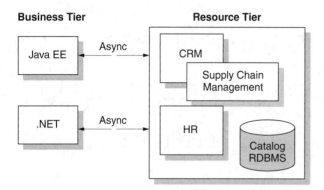

Figure 10-1
Java EE-.NET asynchronous Resource tier integration

Asynchronous integration of the Business Tier with the Resource tier enables the rest of the application logic to execute at a consistent pace. Another benefit of asynchronous integration is that long-running back-end processes do not impact the overall application performance. An ASP.NET application may submit a purchase order to an EJB that processes this request. The EJB makes an asynchronous call, such as a long running query, to the Resource tier and returns an acknowledgement back to the ASP.NET without having to wait for the query to complete. Once the query returns updated, information is rendered on the page. A long-running database transaction does not cause an end user's browser to time out.

Web tier performance is not the only advantage of asynchronous processing. A back-end system may go offline due to an internal failure or for maintenance, while incoming requests get queued for offline processing. With asynchronous communication, reliability, availability, and scalability of the Resource tier can be managed independently from the rest of the application components, which makes it easier to meet required SLAs. There are a number of techniques to manage distributed asynchronous processing. A couple of main techniques include **callback** or **notifications** and **polling**, both of which are discussed in Chapter 8, "Asynchronous Web Services Integration." Asynchronous application-to-application integration does not come without some overhead. The request initiating Business tier often has to encompass a sophisticated error-handling mechanism to ensure that the request either returns back, times out, is resubmitted, or an error is propagated up the invocation chain. Managing distributed transactions and executing compensating logic is also quite involved. Different asynchronous integration techniques are covered in Chapter 8, and there is a distributed transaction discussion in Chapter 12, "Managing Distributed Transactions." This chapter sheds some light on asynchronous integration strategies to develop a scalable SOA model. The discussion starts with asynchronous query execution under Java and .NET.

Asynchronous Query

In both Java and .NET it is possible to create asynchronous queries by creating a thread pool and using individual threads to make calls to the back-end systems. Details of the Java and .NET threading models are explained in Chapter 8, thus this discussion continues on to the asynchronous queries supported by the ADO.NET.

The ADO.NET 2.0 enables asynchronous database programming. The .NET database connection object, `SqlConnection`, takes a Boolean `async` parameter indicating the connection type. Setting this parameter to `true` indicates that the connection on which the command executes will be asynchronous, as shown here:

```
String connectionStr=
  "server=localhost;async=true;uid=sa;psw=admin;database=Warehouse_A"
```

The ADO.NET asynchronous programming model derives from the .NET asynchronous model that spans across the .NET Framework and was introduced earlier in this book. To execute an asynchronous query, the corresponding method is divided into two parts—begin and end—just like the rest of the asynchronous methods in the .NET Framework. The ADO.NET asynchronous method list is a replica of the ADO.NET methods that include ExecuteReader, ExecuteNonQuery, and ExecuteXMLReader. Asynchronous extensions of these methods are shown here:

```
IAsyncResult asyncResult = command.BeginExecuteReader();
...
SQLDataReader reader = command.EndExecuteReader(asyncResult);
```

The IAsyncResult object encapsulates all necessary components to obtain the query result. The WaitHandle property can be used to wait a certain period of time before polling for a response. When executing multiple queries, one can issue WaitHandle.WaitAll or WaitHandle.WaitAny commands to wait until all or any queries complete. IasyncResult also has the IsCompleted property that is set to true once the operation finishes. Calling the end operation ahead of time turns the call into a synchronous one and blocks until the query is complete. After the query result is retrieved, it is necessary to invoke the end method to avoid leaking system resources.

For notification services, the ADO.NET 2.0 SqlNotification API, System.Data.Sql.SqlNotificationRequest, can be used to notify an application of changes [QueryNotifications].

Following are a few strategies on how to leverage asynchronous back-end integration, starting with the Indirect Data Access strategy.

Indirect Data Access Strategy

Business sensitive data often have to remain in a consistent state. This is commonly achieved by having only one enterprise system accessing a database directly to update records. Other applications are restricted from performing a direct update operation. These applications simply use an intermediate placeholder to file required data changes.

Scope

Imagine a scenario where a Java EE e-commerce engine acts as the primary owner of the enterprise data that includes customer and product related information. The e-commerce engine executes the majority of the CRUD operations using optimistic or pessimistic locking, depending on the operation. Additionally, a .NET content management system has to occasionally modify the product-related information such as catalog items or promotional prices with the least disruption to the e-commerce engine. The content management application also has to be notified when the inventory falls low on certain promotional items.

Solution

The Indirect Data Access strategy defines a mechanism to exchange information with the Resource tier without directly connecting to the back-end system—and therefore without impacting the underlying data integrity. There are a couple design techniques you can use to implement this strategy. One way to implement the Indirect Data Access strategy is by using an intermediate file; another way is by creating an intermediate database table. With an intermediate file approach, a .NET content management system can store updates into a file rather than directly modifying the database. A Java EE application, which acts as the primary owner of the data, is authorized to directly access the data source to perform necessary updates. Figure 10-2 depicts an import file that stores changes required by the .NET application. The Java EE application would have a cron job to process the content of the import file.

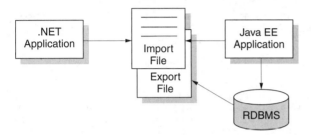

Figure 10-2
Indirect data access

Aside from submitting updates to the database, the .NET content management system may have to receive notifications from the database. A product catalog may have to be updated if certain items don't sell as expected. Figure 10-2 also shows a possible notification technique that uses an export file. The database writes notifications to the export file. The .NET content management system can then poll this file to process incoming notifications or set a file system watcher to detect changes in the file. Commercial database management systems, including Oracle and Microsoft SQL Server, as well as various legacy applications, offer notification services. These services can be used instead of a custom solution. The SQL Server Notification Service [SQLServer_Notification] is designed to dispatch notification events to registered applications. Most of the commercial database and legacy applications are also capable of sending notifications via the SMTP protocol, which eliminates the need for the Export File. In the case of SQL Server HTTP-based notifications are included, so there can be a more direct and immediate methodology. This can be overridden to produce an HTTP POST or a Web service call with the notification, see [SQLServer NotificationFormatting].

Benefits and Limitations

Using an intermediate file/table for asynchronous query processing is a fairly simple solution, straightforward to implement, and is commonly used across the industry. In cases where there is an application that needs to make changes to the database and these changes are not time critical, this strategy fits very well. This strategy, however, will not scale if there are multiple distributed systems that require CRUD queries to be submitted asynchronously as part of a long-running business transaction. Maintaining and updating multiple cron jobs that process intermediate files/tables would be quite involved and time-consuming. Additionally, addressing security and transactional constraints across a multitude of systems can quickly become error prone and a difficult task to maintain.

Related Patterns

There are a number of patterns that can be applied to this strategy. Martin Fowler's File Transfer and Message Broker patterns, [EIP], are among a few relevant ones.

Example

For details on how to integrate Java applications with the SQL Server Notification Server, please refer to [Java_SQLNotifications].

Distributed Mediator Strategy

A more scalable approach to automating business processes compared to the Indirect Database Access strategy is to create a service that processes incoming and outgoing database requests through messaging middleware.

Scope

The complexity of the enterprise landscape requires a high degree of scalability, availability, and reliability. A .NET e-commerce engine may have to submit a purchase order for asynchronous and reliable database processing. A Java EE content management system may need to submit the product catalog changes to the database in an asynchronous manner and register with the database to receive certain event notifications.

Solution

The Distributed Mediator would ensure reliable coordination across distributed applications. Java EE and .NET applications can submit their requests to the Mediator that guarantees messages are delivered only once and arrive in order. This is achieved by using a message queue. The Mediator service incorporates logic to process the queue and ensure data integrity. A traditional business transaction is comprised of multiple operations. If one operation succeeds while another fails, the entire transaction has to roll back. Managing distributed transactions across asynchronous operations is the key functionality of the Distributed Mediator. Its job is to commit any changes upon successful execution or to issue a compensating transaction in case one of the operations fails. The Distributed Mediator service also addresses security constraints that are important to the enterprise by authorizing queue requests prior to their execution.

In the Microsoft world, the idea of a service that extends database functionality with support for long-running business processes and required systemic qualities is referred to as the Service Oriented Database Architecture (SODA), [SODA]. In a nutshell, SODA expands the concept of SOA to encompass the database interactions. A few commercial database management systems, such as SQL Server and Oracle, are extended with a message queue and the corresponding queue processing functionality. Oracle 9i Advanced Queuing, [OracleAQ], is an example of such a solution. Enterprise applications can produce (enqueue) or consume (dequeue) messages via the Oracle AQ component. Applications can communicate with AQ over JMS, HTTP, or e-mail. In addition to asynchronous reliable request processing, applications can register with AQ to receive event notifications. This can be achieved using OCI, PL/SQL, or IDAP APIs. Notifications can be optionally posted in the XML format in the form of an OCI callback, a PL/SQL procedure, an e-mail, or an HTTP post. To integrate with mainframe applications, AQ can propagate messages to the IBM MQ Series. AQ also supports integration with Tibco Rendezvous. Microsoft SQL Server 2005 offers a Service Broker component that processes incoming and outgoing database requests by using a message queue. Asynchronous guaranteed messages can be sent to the Service Broker queue by using extensions to Transact-SQL DML. Service Broker locking mechanisms ensure that individual messages related to the same task are processed only once. This feature allows other instances of the Service Broker to continue processing the remaining messages in the queue. Microsoft Service Broker supports XML-based storing and queue, important to implementing SOA. See [Intro_SQLServer2005_ServiceBroker] for more details. Figure 10-3 depicts this configuration where a Java EE or .NET application communicates with the Distributed Mediator component to asynchronously execute traditional CRUD operations.

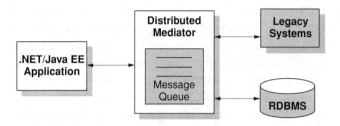

Figure 10-3
Distributed Mediator strategy

Coordinating communication between two applications and a database is not trivial but is a manageable task. Incorporating a multitude of applications into a single business process becomes quite complicated. For elaborate business processes it may be necessary to separate the workflow engine to coordinate business transactions across a distributed application environment. Commercial workflow engines can be of great value, as they feature secure reliable integration points across disparate applications, BizTalk, SeeBeyond, and other commercial integration solutions, already mentioned in Chapter 6, "Resource Tier Synchronous Integration."

Benefits and Limitations

The main advantage of these strategies is that Java EE, .NET, and other enterprise applications can remain loosely coupled and safely share Resource tier components in an asynchronous manner. Of course, managing transactions and security context across multiple back-end applications could propose a challenge. A transaction that is part of the asynchronous workflow may result in an inconsistent data state. Therefore, with asynchronous processing it is always important to define a compensating transaction to roll back data into its original state. From an availability and reliability standpoint, the intermediate data queue should always be available. If an intermediate file or table is not accessible, this may become a bottleneck. If a message queue is used to store queries, the queue may become a single point of failure. Therefore, it is critical to determine a fail over strategy.

Related Patterns

The Gof [GoF] Mediator pattern is derived from the Distributed Mediator strategy. The purpose of the Distributed Mediator is to promote loose cou pling between an enterprise application and the back-end system such as a database. It encapsulates details of asynchronous, reliable, secure processing.

Example

Previous chapters have discussed Java and .NET technologies corresponding to the database and message queue's interaction. These APIs include JDBC and JMS as well as .NET ADO.NET and MSMQ programming APIs. If Oracle or MS SQL Server 2005 are used, the Distributed Mediator functionality is provided out of the box. To manually implement the Distributed Mediator with a database management system like MySQL, the design outlined in Figure 10-4 should be considered:

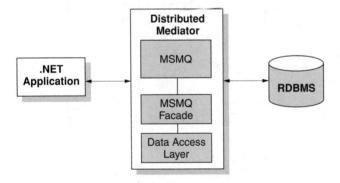

Figure 10-4
Java EE-based Distributed Mediator service

The Java EE Distributed Mediator includes an EJB 2.0-compliant Message Driven Bean (MDB) that processes the message queue. The MDB would dispatch corresponding CRUD operations to the Data Access Object (DAO) that directly talks to the underlying database. The Distributed Mediator can be also used to pass the event notifications back to the Java EE applications. To see some sample code on how to develop asynchronous queries in Java EE by using a JMS provider, please refer to [AsyncQueriesJ2EE].

A similar design would take place on the .NET side, an example of which is detailed in Figure 10-5:

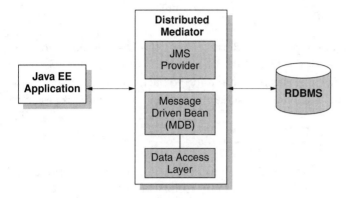

Figure 10-5
.NET-based Distributed Mediator service

In the figure, the MSMQ Façade component is responsible for the message queue processing. The Façade connects to the Data Access Layer that encapsulates a service to execute CRUD operations against the database.

Data Access Proxy Strategy

A simple alternative to the Indirect Data Access strategy entails the use of a shared Data Access Layer, discussed through the rest of the chapter.

Scope

This strategy attempts to solve the same problem as the previous strategy, Distributed Mediator. Multiple applications share a database, while only one of them has primary ownership over the data. The secondary application receives only intermittent access to submit changes.

Solution

The Data Access Proxy component asynchronously invokes a remote DAO to perform underlying CRUD operations. An application can continue its execution without waiting for the underlying database operation to complete. For the Proxy object and the remote DAO component to stay loosely coupled, it is valuable to introduce a Command pattern that the DAO implements. The Command pattern helps to expose a coarse-grained DAO API to the Proxy object and provides a consistent integration point. Figure 10-6 depicts the Data Access Proxy strategy, which can be easily applied to either Java or .NET components.

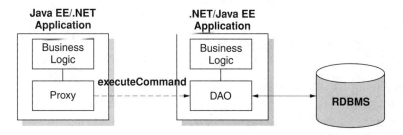

Figure 10-6
Data Access Proxy strategy

The Command object can be passed, encapsulating necessary operations, and return back success, failure, or a result set. For the integration technology, the developer can select the most suitable one for the overall architecture of the distributed environment. Technologies such as .NET Remoting or Web services are among a few to choose from, and this pattern can be used for both synchronous and asynchronous communication. In other words, this pattern needs to be layered on top of a previous Java EE-.NET integration pattern. Is there any reason this is an asynchronous pattern?

Benefits and Limitations

The simplicity of this design is one of its advantages. If Web services or a custom Bridging solution is already being used, implementing the Data Access Proxy strategy should be fairly straightforward. This strategy allows Java and .NET applications to remain loosely coupled as the Proxy component asynchronously connects to the remote Data Access Layer. The limitation of this strategy is that a custom notification or a callback mechanism must be built. For that, it might be beneficial to assign a unique identifier to the command submitted to DAO. This design also involves custom time out and an error handling mechanism. The Data Access Layer design has to be scalable to start with to accommodate requests external to its application. One way to manage the scalability aspect of this design is by creating a separate database connection pool that is dedicated to the external requests. A long-running query submitted by the Proxy component won't affect the internal application's access to the database, as the underlying connections are not shared.

Related Patterns

Data Access Object, [CJ2EEP], and a couple of GoF patterns such as Proxy and Command are used by this strategy.

Example

This example implements the Java Data Access Proxy strategy. A .NET application accesses the Java `DAOFacadeService` Web service that creates a separate thread to asynchronously process the request. This thread checks on the type of command submitted, and given that in this case the command corresponds to inserted Shipment order, the thread executes the following tasks:

- Processes the incoming XML request that contains Shipment order information

- Processes the Shipment order to generate SQL queries

- Updates the database with the corresponding Shipment statement

- Sends `ShippingNotice` back to the .NET application

For the first two tasks the thread invokes the `ShipmentHandler` method, whose responsibility is to unmarshal the XML Shipment order into a Shipment object. `ShipmentHandler` also knows how to parse the Shipment object into the SQL statements. For the third task, the worker thread invokes the DAO object to connect to either MySQL or an SQL Server database and execute the SQL query. Figure 10-7 shows the UML sequence diagram of the `ShipGoods` use case.

For scalability reasons, it is best to delegate the actual command processing to a separate thread, `DAOExecutor`, that invokes DAO component. With this design a .NET client application does not have to wait until a connection to a database gets obtained or until a lengthy query gets executed. The .NET client application receives notification after the asynchronous processing is complete.

To run this example, it is necessary to place corresponding MySQL and SQL Server JDBC libraries under Tomcat's common/lib directory such as C:\tomcat50-jwsdp\common\lib. In addition, the `autodeploy` property of the Tomcat server.xml file, located under tomcat50-jwsdp/conf directory, has to be set to false: `autoDeploy="false"`. The JNDI Context.xml is defined and included as part of the final WAR file. Check the Context.xml file, located under chapter10/etc/server directory to ensure that Resource parameters including JDBC package name, document root, and context path correspond to your configuration.

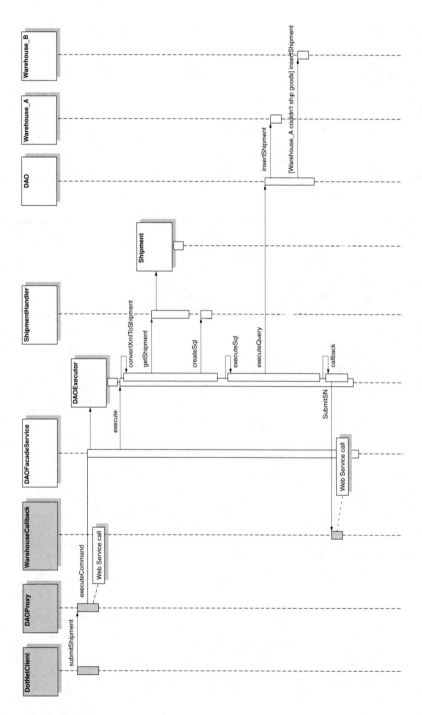

Figure 10-7
Data Access Proxy strategy, *ShipGoods* sequence diagram

The Ship Goods scenario is implemented using a top-down approach, starting with a common XSD schema.

The application is composed out of four distinct steps outlined as follows:

Step 1: Defining XSD Shipment

The top-down Web services design allows both Java and .NET applications to adhere to the same XML schema. Listing 10-1 lists the Shipment schema, from the Shipment.xsd file:

Listing 10-1
The XSD Shipment Schema

```xml
<?xml version="1.0" encoding="UTF-8"?>
<xsd:schema xmlns:xsd="http://www.w3.org/2001/XMLSchema">

<xsd:element name="Shipment">
  <xsd:complexType>
    <xsd:sequence>
      <xsd:element name="id" type="xsd:string" minOccurs="1"
          maxOccurs="1"/>
      <xsd:element name="contact" type="xsd:string"/>
      <xsd:element name="address" type="Address" minOccurs="1" />
      <xsd:element name="items" type="Item" minOccurs="1"
          maxOccurs="100"/>
    </xsd:sequence>
  </xsd:complexType>
</xsd:element>

<xsd:complexType name="Address">
  <xsd:sequence>
    <xsd:element name="name" type="xsd:string"/>
    <xsd:element name="street" type="xsd:string"/>
    <xsd:element name="city" type="xsd:string"/>
    <xsd:element name="state" type="xsd:string"/>
    <xsd:element name="zip" type="xsd:string"/>
    <xsd:element name="country" type="xsd:string"/>
  </xsd:sequence>
</xsd:complexType>
```

```
<xsd:complexType name="Item">
  <xsd:sequence>
    <xsd:element name="id" type="xsd:string" />
    <xsd:element name="name" type="xsd:string"/>
    <xsd:element name="quantity" type="xsd:int"/>
  </xsd:sequence>
</xsd:complexType>

</xsd:schema>
```

Step 2: Building .NET Callback Application

Listing 10-2 is the sample code for the .NET WarehouseCallback.asmx:

Listing 10-2
.NET *WarehouseCallback* Web Service

```
namespace Java EEDotNet.Chapter10.Retailer {

public class WarehouseCallback : System.Web.Services.WebService {

[WebMethod(Description = "WarehouseCallback WebService")]
     public string SubmitSN(String sn) {
         string ack="ShippingNotice sh_id:" +sn+" is Received";
         return ack;
     }
  }
}
```

Because this callback service is not invoked at the end of the processing loop, for testing purposes it is worth creating a standalone Java client to ensure that the service is deployed correctly.

Step 3: Implementing Java *DAOFacade* Application

The core business logic resides in the DAOFacade application. The DAOFacadeService Web service is the frontier to the service request processing. The Web service implementation class, DAOFacadeServiceImpl, delegates the actual request processing to a separate thread, DAOExecutor thread. The service returns the status that the Shipment order has been received and sent for further processing. Listing 10-3 shows the `executeCommand()` method:

Listing 10-3
Java *DAOFacadeService* Web Service

```java
public String executeCommand(int id, int queryType,
    String valueObjectStr) throws RemoteException
{
  String status ="Received command";
  try{
    ThreadPerTaskExecutor executor = new ThreadPerTaskExecutor();
    DAOExecutor executeCommand =
      new DAOExecutor(id, queryType, valueObjectStr);
    executor.execute(executeCommand);
    status = "Request has been submitted for processing";
  }catch(Exception e){
  }
  return status;
}
```

The `ThreadPerTaskExecutor` class is located in the `DAOExecutor.java` file. The `ThreadPerTaskExecutor` class simply extends the `java.util.concurrent.Executor`, as shown in Listing 10-4:

Listing 10-4
Java *ThreadPerTaskExecutor* Class

```java
class ThreadPerTaskExecutor implements Executor {
    public void execute(Runnable r) {
        new Thread(r).start();
    }
}
```

The `DAOExecutor` is responsible for processing the actual command. Listing 10-5 lists its `run()` method that is invoked when the thread starts.

Listing 10-5
Java *DAOExecutor run( )* Method

```
public void run(){
  // Processing received XML file to create SQL queries
  String[] queries = convertXmlToSql(id, queryType, valueObject);

  // Executing SQL queries
  executeSql(queries);

  // Submitting Shipment Notifications
  String sn = "Shipment Order is Submitted Succesfully";
  submitShipmentNotification(sn);
}
```

As is shown, there are two methods that need to be explored: convertXmlToSql() and executeSql(). The first method is responsible for checking on the type of query and because in our case the query corresponds to Shipment order, it creates the ShipmentHandler object to convert XML into the Shipment value object and then generate corresponding SLQ statements based on the content of the Shipment order. The convertXmlToSql is shown in Listing 10-6:

Listing 10-6
Java *DAOExecutor convertXmlToSql( )* Method

```
private String[] convertXmlToSql(int id, int queryType,
      String valueObject){
  String[] sqlStmt=null;

  // If query type == 1, the query corresponds to insert shipment
  if (queryType==1) {
     ShipmentHandler handler = new ShipmentHandler();

     // Creating queries based on the received command
     Shipment shipment = handler.getShipment(valueObject);
     sqlStmt = handler.createSQL(shipment);

  } else {
    // Process other type of queries...
```

continues

Listing 10-6 (continued)

```
  }
  return sqlStmt;
}
```

The `ShipmentHandler` object creates the Shipment object. The Shipment class is auto-generated from the original Shipment XSD.

Before delving into the `ShipmentHandler` implementation, here is a brief look at the `executeSql()` method invoked by `DAOExecutor`. All it does is access the Data Access Object component and iterate over the list of SQL statements to execute them. This is shown in Listing 10-7:

Listing 10-7
Java *DAOExecutor executeSql( )* Method

```
private void executeSql(String[] queries){
  DAO dao = new DAO();

  for (int i=0; i<queries.length;i++)
    dao.executeQuery(queries[i]);
}
```

In putting this all together, the `DAOFacadeService` Web service implementation class, `DAOFacadeServiceImpl`, invokes the `DAOExecutor` to actually process the incoming command. Listing 10-8 includes a complete listing of `DAOExecutor.java`:

Listing 10-8
Java *DAOExecutor.java*

```
package Java EEdotnet.chapter10.retailer;

import shipment.Shipment;
import javax.naming.Context;
import javax.naming.InitialContext;
import javax.sql.DataSource;
import java.util.concurrent.Executor;
import java.io.FileOutputStream;
import java.sql.Connection;
public class DAOExecutor implements Runnable {
  DAO dao;
```

```
int id;
String valueObject;
int queryType;

public DAOExecutor(int id, int queryType, String valueObject) {
  this.id = id;
  this.queryType = queryType;
  this.valueObject = valueObject;
}

public void run(){
  // Processing received XML file to create SQL queries
  String[] queries = convertXmlToSql(id, queryType, valueObject);

  // Executing SQL queries
  executeSql(queries);

  // Submitting Shipment Notifications
  String sn = "Shipment Order is Submitted Succesfully";
  submitShipmentNotification(sn);
}

/*
 * Convert XML object into the corresponding SQL queries
 * based on the query type.
 */
private String[] convertXmlToSql(int id, int queryType,
   String valueObject)
{
  String[] sqlStmt=null;

  // If query type == 1, the query corresponds to insert shipment
  if (queryType==1) {
    ShipmentHandler handler = new ShipmentHandler();

    // Creating queries based on the received command
    Shipment shipment = handler.getShipment(valueObject);
    sqlStmt = handler.createSQL(shipment);

  } else {
    // Process other type of queries...
```

continues

Listing 10-8 (continued)

```
    }
    return sqlStmt;
  }

  private void executeSql(String[] queries){
    DAO dao = new DAO();

    for (int i=0; i<queries.length;i++)
      dao.executeQuery(queries[i]);
  }
}


// Defining a Thread per task executor
class ThreadPerTaskExecutor implements Executor {
    public void execute(Runnable r) {
        new Thread(r).start();
    }
}
```

There are two main references within the `DAOExecutor` class, the `ShipmentHandler` and the `DAO` class. We'll start with the `ShipmentHandler` class that takes a Shipment XML request file and using JAXB APIs, unmarshals that file into the Shipment object. This is shown in Listing 10-9:

Listing 10-9
Java ShipmentHandler getShipment() method

```
public Shipment getShipment(String xmlShipment){
  try {
    JAXBContext jc = JAXBContext.newInstance("shipment");
    Unmarshaller u = jc.createUnmarshaller();
    sh = (Shipment)u.unmarshal(
        new StreamSource(new StringReader(xmlShipment)));
  } catch (Exception exe ) {
    // Log exception...
    // StackTraceElement[] exeElem= exe.getStackTrace();
  }
  return sh;
}
```

After the object has been restored from the XML file, it is time to parse it to create SQL statements, defined in the `createSQL()` method of `ShipmentHandler`. This method is given in Listing 10-10:

Listing 10-10
Java *ShipmentHandler createSQL()* method

```java
public String[] createSQL(Shipment sh){
  String [] queries = null;
  Item item = null;
  String id = null;
  String name = null;
  int qty = -1;

  List items = sh.getItems();
  int size = items.size();
  queries = new String[size];

  for (int i=0; i<size; i++ ) {
    item = (Item)items.get(i);
    id = item.getId();
    name = item.getName();
    qty = item.getQuantity();
    queries[i] =
      "insert into ship_goods values ('"+id+"','"+name+"',"+qty+")";
}
```

The `createSQL()` method retrieves items and creates insert SQL statements with the corresponding values. Similarly, SQL statements can be extended with Address and Contact information encapsulated within the Shipment object. This is it for the `ShipmentHandler` class.

After the Shipment has been processed, the next step is to execute SQL statements. The DAO object is responsible for establishing the actual database connection. In this example, the JNDI Context is used to lookup the `DataSource` and with the help of the `DataSource` create the database connection. Listing 10-11 shows the core logic of the DAO `connect()` method:

Listing 10-11
Creating JNDI Context, Performing a *DataSource* Lookup, and Creating Connection

```
Context initCxt = new InitialContext();
Context envCxt = (Context)initCxt.lookup("java:comp/env");
//Looking up DataSource for WarehouseA, MySql
DataSource dataSource = (DataSource)envCxt.lookup("jdbc/WarehouseA");
// Establishing connection to the database
con = dataSource.getConnection();
```

Once the database connection is established, the update query can be executed:

```
stmt.executeUpdate(query);
```

It is now possible to check with the database that the Shipment order submitted by the .NET application has been correctly processed. In this case, the .NET client application sends two order items that are reflected in the database, as demonstrated in Listing 10-12:

Listing 10-12
Checking Database Records

```
mysql> select * from ship_goods;
+-------------+-----------------+------+
| id          | descr           | qty  |
+-------------+-----------------+------+
| 223         | Sun Fire X4200  |   1  |
| 762         | Sun Fire X4100  |   1  |
+-------------+-----------------+------+
2 rows in set (0.03 sec)
```

Step 4: Building the .NET Client Application

The schema is transformed into the corresponding C# class. Listing 10-13 provides the ant target, "createC#ClassesFromSchema", that generates the corresponding classes by using the xsd.exe .NET tool.

Listing 10-13
Creating C# Classes From XSD Schema

```
<target name="createC#ClassesFromSchema" depends="prepare">
    <echo message="--- creating C# classes of given schema---"/>
    <exec executable="xsd.exe">
    <arg value="${etc.schema}/Shipment.xsd"/>
    <arg value="/classes"/>
    <arg value="/namespace:Java EEDotNet.Chapter10.Retailer"/>
    <arg value="/out:${build.src}"/>
    </exec>
</target>
```

The auto-generated Shipment class, shown in Listing 10-14, is composed of identifier, content, address, and item array:

Listing 10-14
Auto-generated C# Shipment class

```
//
// This source code was auto-generated by xsd, Version=1.1.4322.2032.
//
namespace Java EEDotNet.Chapter10.Retailer {
    using System.Xml.Serialization;
    /// <remarks/>
    [System.Xml.Serialization.XmlRootAttribute(Namespace="",
     IsNullable=false)]
    public class Shipment {

        /// <remarks/>
        [System.Xml.Serialization.XmlElementAttribute
        (Form=System.Xml.Schema.XmlSchemaForm.Unqualified)]
        public string id;

        /// <remarks/>
```

continues

Listing 10-14 (continued)

```
        [System.Xml.Serialization.XmlElementAttribute
        (Form=System.Xml.Schema.XmlSchemaForm.Unqualified)]
        public string contact;

        /// <remarks/>
        [System.Xml.Serialization.XmlElementAttribute
        (Form=System.Xml.Schema.XmlSchemaForm.Unqualified)]
        public Address address;

        /// <remarks/>
        [System.Xml.Serialization.XmlElementAttribute("items",
Form=System.Xml.Schema.XmlSchemaForm.Unqualified)]
        public Item[] items;
    }

    /// <remarks/>
    public class Address {

        /// <remarks/>
        [System.Xml.Serialization.XmlElementAttribute
        (Form=System.Xml.Schema.XmlSchemaForm.Unqualified)]
        public string name;

        /// <remarks/>
        [System.Xml.Serialization.XmlElementAttribute
        (Form=System.Xml.Schema.XmlSchemaForm.Unqualified)]
        public string street;

        /// <remarks/>
        [System.Xml.Serialization.XmlElementAttribute
        (Form=System.Xml.Schema.XmlSchemaForm.Unqualified)]
        public string city;

        /// <remarks/>
        [System.Xml.Serialization.XmlElementAttribute
        (Form=System.Xml.Schema.XmlSchemaForm.Unqualified)]
        public string state;

        /// <remarks/>
```

```
    [System.Xml.Serialization.XmlElementAttribute
    (Form=System.Xml.Schema.XmlSchemaForm.Unqualified)]
    public string zip;

    /// <remarks/>
    [System.Xml.Serialization.XmlElementAttribute
    (Form=System.Xml.Schema.XmlSchemaForm.Unqualified)]
    public string country;
}

/// <remarks/>
public class Item {

    /// <remarks/>
    [System.Xml.Serialization.XmlElementAttribute
    (Form=System.Xml.Schema.XmlSchemaForm.Unqualified)]
    public string id;

    /// <remarks/>
    [System.Xml.Serialization.XmlElementAttribute
    (Form=System.Xml.Schema.XmlSchemaForm.Unqualified)]
    public string name;

    /// <remarks/>
    [System.Xml.Serialization.XmlElementAttribute
    (Form=System.Xml.Schema.XmlSchemaForm.Unqualified)]
    public int quantity;

    }
}
```

The DotNetClient populates the Shipment object and passes it to the .NET DAOProxy. The proxy invokes the Web service executeCommand() method and sends the XML Shipment order as a parameter to the Web service. Listing 10-15 shows the submitShipment() method of the DAOProxy class:

Listing 10-15
C# DAOProxy Class Populating Shipment and Invoking the *DAOFacadeService* Endpoint

```csharp
public string submitShipment (Shipment sh) {
    XmlSerializer serializer = new XmlSerializer(typeof(Shipment));
    StringWriter writer = new StringWriter();
    serializer.Serialize(writer,sh);
    string shXML = writer.ToString();
    Console.WriteLine("Shipment XML: " + shXML);

    // Assuming 1 indicates submit shipment
    int queryType = 1;
    int queryId = 99;
    DAOFacadeService srv = new DAOFacadeService();
    string result = srv.executeCommand(queryId, queryType, shXML);

    return result;
}
```

After the Java Web service is deployed, you can consume it with a .NET
client application.

Listing 10-16 details the output of the .NET client application execution
that includes the XML Shipment file:

Listing 10-16
Result of Executing .NET Client Application

```
app/build/bin>DotNetClient
DotNetClient.Main(): populating Shipment...
Shipment XML: <?xml version="1.0" encoding="utf-16"?>
<Shipment xmlns:xsd="http://www.w3.org/2001/XMLSchema"
xmlns:xsi="http://www.w3.org/2001/XMLSchema-instance">
  <id>932850</id>
  <contact>joe.miller@abc123.com</contact>
  <address>
    <name>Joe Miller</name>
    <street>134 N 1st Street</street>
    <city>San Jose</city>
    <state>CA</state>
    <zip>95111</zip>
```

```
  <country>US</country>
 </address>
 <items>
   <id>223</id>
   <name>Sun Fire X4200</name>
   <quantity>1</quantity>
 </items>
 <items>
   <id>762</id>
   <name>Sun Fire X4100</name>
   <quantity>1</quantity>
 </items>
</Shipment>
Result of executing the Web Service: Request has been submitted for
processing
```

It is also important to check the log file, generated as the result of the callback operation, to ensure that the ShippingNotice acknowledgement successfully arrived. As can be seen in these examples, the client application is quite simple, and most of the business logic resides in Java.

What this example has demonstrated is a simple mechanism to perform asynchronous processing of the database request. Integrating databases with business logic and the Web service may be quite involved; therefore, it is quite helpful to do unit testing to ensure that individual operations are performed correctly. Additionally for ease of troubleshooting, it is important to enable logging at the Web service hosting server, application level, and database.

In addition, building the .NET Data Access Adapter is simpler than doing so in Java, given that one can directly leverage the .NET asynchronous programming model with begin/end method calls. Refer to the Web services and asynchronous programming model under the .NET platform in previous chapters as well as the online examples and walkthroughs that come with Visual Studio.NET for examples on how to do this.

Summary

This chapter introduced methodologies to assure interoperability at a layer that is sometimes forgotten about when it comes to discussions on interoperating applications: the Resource tier. In many cases tiers have connectivity to both Java EE and .NET technologies and are designed to be interoperable across both. For example, database servers typically have ADO.NET and JDBC drivers for them, and as such can be used transparently by applications written for either platform. This chapter introduced strategies and methods through which the Resource tier can be used to provide an interoperability layer within applications. An example demonstrated an end-to-end system that allowed for synchronous integration via database calls as well as asynchronous integration through methodologies such as SQL Notifications within SQL Server—and how these may be used within Java.

References

[AsyncQueriesJ2EE] Kyle Brown. Asynchronous queries in J2EE. March 2004. IBM.

www.javaranch.com/newsletter/200403/AsynchronousProcessingFromServlets. html

[CJ2EEP]D. Alur, et al. *Core J2EE Patterns: Best Practices and Design Strategies*, first edition. Boston: Prentice Hall, 2002.

[EIP]Gregor Hohpe, Bobby Wolfe. *Enterprise Integration Patterns: Designing, Building, and Deploying Messaging Solutions*, Boston: Addison-Wesley, 2004.

[GoF]Erich Gamma, et al. *Design Patterns*, Boston: Addison-Wesley, 1995.

[Intro_SQLServer2005_ServiceBroker] Roger Wolter. An Introduction to SQL Server Service Broker. February 2005.

http://msdn.microsoft.com/library/default.asp?url=/library/ens/dnsql90/html/ sqlsvcbroker.asp

[Java_SQLNotifications] Laurence Moroney. Letting Java in on SQL Server Notifications. May 19, 2005.

www.devx.com/Java/Article/28139/0

[OracleAQ] Oracle Advanced Queuing. 2005. Oracle.

www.oracle.com/technology/products/aq/htdocs/9iaq_ds.html

[QueryNotifications] Bob Beauchemin. Query Notifications in ADO.NET 2.0. DevelopMentor. Microsoft Corporation, April 2005.
http://msdn.microsoft.com/data/dataaccess/whidbey/default.aspx?pull=/library/en-us/dnvs05/html/querynotification.asp

[SODA] David Campbell. Service Oriented Database Architecture: APP server-lite? Microsoft Corporation, June 2005.
http://portal.acm.org/citation.cfm?id=1066157.1066267

[SQLServer_Notification] Microsoft SQL Server Notification Services.
www.microsoft.com/sql/ns/default.mspx

[SQLServerNotificationFormatting] Notification Formatting and Delivery Architecture. © 2005 Microsoft Corporation.
http://msdn.microsoft.com/library/default.asp?url=/library/enus/sqlntsv/htm/ns_overarch_4ou1.asp

Addressing Quality of Service Requirements

353

Addressing Quality of Services

11

Quality of Services—Core Issues

This short introductory chapter discusses the core issues associated with building quality Java EE .NET interoperable applications, and identifies the relevant standards and technologies that address these issues.

Quality of Services is extremely important in managing successful business operations. Availability, scalability, and security are service-level characteristics that determine Quality of Service requirements. These characteristics are highly desirable for business services such as video on-demand or music downloading, which require resources and capacity to be dynamically allocated based on user request. With Quality of Services, businesses can provide **differential** business services and capacity on-demand. This is also one of the key objectives in Utility Computing.

The term "Quality of Services" (QoS) has been widely used in the telecommunications and data center communities to refer to treating different network packets or infrastructure services differently—and not with the same best-effort service. Applying the QoS concept to software engineering, QoS usually refers to the *systemic quality of reliability, availability, scalability, manageability and security for developing and deploying business applications and services*. It is important to design and deploy Java EE and .NET business applications with this systemic quality, particularly Java EE .NET interoperable solutions. Managing the QoS for network services and infrastructure is very different from managing the QoS for Java EE .NET interoperable software applications.

To illustrate the difference, architects and developers might find some common issues in managing service-level objectives for their Java EE .NET interoperable applications:

- Individual Java EE or .NET applications seem to be reliable and scalable. Once they exchange service requests and business data, the performance degrades. It is difficult to easily tell whether the Java EE or .NET applications have any QoS issues.

- You cannot manage QoS of the other parties outside your domain if the QoS problem lies at the other end.

- The QoS design strategy that works for the Java platform does not necessarily apply in .NET, and vice versa.

- There is no standard mechanism to measure and manage QoS.

In a telecommunications context, managing QoS is specific to the network layer and does not need to take into consideration individual business applications (components or factors) within the application layer. Besides, managing QoS does not need to regard the dependencies (for example, a Java EE application function aggregates business data from another Java EE application and a .NET business component) or the integration points (such as the interoperability bridge) inside the application layer. Handling different business applications or components on heterogeneous platforms (particularly when they have dependencies) is rather complex.

This short introductory chapter defines four key attributes of achieving QoS in Java EE .NET interoperable applications—reliability, availability, scalability and performance (RAS) and manageability. These Quality of Services issues are common to both Java EE and .NET applications, as well as to Java EE .NET interoperable solutions. The chapter also introduces some metrics and technology that can help in implementing the Quality of Services attributes. Chapter 14, "Java EE .NET Reliability, Availability, and Scalability," discusses some design strategies for addressing the RAS requirements. Chapter

13, "Java EE .NET Security Interoperability" discusses the details of security requirements and design strategies, and Chapter 15, "Managing Java EE .NET Interoperability Applications," discusses the manageability aspect in detail.

Myths and Truths about Quality of Services

Here are some myths and truths about the QoS:

- *Myth 1*

  Both Java EE and .NET platforms themselves take care of the Quality of Services (QoS). There is no need for developers and architects to worry about the QoS.

  Truth

  Both platforms provide essential elements for QoS and require experienced design and implementation to enable business applications and services to be reliable, highly available, and scalable. Please refer to Chapter 14 for details.

- *Myth 2*

  QoS is a systemic quality for deploying Java EE and .NET applications in the data center. As long as there is reliable, highly available, and scalable infrastructure, developers and architects should be able to scale up (or scale down) the Java EE .NET applications reasonably without major service management issues.

  Truth

  Hardware and system infrastructure in the data center is certainly important to support QoS. It can provide basic availability. However, though machines are clustered for high availability, the infrastructure does not provide application-level session failover. There is also a limitation to scale up a business application simply by increasing resources. For example, adding another two CPUs and 2GB of physical memory do not necessarily double the system response time for a business application running on a 2-CPU machine with 2GB of memory. This is particularly critical for Java EE .NET interoperability because they are running on different infrastructures (hardware and operating systems) and do not share the same QoS capabilities. These applications need to be designed to support better reliability, availability, and scalability.

- *Myth 3*

  Good performance for Java EE .NET interoperability generally refers to high throughput and lower latency. With the availability of high performance and relatively low cost hardware infrastructure, developers do not need to worry about application design for performance.

  Truth

  Low-cost hardware can certainly boost up the performance throughput of Java EE .NET interoperable applications to a certain extent. Good performance for Java EE .NET interoperable applications is heavily dependent on design (for example, XML payload and parsing design) and interoperability strategy (for example, use of .NET Remoting versus asynchronous messaging using Web services). This may vary for different business requirement scenarios.

Understanding the QoS Requirements

Here are some main Quality of Services requirements that are specific to Java EE .NET interoperable applications. It is crucial that architects and developers incorporate these requirements in their interoperability designs or add to their evaluation criteria for their Java EE .NET interoperability products. Security is another important attribute of the Quality of Services requirements. Please refer to Chapter 13 for more details.

Reliability

Reliability for Java EE .NET interoperable applications requires service requests or business data from a sender (say, a service requester) to be transmitted to the target recipient (say, a service provider) successfully and accurately. The target recipient should be able to acknowledge receipt if necessary. The business data needs to be accurate and without errors. Successful transmission can be achieved by resending the service requests and business data until there is a receipt acknowledgement from the recipient or by persisting them in a reliable data store so that the target recipient can pick them up.

Reliability can be **producer-centric** or **consumer-centric**. In the producer-centric scenario, the sender (producer) needs to ensure that the target recipient (consumer) receives the business data. Otherwise, the sender resends the business data until the target recipient sends an acknowledgement. If the target recipient is offline or unavailable, the sender is responsible for resending the business data whenever the target recipient service becomes available. In the consumer-centric scenario, the target recipient (consumer) is responsible for retrieving the business data from the sender (producer). This requires the sender be highly available for information retrieval.

The reliability capability may vary depending on the interoperability technology used. For example, if an IIOP bridge is used, the bridge needs to ensure the connection from the Java EE or .NET application must be reliable. It should be able to persist all service requests or business data for resend and also log all activities for audit review. If a SOAP-based Web service is used, reliable messaging can be achieved by leveraging emerging technologies, such as Enterprise Service Bus, or implementation using WS-Reliability because any delivery failure will be re-sent by the messaging infrastructure.

In essence, reliability for Java EE .NET interoperable applications is expected in different layers or tiers in the application architecture, which includes the following:

- The underlying communication mechanism or data transport layer for both Java and .NET applications needs to be reliable.

- When a sender exchanges some business data with a recipient, the contents of the business data should be reliably transferred. For example, if the business data contain a data type of a large scientific quantity (for example, $23.1234567891 \times 10^{-49}$) or a complex data type (for example, a custom customer account data object), the recipient should receive them verbatim without any data type conversion or XML encoding errors between Java and .NET applications.

- There should be a receipt acknowledgement capability for the Java EE or .NET applications. One of the common design criteria is to enable the timeout on the message or acknowledgement of delivery to avoid applications waiting for an extended period of time.

- Any error or exception thrown should be reliably reflected on the other end. For example, if the recipient application throws a runtime exception (for example, the SOAPFault exception), the sender should be able to catch the exception reliably for appropriate error handling, instead of discarding or ignoring the errors.

- There should be a logging mechanism at both ends of the Java and .NET applications for audit trail and for compliance reporting purpose.

- Guaranteed delivery is not the only characteristic of reliability. Once-and-only-once (also known as idempotence) requirement may also apply to the QoS requirements, meaning that the message can only be delivered one time to its destination.

- Should a message consist of multi-parts, individual parts of the message may have to be delivered in the proper order. Alternatively, there should be aggregation logic available at the receiving end.

- Message routing across heterogeneous Java EE, .NET, and legacy applications often needs to be accompanied by the business flow orchestration. An Enterprise Service Bus solution can be deployed to address complex B2B scenarios.

- Reliable messaging, in cases such as financial data transfer, also requires a high level of security. Therefore, it is important to perform a comprehensive QoS check to ensure that your architecture adequately addresses individual QoS requirements.

Availability

Availability for Java EE .NET interoperable applications requires that the underlying application infrastructure (such as the operating system and the application server container) be online for services (that is, available) all the time. The availability of business applications or services can be measured in percentage over a period of time (for example, 99.99 percent available during 365 days of operation), or in downtime statistics (for example, 53 minutes downtime throughout the 365-day year). Business applications and services can usually achieve high availability by clustering the Java EE or .NET application server containers and enabling session failover from a failing application.

Achieving high availability for Java EE .NET interoperable applications is complex. It requires

- **Detection of Availability Status**   There is a mechanism to detect or look up whether the target recipient (Java EE or .NET application) is online or not.

- **Persistence**   The service request or business data can be persisted for resend later after the target recipient resumes operations from service failure.

- **End-to-end Availability**   For distributed Java and .NET interoperable applications, availability means both the Java and .NET applications should be online and available for service simultaneously. If either side is offline or unavailable, the other side needs to take exception handling routines such as persisting the service request for later resend.

- **Uptime**   Availability for Java EE .NET interoperable applications counts the uptime for both ends of the applications. It is not the average availability percentage of both Java and .NET application servers. For example, if the sender running Java EE applications is 99.99 percent available, and the recipient running .NET application is 99.91 percent available, it cannot simply be assumed that the availability for Java EE .NET interoperable applications is 99.99 percent or the average 99.95 percent.

- **Middleware**   The availability for Java and .NET interoperable applications using an IIOP bridge or Enterprise Service Bus will be highly dependent on the availability of the middleware technology. Thus it is critical to ensure that the bridge is highly available and has recovery or self-healing features to support high availability. Some bridge or bus middleware technologies use software clustering, fault tolerance, or application recovery to ensure availability.

Scalability and Performance

Individual Java EE or .NET applications usually can be tuned for better scalability and performance. However, a Java EE .NET interoperable application depends on the scalability design and performance of both a Java and a .NET application. The same scalability design and performance enhancement strategy do not necessarily work for both platforms.

Scalable Java EE .NET interoperable applications can handle a large volume of service requests and business transactions or can generate higher transaction throughput. An ideal scalability scenario for a Java EE .NET interoperable application is that the performance should be able to scale linearly. For example, there is an existing interoperability solution using Web services approach. If extra physical memory is added (say, 2GB of memory) or the hardware is upgraded (perhaps to 3GHz processor from 2GHz processor) to the existing Java and .NET application servers, they should be able to scale up to handle additional SOAP messages (perhaps 20 percent additional transaction processing rate) simultaneously.

In reality, there are different scalability and performance factors for the Java EE .NET interoperability solution. These include

- **Memory Factor** The Java EE .NET interoperability application should be able to optimize performance by leveraging the available physical memory. .NET and many Java application servers today are able to benefit from the physical memory with proper setting of the configuration parameters. Architects and developers may want to see whether the interoperability strategy has any cache design for better system performance.

- **CPU Factor** Interoperability applications that require intense computing resources should be able to leverage high-end CPU power for linear scalability. For example, message encryption and decryption (such as XML Encryption) require high CPU processing power. If the interoperability application uses an IIOP bridge or Enterprise Service Bus with XML encryption and decryption, a high-end CPU processor will help to improve system performance.

- **Interface (or I/O) Factor** Some interoperability solutions may use a relational or object database to persist all service requesters. In such a case, the interoperability application should be able to leverage the underlying database technology to scale up or to enhance input/output performance, instead of creating its own scalability implementation.

- **Multi-Threading Factor** Either the Java EE or .NET interoperable application should be able to incorporate multi-threading support into their design so that they can use multi-threads to process a large volume of service requests. Not all application design supports multi-threading by default, as the application design needs to handle synchronization issues. One example is that using asynchronous messaging strategy for Java EE .NET interoperability allows multiple threads of the application to process more service requests.

- **Distributed Architecture Factor** The interoperability application design needs to support multiple instances on the same machine or across different machines. This distributed architecture design allows multiple instances of the interoperability application to run simultaneously and can scale up horizontally to handle a large volume of service requests simultaneously. For example, the asynchronous message strategy using Enterprise Service Bus can allow multiple instances of the interoperability application to run because service requests are encapsulated in messages and can be processed by multiple subscribers (service providers).

Manageability

Manageability refers to a Quality of Service attribute that an application or service can be instrumented, monitored, and recovered if it runs into an exception. Because Java applications can support JMX (Java Management Extension APIs) but .NET applications do not, the manageability for Java EE .NET interoperable applications needs to rely on a common measurement and manageability technology (for example, management proxy) or standard (for example, WS-Management). Interoperability strategy using IIOP Bridge and Enterprise Service Bus can play an important role in providing manageability because they can capture system management information from the application centrally. There are a few important manageability requirements that the interoperability solution should support:

- **Visibility**   The Java EE .NET interoperable applications should be able to expose their operation states (for example, active or error) or management information (for example, CPU utilization) for instrumentation and system monitoring. There should be monitoring capability in the interoperability strategy for online status or for service reporting.

- **Detection of Problems**   The interoperability solution should be able to detect if there is any service problem or system failure in both the Java and .NET applications. This may require the interoperability solution to poll the system status or the application itself to send system heart-beat periodically. For example, some Enterprise Service Bus interoperability solutions support JMX and can report any service problems from either the Java EE or .NET application to the management server (running MBean server).

- **Remediation**   The capability to recover the failing system or execute corrective management actions is very crucial to managing Java EE .NET interoperable applications.

- **Adaptability**   The management solution should be easily extendible to additional enterprise applications regardless of their origins, Java EE, .NET, or legacy. Additionally, manageability should be controlled depending on the environment, development, Quality Assurance, staging, and production. Enabling or disabling certain application or system-level logging should be performed outside of the actual application, that is, in the configuration files or centralized management console.

- **Effectiveness**   There should be a balance between logging and application state tracing and the overall system performance.

- **Logging**   Logging information provides basic input to managing the integration points between a Java EE .NET interoperate solution. The solution should be able to collect logging information from individual Java EE and .NET service components, as well as from the integration points (such as Bridge) and correlate for application management of the interoperable solution.

Related Technologies and Standards

Enterprise Service Bus

Enterprise Service Bus is becoming more popular in implementing Java EE .NET interoperability. It supports both synchronous and asynchronous communication. It also persists asynchronous messages for better reliability. It allows priorities to route or process certain tasks first. With an Enterprise Service Bus, architects and developers can centrally maintain security using the bus to apply business or security policies (such as Policy Decision Point or Policy Execution Point).

Metrics for QoS

There is no standard for measuring the QoS for Java EE .NET interoperable applications today. Having a single performance metric for them is difficult and may not be appropriate because we are not sharing the same measurement baseline. In other words, it is not an apple-to-apple comparison. For Java EE .NET interoperability, it is more pragmatic to measure the performance throughput for different interoperability strategies using the same client platform and infrastructure, for example, comparing the system response time of using an IIOP bridge and Web services for the same set of system infrastructure.

Performance metrics specifications exist, but they are specialized for specific technologies such as application server (for example, SPECjAppServer from http://www.spec.org/benchmarks.html) and TPC-App from the TPC (http://www.tpc.org/tpc_app/default.asp). The performance throughput for Java applications can be measured using these specifications—but not for .NET applications. However this is not sufficient for end-to-end measurement for Java EE .NET interoperable applications.

Management of Web Services

Web services technology is a key Java EE .NET interoperability strategy. Web services management can help monitoring and managing Web services end-points and can take appropriate corrective actions to meet service-level objectives. Please refer to Chapter 15 for details.

There is a convergence of WS-Management efforts between industry leaders including Sun Microsystems and Microsoft. OASIS Web Services Distributed Management Technical Committee (http://www.oasis-open.org/committees/tc_home.php?wg_abbrev=wsdm) has recently approved a couple of Web services management standards, namely, management using Web services (MUWS) and management of Web services (MOWS). These specifications define the requirements of how to meter and manage Web services end-points and should be applicable to both Java EE or .NET applications.

Other Web Services Standards and Specifications

Web Services Reliable Exchange (WS-RX) is a specification that continues the work of WS-ReliableMessaging. It is based on Web Services Reliable Messaging Policy Assertion to allow two Web services to express support for reliable messaging and other related useful parameters. Refer to http://www.oasis-open.org/committees/tc_home.php?wg_abbrev=ws-rx for more details.

Summary

Quality of Services is a crucial element in managing service-level objectives for heterogeneous business applications and services. This is especially important for Java EE .NET interoperable applications where there are many technology complexities and dependencies across architecture tiers and layers. Not all Java EE .NET interoperability products are necessarily reliable and scalable by default.

Achieving QoS varies by the inherent application design and the choice of interoperability strategies. It also requires a careful architecture design up front, instead of post-implementation performance tuning. There is no single rule of thumb that can apply to all Java EE and .NET application design. Thus architects and developers need to understand the Quality of Services requirements and implications to each different interoperability strategy.

There are evolving open standards that address the QoS issues, including WS-Management, WS-RM, and WS-Security. These open standards provide a model approach in managing Quality of Services. Architects and developers might find it useful to adhere to these standards wherever possible for better interoperability.

Managing Distributed Transactions

12

Introduction

The management of transactions is a vitally important part of any integration strategy. Why is transactional support important when talking about Java EE and .NET application communication? First, to ensure data integrity when interoperating between Java EE and .NET applications, it is often necessary to operate in the scope of a distributed transaction. Both the Java EE platform and the .NET Framework provide flexible models for parallel access of shared resources and ensure that at the end of a transaction data are not corrupted or lost. The challenge is that supported native mechanisms are neither interoperable nor compliant with each other. This chapter outlines various strategies and considerations pertaining to Java EE and .NET component integration in the scope of an atomic transaction. Specifically, it discusses distributed transaction support across Java EE and .NET using messaging and Web services technologies.

In the context of the Java EE .NET integration, a transaction is used to coordinate multiple operations that span across multiple platforms and control the commit or abort of any changes submitted to the underlying data source. The cross platform transactional support depends on a mechanism selected for application interconnection and the required level of transactional integrity. Before exploring distributed transaction strategies, it is important to get familiar with the concept of transactional integrity as well as the mechanics of Java EE and .NET transaction management.

Foundation of Transactional Integrity

A transaction is often defined as a unit of work that results in either success or failure and fulfills Atomic, Consistent, Isolated, and Durable (ACID) principals [ACID]. For instance, in the procurement system depicted in Figure 12-1, the purchase order processing depends on the inventory check service, which verifies that the selected product is in stock. Once the selected product availability is positively checked, the stock inventory is updated and a purchase order is created. Following is a discussion regarding what individual ACID properties mean and how they apply in the purchase order scenario.

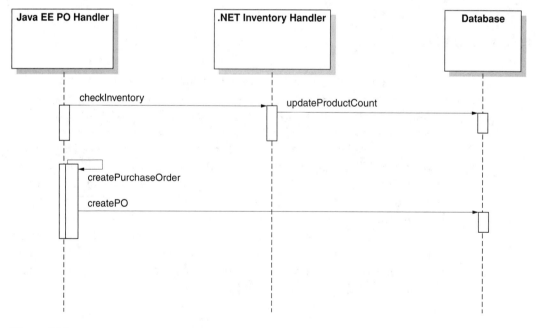

Figure 12-1
Distributed transaction scenario

Atomicity

Individual operations of a transaction should all be successfully completed or rolled back as if they are a single operation. In the preceding example, changes to the product count and the purchase order creation must be all successfully completed or be rolled back, thus appearing as a single, Atomic, unit of work. In case of an application error, the system should restore all modified data to its original state. Similarly, if a purchase order gets cancelled, there should be a corresponding update to the product count in the inventory.

Consistency

Modified or rolled back data must remain in a consistent state across application components that access the data. These application components include objects and records. Consistency helps to ensure that referential and integrity constraints remain in a coherent state. In this example, the inventory system references the Supply Chain Management system, and a new product request is generated when the product count is low. If the product count does not decrement correctly, the Supply Chain Management may not request new products on time. Therefore it is important to maintain consistency across application data by encapsulating business requirements into the application logic or enforcing corresponding constraints at the database level. Transaction systems don't give the guarantee of consistency—it is the responsibility of the application level to handle this.

Isolation

Isolation implies that concurrent users or applications should have the impression of being the only users of the data. At the system level, Isolation is usually implemented with locks. In the purchase order example, when decrementing the product counter, a write lock should be set to avoid potentially overselling a product. An application should deny requests for the product count information while this product count is being modified. Only after all changes are committed or rolled back should the data be available to the rest of the requests. The Isolation property helps to protect uncommitted changes from being accessed by other application components. For performance reasons, so-called Isolation levels allow this property to be relaxed for particular applications. The Isolation level determines how isolated this transaction is from the rest of the transactions. Individual transaction Isolation levels and their effects are discussed in the next section.

Durability

Any modifications to the data have to be permanent regardless of any software or hardware failures occurring after transaction completion. This is often achieved by storing individual transaction steps in a persistent store. For instance, in Figure 12-1, the purchase order is being saved into the database. Once the purchase order transaction commits, all changes made to the data are permanent, and critical information will not be lost. If an error occurs prior to modifications committed to the database, changes should roll back, thus leaving the system in the original state, as per the Atomicity property. There is never a 100 percent guarantee of durability and that the rollback will restore everything perfectly, as there are a number of factors that can cause failures, but transactable managed systems are the best way of getting the best possible durability.

Distributed Transaction

A transaction can span across different applications and resources. In the Distributed Transaction Scenario diagram, Figure 12-1, a transaction encapsulates calls to Java EE and .NET applications. Another example of a distributed transaction involves different resources, that is, databases or file systems. The .NET application can be configured with MSSQL server for storing inventory data, while the Java EE application can be configured with Oracle RDBMS for coordinating a purchase order. Managing a transaction distributed across multiple systems significantly complicates an implementation to adhere to the basic ACID tenets. Synchronizing ACID qualities across multiple transaction managers can be achieved with the Two-Phase Commit (2PC) protocol to ensure atomicity and durability, in combination with two-phase locking (2PL) to ensure isolation. The RDBMS and the program logic are responsible for the consistency. In the context of the Java EE and .NET interoperability, support for distributed transaction varies depending on the integration technology.

Two-Phase Commit (2PC) Protocol

The two-phase commit protocol enables the Atomicity in a distributed transaction scenario. The system module responsible for this protocol is usually called a **transaction manager** or a coordinator. As the name implies, there are two phases to the protocol. In the first phase, the coordinator asks each participant to vote on a commit or a rollback. This is accomplished by sending a so-called `prepare` request to each participant. When a participant votes for a commit, it loses its right to roll back independently, meaning that it has to wait for the final outcome received from the coordinator. The first phase ends when the coordinator receives all votes or if a timeout occurs. The second phase starts with the final decision made by the coordinator. In the case of a timeout or at least one "rollback" vote, the decision to roll back is sent to each participant that voted for "commit" in the first phase. As a result, all data modifications at all places involved are rolled back. Should all participants vote to commit, then and only then, the coordinator decides to perform a global commit and sends a commit notification to all participants. Consequently, all the work at all places is committed.

The complexity of the two-phase commit relates not only to the distributed nature of a transaction, but also to a possible non-atomic outcome of a transaction, i.e. heuristics. For example, the first participant may commit changes during phase two, while the second participant encounters a hardware failure when saving changes to the disk. Being able to roll back or at least notify the errors to recover the system into the original state is an important part of the process.

By persisting intermediate steps of the 2PC, that is, logging `abort`, `ready to commit`, and `commit` messages, the protocol provides a certain degree of reliability in case the coordinator or participants fail in the midst of transaction processing. The two-phase commit protocol can be implemented in a synchronous or asynchronous manner with variations to its actual execution.

ARCHITECT'S NOTE

For the Java EE-.NET integration it is important to determine which transactional characteristics have to be carried out. It is fairly common that not all of the ACID qualities need to be fulfilled at the same time. Business requirements and the Service Level Agreement (SLA) often act as core drivers for selecting or eliminating support for some of the ACID properties. In the purchase order example, overselling a product may be perfectly acceptable from the business, data availability, and performance standpoints. Assessing technical artifacts against well-defined business requirements is essential in determining to which individual characteristics of a transaction the integration scenario has to adhere. Additionally, defining boundaries of a transaction can impact the level of complexity required during the actual implementation.

Java EE and .NET Transaction Support

Java EE Transaction Support

The Java EE container implements support for transactions and facilitates the ACID properties required by the application logic. The container provides an implementation for the two-phase commit protocol between a transaction manager and underlying resources such as the database or messaging provider. The Java EE container is also responsible for the transaction context propagation and provides support for a distributed two-phase commit. With a distributed two-phase commit, a Java EE application can modify data across multiple application servers as if it is a single transaction. The EJB architecture only requires support for flat transactions; however, some of the vendors, such as Arjuna Technologies and Atomikos, provide support for nested transactions. (If nested transactions are not supported and a program creates a nested transaction using the `javax.transaction.UserTransaction` interface, the container will throw a `javax.transaction.NotSupportedException`.)

The Java Transaction API (JTA) and the Java Transaction Service (JTS) act as fundamental components for Java EE transaction support and transactional interoperability. The JTA API specifies an interface, `UserTransaction`, used by applications to delineate transaction boundaries. The Java EE transaction model is quite flexible and allows an EJB to participate in an already created transaction or never participate in a transaction depending on the application logic. The `UserTransaction` is utilized to start and commit and roll back transactions. JTA also defines interfaces used by an application server to communicate with a transaction manager and for a transaction manager to communicate with a resource manager. JTS represents a Java binding of the CORBA Object Transport Service (OTS) specification v1.1. Thus JTS provides transactional interoperability across servers that support the IIOP protocol. Although most of the commercial application servers, such as Sun JES Application Server, BEA's WebLogic, and IBM's WebSphere, implement the JTS API, the EJB specification only mandates JTA API support.

NOTE

Despite the theory, JTS/OTS cross-vendor interoperability has always been a problem in practice; this is another reason why many people are looking at Web services technology as the integrating factor.

The Java EE specification defines three types of transactional resources— JDBC connections, JMS sessions, and resources accessed with the Connector Architecture such as Enterprise Resource Planning (ERP) systems. The Java EE container coordinates resource enlistment, the transaction commit, and delistment from the transaction by invoking the corresponding JTA XAResource API. The XAResource interface represents the industry standard XA interface based on the X/Open CAE Specification, [XASPEC]. For more details on this check out the JTA API page [SunJTA].

At the presentation tier, a transaction can be initiated by components such as Java Server Pages or Servlets that can invoke business tier components, such as Enterprise Java Beans, to participate in a transaction. In a database integration scenario, EJBs or even plain old Java objects (POJOs) connect to transactional resource managers via the JDBC connection API.

At the Business tier, EJBs or POJOs can span a new transaction connecting directly to a resource manager. The code excerpt that follows demonstrates how to demarcate a transaction in the Presentation tier using JTA. In this example the `ProcessRequestServlet` uses the `javax.transaction.UserTransaction` interface to demarcate transaction boundaries. The `UserTransaction` is obtained via the JNDI interface. Refer to Listing 12-1.

Listing 12-1
ProcessRequestService Snippet

```
public ProcessRequestServlet {
    ...
    public createPO() {
      Context initCtx = new InitialContext();
      UserTransaction txn =
          (UserTransaction)initCtx.lookup("java:comp/
          UserTransaction");
      txn.begin();
      // execute required operations
      txn.commit();
    }
    ...
}
```

Programmatic Transaction Support

Presentation tier components such as Servlets and JSPs can directly connect to the underlying resources, or they may invoke Business tier components. The transaction context is automatically propagated from the Servlet/JSP to the Business tier by the Java EE container, which encapsulates transactional services. At the Business tier the EJB transaction support is quite flexible and allows for two ways to demarcate transactions—declaratively Container-Managed Transaction (CMT) and programmatically Bean Managed Transaction model (BMT). For POJOs, transaction demarcation usually has to happen programmatically (although so-called pico-container frameworks like Spring (www.springframework.org) can be used to introduce CMT for POJO-based applications). For EJBs, the javax.ejb.SessionContext (EJBContext) is used to retrieve a `UserTransaction`. The code fragment here shows how to demarcate transactions with the BMT model. The code encapsulated between the `txn.begin()` and `txn.commit()` methods is executed within the scope of a transaction. Refer to Listing 12-2.

Listing 12-2
POHandlerEJB Implementation

```
public POHandlerEJB implements SessionBean {
    SessionContext ctx;

    public createPO() {
      try {
        UserTransaction txn = ctx.getUserTransaction();
        txn.begin();
        Connection = DataSource.getConnection();
        // execute SQL operations
        Connection.close();
        txn.commit();
        } catch (SQLException exp){
            // rollback the transaction
            txn.rollback()
        }
    }
    ...
}
```

The `txn.begin()` call initiates a new transaction. The `getConnection()` method typically enlists the corresponding `XAResource`, such as a database, into the transaction. By enlisting the database in the transaction, the database automatically participates in the 2PC protocol. The `connection.close()` method typically initiates the `XAResource.end()`

method to delist the resource from the transaction. With the `txn.commit()` call, if it is a 2PC protocol (i.e., if more than one resource have been accessed within the transaction), the `XAResource.prepare()` and `XAResource.commit()` are called by the transaction manager. In case of failure or at least one negative prepare, the `XAResource.rollback()` is called to roll back the transaction in each remaining resource. A reasonably sophisticated transaction manager will also be able to optimize for the common case where only one resource is accessed. In that case, only a one-phase commit is necessary, and the overhead of preparation can be avoided. All this logic is transparent to the Java EE application developer, as can be seen in the code sample. A transaction manager is provided as part of the Java EE application server.

The previous example demonstrates how to demarcate transactions in a programmatic manner. Java EE programmatic transaction management is useful when the application relies on a sophisticated level of transaction logic. It is often the case that Java EE applications manage transactions in a declarative manner.

Architect's Note

The decision for whether to use programmatic or declarative transaction support depends on the level of transaction control and complexity required by the application design. With the declarative transaction support, also known as Container-Managed Transaction demarcation (CMT), boundaries and individual properties of a transaction are specified in a deployment descriptor of Enterprise Java Bean. With programmatic support to a transaction, also known as Bean-Managed Transaction demarcation (BMT), application logic encapsulates transactional characteristics in the code. A Session EJB or a message-driven bean can be designed with either of two demarcation models. An Entity Bean must always be designed with container managed transaction demarcation, whereas a POJO object has to use the programmatic transaction demarcation. (However, it has to be noted that with the introduction of pico-containers and so-called "inversion of control" frameworks, CMT is now also available for POJO applications.)

Declarative Transaction Model

With the declarative model, the Java EE container provides transaction demarcation based on the EJB transaction attributes. Transaction attributes are defined in the bean deployment descriptor and direct the container on how to manage transactions of an enterprise bean method. This model is somewhat similar to the one in .NET. In general, CMT is preferred over BMT because of the following reasons:

- CMT allows more flexibility in composing and reusing business components (whether EJB or POJO-based). Indeed, specifying transaction preferences outside of the source code (as in CMT) allows one to change or adapt these preferences without the need for recompilation.
- The Java EE specification implies a significant limitation on the reusability of BMT components, given that BMT components essentially ignore the transaction context in which they are called.

CMT also reduces the amount of transaction-related code developers have to write, test, and maintain, which is certainly beneficial in terms of application design.

Transaction Attributes

There are six values to choose from. Based on the application design, individual methods of an enterprise bean may have different transactional attribute values. Alternatively, all methods may share the same value or, conversely, none of the methods may support transactions.

1. **NotSupported** The transaction context is unspecified. This results in suspending the transaction context that was propagated by the client. The context will be resumed after the enterprise bean method completes its execution.
2. **Required** The container provides a transaction context when invoking a bean's method. If a client is associated with a transaction context, the same context will be used to execute the bean's method. Otherwise, the container starts a new transaction.
3. **Supports** The container will not create any new contexts unless a client is associated with a context. In that case, the context will be used to invoke the bean's method.
4. **RequiresNew** The container invokes the enterprise bean's method with a new transaction context, regardless of the client's context. If a client calls with a transaction context, the container suspends its context and creates a new transaction when invoking the business method. The original transaction is resumed on the thread when the method returns.
5. **Mandatory** A client must always invoke the bean's methods in a client's transaction context, or an exception will be thrown by the container.

6. Never   Clients must not call the bean's methods within a transaction context. The container will throw an exception if a transaction context is detected for a client call.

The purchase order example implemented with CMT demarcation looks similar to the previous example. There is, however, a significant difference pertaining to the lack of transaction processing code. Refer to Listing 12-3.

Listing 12-3
POHandlerEJB Implementation

```
public class POHandlerEJB implements SessionBean {
    EJBContext ejbContext;

    public PurchaseOrder createPurchaseOrder(Product prod,
       UserInfo user) {

        // Create PurchaseOrder based on Product and User information
        PurchaseOrder po = new PurchaseOrder(prod, user);
        // Store PurchaseOrder in the database
        createPO(po);
        return PurchaseOrder;
    }

    protected void createPO( PurchaseOrder po) {
        javax.sql.DataSource dataSource;
        java.sql.Connection  connection;
        java.sql.Statement    stmt;
        java.sql.SQLException exc;

      try {
        InitialContext initialContext = new InitialContext();

        // Obtain a connection and SQL statement
        dataSource = (javax.sql.DataSource)
        initialContext.lookup("java:comp/env/jdbc/ProcurementDB");
        connection = dataSource.getConnection();
        stmt = connection.createStatement();

        // Execute query
        stmt.executeQuery("INSERT INTO
                    PURCHASE_ORDER(USER_ID, PRODUCT_ID)
                    VALUES (123, 345)";
      } catch (SQLException e) {
         ...
      } finally {
      // Release resources
      stmt.close();
      connection.close();
      }
    }
}
```

All transaction processing, such as commit or rollback, is delegated to the Java EE container's transaction manager and specified via transaction attributes. The deployment descriptor corresponding to the POHandlerEJB defines the transaction RequiresNew attribute for all methods of the bean. Transaction attributes can be alternatively defined on a per-method basis. Refer to Listing 12-4.

Listing 12-4
Assembly Descriptor for *POHandlerEJB*

```
<ejb-jar>
  ...
  <assembly-descriptor>
  ...
   <container-transaction>
     <method>
       <ejb-name>POHandlerEJB</ejb-name>
         <method-name>*</method-name>
     </method>
     <trans-attribute>RequiresNew</trans-attribute>
   </container-transaction>
  </assembly-descriptor>
</ejb-jar>
```

Isolation Levels

Besides the ability to delineate transactional boundaries, the Java EE transaction model provides a mechanism to specify the transaction isolation level. Isolation levels allow or disallow changes made to the data within the scope of a transaction to be visible to other concurrently executed transactions. There are five different transaction isolation levels supported by Java EE:

1. **TRANSACTION_NONE**   Transactions not supported.
2. **TRANSACTION_READ_UNCOMMITTED**   Other concurrent transactions can see uncommitted changes made within a scope of transaction (seeing uncommitted data is commonly known as **dirty reads**).
3. **TRANSACTION_READ_COMMITTED**   Changes have to be committed before any other transactions can see changes made by the transaction (this prevents dirty reads). However, data read by one transaction might be changed by a second (concurrently committed) transaction, and when the previous transaction rereads the same data, it receives different values, that is, "non-repeatable reads."

4. **TRANSACTION_REPEATABLE_READ** Prohibits a transaction from reading any uncommitted changes (dirty reads) just like in the previous level. Additionally, this level prohibits non-repeatable reads from happening. However, so-called **phantom reads** can still occur: One transaction reads all records satisfying a predicate condition (that is, where a clause, and then a second transaction, inserts new data satisfying the same predicate condition, causing the first transaction to reread the data and see new records).

5. **TRANSACTION_SERIALIZABLE** Prevents dirty reads, non-repeatable reads, and phantom reads.

Transaction isolation levels can be specified based on the type of the underlying resource. For example, for a database access, an enterprise bean implementing the BMT model can set the isolation level using `java.sql.Connection` interface's `setTransactionIsolation (txn IsolationLevel)` method . All transaction isolation levels are defined as constant by the `java.sql.Connection` interface.

The .NET Transaction Support

.NET transaction support is based on the original Microsoft Transaction Server (MTS) introduced in Windows NT 4.0. Later, MTS became part of the Microsoft Windows 2000 COM+ Services and is now incorporated into Windows Server 2003. The .NET Common Language Runtime (CLR) leverages an automatic distributed transaction model introduced in MTS. At the core of the MTS architecture lays the MTS Executive that hosts individual components such as C# objects or ASP.NET pages. MTS relies on the Distributed Transaction Coordinator (DTC) component to perform the role of transaction manager to coordinate the correct execution of a transaction across multiple resource managers. Interaction between DTC and resource managers is achieved using OLE Transaction interfaces. DTC also supports X/Open Distributed Transaction Processing (DTP) XA standard, see [XASPEC]. You may recall that Java Transaction Service also supports the XA standard. Transactional applications can be built with any of the .NET languages including VB.NET, J++, C#, and ASP.NET. Transactional support can be achieved by one of two mechanisms—implicit via programmatic transaction support or declarative. Starting with .NET Framework 2.0, there is a new transactional API available with System.Transactions namespace. Please refer to [SYSTXN] for more details.

Programmatic Transaction Support

Manual transaction management can be achieved by explicitly calling the `SetComplete` and `SetAbort` methods of the `System.Enterprise Services.ContextUtil` class. If the MTS receives `SetAbort` from any of the objects involved in the transaction, the runtime instructs the transaction coordinator to abort the transaction. Otherwise, MTS waits to receive a `SetComplete` call from all of the components and then instructs the transaction coordinator to commit the transaction. When managing transactions manually, the transaction attribute has to be set to `Disabled`. An object then can make direct calls to the Distributed Transaction Coordinator using OLE Transaction interfaces. The manual mechanism of handling transactions is analogous to the Java EE BMT demarcation. The .NET transaction Isolation Levels are very similar to the ones discussed in the Java EE overview.

There are six Isolation Levels to support transactions: `Chaos`, `ReadCommited`, `ReadUncommited`, `RepeatableRead`, `Serializable`, and `Unspecified`. The `Chaos` isolation level prevents pending changes from more highly isolated transactions from being overwritten. Manual transactions, unlike automatic, can be used to implement pseudo-nested transactions (they are not truly nested as they don't support nested scopes of Moss' locking rules). However, manually managing distributed transaction management, recovery, concurrency, and data integrity in an effective manner is fairly complicated. Microsoft ActiveX Data Objects (ADO), OLE DB, Open Database Connectivity (ODBC), and Message Queuing resource APIs all enable manual transaction processing.

Listing 12-5 demonstrates how to implement a local database transaction using C#. Database access is achieved using ADO.NET API.

Listing 12-5
UpdateProductCount Class

```
private void updateProductCount (int prodId, int newProdCount,
   String connectionInfo ) {

// Create and open database connection
SqlConnection connection = new SqlConnection(connectionInfo);
connection.Open();

// Begin a local database transaction
SqlTransaction txn =
connection.BeginTransaction(IsolationLevel.Serializable);

// Enlist the command in the current transaction
```

```
SqlCommand command = connection.CreateCommand();
command.Transaction = txn;

try {
   // Update product inventory
   command.CommandText = "UPDATE inventory
                        SET product_quantity='
                        & newProdCount & '
                        WHERE product_id=' & prodId '";
   command.ExecuteNonQuery();

   // Commit the transaction
   txn.Commit();

} catch(Exception e) {
   try {
     txn.Rollback();
   } catch (SqlException ex) {
// Process error
   }
   } finally {
   // Release resources and delist connection from the transaction
   connection.Close();
   }
}
```

In this example when creating `SqlCommand`, the `Connection` object automatically enlists resources in an active transaction. This is the default platform setting. By enlisting in a distributed transaction, the transaction commit or abort will be propagated to the resource manager, and changes to the data will be committed or rolled back in the database. The `Connection.EnlistDistributeTransaction()` method can be used to enlist in an existing distributed transaction if automatic settings are disabled. If an application design requires disabling auto-enlist, `SqlConnection` should be created with `Enlist=false`:

```
SqlConnection connection =
 new SqlConnection("Data Source=localhost;
 Initial Catalog=Northwind;Integrated Security=SSPI;Enlist=false");
```

Automatic Transaction Support

.NET CLR automatic transaction support is similar to the CMT demarcation of the Java EE architecture. The .NET Framework relies on MTS/COM+ services to support automatic transactions, which is enabled through the `System.EnterpriseServices` namespace. This namespace provides .NET objects with access to the COM+ services. Any .NET class that derives from `System.EnterpriseServices.ServiceComponent`, [SVCCMP], can be exposed as a COM+ configured component. To participate in automatic transactions, a .NET class must be inherited from the `System.EnterpriseServices.ServicedComponent` class, which enables it to run inside COM+ service.

Declarative Transaction Support

How objects participate in transactions can be controlled declaratively using predefined transaction attributes. Based on the application business logic, a C# class, an ASP.NET page, or an XML Web service method, a value for transaction attribute can be declared accordingly. For example, a method can automatically participate in an already existing transaction or never participate in a transaction. Attributes are similar to the EJB transaction attributes that can be used to demarcate transaction boundaries.

- **NotSupported** An object does not run within the scope of a transaction.

- **Supported** If a component is invoked within the scope of a transaction, that context will be used. Otherwise, no transactional context is created.

- **Required** A new transaction will be started unless a caller is associated with a transaction context, in which case a method will be executed within the existing transaction. This is the default attribute value for C#.

- **RequiresNew** A new transaction will be started regardless of the caller's transaction.

- **Disabled** Automatic transaction settings are removed. To manage transactions, an object should explicitly call the Distributed Transaction Coordinator. Disabled is the default setting for ASP.NET.

Implementing the declarative model to manage a transaction, a C# class that requires a new transaction can be declared in the following way (Listing 12-6):

Listing 12-6
InventoryHandler class in C#

```
[Transaction(TransactionOption.RequiresNew)]
public class InventoryHandler {

  public void checkInventory(PORequest Request) {
      // check inventory and update product count
  }
}
```

.NET distributed transactions allow individual participants to vote for committing or aborting a transaction. This feature is available when using automatic transaction settings with `System.EnterpriseServices.Auto CompleteAttribute`. In the absence of an explicit vote within a method, a vote is automatically set to `Commit`.

There are some limitations to both programmatic and declarative transaction models. All transactions are based on the `System .EnterpriseServices` namespace and automatically rely on distributed transaction coordinator (DTC). This imposes a performance overhead for applications utilizing a single resource, for example a single database. Additionally, there is no way for multiple transactions to participate in the same transaction, as the Enterprise Services are thread-safe. This may be a potential limitation for certain types of applications. Thus, the .NET Framework 2.0 introduces a new transaction manager model.

Managing Transactions with *System. Transactions*

The .NET Framework 2.0 introduces two types of transaction managers, the Lightweight Transaction Manager (LTM) and the OleTx Transaction Manager. The latter one is similar to the DTC, while the Lightweight Transaction Manager, as its name implies, is used for managing transactions across a single application domain and a single resource. The new transaction model is available via the `System.Transactions` namespace. The new transaction model automatically selects a transaction manager for your application. If a single application interacts with a single database, the LTM will be selected. If application changes and a new durable resource is added, the transaction manager is switched to OleTx automatically, see [TXME]. This transaction management escalation model decouples an application from the underlying transaction manager. In addition to the dynamic transaction manager escalation, there is a feature of promotable enlistment of durable resources. This means that if there is only one resource such as a database participating in a transaction, it can take the ownership of the transaction. Additionally, the `System.Transactions` infrastructure supports a number of useful features—for instance, subscribing to a `TransactionCompleted` event to notify an application upon transaction completion. Similarly, you can subscribe to `Distributed TransactionStarted` event. A `WorkerThread` class can be used to execute the transaction in a separate thread from the client application, thus contributing to application performance.

If an application relies on declarative model, there are no changes needed to take advantage of the `System.Transactions`. The application will have to be modified if there needs to be manual programming support for the transaction. The `System.Transactions` libraries are included in the Systems.Transactions.dll. You can refer to [SYSTSAMP] for additional resources.

.NET transaction support is consistent across different .NET languages, which provides transactional interoperability across .NET objects, ASP.NET pages, and Web methods.

Transactional Interoperability Across Java EE and .NET

As it appears from this chapter's earlier discussion on individual platform transactional support, the .NET transaction model is not compatible with the transaction support in Java, which makes it difficult to achieve transactional interoperability. The next few sections explore various strategies on how to propagate a transactional context between Java EE and .NET, thus addressing the challenge of the transactional incompatibility between the two platforms. The first and recommended strategy at this point in time is based on messaging. The next strategy relies on a Web services-based solution. The final strategy explores custom, off-the-shelf, solutions to provide support for transactions.

Transaction Management Using Messaging

Depending on the individual integration scenario, support for transactions can be easily incorporated into a publish-and-subscribe or a point-to-point messaging-based solution. In the purchase order scenario there are two distinct services that communicate with each other. The Java-based Purchase

Order management system, acting as a producer, can send an asynchronous request to the Inventory management system to create a purchase order. The .NET service, acting as a consumer, listens on a point-to-point queue or subscribes to a publish-and-subscribe topic. In the purchase order creation scenario, the point-to-point integration is quite appropriate. The publish-subscribe mechanism could be selected in a situation where an event has to be distributed to multiple recipients. For transaction management with the point-to-point application integration, Java EE and .NET components utilize a message queue. Hereafter, examples demonstrate how to implement transactional support using messaging with Java EE and C# components. Asynchronous Java EE-.NET integration with messaging middleware is discussed in Part III of this book, "Asynchronous Integration Solutions."

Messaging Support in Java EE Components

Session and Entity beans can use JMS to send messages, but their lifecycle model makes them inappropriate for receiving messages.

Instead, Java EE defines a special kind of enterprise bean, referred to as a message-driven bean, whose sole purpose is to asynchronously receive messages from the messaging middleware. Depending on point-to-point or publish-subscribe integration, `javax.jms.Queue` or `javax.jms.Topic` is utilized respectively. If the EJB application needs to receive messages, then a message-driven bean is appropriate (as a matter of fact, the only way to invoke a message-driven bean is by sending a JMS message to it).

This example involves a Java EE application that calls a .NET service. This means that the Java EE application is acting as the sender, so one wouldn't use a message-driven bean but a session EJB here. The session bean is called to check the inventory, and it delegates the call to .NET via a JMS message.

The example in Listing 12-7 demonstrates how to communicate with a JMS connection using a message queue.

Listing 12-7
POHandlerEJB Class

```
public class POHandlerEJB implements SessionBean {
    EJBContext ejbContext;

    public void sendCheckInventoryRequest(String productID,
        int productCount) {
```

continues

Listing 12-7 (continued)

```
    javax.transaction.UserTransaction userTxn;
    javax.jms.QueueConnectionFactory connectionFactory;
    javax.jms.QueueConnection connection;
    javax.jms.Queue queue;
    javax.jms.QueueSession session;
    javax.jms.QueueSender sender;
    javax.jms.MapMessage msg;

  try{
    InitialContext initialContext = new InitialContext();

    // Createa JMS connection and set up Queue Session for
    // transactions
    connectionFactory =
      (javax.jms.QueueConnectionFactory) initialContext.lookup
               ("java:comp/env/jms/QueueConnectionFactory");
    connection = connectionFactory.createQueueConnection();
    // Pass values for boolean transacted and int acknowledgeMode
    session = connection.createQueueSession(true,0);
    queue = (javax.jms.Queue)
    initialContext.lookup("java:comp/env/jms/jmsQueue");
    sender = session.createSender(queue);
    msg = session.createMapMessage();
    msg.setInt(productID, productCount);

    //Get user transaction
    userTxn = ejbContext.getUserTransaction();
    //Start the transaction
    userTxn.begin();
    // Execute transaction
    sender.send(msg);
    //Commit the transaction
    userTxn.commit();
  } catch (SQLException exc) {
      try {
        userTxn.rollback();
      } catch (Exception e){}
  } finally {
    //Release resources
    sender.close();
    session.close();
    connection.close();
  }
 }
}
```

In Listing 12-8, the queue session, `connection.createQueue Session(true, 0)`, is created with a transaction attribute set to true and acknowledgement mode set to zero. The reason for acknowledgement being zero is because the Java EE container ignores this method parameter in transactional use cases. The container handles transactional characteristics of this

JMS session on behalf of a bean. Similarly, `createTopicSession(true, 0)` can be used to utilize a topic rather than a queue.

ARCHITECT'S NOTE

It is important to mention the limitations of messaging-based Java EE .NET integration when it comes to transaction management. With the messaging-based communication, a transaction typically does not span across a messaging channel. In particular, the scope of a transaction is limited to only one party in the message chain. A rollback can only affect at the most one party in that chain. Additionally, transactional support in the messaging environment is not designed for a request-reply type of communication. It is impossible to receive a reply to a request as part of the same transaction. An attempt to do so always results in a time-out and a transaction rollback. The practical consequence of using messaging in the transaction context is to ensure that all of the following requirements are met:

- No reply message is required within the scope of a transaction.
- Once sent, a request is guaranteed to arrive at the recipient.
- Upon arrival of the message, a recipient guarantees to process the message successfully.

Failure to meet one of these requirements can result in violations of the Atomic property, thus transaction management with messaging should be used with the proper care. Having said that, the chapter next explores what it takes to process a message by the .NET application.

Transaction Request Processing with .NET Messaging

On the .NET platform, transactions can be enabled with the `System.Messaging.MessageQueueTransaction` class and automatically managed by the MSMQ engine. Refer to Listing 12-8.

Listing 12-8
Enabling Transactions with *System.Messaging.MessageQueueTransaction*

```
// Check if the queue exists
if ( MessageQueue.Exists(".\\inventoryQueue") {
  // Look up the inventory queue

  // Create new transaction
  MessageQueueTransaction txn = new MessageQueueTransaction();
```

continues

Listing 12-8 (continued)

```
  try {
    // Begin transaction
    txn.Begin()
    // Receive the inventory check reques
    Message msg = inventoryQueue.Receive(txn);
    Sting request = (String)msg.Body;

    // After checking the inventory, send the status back to the
queue

    inventoryQueue.Send("inventory status...", txn);
    txn.Commit();
  } catch ( MessageQueueException exp){
  //abort the transaction
    txn.Abort();
  }

} //End of if statement
```

After sending a message to the queue, the status of the transaction can be verified with the `MessageQueueTransactionStatus` library to determine if a transaction has been committed, aborted, initialized, or if it is pending.

```
if (txn.Status = MessageQueueTransactionStatus.Aborted)
  // Log the status
```

If a transaction has been aborted, sent messages are removed from the queue.

ARCHITECT'S NOTE

Messaging is a practical and mature solution for transactional interoperability across Java EE and .NET. While the Web services transactional support, discussed next, is still evolving, messaging is the most reliable way to ensure integrity of distributed transactions. A disadvantage of messaging pertains to its cost as compared to using Web services. Leveraging transactional characteristics of messaging would be more appropriate if Java EE and .NET applications already relied on messaging as an integration solution or if there were a messaging server already deployed in the company that could be leveraged for other purposes.

Web Services Transaction Strategy

In spite of the high value and simplicity of Web services-based Java EE and .NET component integration, support for distributed transactions with Web services is somewhat problematic. There is no de-facto standard adopted by the industry to address transactional interoperability, although a strong candidate specification has recently been published by a consortium of industry giants—WS-Transactions. However because this is a new evolution at the time of this writing, transactional characteristics of Java EE-.NET Web services integration are very limited and primarily embrace proprietary technologies. Most of today's Web services integrations rely on a simple request-response scenario or a reliable and secure message interchange for B2B transactions. Neither of these scenarios entails a request for distributed transactions.

In some cases, though, distributed transaction integration is necessary, and most of the industry players, realizing its potential value, released a set of specifications to accommodate support for Web services-based distributed transactions. Microsoft, IBM, IONA, Arjuna, and BEA released a proprietary trio of specifications for WS-Coordination, WS-AtomicTransaction, and WS-BusinessActivity, which were previously embraced under an umbrella of the WS-Transaction specification [WS-TX]. This specification set was officially published in version 1.0, open to the public as well as royalty-free to implement. Along the same line, Sun, Oracle, Iona, Arjuna Technologies, and Fujitsu, as part of the Organization for the Advancement of Structured Information Standards (OASIS), are working on the Web Services Composite Application Framework, a.k.a. WS-CAF specification. The OASIS WS-CAF technical committee will define a royalty-free, generic, and open to the public framework to manage Web service distributed transactions [SUNWSCAF]. From a technical standpoint, WS-CAF and WS-Transaction trio resemble each other greatly. Another standard in this space corresponds to OASIS' Business Transaction Process (BTP) standard that addresses distributed transaction across the long living B2B communication. A more detailed discussion of each of these standards follows, providing an understanding of how they can be leveraged for Java EE .NET transaction interoperability with Web services and dive a bit more into details with the WS-AtomicTransaction specification.

WS-Coordination, WS-AtomicTransaction, and WS-BusinessActivity

The industry is gaining momentum around this trio of specifications that defines how Web services can participate in the distributed transaction model, see [WSACOORD]. The first of the trio, WS-Coordination, provides a means to create, register, and coordinate distributed Web services. While WS-Coordination does not require transaction support to protect ACID properties, the latter are essential features of distributed collaborations. WS-AtomicTransaction extends the WS-Coordination specification with support for atomic, all-or-nothing transactions. This specification relies on a transaction coordinator to collaborate with each of the participants to agree on a transaction commit or rollback, thus following a classic two-phase-commit protocol. WS-AtomicTransactions can be used when heterogeneous applications and resources have to participate in a short-lived transaction and the level of trust among transaction participants is fairly high. The WS-BusinessActivity specification is the second type of the transaction coordination. WS-BusinessActivity is designed for a long living business transaction with a low level of trust, and aimed at facilitating transaction execution in a B2B scenario.

Achieving Transactional Interoperability with WS-AtomicTransaction

In light of Java EE .NET integration, this book primarily focuses on how to integrate two intranet applications, Java EE and .NET, and their underlying resources. This implies that a transaction the text is trying to portray is short-lived and is deployed within the boundaries of the same corporation. Therefore, it is expected that the level of trust among transaction participants is high. These characteristics point to the WS-AtomicTransaction as an adequate technology for needed requirements.

The first thing that needs to happen is the creation of a new transaction. In WS-AtomicTransaction, this is done via the Coordinator service. This is a Web service that runs either inside the Java EE server or as a separate Web service on the network. The Coordinator service needs a transaction type for the creation request (because the design of WS-Transactions allows multiple transaction types to be supported by the same Coordinator). For WS-AtomicTransaction, the type is identified by a schema, which can be found at [WS-AT].

As a result of the creation, the Coordinator returns a **ticket** (the so-called `CoordinationContext`, expressed in XML) that describes the transaction and can be passed along with the application-level requests. The fact that a request carries this context in its header signals that it is part of the corresponding transaction. An example of such a context is shown here in Listing 12-9.

Listing 12-9
Example of a Web Services Coordination Context

```
<wscoor:CoordinationContext>
    <wsu:Identifier>http://theInventoryCheck.com</wsu:Identifier>
    <wsu:Expires>2004-12-22T15:10:17-00:00</wsu:Expires>
    <wscoor:CoordinationType>
      http://schemas.xmlsoap.org/ws/2004200410/09/wsat
    </wscoor:CoordinationType>
    <wscoor:RegistrationService>
      <wsu:Address>
        http://RegistrationSrvice_uri
      </wsu:Address>
    </wscoor:RegistrationService>
  </wscoor:CoordinationContext>
```

Any invoked Web service that receives a request with a context header can use the context information to register with the Coordinator's `RegistrationService` (included in the context shown in Listing 12-9) so that the service becomes subject to two-phase commit termination at the end of the transaction. This registration is shown in Listing 12-10.

Listing 12-10
Registering a Database Resource in Web Services Coordination

```
<soapenv>
 <soapheader>
     <!-- WS-Addressing headers to identify target service, and
          the requesting service with its reply information.
 -->
 </soapheader>
 <soapbody>
  <wscoor:Register>

    <ProtocolIdentifier>
      http://xxxx/AtomicTransaction/Completion
      http://schemas.xmlsoap.org/ws/2004/10/wsat/Durable2PC
    </ProtocolIdentifier>
    <ParticipantProtocolService>
      <Address>http://database_address</Address>
```

continues

Listing 12-10 (continued)
```
    </ParticipantProtocolService>
  </wscoor:Register>
 </soapbody>
</soapenv>
```

Upon receiving a registration, the Coordinator (Registration) service returns a reference (address) of the coordination service to the registering party (not shown).

Services can register for two types of termination: Volatile2PC or Durable2PC. Services that register for the former will only receive a notification before 2PC really happens (this is useful for cache managers that only need to flush to other services that take care of the real persistence work). Services that register for the latter will receive full 2PC requests and should also respond accordingly. When the transaction ends, all remote business calls have been done, and consequently all participating services have registered. This means that at the time of termination, the coordinator service knows all the parties involved in the transaction.

To terminate the transaction, some part of the application has to indicate if it wants to commit or roll back. This happens via the Completion service, another service that is exposed by the Coordinator. Application services that want to trigger commit or rollback processing should first register for the Completion Protocol (with the Coordinator). The registration message is similar to the one for 2PC shown earlier; only the protocol URI differs, and the participant service contains the address of the service that wants to trigger termination. This extra registration is provided to allow a Web service other than the transaction creator to trigger the termination process.

NOTE

If the Coordinator is collocated with the transaction creator and the creator also triggers commit, then no extra SOAP message exchange may be needed—instead, an API call will typically do.

Once registration for Completion is finished, the registered application service can request commit or rollback. Assuming that commit is desired, the Coordinator starts the two-phase commit protocol. WS-AtomicTransaction describes the message format and state transitions for this protocol.

Architect's Note

With version 1.0 released in August 2005, WS-Coordination and WS-AtomicTransaction together standardize the protocol messages to be exchanged between cross-vendor, cross-platform Web service transactions. This minimal and yet unambiguous nature should make it a lot easier to achieve interoperability across vendors and platforms, since implementers are not bothered by unnecessary elements in the specification. WS-AtomicTransaction-compliant products are allowed to include proprietary (and purely supplementary) information to enhance the user experience when deployed in a network of single-vendor installations. However, if they follow the protocol guidelines, there should be no implications on interoperability.

Realistically speaking, as with all interoperability technologies, testing will have to make sure that message formats and content are really compliant across vendors. This is inevitable; the same problem exists even at the basic SOAP protocol level.

Web Services Composite Application Framework

This specification is more generic than WS-AtomicTransaction, WS-BusinessActivity, and WS-Coordination, although WS-CAF also addresses the same problem domain space of Web services distributed transaction support. The WS-CAF specification encompasses three specifications, all of which are still works in progress at the time of writing. The first one pertains to the Web Service Context (WS-CTX), which defines a means for Web services to manage, share, and access Web services context—for instance, coordinating a state of a shopping cart across different Web services at the application level. Another example of the Web Service Context is to manage Web service transaction information at the system level. The second WS-CAF specification, Web Service Coordination Framework (WS-CF), coordinates distributed transaction support. For example, if a 2PC commit failed at one of the Web services, the coordinator is responsible for propagating the rollback across all participants. Finally, the Web Service Transaction Management (WS-TXM) defines a plug-in model for transaction managers.

Architect's Note

As a result of the fairly generic set of specifications, WS-CAF inevitably leads to added complexity, which, in turn, could complicate interoperability.

In addition to discussed specifications, there is a Business Transaction Processing Protocol (BTP), [BTP], which outlines a mechanism to conduct a business-to-business transaction across multiple parties.

Java Support of Web Services Transaction Standards

There are two Java Specification Requests, JSR 156 and JSR 95, that have been submitted to address Java EE support for distributed transactions using Web services.

- **JSR 156 XML Transactioning API for Java (JAXTX)**   This JSR intends to extend Java transactional support with Web services transaction models including OASIS BTP and WS-Transaction. Mapping of the transaction context between Java and SOAP message headers or Java and WS-Transaction would simplify transaction processing of loosely coupled applications.

- **JSR 95 Java EE Active Service for Extended Transactions**   This JSR intends to extend Java EE frameworks with support for activities, where an activity can be anything from an ACID transaction to a workflow task. This JSR extends JTA/JTS with support for OMG's Activity Service standard and is fairly generic (that is, very low-level and therefore probably not useful for mainstream Java EE application developers).

Web Services Transaction Support Future Directions

Considering Sun and Microsoft announcements regarding technology interoperability, it would not be surprising if Web services transactional interoperability improves. Once WS interoperability gets better, the distributed transaction design spanning across Java EE and .NET Web services will become easily realizable because there will be corresponding product support such as Java EE containers and .NET CLR. In this example, the PO Handler prepares to call the Inventory Handler Web service and initiates a transaction. At that point all members of the transaction register with the distributed transaction coordinator. The Java EE transaction coordinator coordinates the 2PC across different transaction managers. Figure 12-2 shows how distributed transaction can be achieved with Web services, once the interoperability is implemented in Java EE and .NET containers.

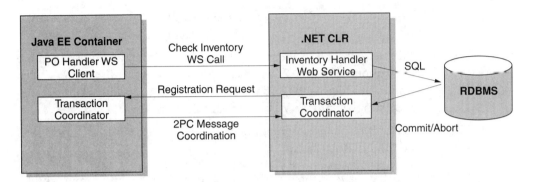

Figure 12-2
Web services distributed transaction

For additional information on Web services and transaction, please see [WSTXN].

Commercial Products

There are a number of vendors that provide solutions in the transaction interoperability space.

- Arjuna Technologies implements the WS-Transaction specification into the Arjuna XML Transaction Service. This solution is based on the JAXTX API discussed as part of JSR 156 and provides a reliable coordination infrastructure to support distributed transactions that span across multiple Web services.

- Atomikos provides support for the WS-Transaction standard with its product "Transactions," and is committed to adding any other future transaction standards, should the need arise. On the (Java EE) server side, Atomikos also offers the possibility to plug-in custom application logic for the global commit and/or rollback events of a Web service transaction (the so-called compensating transaction handler pattern). In addition, Atomikos Transactions offer bridging between different transaction protocols—for instance, a SOAP message can be received with a WS-T transaction context, and this transaction can then be transparently exported over RMI/IIOP with any remote RMI call made during the processing of the message.

- Choreology is another player in this space that provides implementation to the Business Transaction Protocol, among other standards.

- IBM released the Web Services Atomic Transaction for the WebSphere Application Server 5.0.2 Technical Preview (WSAT) distribution. This technical preview is the initial step toward building a distributed transaction support into the WebSphere application server.

- Microsoft also plans to integrate support for Web services transactions into the .NET platform.

Once industry players come within reach of transactional interoperability, achieving seamless integration across different vendors will become much simpler. In addition to the Web services-based transactional support, it is important to note that commercial vendors that provide the .NET Remoting implementation in Java also offer support for distributed transactions. For example, the JNBridgePro solution allows transaction propagation across Java EE and .NET.

Related Patterns

After having discussed the technologies of building distributed transactions across the Java EE and .NET space, the chapter now takes a look at the patterns that can be leveraged in this space when designing enterprise applications. There are a couple of patterns that can simplify the application architecture, including Transaction Handler and the Coarse-Grained Transaction Façade.

Transaction Handler

Problem Domain

When building distributed transactions, it is often necessary to have a transaction coordinator at the application level. For example, in order to create a Purchase Order, an Atomic Transaction may have to encapsulate multiple calls spanned across Java EE and .NET services, which requires the need for a transaction coordinator that resides at the application level. This may become necessary when the Java EE and .NET applications are integrated using Web services and do not rely on third-party transaction support.

Solutions

Global Transaction Handler

One solution to this problem is to create a distributed transaction coordinator, which can be realized in the form of the Global Transaction Handler. This component knows what services need to be invoked as part of a distributed transaction. The handler implements logic to create a purchase order to cancel the order in case there is an error. It also is responsible for invoking application logic components in a particular order. The Global Transaction Handler is implemented as part of the system that originates the transaction. If a Java EE application initiates a distributed transaction, then the Global Transaction Handler will be implemented in Java. The handler acts as a core manager responsible for the transaction workflow. This coordinator is agnostic to what technology is used to achieve transactional interoperability. Its core logic is to control application-level transactional lifecycles. A Global Transaction Handler can be implemented as a Singleton and should encapsulate a transaction identifier to uniquely identify a transaction. The Purchase Order Transaction Handler will have the following methods defined: `createOrder(TxnID txnId, PurchaseOrder order)`, `cancelOrder(TxnID txnId)`, and `commitOrder(TxnID txnId)`.

A disadvantage of this solution is that the Java EE or a .NET transaction handler has to have an explicit knowledge of when and how to cancel an ongoing transaction. More importantly, because the Global Transaction Handler is defined at the initiator side, the supplier Web service provider depends on the ability and the goodwill of the initiator to perform the cancellation when appropriate. This opens up opportunities for denial-of-service style attacks and implies a significant level of trust between initiator and supplier services.

Compensating Transaction Handler

An alternative solution would encompass a compensating transaction for the application-level two-phase commit. This solution can be implemented with a Compensating Transaction Handler pattern. In this scenario, if a failure or a time out occurs at any endpoint, the handler that coordinates the transaction issues a compensating transaction. A compensating transaction does not undo the failed transactions but negates their effect by compensating for it. In this example, a decrement to the product count succeeds where the purchase order creation fails. This would be followed by an instruction to reverse, or compensate, creation of the purchase order.

A compensating transaction can be applied when the initiator does not know when and how to cancel the endpoint transaction or if the cancel logic is not exposed to the client application in the first place. A compensating transaction also contributes toward better performance compared to the distributed two-phase commit protocol. The disadvantage of this approach is that the compensation occurs after the initial transaction has been committed and is visible to other applications and users, thus giving up isolation of the distributed transaction.

Coarse-Grained Transaction Façade

Problem Domain

In an application design where a distributed transaction encapsulates multiple calls to remote systems or services, it is important to ensure that those calls are fairly coarse-grained. Should a .NET application make multiple calls to the Java EE application as part of the transaction, it is important to evaluate the use case and possibly consolidate those calls into a single call. The main force for this pattern is to address performance and scalability concerns when building a distributed transaction.

Solution

To reduce a number of operations within an Atomic Transaction, it is useful to consolidate multiple transaction calls into a single call represented by a Transaction Façade. This approach is similar to a number of documented patterns such as Session Façade from the Core Java EE Pattern Catalog or a Transaction Script from Martin Fowler's "Patterns of Enterprise Application Architecture" [POEAA]. The main difference is that the Transaction Façade acts as a gateway to the .NET or Java EE business component rather than a database or an Entity Bean.

Best Practices and Pitfalls

The following recapitulates some best practices and pitfalls regarding the interoperability of managing transactions using Java EE and .NET platforms.

Performance and Scalability

A common 2PC might cause a performance overhead if the 2PC is used with a pessimistic locking. Individual resources hold a lock on a record for the duration of the transaction and prevent access to these records by other requests. In this scenario, multiple requests to the same product will not be successful because during the execution of the Inventory look-up call, that product record has to be locked to check availability and decrement its quantity. Therefore, an application architect has to make provision for data availability when addressing data integrity risks. In some cases an optimistic locking can be used in lieu of a pessimistic lock. Alternatively, a compensation-based approach can eliminate locking overhead. It is important to specify measurable Service Level Agreements (SLAs) when establishing the application integration criteria. In a purchase order example, the product availability lookup and the counter decrement should not take more than a few milliseconds, particularly when the integration occurs on an internal network. Similarly, throughput parameters may need to be available to ensure that the flow of requests does not cause a bottleneck.

Security

A Purchase Order application has to "trust" the Inventory application to perform a product availability check on its behalf. Along the same line, an Inventory application has to be authorized to make an Inventory call and access the underlying resources. From a best practices standpoint, it is important to ensure an adequate level of trust among all parties participating in a distributed transaction.

Reliability

Distributed transactions often have to be interoperable with the reliable messaging mechanism. In this chapter's example, the .NET Inventory Check service may require reliability to guarantee delivery of the request. Therefore, when assessing requirements it is imperative to make provision for reliability when selecting a distributed communication technology.

Summary

This chapter has explained how to implement distributed transactions between Java EE and .NET applications. With respect to best practices, messaging remains the main method to realize distributed transactions across two heterogeneous applications. With messaging, a critical factor pertains to whether all correct requirements are met (no reply, guaranteed delivery, and successful execution at the receiver). As the Web services transaction marketplace matures and gains wide product support, transactional interoperability with Web services will become another viable way to integrate Java EE and .NET systems. Unlike the messaging strategy, integration with Web services will not be bound to the same three requirements. The request-reply style of communication is possible within a transaction scope. The message delivery does not have to be reliable. Finally, the successful request execution is no longer required, but rather handled by the transaction manager.

Aside from the integration technology, there are at least a couple of considerations that have to be taken into account when implementing distributed transactions across Java EE and .NET. It is important that the designer of the integration use case attend to systemic qualities including performance, scalability, security, and reliability.

References

[ACID] The All App Labs Glossary.
http://www.allapplabs.com/glossary/acid.htm

[BTP] Business Transaction Protocol v1.0.
http://www.choreology.com/downloads/2002-0603.BTP.Committee.spec.1.0.pdf

[POEAA] Martin Fowler. Patterns of Enterprise Application Architecture. Addison-Wesley. September 2003. ISBN 0321127420

[SUNJTA] JTA API Home Page.
http://java.sun.com/products/jta/

[SUNWSCAF] Web Services Specifications to Co-Ordinate Business Applications.
http://developers.sun.com/techtopics/webservices/wscaf/

[SVCCMP] MSDN .NET Framework Library. ServicedComponent Class.
http://msdn.microsoft.com/library/default.asp?url=/library/enus/cpref/html/frl
rfSystemEnterpriseServicesServicedComponentClassTopic.asp

[SYSTSAMP] ADO.NET and System Transactions.
http://msdn.microsoft.com/msdnmag/issues/05/02/DataPoints/

[SYSTXN] System.Transactions Specifications.
http://www.microsoft.com/downloads/details.aspx?FamilyId=AAC3D722-444C-4E27-8B2E-C6157ED16B15&displaylang=en

[TXME] MSDN Resources on Transaction Management Escalation.
http://msdn2.microsoft.com/library/ms229978.aspx

[WSACOORD] Co-ordinating Web services activities.
http://msdn.microsoft.com/library/default.asp?url=/library/enus/dnwebsrv/html/wsacoord.asp

[WS-AT] Web Services Atomic Transaction.
http://schemas.xmlsoap.org/ws/2004/10/wsat/

[WS-TX] Web Services Transactions Specifications.
http://www-128.ibm.com/developerworks/library/specification/ws-tx/

[WSTXN] Web Services Transactions and Heuristics.
http://www.webservices.org/weblog/mark_little/web_services_transactions_and_heuristics

[XASPEC] Distributed Transaction Processing Specification.
http://www.opengroup.org/onlinepubs/009680699/toc.pdf

Java EE .NET Security
Interoperability

13

Security by Default

Security exploits and vulnerabilities are often causes of huge financial loss and disruption of business services. The Computer Security Institute (refer to [CSI] for details) has reported a worldwide financial loss of circa US$130 million that resulted from virus, unauthorized access, and theft of proprietary information in 2005, a US$7.3 million loss (compared to US$65 million loss in 2003) due to denial of service attacks, and an average US$355,552 (2005) loss per incident for proprietary information theft in 2003. A business application that was considered "secure" running on a Unix or Windows platform (for example, protected by firewall and anti-virus application) is not necessarily vulnerability-free when exchanging sensitive business data with another business application running on a different platform. This is because the interoperable solution is exposed to security vulnerabilities if one of the applications (either the sender or recipient) is exploited or is being attacked by hackers.

There are historic incidents of vulnerabilities in the Windows platform (such as flaw authentication [WindowsAuthFlaw]) or Java platform (such as a flaw in the JVM in [JavaVMFlaw]). These incidents are critical and can become the "Achilles' heel" (a critical problem that causes financial loss or disruption to the business service) for the mission-critical Java EE .NET interoperable solutions. Although the individual vulnerability incident may not be a direct root cause to security exploits of a Java EE .NET interoperable solution, any vulnerability exposed on either Solaris OE, Unix, Linux, or Windows platform becomes a "weakest link" to the security of the interoperable solution.

Web Services Interoperability (WS-I) identifies the following security threats that can impact Java EE .NET interoperability:

- **Message alteration**   changing the message header or body during the transit.

- **Attachment alteration**   changing the SOAP attachment during the transit.

- **Confidentiality**   the capability to ensure no unauthorized access is made to the message.

- **Falsified messages**   the message is falsified by using a different identity of the sender.

- **Man-in-the-middle**   the message is being spoofed or tampered with during transit.

- **Principal spoofing**   the information about the user or subject is being spoofed during transit.

- **Repudiation**   the sender or recipient denied or repudiated about the message being sent or received.

- **Forged claims**   the claim about sending the message is forged by tampering with the message content.

- **Message replay (or replay of message parts)**   the message was once spoofed and modified for resending the message.

- **Denial of service**   a malicious action to replay a message continuously or to overload the target service provider until the service provider is out of service.

To make a Java EE .NET interoperable solution *secure by default*, security architects and developers should consider the following security requirements. Also refer to [WSI-countermeasure] for the details of security scenarios and the counter-measures to the security threats.

- **Always Customize Security Settings** Do not take the default security settings of vendor products in the operating environment. Many business applications are not designed and deployed with security by default—they are designed with unused system services turned on when deployed, which may be open to security exploits and vulnerabilities that can severely impact the interoperable solution.

- **Use Open Standards for Interoperability** Web services security is currently an open standard for SOAP-based Web services. WS-I Basic Security Profile (BSP) 1.0 addresses these security threats. In essence, BSP 1.0 extends Web services security to handle SOAP attachments. These standards ensure that the applications are interoperable.

- **Use Strong Authentication Mechanisms.**

- **Use Secure Transport Mechanisms** Use of secure transport mechanisms such as SSL/TLS should address principal spoofing.

- **Use Digital Signature** Use of digital signature should address the security risks of message alteration, attachment alteration, confidentiality, repudiation, and forged claims. Signing the SOAP message header once, creation time, and optional user data over secure transport layer such as SSL/TLS are able to address the security risk of message replay.

- **Use Encryption** Use of encryption should address the security risks of confidentiality.

This chapter recapitulates the features of Java and .NET security that make interoperability easier. It also discusses different technologies (such as authentication in the Presentation tier) and the open standards (such as Web services security) where Java and .NET applications can interact. Finally, two interoperability strategies are discussed.

Java Security by Design

Application security is critical in Java technology. The Java runtime environment (aka JVM) provides a tightly guarded security environment for runtime execution. (Refer to [J2EE14], [J2EE14Tutor], and [LiGong] for more details.) Figure 13-1 depicts a high-level security overview. Inside the JRE, the Security Manager is responsible for code runtime verification and access control. The code runtime verification is managed by the Protection Domain, where different class files (namely, bootstrap class, system class, and user class) are verified by bootstrap class loader, system class loader, class loader, and the bytecode verifier. The Access Module is responsible to authenticate and authorize the principal (user or service requester) against the security policy files (namely, java.security and java.policy files). The JRE supports a variety of authentication mechanisms, including JAAS login module, database security (using JDBC), or LDAP (using JNDI).

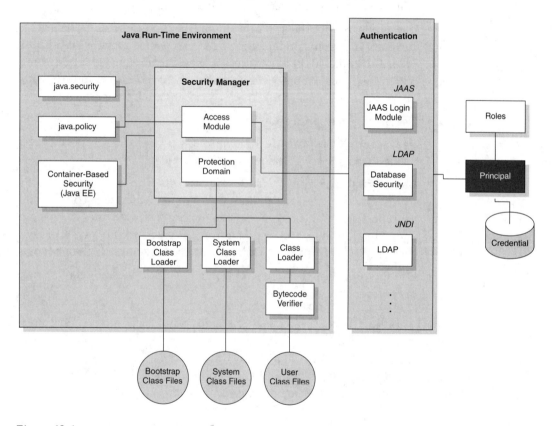

Figure 13-1
Java security overview

Java Runtime Security

Java SE provides a Java "sandbox" to restrict applets from accessing file systems and networks and untrusted applets from accessing all of the API functionality. The "sandbox" security architecture (refer to Figure 13-1) consists of three key components:

- **Bytecode Verifier** It verifies Java bytecodes that are compiled from Java source codes prior to execution. It ensures that the bytecodes do not violate permission policies or access system resources using incorrect type information.

- **Class Loader** The "primordial" (root) class loader bootstraps the class loading process and protects the runtime environment from loading harmful codes locally or remotely by hackers during the class loading process (so-called "code-spoofing"). It loads the initial classes required by all Java programs. The secure class loader `java.security.SecureClassLoader` then kicks off assembling and loading other classes locally, for example, bootstrap class files, system class files, and user class files.

  Class loading works under a class loader hierarchy. A child class must delegate to the parent class to load a specific class. If the parent class cannot load the specific class, then the child class loads it. Remote classes from the network are instantiated and loaded by the parent class loader as a new class. Thus hackers are not able to spoof attack by loading a malicious class directly into the JVM. For instance, hackers are able to insert a malicious version of `System.out.print` or `java.lang.String` into the application because the class loader loads a local version of `System.out.print` or `java.lang.String` under this class loading process. A Java archive (JAR) signer is a utility that seals packages for protection from tampering and verifies remote classes prior to loading to the JVM.

- **Security Manager** The security manager (`java.lang.SecurityManager`) performs runtime checks on any method or any code accessing sensitive system resources (for example, file or network access), and generates a security exception for any security policy violation. It delegates the permission check to the `java.security.AccessController` by calling the `checkPermission` method. The security manager can be invoked by specifying the system property while starting the JVM (for example, `java -Djava.security.manager myApps.class`) or creating an instance in the program code (for example, `System.setSecurityManager(new SecurityManager());)`

The security manager has a security policy database where security policies are maintained. The security policy database stores permission rules for authorization and key stores for authentication. A security policy relates to a set of permissions for a domain (system or application), which encloses a set of classes. Developers can also customize any additional protection of resources within the domain boundary, say, using the `SignedObject` class.

The **protection domain** (`java.security.ProtectionDomain` class) is another important security concept. It refers to the system and application components (for example, a group of classes) of the runtime environment that can be secured according to the predefined security policy. There are two types of protection domain: **static** (grant permissions specified only when constructed) and **dynamic** (grant permissions specified when constructed and permissions granted by the security policy). The protection domain extends the "sandbox" security architecture by associating a group of principals with permissions. For example, a protection domain associates permissions with a **code source** (URL where the class file comes from), such that any classes originating from the same URL will have the same signature and key placed in the same domain, and thus granted the same permissions and access rights. This enhances the current mechanism to load a class. Moreover, the security policy allows defining an association between the principals and permissions for the classes (via the code source). It can be passed as a parameter to the application, which can use different protection domains wherever necessary.

Java SE security introduces a set of additional security concepts (see [LiGong] for details), which includes the concepts of a **Principal** (an entity that a security service can authenticate with an authentication protocol) and **security domain** (the scope related to a set of security policies defined by the administrator of a security service). There are two important files under JVM that store security policy information: `java.policy` and `java.security` under the directory, %J2SE%/lib/security, where %J2SE% is the file location for the JVM.

Authentication Mechanisms

Figure 13-1 shows an example of three different authentication mechanisms. A subject (user) has multiple principals, or multiple user names or identities. Suppose one of his principals (using the `java.security.Principal` class) possesses a digital certificate as a credential. Under the Java SE security architecture, the principal can use the credential to authenticate with the applications via JAAS (using the `javax.security.auth.login.*` class), JNDI (using the LDAP directory server), or JDBC (using back-end database security). In this example, the security manager is used. Upon successful authentication, the security manager will check permission, and pass control to the access module. The access module (using the `java.security.AccessController` class) checks permission by checking the `java.security` file, which contains the policy URL (`policy.url.1`) and keystore information (`keystore.type`). The `java.security` file associates the permission (`grant ... permission ...`) with the principals. If the principal-permission relationship is found, then the access module grants access to the principal for the application resources to the principal

Apart from the "sandbox" security architecture, Java SE also provides some authentication and encryption services that work with JCA and JCE layers. These security services include JAAS, JSSE, JGSS, and CertPath. Applications or security packages can also customize their security APIs using these security services.

Container-Based Security

The Java EE container provides a comprehensive application-level security that is related to the application component deployment and runtime environment.

- **Declarative Security**   According to [J2EE14], Java EE security has the notion of declarative security. In other words, the application's security structure, including security roles, access control, and authentication requirements in a form external to the application, is expressed in the deployment descriptor. The **deployment descriptor** is in effect a contract between the application component provider and the deployer or application assembler, where the application security policy is mapped to the security structure of the relevant operating environment.

- **Programmatic Security**   Java EE security architecture also provides some APIs (programmatic security) to manipulate the roles and principals, in addition to the declarative security. This supports both servlets (`isUserInRole` and `getUserPrincipal` using the interface `HttpServletRequest`) and EJBs (`isCallerInRole` and `getCallerPrincipal` using the interface `EJBContext`).

Security Interoperability Features

Java technology has provided several interoperability features to secure business applications. The following highlights a few major security interoperability features:

- "Building block" security components to support interoperability, for example, JAAS and JSSE.

- JSR implementation that enables interoperability, for example, JAX-RPC 2.0 and WS-I Basic Security Profile 1.0/1.1.

- Support of single sign-on using Web SSO protocol, WS-MEX protocol, Liberty, and SAML.

- Support of security interoperability standards, for example, OASIS's Web services security.

- Support of WS-Policy by Java Web Services Developer Pack 2.1 or later.

.NET Security by Design

.NET security is targeted at developers. The .NET Framework provides a developer-centric and runtime security model on top of the Windows operating system security. It supports a *role-based security* that defines the access rights for resources using a role or a group. Role-based security addresses the security risk of broken access control for applications. At the software code level, the .NET Framework has **Code Access Security**, also known as **evidence-based security**, that defines whether or not a user can be trusted to access a resource. Code Access Security addresses the security risk of tampering or the use of a Trojan horse when downloading codes from external sources or Internet. Refer to [Watkins] for an overview of the .NET Framework security.

Figure 13-2 depicts a high-level security overview of the .NET Framework. The .NET Common Language Runtime (CLR) provides a runtime environment under the Windows hosting environment. When a .NET application is deployed, the .NET Framework assembles and deploys the .NET application to the target runtime environment in MSIL (Microsoft Intermediate Language) with the associated metadata. MSIL is an object-oriented assembly language that can be compiled to x86 native codes by a just-in-time compiler for execution in the CLR environment. **metadata** is a set of tables, also known as contract or blueprint, that depict the assembly's types, their methods, fields, signatures, and dependencies on other assemblies.

The .NET Common Language Runtime also provides a runtime security system that uses a policy manager to evaluate what permission should be granted to a service request. A Principal interacts with a .NET application and issues a service request to access resources. The security system in the CLR evaluates the service request based on the evidence, which is a set of information that constitutes input to security policy decisions, for example, origin of the codes and digital signature of the assembly, in the Windows hosting environment and the security policies defined in the CLR's policy levels and permission set.

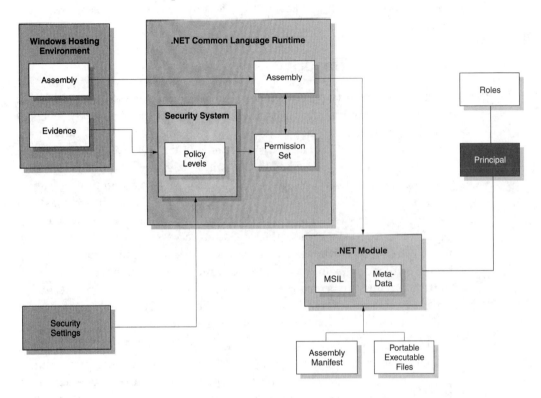

Figure 13-2
.NET security overview

A .NET application is composed of an assembly and one or more .NET modules. An **assembly** is the unit of code deployment in the .NET Common Language Runtime environment. It consists of an **assembly manifest** (a list of the assembly layout and global attributes) and one or more .NET modules. .NET modules are either DLLs or EXE Windows portable executable files. They contain the Microsoft Intermediate Language (MSIL), the associated metadata, and optionally the assembly manifest.

In the .NET CLR environment, an assembly uses the basic permission set class `System.Security.PermissionSet` to grant permissions to codes that are defined in the policy levels of the security system. Permissions can be code access permissions, which protect the resources directly, or identity permissions, which represent evidence that is granted to assemblies.

A Principal authenticates with the Windows system and invokes a .NET application to access a system resource. The CLR environment evaluates the security policies to determine whether the Principal has appropriate permission and access rights to execute the program codes and access the system resources.

Code Access Security

Code Access Security (CAS) is a key security feature of .NET Framework. It supports the requirement that different code should have different levels of trust. Using CAS, the security access control is based on the identity of the code, not individual user identity (such as user id), who executes or runs the software codes. This addresses the limitation of access control for different software codes by username-password, which is at a coarse granularity level. For example, developers can define code access security policies to constrain the ability of an assembly to perform file input/output and restrict file input/output to a specific directory. Code access security addresses the insufficiency of guarding against malicious or faulty codes that may have been downloaded from e-mail or the Internet that can damage files, though the user has already been authenticated and authorized to run the executable codes. In other words, CAS addresses the gap of protection against malicious codes and is complementary to role-based security.

CAS has three key elements: evidence, security policy, and permissions. Evidence refers to the set of information that constitutes input to security policy decision. This includes the characteristics of an assembly, such as the Web site from where an assembly is loaded. Security policy (also refer to next section for details) is a set of rules used by the runtime **policy resolution process**, also known as the Policy Decision Point, to determine which permissions an assembly can be granted. Permissions refers to the authority of an assembly's code to access protected operations and resources. There are three different permission classes in .NET: code-access permissions, for example, file input/output access granted to an assembly; identity permissions, where an assembly presents a certain host evidence value to the runtime policy resolution process as "identity;" and role-based permissions, when access is granted to a role, such as system administrator.

To illustrate how CAS works, consider a sample .NET application, "myinterop.exe," by re-using the architecture diagram in Figure 13-2. When a user runs the application "myinterop.exe," the .NET Common Language Runtime loads the "myinterop.exe" assembly from the Windows hosting environment. The runtime then evaluates its evidence and determines what permissions to grant the application against the defined security policies. For instance, the application, myinterop.exe, has a permission request to write to the text file "userpassword" in the local hard drive. The runtime's policy resolution process determines what permission should be granted to the assembly based on the security policies as well as the permission set assigned to the assembly (for example, `FileIOPermission` object defined in the myinterop.exe assembly). Once the runtime confirms that the application has the necessary permission to write to the text file, "userpassword," the runtime responds with a positive result to the `File.Write` method. Otherwise, the runtime throws a `System.Security.SecurityException` if the permission is not granted.

CAS is about the understanding of the relationship between evidence, policies, and permission, the details of which are beyond the scope of this chapter. Please refer to the References section for more resources.

Security Policies

Security policies in the .NET Framework refer to the mechanism for administrators to express the level of trust for different codes. There are four key elements of the .NET security policies:

- **Membership conditions** A membership condition resembles an object that answers "yes" or "no" when asked if an assembly matches its membership test. The membership conditions turn the evidence of an assembly into a grant set

- **Code groups** Code groups map the .NET Framework code to specific levels of trust. They are bindings between membership conditions and permission sets. If code matches the membership condition in a code group, it is ranked a permission set.

- **Policy levels** The `System.Security.Policy.PolicyLevel` class defines policy levels using a list of named permission sets, a code group hierarchy, and a list of "full trust" assemblies. There are four policy levels supported: enterprise, machine, user, and application domain. During the policy resolution of an assembly, the Policy Manager evaluates the assembly's evidence against each individual policy level via the `SecurityManager.ResolvePolicy` method.

- **Default security policy** This is the culmination of the default policies of all four policy levels, where each policy level has a hard-coded default. All default policy levels are identical with reference to the permission set lists and assembly lists. The permission set lists contain all the named permission sets.

Execution-Time Security

When an assembly is deployed to a target machine, the Assembly Loader loads the assembly in the CLR environment with the context of a trusted host, that is, the host is the trusted piece of code that is responsible to launch the runtime. The Policy Manager evaluates the current security policy, the evidence known about the assembly, and the set of permission requests, if any, made in the assembly metadata. It determines what permissions should be granted to the service requester based on the security policies for code access. Upon evaluation by the Policy Manager, the Class Loader loads the class for the JIT compiler to verify the codes prior to execution. The Code Manager then translates the classes into native code for execution.

Security Interoperability Features

.NET technology has provided several interoperability features to secure business applications. The following highlights a few major security interoperability features:

- Support of WS-I Basic Security Profile 1.0 via Web Services Enhancement (WSE).

- Support of single sign-on using Web SSO protocol via Active Directory Federation Services and the WS-MEX (metadata Exchange) protocol via Microsoft Windows Communication Foundation (WCF) or formerly Indigo.

- Support of security interoperability standards, for example, OASIS's Web Services Security.

- Support of WS-Policy. WSE is an add-on to the .NET Framework and provides a policy editor that allows defining policies for Web services using WS-Policy.

Security for Interoperability

Previous chapters have discussed that Java and .NET applications can interoperate synchronously or asynchronously in different architecture tiers. As security is end-to-end, security for interoperability should not be limited to a single application component (for example, .NET bridge) or a specific architecture tier (for example, Web tier). Further, the security requirements for interoperability in each architecture tier are different. This section discusses the security requirements and what enabling technologies and security standards are available to address these requirements. The details of security standards for interoperability are discussed in the next section. Adopting interoperability technologies that support security standards allows wider choice of vendor products and easier implementation.

Figure 13-3 depicts the areas of security for interoperability that have support for security standards such as WS-I Basic Security Profile and WS-Security. A Java client should be able to perform a single sign-on with the .NET application and similarly for a .NET client with a Java application. To ensure client-to-server communication is secure, developers can use HTTPS or SSL/TLS to encrypt the communication channel.

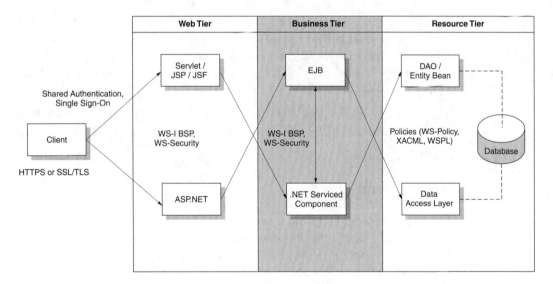

Figure 13-3
Security for interoperability

In both the Web and the Business tiers, the client should be able to initiate service requests or exchange business data synchronously or asynchronously using Web services (with WS-I BSP and WS-Security). This should allow a servlet, JSP, or JSF component under the Web tier to interoperate with a .NET service component under the Business tier—or an ASP.NET page under the Web tier to interoperate with an EJB object under the Business tier.

In the Resource tier, a Java servlet or EJB component can also request access to resources such as business data and database objects implemented by means of the Data Access Layer using a policy language such as

WS-Policy, XACML, and Web Services Policy Language (refer to next section for more details). Similarly, a .NET-serviced component can also share the same policy language (provided that they are available in both .NET and Java language) when requesting access to resources via Data Access Objects or Entity Beans.

There are always business scenarios in the existing or legacy environment that Figure 13-3 does not cover. As most of these scenarios use nonstandard interoperability technologies that are usually proprietary or highly customized on a case-by-case basis, they require additional cost and efforts to analyze the potential security risks and to mitigate the vulnerabilities. For example, if a bridge technology is used for Java EE .NET interoperability, developers and security architects need to analyze the risks of the bridge technology and the customized application codes that connect to the bridge. The bridge would become an easier target for hacking or the single point of failure attacks. Even though the security for the bridge is strong, there may be considerable unknown risks for the customized application codes related to it.

The following sections elaborate on the security requirements of the Java EE .NET interoperability and discuss the technologies available to mitigate the security risks.

Secure Transport

The client-to-server session is often a target of security spoofing. A basic security requirement for interoperability when exchanging user credentials or sensitive business data is secure data transport. Java and .NET applications can use HTTPS or SSL/TLS in the data transport layer to secure the client-to-server session. Secure data transport can ensure confidentiality and reduce the risk of principal spoofing.

Security Interoperability by Tiers

Interoperability at the Web Tier

A Java client can authenticate with an Active Directory or a Directory Server using a JAAS login module. Similarly, a .NET client can authenticate with a Directory Server. Digital certificates can be used as a common user credential; however, Java and .NET clients need to create shared session state in order to interoperate in a heterogeneous environment. The capability to authenticate with both Java and .NET application servers and to create shared common session data are key security requirements for interoperability. These security requirements allow the Principal to share session information between the Java and .NET environments and not necessitate relogin.

A Java client can authenticate with a .NET application using the shared authentication approach. Similarly, a .NET client can also authenticate with a Java application using the same shared authentication approach. Shared authentication here refers to the use of form-based authentication and customization of shared session data for both Java and .NET applications. Form-based authentication allows page-level authentication to a Web application. Shared session data can be stored in a customized shared session state database or a Directory Server using existing session APIs in both Java and .NET platforms—for example, Java has many APIs under the `javax.servlet.http.HttpSession` class, and .NET has `Shared Session` object.

Nevertheless, customized processing logic for shared authentication and shared session data are often proprietary and are specific to certain implementation. The use of Web SSO MEX (Single Sign-on metadata Exchange) protocols is a proposed standard for Java EE .NET interoperability to achieve single sign-on and should be recommended. Please refer to the following section for more details.

Shared authentication, shared session data, and single sign-on using Web SSO MEX protocol are mechanisms to address broken authentication and session management. They also rely on strong authentication mechanisms, for example, use of digital certificates and strong user passwords, and reliable authentication infrastructure such as Directory Server. For Web services such as asynchronous SOAP messages, it is critical to use the WS-I Basic Security Profile (BSP) and WS-Security standards. WS-I BSP ensures that both Java and .NET applications are using a common semantic for SOAP messages. WS-Security supports service requests or replies that are digitally signed and/or encrypted to ensure confidentiality. It addresses the risk of message alteration, attachment alteration, falsified messages, repudiation, forged claims, and message replay.

Interoperability at the Business Tier

Security interoperability requirements for the Business tier are similar to those for the Web tier. The key difference is that the Business tier interaction is often server-to-server, not client-to-server. Interaction between .NET-serviced components and EJBs or service requests from the Web tier are often point-to-point, and these components do not use SSL/TLS, which is used for client-to-server communication. Customized and point-to-point security processing logic (for example, encrypted transactions) that secures the business transactions in the Business tier is usually proprietary and is unlikely to be reusable in another environment. For interoperability using Web services, WS-I BSP and WS-Security provide an open standard to secure business transactions. For interoperability using a bridge technology, developers need to rely on customized encryption or proprietary security mechanism.

Interoperability at the Resource Tier

Both Java and .NET platforms support a variety of access control mechanisms to determine which resources are accessible to the service requesters. They may either embed the access control processing logic into the programming codes or use a policy framework. Using a policy framework, developers can decouple the custom access control processing logic from the application codes. Because the access control processing logic is separate from the application codes, it will be more flexible, allowing management of changes without the need to recompile or retest the entire application for every security policy change.

Without a common policy framework, an interoperability solution needs to rely on two different access control systems. If the two policy frameworks are "out of sync," the service requester may be denied access. It is also time-consuming to troubleshoot which side of the policy framework is problematic.

The use of common and standard security policies, such as WS-Policy and XACML, across Java and .NET platforms addresses the risk of broken access control. For example, Microsoft's Web Services Enhancement provides support for WS-Policy, and Sun's XACML Kit is available on both Java and .NET platforms. Please refer to the next section for details on these policy frameworks.

Support of Audit Control and Compliance

In recent years, support of audit control and compliance (for example, Sarbanes-Oxley, Gramm-Leach-Bliley Act of 1994, HIPPA or Health Insurance Privacy and Portability Act of 1996) has become a key security interoperability requirement. These compliance requirements are focused in building the capability for tracking unusual or suspicious user activities, ranging from unauthorized access to suspicious high volume business transactions. They also require a timely report of the unusual or suspicious security events, and tracing the source of the service requesters. Thus, it is extremely important that the Java and .NET interoperability design should be able to have risk mitigation mechanisms for security attacks, and to build up capability for "track and trace" of any unusual security events and service requests.

Security Standards for Interoperability

One of the purposes of creating security standards is the ease of interoperability. Using security standards, developers have more flexibility to interoperate between Java and .NET applications and do not lock in with a specific vendor product. This section introduces security standards and specifications for interoperability using Web services with details: WS-Security, WS-I Basic Security Profile, XACML, WS-Policy, Web Services Policy Language, and Single Sign-on Metadata Exchange (SSO MEX). Table 13-1 provides a list of security standards and specifications that are relevant for Java EE .NET interoperability. Although WS-Policy and SSO MEX are not a security standards yet, they are important security specifications for Java EE .NET interoperability.

Table 13-1
List of Security Standards and Specifications for Interoperability

	Security Standards	Security Specifications
Application Security	Web Services Security (OASIS)	
	WSI Basic Security Profile (WSI)	
Policy	XACML (OASIS)	
	Web Services Policy Language (OASIS)	WS-Policy
Single Sign-on		SSO MEX
Others (not covered in this chapter)		WS-Trust
		WS-SecureConversation

Web Services Security

Web services security (WS-Security) is an approved standard to secure SOAP messages under OASIS. It leverages XML Digital Signature and XML Encryption for message integrity and confidentiality. WS-Security provides an abstract message security model that specifies how to protect a SOAP message in terms of a security token and digital signature. Security tokens are simply assertions of claims about the user identity and can be used to assert the binding between the authentication secrets, keys, or security identities. WS-Security currently supports a variety of security tokens, for example, user name token (aka password), binary token (such as the X.509v3 certificate or Kerberos ticket), and XML tokens.

From a Java EE .NET interoperability perspective, WS-Security plays a key role because it defines a standard format where a Java and .NET application can exchange business data. Listing 13-1 shows a .NET program excerpt how to sign a message using a X.509 certificate.

Listing 13-1
Sample .NET Program Excerpt Showing How to Sign a Message with an X.509 Certificate

```
using System;
using Microsoft.Web.Services2.Security;
using Microsoft.Web.Services2.Security.Tokens;
using Microsoft.Web.Services2.Security.X509;
using Microsoft.Web.Services2.QuickStart;

namespace X509SigningClient {
    /// <summary>
    /// This is a sample which allows the user to send a message to
    /// a Web
    /// service that has been signed with an x.509 certificate.
    /// </summary>
    class X509SigningClient : AppBase {

        [MTAThread]
        static void Main(string[] args) {

            X509SigningClient client = null;
            try {
                client = new X509SigningClient();
```

```
            client.Run();
        } catch (Exception ex) {
            Error(ex);
        }
        Console.WriteLine( "Sample   .NET X.509 Signing Client" );
        Console.WriteLine();
    }

    public void Run() {
        // Create and configure Web service proxy
        //
        //ManufactureDelegate serviceProxy = new
            ManufactureDelegate(...);
        //ConfigureProxy(serviceProxy);
        ...
        // Fetch X.509 security token and generate asymmetric key
        // 'false' forces to use WSE sample certificate
        X509SecurityToken token =
            AppBase.GetClientToken(false);

        if (token == null)
            throw new ApplicationException
                ("Cannot retrieve security token!");

        // Add the signature element to a security section on the
        // request
        // to sign the request
        serviceProxy.RequestSoapContext.Security.Tokens.Add(token);
        serviceProxy.RequestSoapContext.Security.Elements.
            Add(new MessageSignature(token));

        // Invoke business service
        ...
    }
}
```

A Java platform provides low-level and fine-grained programming APIs that generate XML signatures using the JSR 105 (XML signature) API (refer to Listing 13-2 for an example). In practice, developers do not use these fine-grained APIs directly to sign a message in WS-Security. There are tools available to implement WS-Security with coarse-grained programming APIs. For example, JWSDP version 1.5 provides a useful WS-Security security handler, `SecurityEnvironmentHandler`, that refactors the encryption, decryption, and the digital signing processing logic into handlers. It does not require developers to embed the common security processing logic into the application. Developers can simply turn on or off the security processing logic in a configuration file (refer to the next section, "Secure Object Handler Strategy").

Listing 13-2
Sample Java Program Excerpt Generating a Digital Signature

```java
import javax.xml.crypto.*;
import javax.xml.crypto.dsig.*;
import javax.xml.crypto.dom.*;
import javax.xml.crypto.dsig.dom.DOMSignContext;
import javax.xml.crypto.dsig.keyinfo.*;
import java.io.FileInputStream;
import java.io.FileOutputStream;
import java.io.OutputStream;
import java.security.*;
import java.util.Arrays;
import java.util.Collections;
import javax.xml.parsers.DocumentBuilderFactory;
import javax.xml.transform.*;
import javax.xml.transform.dom.DOMSource;
import javax.xml.transform.stream.StreamResult;
import org.w3c.dom.Document;
import org.w3c.dom.Node;

public class SigningClient {

    public static void main(String[] args) throws Exception {

        // Create digital signature factory
        String providerName = System.getProperty
            ("jsr105Provider",
```

```
     "org.jcp.xml.dsig.internal.dom.XMLDSigRI");
XMLSignatureFactory dsigFactory =
    XMLSignatureFactory.getInstance("DOM",
    (Provider) Class.forName(providerName).newInstance());

// Create document factory and object reference using SHA1
// digest
Reference ref = dsigFactory.newReference("#object",
    dsigFactory.newDigestMethod(DigestMethod.SHA1, null));

DocumentBuilderFactory docFactory =
    DocumentBuilderFactory.newInstance();
docFactory.setNamespaceAware(true);
Document doc = docFactory.newDocumentBuilder().newDocument();
Node text = doc.createTextNode("PO number");

XMLStructure content = new DOMStructure(text);
XMLObject obj = dsigFactory.newXMLObject
    (Collections.singletonList(content), "object", null, null);

// Create the SignedInfo
SignedInfo signedInfo = dsigFactory.newSignedInfo(
    dsignFactory.newCanonicalizationMethod
    (CanonicalizationMethod.INCLUSIVE_WITH_COMMENTS, null),
        dsignFactory.newSignatureMethod(SignatureMethod.DSA_SHA1,
        null),
    Collections.singletonList(ref));

// Create a DSA KeyPair
KeyPairGenerator keyPairGen =
    KeyPairGenerator.getInstance("DSA");
keyPairGen.initialize(512);
KeyPair keyPair = keyPairGen.generateKeyPair();

// create key value using DSA public key
KeyInfoFactory keyInfoFactory =
    dsigFactory.getKeyInfoFactory();
KeyValue keyValue =
    keyInfoFactory.newKeyValue(keyPair.getPublic());
KeyInfo keyInfo =
```

continues

Listing 13-2 (continued)
```
keyInfoFactory.newKeyInfo(Collections.singletonList(keyValue);

    // create XML signature
    XMLSignature signature = dsigFactory.newXMLSignature(signedInfo,
        keyInfo,Collections.singletonList(obj), null, null);

    // create context using DSA private key
    DOMSignContext signContext = new
        DOMSignContext(keyPair.getPrivate(), doc);

    // Generate enveloping signature using private key
    signature.sign(signContext);
    ...


    }
}
```

WS-I Basic Security Profile

Web Services Interoperability (WS-I)'s Basic Security Profile (BSP) version 1.0 (refer to [BSP] for details) is a draft specification that defines the semantics of using the elements of OASIS's Web Services Security and places constraints on its use to achieve interoperability. BSP includes the following key characteristics:

- **Elements of a Secure SOAP Message** BSP uses elements defined in the Web Services Security 1.0 specification and includes a secure envelope, secure message, security header, reference, digital signature, encrypted key, encryption reference list, encrypted key reference list, encrypted data, security token reference, internal security token, and timestamp.

- **Secure Transport Layer** HTTP over TLS 1.0/SSL 3.0 should be used for transport layer security. Though BSP does not prohibit use of any specific TLS or SSL ciphersuites, it recommends ciphersuites that support the AES encryption algorithm, for example, TLS_RSA_WITH_AES_128_CBC_SHA, and discourages ciphersuites that are vulnerable to man-in-the-middle attacks, for example, SSL_RSA_WITH_NULL_SHA.

- **SOAP Message Security**   BSP places some constraints in the use of binary security tokens, for example, only `Base64Binary` encoding type is supported, and `<wsse:BinarySecurityToken>` with a single X.509 certificate in the element `<wsu:Id>` must have the `ValueType` value http://docs.oasis-open.org/wss/2004/01/oasis-200401-wss-x509-token-profile-1.0#X509v3. The `ValueType` element is interesting and important from the perspective of ensuring openness and interoperability because it is used to define customer bearer tokens, which is used, for instance, by the Liberty Alliance for single sign-on. Moreover, BSP defines the semantics of a creation timestamp (`<wsu:Timestamp>`) element to be used for each `<wsu:Created>` element but does not allow leap seconds. BSP also specifies the order of processing the signature and encryption blocks (that is, signature, encrypted key, and encryption reference list) within the `<wsse:Security>` headers so that the recipient gets the correct result by processing the elements in the order they appear.

- **Username Token Profile**   BSP specifies the semantics regarding the use of a username token, for example, the `<Type>` attribute (such as `Type='http://docs.oasis-open.org/wss/2004/01/oasis-200401-wss-username-token-profile-1.0#PasswordText')` must be specified to avoid any ambiguity of the element, `<wsse:Password>`. Another example is that Web Services Security does not fully describe the proper `ValueType` for the username token, and BSP uses the value `http://docs.oasis-open.org/wss/2004/01/oasis-200401-wss-soap-messagesecurity-1.0#User nameToken for the attribute wsse:SecurityTokenReference/wsse:Reference/@ValueType`.

- **X.509 Certificate Token Profile**   Web Services Security supports three token types (namely, X509v3, x509PKIPathv1, and PKCS7) in the X.509 certificate token profile. BSP places some constraints to the profile, for example, when certificate path information is provided via either X509PKIPathv1 or PKCS7 formats, the sender must provide one of the X509PKIPathv1 or PKCS7 token types. In addition, when the element, `<wsse:KeyIdentifier>`, is used within a security token reference to denote an X.509 certificate token, the element, `<wsse:KeyIdentifier>`, must use the value `http://docs.oasis-open.org/wss/2004/01/oasis-200401-wss-x509-token-profile-1.0#X509SubjectKeyIdentifier` in the `<ValueType>` attribute.

- **Use of XML Signature**   BSP places some constraints on the use of XML Signature—for example, the enveloping signature is not allowed, and a detached signature should be used instead. BSP also recommends two key signature algorithms (hmac-sha1 and rsa-sha1) and one digest algorithm (SHA1) for interoperability.

- **Use of XML Encryption**   BSP adds some constraints on the use of XML Encryption—for example, an encrypted key `<xenc:Encrypted Key>` must precede any encrypted data in the same security header.

- **Attachment Security**   BSP specifies some constraints on the SOAP with Attachments for interoperability, one of which is that secure message must conform to WS-I Attachment Profile 1.0. BSP also defines the semantics around the signed attachments—for example, reference to a signed MIME part must use a URI attribute of the form `"cid:partToBeSigned"`, and encrypted attachments—for example, encrypted data referencing a MIME part must include a type attribute with the value of either `"...#Attachment-Content-Only"` or `"...#Attachment-Complete"`.

XACML

Business applications usually have custom security policies to determine which resources or business data a service requester can access. Some applications may tightly couple the access control processing logic with the business processing logic. This would make the access control policies very difficult to extend or customize. For Java and .NET applications running on different platforms, it is fairly important to have a generic, flexible, and adaptive policy framework that operates on both Java and .NET applications. When there is a change of access control policy, developers do not need to modify their program logic or recompile their programs.

eXtensible Access Control Markup Language (XACML) version 2.0 is an approved security policy management standard under OASIS (refer to [XACML2]). Currently, it has both Java and .NET implementations. XACML is both a policy language and an access control decision request-response language encoded in XML. It is used to express authorization rules and polices and to evaluate rules and policies for authorization decisions. Moreover, XACML is used to make authorization decision requests and responses.

In a typical application environment, a user wants to make a request to access certain resources. The Policy Enforcement Point (PEP) is a system or application that protects the resources. The PEP needs to check whether the service requester is eligible to access the resources. It sends the resources request to the Policy Decision Point (PDP), which looks up the security access control policies. XACML provides both a policy language and an access control decision request-response language to meet the security access control requirements. With XACML, the PEP forms a query language to ask the PDP whether or not a given action should be allowed. The PDP responds by returning the value of either `Permit`, `Deny`, `Indeterminate` (decision cannot be made due to some errors or missing values), or `Not Applicable` (the request cannot be answered by this service).

XACML Components

XACML provides a rich policy language data model to define flexible and sophisticated security policies. The following summarizes the key components in an XACML data model, [XACML2]:

- **Policies** A policy represents a single access control policy, expressed through a set of rules. Policies are a set of rules together with a rule-combining algorithm and an optional set of obligations. Obligations are operations specified in a policy or policy set that should be performed in conjunction with enforcing an authorization decision. Each XACML policy document contains exactly one Policy or PolicySet root XML tag.

- **Policy Set** A Policy Set is a set of policies or other Policy Sets and a policy-combining algorithm, and a set of optional obligations.

- **Rules** Rules are expressions describing conditions under which resource access requests are to be allowed or denied. They apply to the target (`<Target>`), which can specify some combination of particular resources, subjects, or actions. Each rule has an effect (which can be `permit` or `deny`) that is the result to be returned if the rule's target and conditions are true. Rules can specify a condition (`<Condition>`) using Boolean expressions and a large set of comparison and data-manipulation functions over subject, resource, action, and environment attributes.

- **Target** A Target is basically a set of simplified conditions for the Subject, Resource, and Action that must be met for a PolicySet, Policy, or Rule to apply to a given request. These use Boolean functions (explained more in the next section) to compare values found in a request with those included in the Target. If all the conditions of a Target are met, then its associated PolicySet, Policy, or Rule applies to the request. In addition to being a way to check applicability, Target information also provides a way to index policies, which is useful if several policies need to be stored and then quickly sifted through to find which ones apply.

• **Attributes**   Attributes are named values of known types that may include an issue identifier or an issue date and time. Specifically, attributes are characteristics of the Subject, Resource, Action, or Environment in which the access request is made. For example, a user's name, their group membership, a file they want to access, and the time of day are all attribute values. When a request is sent from a PEP to a PDP, that request is formed almost exclusively of attributes, which are compared to attribute values in a policy to make the access decisions.

Example

Listing 13-3 depicts a service request to access the URL http://www.supply-chain.com/purchaseorder.html. The service requester is a buyer with the subject buyer@javadotnetinterop.com and the access rights group `tradingPartner`.

Listing 13-3
Sample Service Request to Access a URL

```
<?xml version="1.0" encoding="UTF-8"?>
<Request xmlns="urn:oasis:names:tc:xacml:2.0:context"
        xmlns:xsi="http://www.w3.org/2001/XMLSchema-instance">
   <Subject>
     <Attribute
        AttributeId=
  "urn:oasis:names:tc:xacml:2.0:subject:subject-id"
        DataType=
"urn:oasis:names:tc:xacml:2.0:data-type:rfc822Name">
      <AttributeValue>
          buyer@javadotnetinterop.com
      </AttributeValue>
     </Attribute>
     <Attribute
        AttributeId="group"
           DataType=
        http://www.w3.org/2001/XMLSchema#string
           Issuer=
```

```
                    "admin@javadotnetinterop.com">
          <AttributeValue>tradingPartner</AttributeValue>
        </Attribute>
      </Subject>
      <Resource>
        <Attribute AttributeId=
        "urn:oasis:names:tc:xacml:2.0:resource:resource-id"
                DataType=
            "http://www.w3.org/2001/XMLSchema#anyURI">
          <AttributeValue>
http://www.supplychain.com/purchaseorder.html
</AttributeValue>
        </Attribute>
      </Resource>
      <Action>
        <Attribute
           AttributeId=
      "urn:oasis:names:tc:xacml:2.0:action:action-id"
           DataType=
      "http://www.w3.org/2001/XMLSchema#string">
          <AttributeValue>execute</AttributeValue>
        </Attribute>
      </Action>
    </Request>
```

Listing 13-4 defines the security policy in XACML. The policy indicates that only service requesters with the e-mail address javadotnetinterop.com and the access rights group tradingPartner can access the URL, http://www.supplychain.com/purchaseorder.html.

Listing 13-4
Sample XACML Policy

```
<?xml version="1.0" encoding="UTF-8"?>
<Policy xmlns="urn:oasis:names:tc:xacml:2.0:policy"
      xmlns:xsi="http://www.w3.org/2001/XMLSchema-instance"
      PolicyId="MemberCanPlaceOrder_ObligationPolicy"
      RuleCombiningAlgId=
      "urn:oasis:names:tc:xacml:2.0:rule-combining-algorithm:permit-
overrides">
```

continues

Listing 13-4 (continued)

```
<Description>
    This policy states that trading partners with a valid domain name
    @javadotnetinterop.com should be able to submit purchase order
    online using the URL http://www.supplychain.com/purchaseorder.html
    Both successful and invalid read request are logged using
    Obligation.

    If users have a different domain name other than
    @javadotnetinterop.com, this policy will deny access.
    If users with a domain name @javadotnetinterop.com who
    are NOT trading partners this policy also deny their access.

    This policy illustrates use of "Condition" within a
    "Target" element to apply constraints to the read access
    for the requester who are Administrator only. It also
    provides an example of "Obligation"
    to log successful read and log invalid access.
</Description>

<Target>
  <Subjects>
    <Subject>
      <SubjectMatch MatchId=
          "urn:oasis:names:tc:xacml:2.0:function:rfc822Name-match">
        <AttributeValue
          DataType=
          "http://www.w3.org/2001/XMLSchema#string">
          javadotnetinterop.com
        </AttributeValue>
        <SubjectAttributeDesignator
          DataType=
          "urn:oasis:names:tc:xacml:2.0:data-type:rfc822Name"
          AttributeId=
          "urn:oasis:names:tc:xacml:2.0:subject:subject-id"/>
      </SubjectMatch>
    </Subject>
  </Subjects>
  <Resources>
    <Resource>
      <ResourceMatch
        MatchId=
```

```
          "urn:oasis:names:tc:xacml:2.0:function:anyURI-equal">
        <AttributeValue
          DataType=
          "http://www.w3.org/2001/XMLSchema#anyURI">
          http://www.supplychain.com/purchaseorder.html
        </AttributeValue>
        <ResourceAttributeDesignator
          DataType=
          "http://www.w3.org/2001/XMLSchema#anyURI"
          AttributeId=
          "urn:oasis:names:tc:xacml:2.0:resource:resource-id"/>
      </ResourceMatch>
    </Resource>
  </Resources>
  <Actions>
    <AnyAction/>
  </Actions>
</Target>

<Rule RuleId="ExecuteRule" Effect="Permit">
  <Target>
    <Subjects>
      <AnySubject/>
    </Subjects>
    <Resources>
      <AnyResource/>
    </Resources>
    <Actions>
      <Action>
        <ActionMatch
          MatchId=
          "urn:oasis:names:tc:xacml:2.0:function:string-equal">
          <AttributeValue
            DataType="http://www.w3.org/2001/XMLSchema#string">
            execute
          </AttributeValue>
        <ActionAttributeDesignator
          DataType=
          "http://www.w3.org/2001/XMLSchema#string"
          AttributeId=
          "urn:oasis:names:tc:xacml:2.0:action:action-id"/>
```

continues

Listing 13-4 (continued)

```
        </ActionMatch>
      </Action>
    </Actions>
  </Target>
      <Condition
        FunctionId=
        "urn:oasis:names:tc:xacml:2.0:function:string-equal">
    <Apply FunctionId=
    "urn:oasis:names:tc:xacml:2.0:function:string-one-and-only">
      <SubjectAttributeDesignator
        DataType="http://www.w3.org/2001/XMLSchema#string"
        AttributeId="group"/>
    </Apply>
    <AttributeValue
      DataType=
      "http://www.w3.org/2001/XMLSchema#string">
      tradingPartner
    </AttributeValue>
    </Condition>
</Rule>

<Rule RuleId="DenyOtherActions" Effect="Deny"/>

<Obligations>
  <Obligation
    ObligationId="LogSuccessfulExecute"
    FulfillOn="Permit">
    <AttributeAssignment
      AttributeId="user"
      DataType=
      "http://www.w3.org/2001/XMLSchema#anyURI">
        urn:oasis:names:tc:xacml:2.0:subject:subject-id
    </AttributeAssignment>
    <AttributeAssignment
      AttributeId="resource"
      DataType="http://www.w3.org/2001/XMLSchema#anyURI">
      urn:oasis:names:tc:xacml:2.0:resource:resource-id
    </AttributeAssignment>
  </Obligation>
  <Obligation
```

```
      ObligationId="LogInvalidAccess"
      FulfillOn="Deny">
     <AttributeAssignment
        AttributeId="user"
        DataType="http://www.w3.org/2001/XMLSchema#anyURI">
        urn:oasis:names:tc:xacml:2.0:subject:subject-id
     </AttributeAssignment>
     <AttributeAssignment
        AttributeId="resource"
        DataType="http://www.w3.org/2001/XMLSchema#anyURI">
        urn:oasis:names:tc:xacml:2.0:resource:resource-id
     </AttributeAssignment>
     <AttributeAssignment
        AttributeId="action"
        DataType="http://www.w3.org/2001/XMLSchema#anyURI">
        urn:oasis:names:tc:xacml:2.0:action:action-id
     </AttributeAssignment>
    </Obligation>
   </Obligations>

</Policy>
```

When applying the XACML security policy using Sun XACML Kit's sample policy engine (SimplePDP), the policy engine shows a positive policy evaluation result, and the service requester is granted access to the URL in question. Refer to Listing 13-5.

Listing 13-5
Evaluating an XACML Policy

```
C:\XACML2\sunxacml-1.2\sample>java SimplePDP request\request.xml
policy\policy.xml
<Response>
  <Result ResourceID=
       "http://www.supplychain.com/purchaseorder.html">
    <Decision>Permit</Decision>
    <Status>
      <StatusCode
        Value="urn:oasis:names:tc:xacml:2.0:status:ok"/>
    </Status>
    <Obligations>
```

continues

Listing 13-5 (continued)

```
    <Obligation
        ObligationId="LogSuccessfulExecute"
        FulfillOn="Permit">
      <AttributeAssignment
          AttributeId="user"
          DataType=
          "http://www.w3.org/2001/XMLSchema#anyURI">
          urn:oasis:names:tc:xacml:2.0:subject:subject-id
      </AttributeAssignment>
      <AttributeAssignment
          AttributeId="resource"
          DataType=
          "http://www.w3.org/2001/XMLSchema#anyURI">
          urn:oasis:names:tc:xacml:2.0:resource:resource-id
      </AttributeAssignment>
    </Obligation>
   </Obligations>
  </Result>
</Response>
```

WS-Policy

Policies are useful in specifying the conditions or assertions regarding inter-actions between Java and .NET interoperable applications. These policies can be defined for authentication, authorization, quality of protection, quality of service, privacy, reliable messaging, and service-specific options (such as bandwidth guarantee). For Java EE .NET interoperable solutions using Web services, there are two emerging policy-related specifications: WS-Policy and WSPL (Web services policy language).

WS-Policy (Web Services Policy) framework is part of the Web Services roadmap and specifications (a.k.a., WS*) proposed by Microsoft, IBM, VeriSign, and others. It is primarily a policy language that defines polices for Web services. WS-Policy encodes the policy definition in XML using SOAP messages for data exchange. These Web services policies are a collection of "policy alternatives," which are a collection of policy assertions such as authentication scheme, privacy policy, and so forth. This policy framework is a flexible mechanism to define rules for executing Java and .NET applications even though they run on different software platforms and different underlying implementations. Currently, there is a draft JSR 265 specification for Web services policy (refer to www.jcp.org/en/jsr/detail?id=265 &showPrint for details).

Please note that WS-Policy is still not yet an open standard. Some extensions and usage of WS-Policy are now defined in the WS-SecurityPolicy specification. The new OASIS Web Services Secure Exchange (WS-SX) Technical Committee (http://www.oasis-open.org/committees/tc_home .php?wg_abbrev=ws-sx) is working on finalizing a set of specifications based on WS-SecureConversation, WS-SecurityPolicy, and WS-Trust specifications.

Unlike XACML, the WS-Policy specification does not restrict the policy definitions to access control or privacy. WS-Policy can be used to specify the type of security token, digital signature algorithm, and encryption mechanism for a SOAP message (for example, a purchase order message) or even partial contents of a SOAP message (a credit card number, for example). In addition, it can also specify data-privacy or data-confidentiality rules. Nevertheless, WS-Policy does not specify how to discover policies or how to attach a policy to a Web service. It relies on other WS* specifications (for example, WS-PolicyAttachment) to provide full functionality of policy management.

Listing 13-6 shows an example of a WS-Policy that uses Triple DES and RSA OAEP (RSA Optimal Asymmetric Encryption Padding) encryption key algorithms.

Listing 13-6
Sample WS-Policy File

```
<?xml version="1.0" encoding="utf-8"?>
<configuration>
  <configSections>
    <section name="microsoft.web.services2"
type="Microsoft.Web.Services2.Configuration.WebServicesConfiguration,
Microsoft.Web.Services2, Version=2.0.0.0, Culture=neutral,
PublicKeyToken=31bf3856ad364e35" />
  </configSections>
  <microsoft.web.services2>
    <security>
      <x509 storeLocation="CurrentUser" allowTestRoot="true"
          allowRevocationUrlRetrieval="false" verifyTrust="true" />
      <binarySecurityTokenManager
          valueType="http://docs.oasis-open.org/wss/2004/01/oasis-
200401-wss-x509-token-profile-1.0#X509v3">
```

continues

Listing 13-6 (continued)

```
        <sessionKeyAlgorithm name="TripleDES" />
        <keyAlgorithm name="RSAOAEP" />
      </binarySecurityTokenManager>
      <securityTokenManager
          xmlns:wsse="http://docs.oasis-open.org/wss/2004/01/oasis-
200401-wss-wssecurity-secext-1.0.xsd"
          qname="wsse:UsernameToken" />
    </security>
    <diagnostics>
      <trace enabled="true" input="InputTrace.webinfo"
          output="OutputTrace.webinfo" />
    </diagnostics>
    <policy>
      <cache name="policyCache.config" />
    </policy>
    <tokenIssuer>
      <autoIssueSecurityContextToken enabled="true" />
    </tokenIssuer>
  </microsoft.web.services2>
</configuration>
```

Under WS-Policy, there is a set of policy assertions for each policy domain. For example, the assertions for use with WS-Security are defined in WS-SecurityPolicy. Each specification or schema to be controlled or managed by WS-Policy requires definition of a new set of assertions.

Under the WS-Policy model, a policy for Web services denotes conditions or assertions regarding the interactions between two Web services endpoints. The service provider exposes a Web services policy for the services they provide. The service requester decides, using the policies, whether it wants to use the service, and if so, the "policy alternative" it chooses to use. In other words, WS-Policy does not have the notion of a Policy Enforcement Point, which enforces policies, and a Policy Decision Point, which also determines policies. It leaves the policy enforcement and decision to the service providers and service requesters.

Web Services Policy Language

WSPL (Web Services Policy Language) is based on XACML and is currently a working draft in the OASIS XACML technical committee. It uses a strict subset of XACML syntax (restricted to Disjunctive Normal Form) and has a different evaluation engine than XACML. XACML evaluates the access-control policies with a given set of attributes and policies, while WSPL determines what the mutually acceptable sets of attributes are when given two policies. For a good introduction on WSPL refer to [Anne3].

WSPL has provided similar functionality to define policies for Web services. WSPL has the semantics of policy and operators, which allow comparison between an attribute of the policy and a value or between two attributes of the policy. The policy syntax also supports rule preference. There are three distinctive features in WSPL. First, it allows policy negotiation, which can merge policies from two sources. Second, policy parameter allows fine-grained parameters such as time of day, cost, or network subnet address to be defined in a policy for Web services. Third, the design of WSPL is flexible enough to support any type of policy by expressing the policy parameters using standard data types and functions.

One main problem WSPL has addressed is the negotiation of policies for Web services. Negotiation is necessary when choices exist or when both parties, Web services consumers and service providers, have preferences, capabilities, or requirements. In addition, it is necessary to automate service discovery and connection related to policies.

WSPL shares similar policy definition capabilities with WS-Policy. Listing 13-7 shows a policy defined in WS-Policy, which specifies the security token usage and type for the Web services. It uses the element, `<ExactlyOne>`, to denote the security token usage.

Listing 13-7
Policy for a Security Token Usage and Type Defined in WS-Policy

```
<wsp:Policy>
   <wsp:ExactlyOne>
      <wsse:SecurityToken>
         <wsse:TokenType>wsse:Kerberosv5TGT
         </wsse:TokenType>
      <wsse:/SecurityToken>
      <wsse:SecurityToken>
         <wsse:TokenType>X509v3
         </wsse:TokenType>
      <wsse:/SecurityToken>
   </wsp:ExactlyOne>
</wsp:Policy>
```

Listing 13-8 shows that the same policy can be expressed in WSPL. WSPL translates the policy requirements into two rules. This makes it more descriptive and extensible in the event that security architects and developers need to add more operators or constraints.

Listing 13-8
Sample WSPL Policy Showing Two Rules that Need to Be Satisfied

```
<Policy PolicyId="policy:1" RuleCombiningAlgorithm="&permit-
overrides;">
  <Rule RuleId="rule:1" Effect="Permit">
    Condition FunctionId="&function;string-is-in">
     <AttributeValue DataType="&string;">Kerberosv5TGT</AttributeValue>
     <ResourceAttributeDesignator
        AttributeId="&SecurityToken;"
        DataType="&string;"/>
    </Condition>
  </Rule>

  <Rule RuleId="rule:2" Effect="Permit">
    <Condition FunctionId="&function;string-is-in">
      <AttributeValue
        DataType="&string;">X509v3</AttributeValue>
      <ResourceAttributeDesignator
        AttributeId="&SecurityToken;"
        DataType="&string;"/>
    </Condition>
  </Rule>
</Policy>
```

WS-Policy and WSPL share similar functional features for interoperable Java EE .NET solutions. Anderson has identified a few technical limitations of WS-Policy when compared with WSPL (refer to [Anne2] for details):

- **Negotiation** WS-Policy does not specify a standard merge algorithm or standard way to specify policy negotiation (for example, for merging policies from two sources). Specifications for domain-specific WS-Policy Assertions may describe how to merge or negotiate assertions, but these methods are domain-specific.

- **Assertion Comparison**   Because there is no standard language for defining Assertions in WS-Policy, there is no standard way to describe requirements such as `minimumPurchaseQuantity > 3000`. Again, specifications for domain-specific WS-Policy Assertions may describe schema elements for such comparisons, but the implementation of these elements must be done on a domain-by-domain basis given there is no standard.

- **Dependency**   WS-Policy is designed to depend on extensions. Each extension must be supported by a custom evaluation engine.

Web Single Sign-On Metadata Exchange (SSO MEX)

Both Java and .NET platforms have different approaches in achieving single sign-on. Liberty and SAML protocols are open standards that have wide Java-based implementations. On the .NET side, WS-Federation is used to provide single sign-on functionality. To enable both sides of the single sign-on technologies to interoperate, a new protocol is defined to enable browser-based Web single sign-on between security domains that use different protocols such as Liberty ID-FF and WS-Federation. The Web Single Sign-on Metadata Exchange (Web SSO MEX) primarily specifies a protocol that is independent of the stack and a profile specifying the interoperability between Liberty Identity Federation Framework and WS-Federation. It is not restricted to .NET (or WCF) and Liberty.

The Web SSO MEX protocol defines how a service queries an identity provider for the metadata regarding the identity-federation protocol suites supported by that identity provider. The Web Single Sign-on interoperability profile further describes how the Web SSO MEX protocol is used to enable interoperability between two particular protocol stacks: Liberty's ID-FF 1.2 browser POST profile and WS-Federation Passive Requestor Interoperability profile.

Technology Challenges

A service provider's identity provider may be supporting multiple identity providers, such as Liberty-based and WS-Federation-based identity federation solutions. Both identity management solutions have very different designs and implementations for account federation. For example, Liberty federates different accounts via identity mapping using opaque identifiers, while WS-Federation federates accounts via identity mapping using the

Pseudonym Service. Handling of security tokens can be designed and implemented in different ways as well. For example, Liberty extends SAML assertions for communicating authentication and authorization security tokens between security providers, while WS-Federation uses X.509v3 and Kerberos profiles from the WS-Security specification. For details on the differences between Liberty and WS-Federation, please refer to [LibertyWSFed].

Use Case Scenario

A sample use case scenario (refer to Figure 13-4) would be a Web supply chain portal that supports both Liberty-based and WS-Federation-based identity federation infrastructures. A buyer browses through the online catalog and places purchase orders with two different suppliers. One supplier uses Liberty identity federation framework, denoted in the circles in Figure 13-4, for their supply chain system, and the other supplier uses the WS-Federation identity federation protocol for their order management system, denoted in the triangles in the figure.

Using the Web SSO MEX protocol, the Web portal, acting as the Identity Provider in this scenario, can identify which single sign-on protocol to work with. Each identity federation infrastructure manages its own security token information (such as single sign-on token, SAML assertion, session information, and authentication information). However, there is no data conversion, data exchange, or security token mapping between the two single sign-on systems. Many security vendors are creating products for security token mapping soon. For example, Sun Java System Access Manager (http://www.sun.com/software/products/access_mgr/) now can provide single sign-on token information between the two identity federation infrastructures.

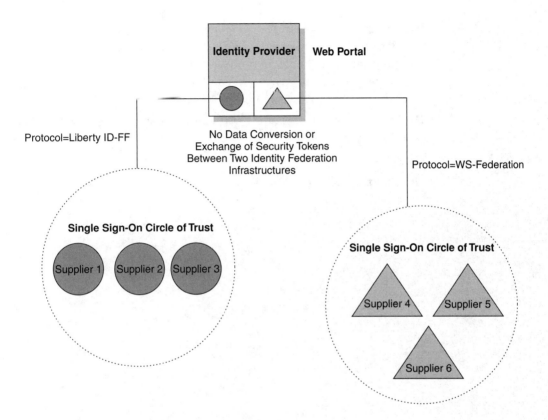

Figure 13-4
Web portal use case scenario

Figure 13-5 depicts a sequence diagram for the message flow between the client (buyer), the service provider (supplier), and the identity provider (Web portal):

- Upon successful authentication, the client selects the Target Service from the Web portal.

- The client indicates its Identity Provider to the Target Service (Step 1).

- The Target Service formulates the Identity Provider (Step 2) and issues a request for the supported identity federation protocol from the Identity Provider (Step 3).

- The Identity Provider returns the protocol suite document to the Target Service.

- The Target Service determines the appropriate protocol suite (Step 4).

- The Target Service begins to exchange documents or messages using the common protocol suite-based single sign-on operations (Step 5). In this step, multiple single sign-on operations are required, and these operations, such as authentication and authentication assertions, vary according to the single sign-on protocols used.
- The Target Service is now able to provide business service based on the user identity (Step 6).

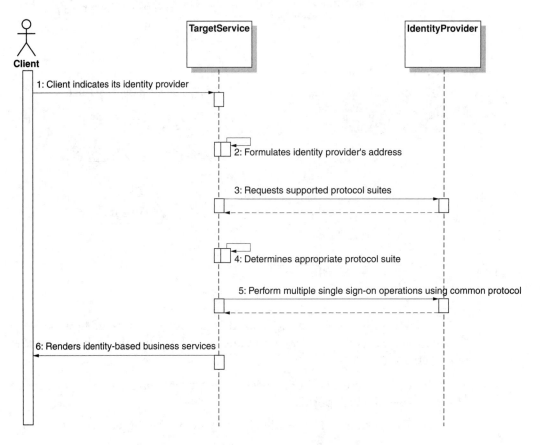

Figure 13-5
Web SSO sequence diagram

The service provider indicates an identity provider by any of the following four methods:

- Special header in the HTTP request (EPR-base64)
- Query string parameter in the URL
- Custom mechanism (such as mapping table, user prompt)
- EPR constructed using DNS name for the requester (client)

Sample Web SSO MEX Message

Listing 13-9 depicts a request message for Web SSO.

Listing 13-9
Sample Web SSO MEX Message

```
<s12:Header>
   <wsa:Action>
   http://schemas.xmlsoap.org/ws/2004/09/mex/GetMetadata/Request
   </wsa:Action>
   <wsa:MessageID>
   uuid:53daedfc-4c3c-38b9-ba46-2480caee43e9
   </wsa:MessageID>
   <wsa:ReplyTo>
      <wsa:Address>
      http://client.javadotnetinterop.com/Endpoint
      </wsa:Address>
   </wsa:ReplyTo>
   <wsa:To>http://service.sun.com/IdentityProvider</wsa:To>
   <ssi:SsiProtocolSuiteHandler/>
</s12:Header>
<s12:Body>
   <wsx:GetMetadata>
      <wsx:Dialect>
      http://schemas.xmlsoap.org/ws/2005/04/SsiSuites
      </wsx:Dialect>
   </wsx:GetMetadata>
</s12:Body>
```

Listing 13-10 shows a response message to the MEX request message.

Listing 13-10
Sample Web SSO MEX Reply

```
<s12:Header>
   <wsa:Action>
   http://schemas.xmlsoap.org/ws/2004/09/mex/GetMetadata/Response
   </wsa:Action>
   <wsa:MessageID>
   uuid:73d7edfc-5c3c-49b9-ba46-2481caee4177
   </wsa:MessageID>
   <wsa:RelatesTo>
   uuid:73d7edfc-5c3c-49b9-ba46-2480caee43e9
   </wsa:RelatesTo>
   <wsa:To>http://client.javadotnetinterop.com/MyEndpoint</wsa:To>
</s12:Header>
<s12:Body>
   <wsx:Metadata>
     <wsx:MetadataSection
     Dialect='http://schemas.xmlsoap.org/ws/2005/04/SsiSuites' >
       <wsp:ExactlyOne>
       . . .
       </wsp:ExactlyOne>
     </wsx:MetadataSection>
   </wsx:Metadata>
</s12:Body>
```

Secure Object Handler Strategy

Problems

It is not uncommon for developers to embed the security processing logic (such as verifying the access rights of the requester and signing the message) in the application code. Such practice allows easy testing of both business functionality and security requirements, without dependency on external program units that provide security functions. This becomes convenient when building Java EE .NET interoperable applications where each platform has its own security processing requirements. However, when the business application grows larger in scale or becomes highly distributed, the maintenance effort and support to manage a change in the security processing logic is enormous. For example, a change in the message digest algorithm or in the access rights processing logic may require considerable program changes in each application program, recompilation and subsequent retesting.

Handlers are processes that can take the service request from the requester's object and process it. For example, a handler can be customized to digitally sign a SOAP message when a service request is created. Thus there is no need to embed the digital signing processing logic in the service requester's application. In essence, handlers are internal representations of actions when an event is triggered or a service request is received. When applied to Java EE .NET interoperability, handlers can be used to execute security processing actions such as digital signing of the SOAP messages, executing the access rights control for a service request, or creating an audit event for the Java EE .NET interoperability actions. Using a secure object handler can decouple the security process from the business processing logic so that the Java EE .NET interoperability solution can be scalable and more manageable.

Solution

The Secure Object Handler strategy applies to both synchronous, asynchronous and bridge interoperability strategies. In essence, the secure object handler intercepts the service request and adds custom processing logic, such as adding a digital signature, to the incoming business data object. Using the object handler strategy, developers do not need to rewrite the application processing logic because they can modify existing handlers directly or add new handlers, or chained handlers.

With synchronous or asynchronous integration, the Secure Object Handler can take the service requester's message or object, and apply the handler action, such as digital signing, encryption/decryption, or tracking the security actions for security audit or compliance reasons. Using a bridge interoperability strategy via, for example, an Enterprise Service Bus, the Secure Object Handler can act as a "service engine" or transformer process for the inbound or outbound service provider.

Although using a handler is a neat strategy, not all interoperability technologies can support the same implementation approach of creating a Secure Object Handler. The following sections discuss different types of technology options for each interoperability strategy that can implement a Secure Object Handler.

Synchronous Integration

Synchronous integration enables a Java client to interoperate with a .NET application in a synchronous mode, and vice versa for a .NET client with a Java application. In the synchronous communication between the service requester (client) and the service provider (application), the client waits in a "blocked state," in which no processing or communication with other processes are made until the service provider completes the service request.

.NET Remoting and RPC-style Web services are examples of synchronous integration technologies. .NET implemented in C#, for example, implements the notion of a handler programmatically at the application code level. The client needs to invoke the handler explicitly. If a developer needs to change the handler or update the processing logic in the handler, he or she needs to modify the application codes, recompile, test, and deploy them again.

Listing 13-11 shows a sample secure object handler code that processes a group of service requests (in string array). If the incoming service request contains the string password, then the client invokes the handler Encrypting to encrypt the service request. If the incoming service request contains the string creditCard or cashPayment, then the client invokes the handler DigitalSigning to perform digital signature. If the service request contains the string news, the client invokes the handler SecureLogging to log the service request for audit control.

Listing 13-11
Sample Secure Object Handler in .NET Using Synchronous Integration

```
using System;

/// <summary>
///     Abstract class definition for handler
/// </summary>
abstract class Handler {

  protected Handler succeedBy;

/// <param name="succeedBy" type="Handler">
///set next successor to the current method</param>
  public void SetSuccessor(Handler succeedBy) {
    this.succeedBy = succeedBy;
  }
```

```
/// <param name="serviceRequest" type="string">
///invoking secure object handler</param>
   abstract public void SecureObjectHandler(string serviceRequest);
}


/// <summary>
///      Encrypting handler will encrypt the data object or message
///      using XML-Encryption and WS-Security
/// </summary>
class Encrypting: Handler {

/// <param name="serviceRequest" type="string">
///invoking secure object handler for Encrypting</param>
   override public void SecureObjectHandler(string serviceRequest) {
      if (serviceRequest == "password")
      //
      // add your encryption processing logic
         Console.WriteLine("'{0}' secure object handler processed for
'{1}'",
            this, serviceRequest);
      else if (succeedBy != null)
         succeedBy.SecureObjectHandler(serviceRequest);
   }
}


/// <summary>
///    Digital Signing handler will digitally sign the data
///    object or message using
///    XML-Signature and WS-Security
/// </summary>

class DigitalSigning : Handler {

/// <param name="serviceRequest" type="string">
///invoking secure object handler DigitalSigning</param>
   override public void SecureObjectHandler(string serviceRequest) {
      if ((serviceRequest == "cashPayment") ||
         (serviceRequest == "creditCard"))
      //
      // add your digital signing processing logic
```

continues

Listing 13-11 (continued)

```
        Console.WriteLine("'{0}'
          secure object handler processed for '{1}'",
          this, serviceRequest);
      else if (succeedBy != null)
        succeedBy.SecureObjectHandler(serviceRequest);
    }
}


/// <summary>
///     SecureLogging handler will log the user info and business
///     transaction reference
///     for audit trail and/or compliance
/// </summary>
class SecureLogging : Handler {

/// <param name="serviceRequest" type="string">
///invoking secure object handler SecureLogging</param>
   override public void SecureObjectHandler(string serviceRequest) {
      if (serviceRequest == "news")
      //
      // add your secure logging processing logic
        Console.WriteLine("'{0}' secure object handler processed for
'{1}'",
           this, serviceRequest);
      else if (succeedBy != null )
        succeedBy.SecureObjectHandler(serviceRequest);
    }
}



/// <summary>
///     Client class to invoke a business transaction or service
///     request.
///     The secure object handler will be invoked.
/// </summary>

public class Client {


/// <summary>
```

```
///     Main method for Client class
/// </summary>
  public static void Main(string[] args) {

    // Setup Chain of Responsibility
    Handler encrypting = new Encrypting();
    Handler digitalSigning = new DigitalSigning();
    Handler secureLogging = new SecureLogging();
    encrypting.SetSuccessor(digitalSigning);
    digitalSigning.SetSuccessor(secureLogging);

    // Generate and process serviceRequest
    string[] serviceRequests = {"password", "creditCard", "cashPayment",
"news", "others"};

    Console.WriteLine("Secure Object Handler for Synchronous Integration
- Example");
    Console.WriteLine();
    Console.WriteLine();

    foreach (string serviceRequest in serviceRequests)
      encrypting.SecureObjectHandler(serviceRequest);

    Console.Read();
  }
}
```

RPC-style synchronous Web services usually have support of handlers at the container level. For example, Sun Java Web Services Developer Pack (JWSDP) version 1.6 and Apache Axis version 1.2 allow developers to add handlers without modifying the application codes. In JWSDP, developers can specify a configuration file for their server security environment configuration, such as the certificate alias of the digital signature and the name of the handler. Refer to Listing 13-12 for the sample configuration file. The sample handler SecurityEnvironmentHandler.java is an implementation of a CallbackHandler that provides digital signature and encryption functionality. The application codes do not need to embed any of the security processing logic.

Listing 13-12
Sample Security Environment Configuration File *wsse.xml* in JWSDP

```xml
<xwss:JAXRPCSecurity
xmlns:xwss="http://java.sun.com/xml/ns/xwss/config">

<xwss:Service>
    <xwss:SecurityConfiguration dumpMessages="true">

    <xwss:Sign>
        <xwss:X509Token certificateAlias="slas"/>
    </xwss:Sign>

    <xwss:Encrypt>
        <xwss:X509Token certificateAlias="wse2client"/>
    </xwss:Encrypt>

    </xwss:SecurityConfiguration>
</xwss:Service>

<xwss:SecurityEnvironmentHandler>
    com.sun.xml.wss.sample.SecurityEnvironmentHandler
</xwss:SecurityEnvironmentHandler>

</xwss:JAXRPCSecurity>
```

When building secure object handlers for synchronous integration, developers need to ensure the client is properly authenticated with the server and authorized for the business services prior to invoking the services. This is to ensure that no unauthorized user can invoke the business service. Having these security measures in place addresses the risks of confidentiality, principal spoofing, repudiation, broken authentication, and broken access control.

Asynchronous Integration

Asynchronous integration is loosely coupled interaction between the service requester (client) and the service provider (server). Unlike synchronous integration, asynchronous integration does not require that the client go into a blocked state until the processing of the service request is complete.

Document-style Web service is a common example of asynchronous integration using Web services. It encapsulates the service request or the reply in the form of a message, which can be encrypted or decrypted for confidentiality and digitally signed for non-repudiation. Synchronous integration also uses the same handler mechanism in the Web services container, such as JWSDP or Axis, as discussed earlier, to encapsulate the security processing logic.

When building secure object handlers, asynchronous integration requires similar security requirements, such as authenticating the service requester with the server, as in synchronous integration. The emphasis is on securing the message instead of securing the service requester or the service provider. The sender of the message can be authenticated prior to sending the message. Alternatively the message can be authenticated, digitally signed with a valid certificate for example, and verified intact or not being modified upon receipt to ensure that it is a valid message. Having these security measures in place would address the risks of message alteration, message replay, and repudiation.

Integration Using Enterprise Service Bus

Java EE .NET interoperability using a bridge or an Enterprise Service Bus (ESB) supports both synchronous and asynchronous integration strategies. The bridge or ESB acts as an intermediary between the Java and .NET platform. The security requirements of both synchronous and asynchronous integration strategies discussed earlier also apply to the ESB integration strategy.

ESB has recently become a common example of interoperability in a Service Oriented Architecture (SOA) environment probably because of the multi-messaging protocol and agility in integrating heterogeneous platforms. Not all ESB products support the implementation of a handler. In the example of Mule ESB (http://mule.codehaus.org), Mule allows handlers to be added to an inbound or outbound process. Listing 13-13 shows an example of a Mule ESB configuration where the tag inboundTransformer can specify a secure object handler. The object SecureObjectHandler is a Java class in the current class path that can be programmed to perform security processing such as digital signature for the incoming messages or service requests. Similarly, a secure object handler can be added under the tag outboundTransformer to embed any security processing for outbound messages or reply. For example, all replies to the service requests need to be encrypted and digitally signed using a Secure Object Handler.

Listing 13-13
Sample Mule ESB Configuration to Specify a Secure Object Handler

```xml
<?xml version="1.0" encoding="UTF-8"?>
...
<mule-configuration id="sampleProperties" version="1.0">
   <connector name="SystemStreamConnector"
className="org.mule.providers.stream.SystemStreamConnector">
      <properties>
        ...
      </properties>
   </connector>

   <model name="MuleClient">
      <mule-descriptor name="ESBClient"
         inboundEndpoint="stream://System.in"
         inboundTransformer="SecureObjectHandler"
         outboundEndpoint="vm://mule/receive"
         implementation="com.sun.esb.samples.MuleClient">
      </mule-descriptor>
   </model>
</mule-configuration>
```

The technology details for creating a handler vary depending on the ESB
product used. It is important to ensure that the client using the ESB is properly authenticated. Moreover, the ESB product adopted should allow adding
or modifying Secure Object Handlers without changing the application processing logic.

Creating Handlers

There is no common or standard way to implement handlers. For example,
developers can use a callback handler design approach to include the
security processing logic. For instance, JWSDP has a sample handler
SecurityEnvironmentHandler.java in the samples directory. Each platform or product may have different mechanisms to implement and customize Secure Object Handlers. The following design considerations can
apply regardless of the platform chosen:

- Decouple the security processing logic from the business processing logic. Factor the common security processing logic, such as digital signing, into a Secure Object Handler.

- Use the application server infrastructure, such as JWSDP with Sun Java System Application Server, to support chained handlers if possible. Refer to earlier sample configuration files.

- Use a policy framework to implement handlers because policy is declarative and is easier to make changes to when compared to implementing handlers programmatically. Listing 13-14 shows an example of specifying the handler in the application configuration file `policyCache.config`, which can be generated by using the built-in WSE policy editor.

Listing 13-14
Sample *policyCache.config* File

```
<?xml version="1.0" encoding="utf-8"?>
<policyDocument
    xmlns="http://schemas.microsoft.com/wse/2003/06/Policy">

  <mappings
      xmlns:wse="http://schemas.microsoft.com/wse/2003/06/Policy">
    <!--The following policy describes the policy requirements for the
service: http://localhost:8080/OrderService/OrderService .-->
    <endpoint uri="http://localhost:8080/OrderService/OrderService">
      <defaultOperation>
        <request policy="#Sign-X.509" />
        <response policy="" />
        <fault policy="" />
      </defaultOperation>
    </endpoint>
  </mappings>

  <policies
      xmlns:wsu="http://docs.oasis-open.org/wss/2004/01/oasis-200401-
wss-wssecurity-utility-1.0.xsd"
      xmlns:wsp="http://schemas.xmlsoap.org/ws/2002/12/policy"
      xmlns:wssp="http://schemas.xmlsoap.org/ws/2002/12/secext"
      xmlns:wse="http://schemas.microsoft.com/wse/2003/06/Policy"
      xmlns:wsse="http://docs.oasis-open.org/wss/2004/01/oasis-200401-
```

continues

Listing 13-14 (continued)

```
wss-wssecurity-secext-1.0.xsd"
    xmlns:wsa="http://schemas.xmlsoap.org/ws/2004/03/addressing">

 <wsp:Policy
      wsu:Id="Sign-X.509">
    <!--MessagePredicate is used to require headers. This assertion
should be used along with the Integrity assertion when the presence of
the signed element is required. NOTE: this assertion does not do
anything for enforcement (send-side) policy.-->

     <wsp:MessagePredicate
        wsp:Usage="wsp:Required"
        Dialect="http://schemas.xmlsoap.org/2002/12/wsse#part">
        wsp:Body()
        wsp:Header(wsa:To)
        wsp:Header(wsa:Action)
        wsp:Header(wsa:MessageID)
        wse:Timestamp()
     </wsp:MessagePredicate>
    <!--The Integrity assertion is used to ensure that the message is
signed with X.509. Many Web services will also use the token for
authorization, such as by using the <wse:Role> claim or specific X.509
claims.-->
     <wssp:Integrity
        wsp:Usage="wsp:Required">
       <wssp:TokenInfo>
        <!--The SecurityToken element within the TokenInfo element
describes which token type must be used for Signing.-->
         <wssp:SecurityToken>
           <wssp:TokenType>
             http://docs.oasis-open.org/wss/2004/01/oasis-200401-wss-
x509-token-profile-1.0#X509v3
           </wssp:TokenType>
           <wssp:TokenIssuer>
             CN=Root Agency
           </wssp:TokenIssuer>

         <wssp:Claims>
           <!--By specifying the SubjectName claim, the policy system
can look for a certificate with this subject name in the certificate
store indicated in the application's configuration, such as LocalMachine
```

or CurrentUser. The WSE X.509 Certificate Tool is useful for finding the correct values for this field.-->

```
                <wssp:SubjectName
                    MatchType="wssp:Exact">
                    CN=WSE2QuickStartClient
                </wssp:SubjectName>
                <wssp:X509Extension
                    OID="2.5.29.14"
                    MatchType="wssp:Exact">gBfo01471M6cKnTbbMSuMVvmFY4=
                </wssp:X509Extension>
            </wssp:Claims>

        </wssp:SecurityToken>
        </wssp:TokenInfo>

        <wssp:MessageParts
            Dialect=
              "http://schemas.xmlsoap.org/2002/12/wsse#part">
            wsp:Body() wsp:Header(wsa:Action)
            wsp:Header(wsa:FaultTo)
            wsp:Header(wsa:From)
            wsp:Header(wsa:MessageID)
            wsp:Header(wsa:RelatesTo)
            wsp:Header(wsa:ReplyTo)
            wsp:Header(wsa:To)
            wse:Timestamp()
        </wssp:MessageParts>

      </wssp:Integrity>
    </wsp:Policy>
  </policies>
</policyDocument>
```

WSE 2.0 provides a configuration editor that reads the input from the app.config or Web.config file and generates the policy cache file in Listing 13-14. (Refer to the "Example" section later in the chapter for more details.) The policy Sign-X.509 and the handler details are referenced in the app.config or Web.config file. If the incoming SOAP request with the element <wsse:BinarySecurityToken> does not contain the appropriate binary security token that meets the policy defined here, an exception is thrown.

If a developer wants to a add new handler, he can write a custom policy assertion handler that is derived from the `Microsoft.Web.Services.Policy.PolicyAssertion` class and register it in the `app.config` or `Web.config` file. Refer to Listing 13-15 for an example.

Listing 13-15
Adding a Custom Handler in the *app.config* or *Web.config* Configuration Files

```
using Microsoft.Web.Services.Policy;
public class MySecureObjectHandler : PolicyAssertion {
   // add your customized security processing logic here
   // to override the member functions
}
```

In the app.config or Web.config configuration file, you need to add an assertion element to the policy section. This assertion element maps a policy assertion element name (such as wsp:MessagePredicate) and registers it in the configuration file.

```
<?xml version="1.0" encoding="utf-8"?>
<configuration>
  <configSections>
   ...
  </configSections>
  <microsoft.web.services>
   <policy>
     <receive>
       <cache name="policyCache.xml"/>
     </receive>
     <assertion name="wsp:MessagePredicate"
               type="SecureObjectHandler"
               xmlns:wsp="..." />
   </policy>
  </microsoft.web.services>
   ...
</configuration>
```

In JWSDP, a handler can be customized to extend a callback handler. Listing 13-16 shows a sample template where you can customize your handlers under the public method "handle." For details, please refer to the JWSDP API documentation to implement a callback handler.

Listing 13-16
Sample *SecurityEnvironmentHandler* Callback Handler Template in JWSDP

```
import javax.security.auth.callback.Callback;
import javax.security.auth.callback.CallbackHandler;
import javax.security.auth.callback.UnsupportedCallbackException;
import com.sun.xml.wss.impl.callback.CertificateValidationCallback;
import com.sun.xml.wss.impl.callback.DecryptionKeyCallback;
import com.sun.xml.wss.impl.callback.EncryptionKeyCallback;
import com.sun.xml.wss.impl.callback.PasswordCallback;
import com.sun.xml.wss.impl.callback.PasswordValidationCallback;
import com.sun.xml.wss.impl.callback.SignatureKeyCallback;
import com.sun.xml.wss.impl.callback.SignatureVerificationKeyCallback;
import com.sun.xml.wss.impl.callback.UsernameCallback;
import com.sun.org.apache.xml.security.utils.RFC2253Parser;
// insert your additional Java class libraries...
...

public class SecureObjectHandler implements CallbackHandler {
    // ...

    public SecureObjectHandler() throws Exception {
        // define your constructor details
    }

    public void handle(Callback[] callbacks) throws IOException,
UnsupportedCallbackException {
        for (int i=0; i < callbacks.length; i++) {

            if (callbacks[i] instanceof PasswordValidationCallback) {
                // implement your own password validation processing
                // logic
            } else if (callbacks[i] instanceof
SignatureVerificationKeyCallback) {
                // implement your own digital signature verification
                // processing logic
```

continues

Listing 13-16 (continued)

```
        } else if (callbacks[i] instanceof SignatureKeyCallback) {
            // implement your own signature key processing logic
        } else if (callbacks[i] instanceof DecryptionKeyCallback) {
            // implement your own decryption key processing logic
        } else if (callbacks[i] instanceof EncryptionKeyCallback) {
            // implement your own encryption key processing logic
        } else if (callbacks[i] instanceof
CertificateValidationCallback) {
            // implement your own digital certificate validation
            //  processing logic
        } else {
            throw unsupported;
        }
      }
    }
    // ...
}
```

It's best to use known interoperable encryption key or session algorithms. For example, RSA Optimal Asymmetric Encryption Padding (RSAOREA) and Triple DES are interoperable between .NET and JWSDP.

Example

This example illustrates a .NET client (Retailer) placing a purchase order with the service provider (Manufacturer). The .NET client invokes a purchase order Web service from a Java application service with the details of the account number, SKU number, supplier item number, and quantity. Upon completion of the purchase order submission, the service provider returns a receipt number.

The .NET client uses the installed X.509 certificate to sign the service request and encrypt the business data. The JWSDP server validates the message digest and decrypts the business data. This example demonstrates the interoperability of the digital signature and the encryption/decryption between the .NET client and the JWSDP server using Web services security.

Gates provides a comprehensive example for Java EE .NET interoperability. See [SGuest] for more details.

Assumptions

The following software components need to be installed and configured on the same machine:

- **Java Web Services Developer Pack (JWSDP) version 1.5 (http://java.sun.com/webservices/downloads/webservicespack.html)** A Tomcat container *customized* for JWSDP (http://java.sun.com/webservices/containers/tomcat_for_JWSDP_1_5.html) also must be installed. Please note that the standard Apache Tomcat server is not compatible here. In this example, the product is installed under C:\Tools\Tomcat. Please refer to the product installation documentation for details.

- **Web Services Enhancement 2.0 SP1 (http://msdn.microsoft.com/webservices/)** In this example, the product is installed under the default directory C:\Program Files\Microsoft WSE\v2.0. Please refer to the product installation documentation for details.

- **.NET Framework SDK version 1.1 (http://msdn.microsoft.com/netframework/downloads/framework1_1)** In this example, the product is installed under the default directory C:\Program Files\Microsoft.NET\SDK\v1.1. Please refer to the product installation documentation for details.

- **Java 2 Standard Edition SDK version 1.5.0_03 http://java.sun.com/j2se/1.5.0/download.jsp)**

Prerequisites

To illustrate security interoperability using Web services security, this example requires the following:

- .NET client installs a sample X.509 certificate entitled WSE2QuickStartClient ("Client Private.pfx") from the WSE 2.0 (under C:\Program Files\Microsoft WSE\v2.0\Samples\Sample Test Certificates). The public key of the client certificate also must be imported into the Java Keystore via Microsoft Management Console (mmc.exe) as the name "wse2client.cer" under C:\Tools\JWSDP\xws-security\etc.

- Using the WSE2QuickStartClient certificate, the root agency must be exported to a file wse2ca.cer under C:\Tools\JWSDP\xws-security\etc.

- JWSDP server uses the sample X.509 certificates from the JWSDP distribution. Export the JWSDP server (`server.cer`) and root agency (`ca.cer`) certificates from the keystores `server-keystore.jks` and `server-truststore.jks` under the same directory `C:\Tools\JWSDP\xws-security\etc`).

- Install a JCE RSA provider. In this example, the latest Bouncy Castle JCE provider (BCP) for Java 2 SE SDK (aka JDK) version 1.5 (www.bouncycastle.org/latest_releases.html) is used. Ensure that the BCP version (such as BCP for JDK 1.5) matches the same JDK version number (such as JDK 1.5) for compatibility.

- The .NET client is configured with a WS-Security setting of XML signature and encryption using the built-in WSE Configuration Editor.

- The JWSDP server is configured with the default `SecurityEnvironmentHandler` to provide XML signature and decryption/encryption.

Procedures

1. **Install .NET Client Certificate.**
   Go to `C:\Program Files\Microsoft WSE\v2.0\Samples\ Sample Test Certificates` and double-click the file `Client Private.pfx`. This should start the Certificate Import Wizard to install the certificate and private key. The Certificate Import Wizard prompts you for the password (which is *wse2qs*). Select the target folder location as "`Personal`."

   To verify the import operation, you can open Microsoft Management Console (`mmc.exe`) to browse the entry `WSE2QuickStart.Client` from the Personal folder. This can be done by running the command `mmc.exe` from the Start/Run of the Windows environment. Then select File/Add/Remove Snap-in.../Add/Certificates/My User Account. Microsoft Management Console (MMC) should then show a hierarchy of certificates folders under "Console Root"/"Certificates – Current User" (refer to Figure 13-6).

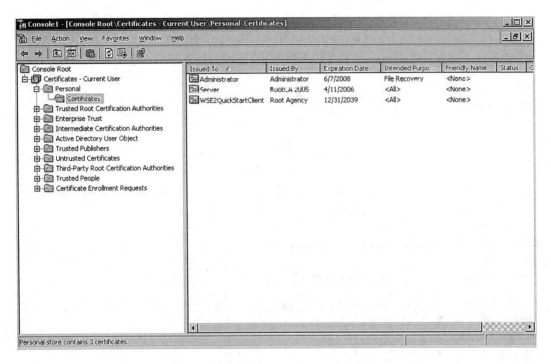

Figure 13-6
Verifying client certificate that is imported

Now you can export the public part of the `WSE2QuickStartClient` certificate to the Java keystore under `C:\Tools\Tomcat\xws-security\etc`. Open the Microsoft Management Console (as depicted earlier in Figure 13-6). From the MMC, right-click the `WSE2QuickStartClient` entry and select "All Tasks | Export" to export the private key in "Base 64 CER" export type under the file name `C:\Tools\Tomcat\xws-security\etc\wse2client.cer`.

After that, double-click the `WSE2QuickStartClient` certificate again, select the Certification Path tab and double-click the `Root Agency` certificate. Then click the Details tab and select the Copy to File button to save the root agency certificate as `C:\Tools\Tomcat\xws-security\etc\wse2ca.cer`.

To import these client certificates into Java keystore `server-trust-store.jks` so that the JWSDP server application can process the XML signature and decryption using the public key, invoke the following commands:

```
keytool -import -file wse2client.cer -alias wse2client
-keystore server-truststore.jks

keytool -import -file wse2ca.cer -alias wse2ca -key-
store server-truststore.jks
```

You can verify the import operation by the following commands (refer to Listing 13-17):

Listing 13-17
Verifying Import of .NET Client Certificate

```
C:\Tools\Tomcat\xws-security\etc>keytool -printcert -file
wse2client.cer
Owner: CN=WSE2QuickStartClient
Issuer: CN=Root Agency
Serial number: -3abb68e8ca769e74b1998659471cf56e
Valid from: Tue Jul 08 11:47:59 PDT 2003 until: Sat Dec 31 15:59:59 PST
2039
Certificate fingerprints:
        MD5:   72:52:48:7C:00:45:53:94:38:BE:47:5B:15:00:80:37
        SHA1:
CA:76:01:38:1B:45:78:50:2B:62:B8:80:98:25:66:4F:1E:78:DF:A2


C:\Tools\Tomcat\xws-security\etc>keytool -printcert -file wse2ca.cer
Owner: CN=Root Agency
Issuer: CN=Root Agency
Serial number: 6376c00aa00648a11cfb8d4aa5c35f4
Valid from: Tue May 28 15:02:59 PDT 1996 until: Sat Dec 31 15:59:59 PST
2039
Certificate fingerprints:
        MD5:   C0:A7:23:F0:DA:35:02:6B:21:ED:B1:75:97:F1:D4:70
        SHA1:
FE:E4:49:EE:0E:39:65:A5:24:6F:00:0E:87:FD:E2:A0:65:FD:89:D4
```

2. **Install JWSDP Server Certificate.**

Go to C:\Tools\Tomcat\xws-security\etc and run the following commands to export the sample JWSDP server certificates:

```
keytool -export -file server.cer -alias s1as -keystore
server-keystore.jks

keytool -export -file ca.cer -alias certificate-
authority -keystore server-truststore.jks
```

To verify the export operation, you can use the following commands (refer to Listing 13-18):

Listing 13-18
Verifying Export of JWSDP Server Certificate

```
C:\Tools\Tomcat\xws-security\etc>keytool -printcert -file server.cer
Owner: CN=Server, OU=JWS, O=SUN, ST=Some-State, C=AU
Issuer: CN=RootCA 2005, OU=JWS, O=SUN, ST=Some-State, C=IN
Serial number: 2
Valid from: Mon Apr 11 22:37:29 PDT 2005 until: Tue Apr 11 22:37:29 PDT
2006
Certificate fingerprints:
        MD5:   5E:F1:DB:6F:66:22:C6:AC:E8:C3:D9:73:35:C7:2C:AC
        SHA1:
F0:67:9A:4E:1C:FD:F5:F0:C7:39:F7:94:08:3A:EF:54:B3:14:71:12

C:\Tools\Tomcat\xws-security\etc>keytool -printcert -file ca.cer
Owner: CN=RootCA 2005, OU=JWS, O=SUN, ST=Some-State, C=IN
Issuer: CN=RootCA 2005, OU=JWS, O=SUN, ST=Some-State, C=IN
Serial number: 0
Valid from: Mon Apr 11 22:28:27 PDT 2005 until: Thu Apr 09 22:28:27 PDT
2015
Certificate fingerprints:
        MD5:   3D:B5:3C:93:F5:65:D5:3D:B5:C5:2E:23:F5:2E:3A:E9
        SHA1:
98:5F:43:96:C0:ED:A5:88:19:DC:D2:1A:2F:8A:5E:0E:44:42:D7:A1
```

---

3. **Install JCE RSA Provider.**
Install the Bouncy Castle JCE provider under the Java 2 SE SDK (JDK) directory. In this example, install under `C:\Tools\JDK15\jre\lib\ext`. Edit your `java.security` policy file under the JDK installation to add the new JCE provider. Please note that the order of the JCE provider may cause compatibility issues. From experience, add the Bouncy Castle JCE provide after the Sun RSA provider (refer to Listing 13-19).

Listing 13-19
Adding Bouncy Castle JCE Provider in *java.security*

```
#
# List of providers and their preference orders (see above):
#
security.provider.1=sun.security.provider.Sun
security.provider.2=sun.security.rsa.SunRsaSign
security.provider.3=com.sun.net.ssl.internal.ssl.Provider
security.provider.4=com.sun.crypto.provider.SunJCE
security.provider.5=org.bouncycastle.jce.provider.BouncyCastleProvider
security.provider.6=sun.security.jgss.SunProvider
security.provider.7=com.sun.security.sasl.Provider
```

4. **Configure .NET Client Policy.**
Open the .NET WSE configuration file `app.config` or `Web.config` using the WSE Configuration Editor (refer to Figure 13-7). This should enable the .NET client side to support XML signature and XML encryption for Web services security.

5. **Configure JWSDP Security Handler.**
On the JWSDP server side, edit the `wsse.xml` configuration file that JWSDP uses to configure Web services security. The previous shows an example of the configuration file content with both XML signature and XML encryption turned on.

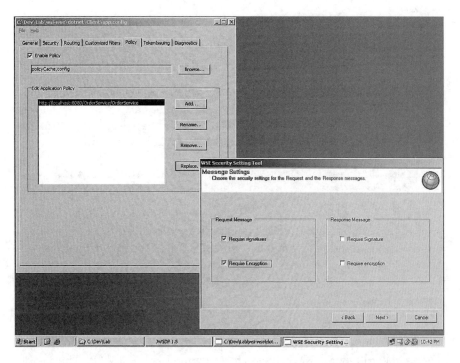

Figure 13-7
Using WSE Configuration Editor to define XML signature and XML encryption

6. **Compile and Deploy JWSDP Application.**
   After the Web services security features are turned on in the JWSDP server application, you can compile and deploy your server application. This example uses an `ant` script to compile and deploy to JWSDP. For example

```
C:\Dev\Lab\wsi-wse\wsdp\service>ant build-all
Buildfile: build.xml
...
build-all:

BUILD SUCCESSFUL
Total time: 19 seconds
```

7. **Compile and Invoke .NET Client.**

Once the Web services security features are turned on in the .NET client, you can compile your client application, for example:

```
C:\Dev\Lab\wsi-wse\dotnet\Client>csc /out:Client.exe
*.cs proxy\OrderProxy.cs /r:"c:\program
files\microsoft wse\v2.0\Microsoft.Web.Services2.dll"
Microsoft (R) Visual C# .NET Compiler version
7.10.6310.4
for Microsoft (R) .NET Framework version 1.1.4322
Copyright (C) Microsoft Corporation 2001-2002. All
rights reserved.
```

In this example, the .NET client application is called `Client.exe`, which is compiled from the existing C# programs in the directory `C:\Dev\Lab\wsi-wse\dotnet\Client`.

Result

The .NET client generates a service request to create a purchase order and renders the following XML message (refer to Listing 13-20). The header contains the key Web Services Security information `<wsse:Security>`, which includes the elements `<wsse:BinarySecurityToken />` and `<ds:Signature />`. The body contains the core business data `<submitOrderResponse />`.

Listing 13-20
Service Request to Create a Purchase Order from a .NET Client

```
<?xml version="1.0" encoding="utf-8"?>
<log>
<env:Envelope xmlns:env="http://schemas.xmlsoap.org/soap/envelope/"
   xmlns:enc="http://schemas.xmlsoap.org/soap/encoding/"
   xmlns:ns0="http://wss.samples.microsoft.com"
   xmlns:xsd="http://www.w3.org/2001/XMLSchema"
   xmlns:xsi="http://www.w3.org/2001/XMLSchema-instance">

<env:Header>
  <wsse:Security
     xmlns:wsse="http://docs.oasis-open.org/wss/2004/01/oasis-200401-
wss-wssecurity-secext-1.0.xsd"
```

```
    env:mustUnderstand="1">
    <wsse:BinarySecurityToken
        xmlns:wsu="http://docs.oasis-open.org/wss/2004/01/oasis-
200401-wss-wssecurity-utility-1.0.xsd"
        EncodingType="http://docs.oasis-open.org/wss/2004/01/oasis-
200401-wss-soap-message-security-1.0#Base64Binary"
        ValueType="http://docs.oasis-open.org/wss/2004/01/oasis-
200401-wss-x509-token-profile-1.0#X509v3"
        wsu:Id="Id-4853980734745059755">
            MIIC8zCCAlygAwIBAgIBAjAN
            ...
            Q3u1+58HZRLS97o+vmKy84OE
    </wsse:BinarySecurityToken>

    <ds:Signature
        xmlns:ds="http://www.w3.org/2000/09/xmldsig#">
        <ds:SignedInfo>
            <ds:CanonicalizationMethod
                Algorithm="http://www.w3.org/2001/10/xml-exc-c14n#" />
            <ds:SignatureMethod
                Algorithm=
                    "http://www.w3.org/2000/09/xmldsig#rsa-sha1" />
            <ds:Reference
                URI="#Id-1069588494982330250">
                <ds:Transforms>
                    <ds:Transform
                        Algorithm=
                            "http://www.w3.org/2001/10/xml-exc-c14n#" />
                </ds:Transforms>

                <ds:DigestMethod
                    Algorithm=
                        "http://www.w3.org/2000/09/xmldsig#sha1" />
                <ds:DigestValue>
                    FD+aZWI8zxgIuqsE9/LbHeGkiuI=
                </ds:DigestValue>
            </ds:Reference>

            <ds:Reference
                URI="#Id1298574802901223328">
                <ds:Transforms>
```

continues

Listing 13-20 (continued)

```
            <ds:Transform
                Algorithm=
                    "http://www.w3.org/2001/10/xml-exc-c14n#" />
            </ds:Transforms>

            <ds:DigestMethod
                Algorithm=
                    "http://www.w3.org/2000/09/xmldsig#sha1" />
            <ds:DigestValue>
                0joA2wLLMj9ZzPMRPEufAv14keI=
            </ds:DigestValue>
        </ds:Reference>
    </ds:SignedInfo>

    <ds:SignatureValue>
        qeYG9xwdSxIMYXi7c4wby5bQkPsqVdOIgi0RbQHW237 …
    </ds:SignatureValue>

    <ds:KeyInfo>
        <wsse:SecurityTokenReference>
            <wsse:Reference
                URI="#Id-485398073474505 9755"
                ValueType=
                    "http://docs.oasis-open.org/wss/2004/01/oasis-
200401-wss-x509-token-profile-1.0#X509v3" />
        </wsse:SecurityTokenReference>
    </ds:KeyInfo>
</ds:Signature>

<wsu:Timestamp
    xmlns:wsu=
        "http://docs.oasis-open.org/wss/2004/01/oasis-200401-wss-
wssecurity-utility-1.0.xsd"
    wsu:Id="Id1298574802901223328">

    <wsu:Created>
        2005-06-28T14:46:42Z
    </wsu:Created>
    <wsu:Expires>
        2005-06-28T14:51:42Z
```

```
        </wsu:Expires>
      </wsu:Timestamp>
    </wsse:Security>
</env:Header>


<env:Body
    xmlns:wsu=
      "http://docs.oasis-open.org/wss/2004/01/oasis-200401-wss-
wssecurity-utility-1.0.xsd"
    wsu:Id="Id-1069588494982330250">
  <ns0:submitOrderResponse>
      <result>2233444</result>
  </ns0:submitOrderResponse>
 </env:Body>
</env:Envelope>
</log>
```

The JWSDP server application receives the service request and returns a receipt number in XML (refer to Listing 13-21):

Listing 13-21
Response to the Purchase Order Request by JWSDP Server Application

```
<?xml version="1.0" encoding="utf-8"?>
<log>
<soap:Envelope
   xmlns:soap="http://schemas.xmlsoap.org/soap/envelope/"
   xmlns:xsi="http://www.w3.org/2001/XMLSchema-instance"
   xmlns:xsd="http://www.w3.org/2001/XMLSchema"
   xmlns:wsa="http://schemas.xmlsoap.org/ws/2004/03/addressing"
   xmlns:wsse=
     "http://docs.oasis-open.org/wss/2004/01/oasis-200401-wss-
wssecurity-secext-1.0.xsd"
   xmlns:wsu=
     "http://docs.oasis-open.org/wss/2004/01/oasis-200401-wss-
wssecurity-utility-1.0.xsd">


<soap:Header>
   <wsa:Action
     wsu:Id="Id-8f3d108c-3186-4eac-bd30-8584e82fa38d">
   </wsa:Action>
```

continues

Listing 13-21 (continued)

```
<wsa:MessageID
    wsu:Id="Id-c00ca163-3d7b-4cec-8e7a-791546d41e15">
        uuid:119831ce-58be-4cd1-b70f-77e7ad96552f
</wsa:MessageID>

<wsa:ReplyTo
    wsu:Id="Id-42f224be-c812-473e-b243-eea1f2dd7e66">

    <wsa:Address>
http://schemas.xmlsoap.org/ws/2004/03/addressing/role/anonymous
    </wsa:Address>
</wsa:ReplyTo>

<wsa:To
    wsu:Id=
        "Id-1f1db802-65c0-43d3-9af1-167208ce98e4">
    http://localhost:8080/OrderService/OrderService
</wsa:To>

<wsse:Security soap:mustUnderstand="1">
    <wsu:Timestamp wsu:Id=
        "Timestamp-d65bb998-7c43-4efc-808c-2304d8a13d79">
      <wsu:Created>2005-06-28T14:45:59Z</wsu:Created>
      <wsu:Expires>2005-06-28T14:50:59Z</wsu:Expires>
    </wsu:Timestamp>
    <wsse:BinarySecurityToken
        ValueType=
            "http://docs.oasis-open.org/wss/2004/01/oasis-200401-wss-
x509-token-profile-1.0#X509v3"
        EncodingType=
            "http://docs.oasis-open.org/wss/2004/01/oasis-200401-wss-
soap-message-security-1.0#Base64Binary"
        xmlns:wsu=
            "http://docs.oasis-open.org/wss/2004/01/oasis-200401-wss-
wssecurity-utility-1.0.xsd"
        wsu:Id=
            "SecurityToken-1ecd5e58-9ba6-4239-a9fb-
250e15dc3769">MIIBxDCCAW6gAwIBAgIQxUSXFzWJYYtOZnmmuOMKkjANBgkqhkiG9w0BA
Q...F5qkh6sSdWVBY5sT/txBnVJGziyO8DPYdu2fPMER8ajJfl
    </wsse:BinarySecurityToken>
```

```
<Signature
   xmlns="http://www.w3.org/2000/09/xmldsig#">
 <SignedInfo>
  <ds:CanonicalizationMethod
     Algorithm="http://www.w3.org/2001/10/xml-exc-c14n#"
     xmlns:ds="http://www.w3.org/2000/09/xmldsig#" />
  <SignatureMethod
     Algorithm=
        "http://www.w3.org/2000/09/xmldsig#rsa-sha1" />
  <Reference
     URI="#Id-8f3d108c-3186-4eac-bd30-8584e82fa38d">
   <Transforms>
    <Transform Algorithm=
      "http://www.w3.org/2001/10/xml-exc-c14n#" />
   </Transforms>
   <DigestMethod
      Algorithm="http://www.w3.org/2000/09/xmldsig#sha1" />
   <DigestValue>
      yHqfuGhCwnU/guHlvPy5j8vZDC0=
   </DigestValue>
  </Reference>
  <Reference
     URI="#Id-c00ca163-3d7b-4cec-8e7a-791546d41e15">
   <Transforms>
    <Transform Algorithm=
        "http://www.w3.org/2001/10/xml-exc-c14n#" />
   </Transforms>
   <DigestMethod
      Algorithm=
        "http://www.w3.org/2000/09/xmldsig#sha1" />
   <DigestValue>
      yM82YC9rZzfb3AWD0iYbNmBT4UM=
   </DigestValue>
  </Reference>
  <Reference
     URI="#Id-42f224be-c812-473e-b243-eea1f2dd7e66">
   <Transforms>
    <Transform Algorithm=
        "http://www.w3.org/2001/10/xml-exc-c14n#" />
   </Transforms>
   <DigestMethod
```

continues

Listing 13-21 (continued)

```
        Algorithm="http://www.w3.org/2000/09/xmldsig#sha1" />
    <DigestValue>
        5GDwT3MA0YOx4GqugDBtWUyjMnw=
    </DigestValue>
</Reference>
<Reference
    URI="#Id-1f1db802-65c0-43d3-9af1-167208ce98e4">
    <Transforms>
     <Transform
        Algorithm=
        "http://www.w3.org/2001/10/xml-exc-c14n#" />
    </Transforms>
    <DigestMethod
      Algorithm=
        "http://www.w3.org/2000/09/xmldsig#sha1" />
    <DigestValue>
        nG7Lkpn0W1pMB/BRWiQGltfbyRA=
    </DigestValue>
</Reference>
<Reference
    URI=
        "#Timestamp-d65bb998-7c43-4efc-808c-2304d8a13d79">
    <Transforms>
     <Transform
        Algorithm=
            "http://www.w3.org/2001/10/xml-exc-c14n#" />
    </Transforms>
    <DigestMethod
      Algorithm="http://www.w3.org/2000/09/xmldsig#sha1" />
    <DigestValue>
        9udH1FbnHV0eq6BQ8wJUof3V+UA=
    </DigestValue>
</Reference>
<Reference
    URI="#Id-42767f08-d88f-4394-a4f3-06bf14b00916">
    <Transforms>
     <Transform
        Algorithm=
        "http://www.w3.org/2001/10/xml-exc-c14n#" />
    </Transforms>
```

```xml
                <DigestMethod
                    Algorithm="http://www.w3.org/2000/09/xmldsig#sha1" />
                <DigestValue>
                    g1QqF2amKSwrGc4EHjgvhpvI4jE=
                </DigestValue>
            </Reference>
        </SignedInfo>
        <SignatureValue>
            KlJ1j0…POB6KzPO00=
        </SignatureValue>
        <KeyInfo>
            <wsse:SecurityTokenReference>
                <wsse:Reference
                    URI=
                        "#SecurityToken-1ecd5e58-9ba6-4239-a9fb-
250e15dc3769"
                    ValueType=
                        "http://docs.oasis-open.org/wss/2004/01/oasis-
200401-wss-x509-token-profile-1.0#X509v3" />
            </wsse:SecurityTokenReference>
        </KeyInfo>
    </Signature>
  </wsse:Security>
  </soap:Header>

<soap:Body
    wsu:Id="Id-42767f08-d88f-4394-a4f3-06bf14b00916">
    <submitOrder
        xmlns="http://wss.samples.microsoft.com">
        <OrderImpl_1 xmlns="">
            <accountNumber>LUCKY-200-300-101</creditCardExpM>
            <quantity>200</quantity>
            <supplierItemNumber>99882388</supplierItemNumber>
            <SKU>2233888</SKU>
        </OrderImpl_1>
    </submitOrder>
</soap:Body>

</soap:Envelope>
</log>
```

Benefits and Limitations

Secure Object Handler is a generic implementation approach to abstract common security processing logic and decouple from the application processing logic. It can be used with various Java EE .NET interoperability technologies and has the following benefits:

Maintainability

Common security processing logic can be refactored into Secure Object Handlers to perform pre-processing or post-processing tasks. Developers just need to maintain the handlers centrally instead of modifying massive numbers of applications that have security processing logic embedded.

Scalability

The Java EE .NET interoperability solution can be more manageable if the security processing logic is decoupled from the business processing logic. This allows Java and .NET applications to extend their security processing logic by either extending existing handler functionality or adding a chain of handlers (if the underlying platform or product supports the handlers).

Limitations

There are a few limitations when using handlers. First, there may be existing legacy applications that do not support the use of handlers. For example, .NET applications that do not use WSE do not benefit from the WS-Policy framework. Developers have to modify the applications to add custom handlers, which may cause considerable change on impact and implementation risks.

Second, some integration strategies' implementations can only support one single handler and not multiple handlers. Thus developers need to consolidate all security processing logic into a single handler. This will overload the handler design in one single implementation.

Secure Tracer Strategy

Problems

Audit control and compliance requirements always expect a good collection of transaction logging information. Sometimes a copy of the SOAP messages may be retained so that raw data can be available for complicated security analysis and reporting when needed. In practice, too much data may not be helpful if administrators need to find out whether there is any suspicious identity theft from signs of identity spoofing or man-in-the-middle attacks. Further, many security audit reports do not correlate the business transactions into sender/recipient pairs or provide the flexibility to apply specific security processing rules, such as a recipient's message timestamp should be later than the sender's message timestamp.

If the sender and the recipient are operating on different platforms, the security reporting and tracing of suspicious business transactions are more complicated because administrators need to collate the service requester and the response messages together to correlate them. If the business data are encrypted, administrators are not able to scan and trace raw data manually. They need to rely on some tools to identify whether there are any sender's or recipient's messages that have invalid user credentials, such as invalid X.509 certificates, or suspicious message timestamp, for example, recipient's message timestamp is earlier than sender's message timestamp, which may suggest a message alteration or spoofing.

The Secure Tracer strategy is intended to address the challenge of tracing business transactions for suspicious activities. It allows administrators to correlate the sender's and recipient's messages in pairs and applies some security processing rules to identify any suspicious messages or to trace the source details from the central logging repository.

Solution

The Secure Tracer Strategy applies to both synchronous, asynchronous, and bridge interoperability strategies that utilize Web services. It intercepts service requests and replies in SOAP messages (whether synchronous or asynchronous) and correlates them in pairs. This also includes bridge strategy that supports Web services. In either strategy, a central logging mechanism needs to be in place.

The secure tracer strategy depends on a central logging mechanism to pull both the sender and the recipient log messages together. This can be implemented by a variety of middleware such as a basic file transfer facility, ftp, for example, or ESB.

Once the central logging mechanism is implemented, a simple message matching application can be built to correlate the sender and the recipient messages that refer to the same service request together. Figure 13-8 depicts a sequence diagram that illustrates a secure tracer strategy.

- Administrators start secure tracing activities (Step 1).

- Upon sending the service request (Step 2), the Sender issues a log message to the central logging system (Step 3).

- Central Logging creates a message correlation identifier for easy identification and mapping of the service request and the corresponding reply messages (Step 4).

- Upon completion of processing the service request (Step 5), the Recipient issues a log message to the central logging system (Step 6).

- The central logging system correlates the sender's message with the recipient's message by message id, message timestamp, and reference and creates a grouping between the two (Step 7).

- The central logging system also applies some security processing rules to ensure the message is authentic and genuine (Step 8). For example, it verifies the digital signature of both the sender's and recipient's messages and checks whether the recipient's timestamp is earlier than the sender's timestamp.

- Suspicious messages are flagged for administrator's attention by putting these messages under the alert queue (Step 9). Optionally, the central logging system should notify the administrator by e-mail or other predefined communication mechanism (such as fax or instant messaging).

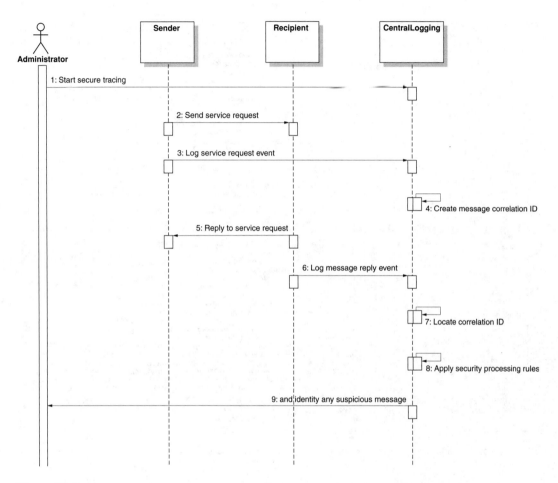

Figure 13-8
Secure Tracer sequence diagram

Example

Figure 13-9 shows WSE Trace Tool (downloadable from www.gotdotnet.com/workspaces/workspace.aspx?id=ab938e2f-cabf-4145-b0e9-dbeeaf51dbe5), which correlates the incoming service request message with the outgoing reply message. It is not an implementation of the secure tracer strategy, but it illustrates a good example of correlating the service request and reply messages for manual inspection.

Figure 13-9
WSE Trace tool correlates the service requester and the response messages together.

Benefits and Limitations

Secure tracer strategy is a simple audit log reporting function that is intended to address basic security auditing, such as track and trace the secure transactions, and compliance requirements. It has the following benefits:

Support Compliance Requirements

With the changing requirements of local compliance, it is crucial to provide a secure tracing capability to meet audit control and compliance needs.

Proactive Reporting of Suspicious Activities

The capability to identify suspicious messages that may have been tampered with or to scan for any problematic digital signature in the messages can allow suspicious or potential security vulnerabilities to be detected proactively.

Limitations

The extensibility of the secure tracer implementation depends on the central logging mechanism and the processing logic for the message correlation. Not all messages can be correlated. For example, the secure tracer implementation has no clue how to correlate a collection of encrypted SOAP messages, given that the message identifiers and message digest do not show any correspondence.

Related Patterns

- **Chain of Responsibility Pattern**   The Chain of Responsibility pattern (refer to [CoR1] and [CoR2] for details) allows a handler object to handle the service request without coupling the sender of the service request to the recipient. By using the handler object, this pattern chains together the receiving objects and passes the service request along the chain of processes. The Chain of Responsibility pattern is generic to Java or .NET platforms and can be applied to security processing logic specific to Java EE .NET interoperability, assuming that the technical details need to be hashed out.

- **Message Inspector Pattern**   The Message Inspector pattern (refer to [CSP] for details) introduces the concept of a message handler chain of security processing actions to pre-process and post-process SOAP messages. These actions can include verifying user identity, validating messages for compliance with Web services standards, validating digital signatures, encrypting and decrypting business data, and auditing and logging. This design strategy is specialized for Web services running on the Java platform and does not cover the details of Java EE .NET interoperability or related technologies.

- **Secure Logger Pattern**   The Secure Logger pattern (refer to [CSP] for details) introduces some best practices to create secure logs for business transactions using message digest, cipher, signature, and UID generator classes. This pattern is targeted for Java applications developed for the Web tier and does not cover the details of Java EE .NET interoperability or related technologies.

Best Practices and Pitfalls

The following recapitulates some best practices and pitfalls regarding the use of WS-Security for interoperability.

Best Practices

- Use compatible or certified software component versions. Don't assume the latest version of open source components always work with the existing code base.

- Use specific encryption and digest algorithms that are proven to work for Java EE .NET interoperable products. Use Triple DES for session key encryption to enable WSE in the app.config for interoperability.

```
<binarySecurityTokenManager
   valueType=
   "http://docs.oasis-open.org/wss/2004/01/oasis-200401-wss-x509-token-
profile-1.0#X509v3">
   <sessionKeyAlgorithm name="TripleDES" />
</binarySecurityTokenManager>
```

- Use Optimal Asymmetric Encryption Padding (RSAOAEP RSA) as the encryption key algorithm to enable WSE in the app.config file for interoperability.

```
<binarySecurityTokenManager
   valueType="http://docs.oasis-open.org/wss/2004/01/oasis-200401-wss-
x509-token-profile-1.0#X509v3">
   <keyAlgorithm name="RSAOAEP" />
</binarySecurityTokenManager>
```

- Use built-in handlers or security policies wherever possible, instead of rewriting your own security processing logic. If you want to customize your own security processing logic, you may consider extending the existing handlers.

Pitfalls

- **Certificate management on both platforms can be problematic**   For example, if the digital certificate is expired, the error messages may disguise the problem as being invalid credentials or keys but not the expired certificates.

- **Use of security exception**   Don't just catch the exception. Make the error message meaningful. For example, the exception "no policy found" can be ambiguous and does not tell what the root cause is.

Summary

Interoperability for security is a challenging subject, and dealing with security on one single platform is already complex. Making two different application platforms interoperate on the security is more complicated. Thus adopting open standards for security interoperability would be a good approach. Web services security certainly is a turning point for Java EE .NET security interoperability. With the availability of Web SSO MEX specification, security interoperability would be viable for users to keep the best of both identity federation infrastructures.

There are many reference materials and documentation about Java EE and .NET security. Nevertheless, the availability of references for the security interoperability is limited probably because the interoperability standards and the supporting technologies are evolving. The good news is that free interoperability software kits (such as WSE and JWSDP) are available for public download.

In this chapter, Secure Object Handler and secure tracer strategies introduce essential best practices to managing interoperability. These two strategies can be implemented in both Java and .NET platforms.

References

[Anne2] Anne Anderson. "IEEE Policy 2004 Workshop 8 June 2004—Comparing WSPL and WS-Policy." IEEE Policy 2004.

http://www.policy-workshop.org/2004/slides/Anderson-WSPL_vs_WS-Policy_v2.pdf

[Anne3] Anne Anderson. "An Introduction to the Web Services Policy Language (WSPL)." Sun Microsystems Laboratories, 2004.

http://research.sun.com/projects/xacml/Policy2004.pdf

[BSP] Web Services Interoperability Organization. Basic Security Profile Version 1.0. Working Group Draft. May 15, 2005.

www.ws-i.org/Profiles/BasicSecurityProfile-1.0.html

[CoR1] Mark Grand. "Pattern Summaries: Chain of Responsibility."

www.developer.com

and

www.developer.com/java/other/article.php/631261

[CoR2] data & object factory. "Chain of Responsibility."

www.dofactory.com/Patterns/PatternChain.aspx

[CSI] Computer Security Institute. CSI/FBI Computer Crime and Security Survey. Computer Security Institute 2005.

[CSP] Chris Steel, Ramesh Nagappan, Ray Lai. *Core Security Patterns: Best Practices and Strategies for J2EE, Web Services, and Identity Management.* Boston: Prentice Hall, 2006.

[J2EE14] Bill Shannon. "Java™ 2 Platform Enterprise Edition Specification, v1.4." Proposed Final Draft 3. Sun Microsystems, April 2003.

http://java.sun.com/j2ee/j2ee-1_4-pfd3-spec.pdf

[J2EE14Tutor] Eric Armstrong, et al. "The J2EE 1.4 Tutorial." Sun Microsystems, 2003.

http://java.sun.com/j2ee/1.4/docs/tutorial/doc/

[JavaVMFlaw] Security Focus. "Security Vulnerability in Sun's Java Virtual Machine Implementation." Security Focus. October 23, 2003.

www.securityfocus.com/archive/1/342147

[LibertyWSFed] Liberty Alliance. "Liberty Alliance & WS-Federation: A Comparative Overview." Liberty Alliance Project White Paper. October 14, 2003.

www.projectliberty.org/resources/whitepapers/wsfed-liberty-overview-10-13-03.pdf

[LiGong] Li Gong. "Java Security Architecture." in "Java 2 SDK, Standard Edition Documentation Version 1.4.2." Sun Microsystems, 2003.

http://java.sun.com/j2se/1.4.2/docs/guide/security/spec/securityspec.doc1.html

and

http://java.sun.com/j2se/1.4.2/docs/guide/security/spec/securityspec.doc2.html.

[SGuest] Simon Guest. "WS-Security Interoperability Using WSE 2.0 and Sun JWSDP 1.5." Microsoft, May 2005.

http://msdn.microsoft.com/library/default.asp?url=/library/enus/dnbda/html/wssinteropjwsdp15.asp

[Watkins] Dr. Demien Watkins. "An Overview of Security in the .NET Framework." MSDN Library, January 2002.

http://msdn.microsoft.com/library/default.asp?url=/library/enus/dnnetsec/html/netframesecover.asp

[WindowsAuthFlaw] Microsoft. "MS02-011: An Authentication Flaw Could Allow Unauthorized Users to be Authenticated on the SMTP Service." Article 310669. Revision 7. Microsoft Support, April 13, 2004.

http://support.microsoft.com/default.aspx?scid=kb;EN-US;Q310669

[WSI-countermeasure] Jerry Schwarz, et al., ed. "Security Challenges, Threats and Countermeasures Version 1.0" Final Material. Web Services Interoperability Organization, May 7, 2005.

http://www.ws-i.org/Profiles/BasicSecurity/SecurityChallenges-1.0.pdf

[XACML2] OASIS. eXtensible Access Control Markup Language (XACML) Version 2.0. February 1, 2005.

http://docs.oasis-open.org/xacml/2.0/XACML-2.0-OS-ALL.zip

Java EE .NET Reliability, Availability, and Scalability

14

Java EE .NET Applications on Steroids

Quality of Services is essential to providing production quality and robustness for business applications. Both Java and .NET platforms have features that developers can use to build reliable, highly available, and scalable interoperable solutions. On the positive side, a well architected Java EE .NET interoperability solution can optimize the current hardware infrastructure for best system performance and high availability and can allow business data to be reliably exchanged. This is like putting the interoperability solution on steroids. However, a fast and highly scalable producer (whether a Java or .NET application) can be impeded or severely impacted by a poorly designed consumer, which causes the system to crash or lose business data. If the consumer cannot handle large volume business transactions during the peak hours (that is, consumer is not scalable), then the entire interoperable solution will not function effectively, and it will likely break the service level agreement.

Chapter 11, "Addressing Quality of Services," discusses some of the myths and truths about Quality of Services. It argues that Quality of Services need to be addressed *early* in the application design of the interoperable solution, instead of solely relying on the Java or .NET platform capability after application deployment. This chapter begins with a sample business scenario and discusses the current state-of-the-art technologies that enable reliability, availability, and scalability (RAS). In particular, it discusses scalability and performance, which are two key and visible aspects of Quality of Services. They easily change the perception of how good or how bad an interoperable solution is.

Business Scenario

Consider the familiar Supply Chain Business scenario where a buyer is sending a purchase order to the supplier. The buyer is using a .NET client to place a purchase order in the shopping cart for procuring some merchandise from a supplier. The .NET application runs on Windows 2003 Server with lots of physical memory on a high-end fast processor. The supplier back-end system is a Java-based application running on an entry-level Solaris operating environment. Developers need to determine which interoperability and integration strategies should be used to achieve the goals of

- Reliable delivery of the service request to the recipient and return of the processing result
- Reasonably fast end-to-end system performance
- Highly available end-to-end interoperable solution

Technical Challenges

One design approach for RAS features is to leverage the platform features of providing reliability and high availability. In other words, developers and architects can rely on application server clustering for availability and the resilience of the middleware (such as bridge, Enterprise Service Bus/ESB, and message queue) to achieve reliability. This leaves the core design job to focus on the scalability aspect by micro-tuning the network bandwidth, I/O, CPU, and memory. A hardware upgrade (such as adding more physical memory and more CPUs on both the producer and the consumer machines) is a common example of up-scaling the interoperability solutions.

However, such a RAS design approach may be good for traditional business applications on standalone machines but may not be appropriate for Java EE .NET interoperable solutions. There are a few important issues:

- **System Performance Symptoms**   RAS problems may manifest themselves in slow system performance symptoms, but the root cause resides in the application design. For example, a slow consumer (say, a Java application running on an entry-level machine) may manifest a problem in long network latency or slow system performance on the consumer side, but the root cause could be an XML data serialization issue, where the consumer gobbles incompatible data types from a .NET client.

- **Hardware Upgrade**   Hardware upgrade does not necessarily address the RAS problem in an interoperable solution. CPU and memory upgrade would enhance system performance for CPU-intensive and memory-intensive tasks such as XML encryption to some extent. Nevertheless, upgrading from a 2-CPU machine to an 8-CPU machine in the Java back-end system does not necessarily mean that the interoperable solution can improve the system performance by four times.

- **Application Architecture Issues**   A Java application running on a Java EE Application Server cluster does not necessarily ensure the Java EE .NET interoperable solution is highly available, unless both the producer and consumer sides have design elements to support session failover and shared session data (say, persistence of session data). Another example is when a single, point-to-point connection from a Java client to a .NET application is fast. However, the connectivity may not be scalable when hundreds (or thousands) of Java clients are connected simultaneously if the .NET application is not well architected. Thus it is extremely important to ensure the end-to-end interoperable application architecture is scalable.

- **Performance Issues**   Performance problems in the interoperability middleware may be a manifestation of a design issue in the overall Java EE .NET interoperability solution. For example, a bridge integration solution may have many performance issues if the bridge client is not well designed. Sometimes, the synchronous Web services integration solution may not be appropriate for the application requirements, and CORBA-IIOP bridge integration is more efficient if the former requires intensive data serialization as well as high overhead of data marshaling and unmarshaling. Thus it is useful to revisit the interoperability application design for performance problems.

Design Factors for RAS

The technical challenges discussed suggest that RAS could be very specific to Java EE .NET interoperable solutions. Chapter 11 identifies the core requirements for RAS. Those RAS requirements apply to Java EE, .NET and the interoperability solutions. In a real-world environment, not all RAS requirements are needed. Thus it is useful to have a general "rule of thumb" when architecting end-to-end Java EE .NET interoperable solutions. The following outlines some key design factors when architecting reliability, availability, and scalability of the interoperable solutions:

Reliability

- **Receipt Acknowledgement** The interoperable solution requires a receipt acknowledgement of the service request.

- **Automatic Retries** The interoperable solution requires automatic resending of the service request or automatic reprocessing of the transactions after service recovery.

- **Verification of Business Transactions** The interoperable solution requires verification of the producer or consumer. Moreover, the interoperability middleware (such as bridge and ESB) should verify the XML schema and data types being exchanged.

Availability

- **Session Failover**   If both the .NET and Java applications are deployed on clusters, how will the interoperable solution handle session failover? If the Java application session fails over to another application server instance, the .NET client should be able to recover the session data. The .NET client should be also explicitly programmed to retry connecting to the Java application a few times in case a session failover is detected.

- **Persistence**   Does the interoperable solution require persistence of the service request and business transactions in a data store? If yes, does it need to persist data in every component (for example, .NET client, MSMQ node, bridge middleware, Java application server, or JDBC resources)? The middleware (or integration point) should provide system-level support for persistence, or developers have to customize the persistence processing logic in each design element. If data are persisted at every design element, they should be recovered after the recovery of a faulty service component. The design details may involve complex data synchronization and two-phase commit issues.

Scalability

- **Data**   When exchanging business data between .NET and Java applications, are both primitive data types and custom complex data types involved? The data types should be mapped correctly, and any incompatible data types should have data type conversion. Do all the data need to be serialized or encrypted? XML data serialization and XML encryption/decryption have performance implications.

- **Middleware**   How scalable (say, the number of simultaneous client connections and messages processed per second) is the bridge or ESB middleware?

- **Infrastructure**   Can the machine (such as CPU and memory) and infrastructure (such as network bandwidth) be upgraded? How much faster can the Java or .NET applications run if additional CPUs or physical memory are added? How many simultaneous connections can the producer/consumer make (using the existing network adapter card or server infrastructure)?

The next section discusses the current state of the interoperability technologies for RAS and how they can be best used to meet the RAS requirements. It also compares how different integration strategies support reliability, availability, and scalability requirements.

Understanding the Current State of Technology

Chapters 1, "Java EE Platform Interoperability Essentials," and Chapter 2, ".NET Platform Interoperability Essentials," covered the essentials of Java and .NET technologies and how they enable interoperability. Subsequent chapters (Chapters 3 through 12) introduced different integration and interoperability technologies. This section assesses what these integration and interoperability technologies can do and cannot do to make reliable, available, and scalable business applications.

Reliability

There are two essential reliability requirements that developers are concerned with. First, the service requests are reliably sent to the target recipient. Similarly, the processing results are reliably returned to the service requester. Second, the business data from one system should be accurately transmitted and delivered to another system without loss. This section discusses the current states of messaging interoperability technologies and how data types should be mapped between Java and .NET platforms.

JMS and MSMQ

Messaging technologies such as JMS and MSMQ are designed to allow business applications to exchange business data reliably. However, these messaging technologies are vendor-specific (they have different underlying data transport implementations), and they are not practically interoperable between two different vendor implementations. There may be a misunderstanding that both JMS and MSMQ are message queue-based technologies, and they can interoperate if a common queue name is used. Developers should not assume that a Java application using JMS can interoperate directly with a .NET application using MSMQ. For example, business data written to a JMS queue using Weblogic JMS implementation cannot be retrieved by using IBM WebSphere MQ JMS API or MSMQ because they use different underlying data transport and data formats.

MSMQ Interoperability

MSMQ is a reliable messaging mechanism available in the .NET platform. It is possible to wrap a WebSphere MQ client (or JMS client, architecturally speaking) by ActiveX Control, so that a WebSphere MQ client (which is a Java application) can exchange business data reliably with a MSMQ client (.NET application). In the case of WebSphere MQ, IBM provides MQ classes for .NET, which allows a .NET application to create some administrative commands (also known as Programmable Control Facility) to the WebSphere MQ Queue Manager using send and receive APIs. Refer to [DotNetMQ] for details.

Data Type Accuracy

Not all data types have identical data type mapping in Java and .NET. Business data will not be rendered correctly if the data types are wrongly mapped between Java and .NET applications. Data type accuracy is an important element in ensuring data reliability in Java EE .NET interoperability.

For example, unsigned integer type is supported in .NET but not in Java. Thus an XML schema with an unsigned integer type will not be interoperable without proper data mapping or data conversion. Array handling also varies in .NET, which will create only the header element if an empty array is serialized but will not serialize any XML element if a null array is serialized. In contrast, Java will serialize the XML element for both types of array. Thus when dealing with data types mapped to an XML schema, it is important to understand the differences between Java and .NET and their exceptions.

Table 14-1 depicts the data mapping between XML Schema, Java data types and .NET data types. Java SE (Java 2 Platform, Standard Edition) version 5.0 now supports a natural mapping of XML Schema to Java types using JAXB (Java Architecture for XML Binding), which is defined by JSR 31. The JAXB data types under the package javax.xml.datatype are prefixed by the namespace xs in Table 14-1. For example, the integer type int in an XML schema will be resembled by int in Java and Int32 in .NET. In other words, int (in Java) will have the same data type value as in Int32 (in .NET).

Table 14-1
Data Mapping Between XML Schema, Java Data Types, and .NET Data Types

Data Types in XML Schema	Java Data Type	.NET Data Type
int	int	Int32
long	long	Int64
short	short	Int16
nonPositiveInteger	integer	String
negativeInteger	integer	String
nonNegativeInteger	integer	String
unsignedLong	long	UInt32
positiveInteger	integer	UInt64
unsignedInt	integer	UInt32
unsignedShort	short	UInt16
unsignedByte	byte	Byte
double	double	Double
decimal	decimal	Decimal
float	float	Single
hexBinary	hexBinary	Byte[]
base64Binary	base64Binary	Byte[]
boolean	Boolean	Boolean or bool
string	string	String
anyURI	java.net.URL	System.Uri

Enterprise Service Bus

Enterprise Service Bus (ESB) provides reliable messaging features for inter-operability. A business process (say, implemented by a .NET application using synchronous Web services) can issue a service request to another business process (for example, implemented by a Java application using asynchronous Web services) via the ESB. A typical synchronous service call does not generate receipt acknowledgement as in an asynchronous messaging protocol. If there is a service failure in the underlying data transport (for example, SOAP over HTTP), the synchronous service request is lost. Using the ESB, the multi-protocol messaging middleware can intercept a synchronous incoming service request and reliably route (bind to the underlying JMS for reliable message routing) to another business process, which only accepts service requests asynchronously. Some ESB implementations (such as Mule ESB) can also invoke a synchronous call asynchronously. Please refer to Chapter 9, "Messaging," for more details.

Not all ESB products support .NET platform. For example, IONA Artix (www.iona.com/products/artix/features.htm) and Sonic ESB (www.sonic-software.com/products/docs/sonic_esb.pdf) support both Java and .NET platforms, but Mule ESB (http://mule.codehaus.org/) only supports Java platform and does not support .NET client. Mule ESB version 1.1 is capable of orchestrating Web services generated from a .NET application. Developers may want to research specific vendor product implementation details.

WS-Reliability and WS-ReliableMessaging

WS-Reliability is an OASIS standard specification (www.oasis-open.org/committees/tc_home.php?wg_abbrev=wsrm) that provides a standard and interoperable way to guarantee message delivery to business applications or Web services. This includes guaranteed message delivery (such as acknowledgement messages or resending messages), no duplicates of messages sent or delivered, and guaranteed message ordering using a sequence number mechanism. Currently, RM4GS is a sample software implementation produced by Fujitsu, Hitachi, and NEC (refer to http://xml.coverpages.org/ni2004-03-11-a.html), but there is no .NET implementation yet. There is a summary of the WS-Reliability specification available at [LuefPichler].

WS-ReliableMessaging is a similar Web services specification from Microsoft, IBM, BEA, and TIBCO for supporting SOAP messages to be sent and received reliably over different data transport mechanisms, particularly SOAP over HTTP. There are two major components: core messaging protocol and a related policy assertion specification. WS-ReliableMessaging uses a unique identifier (aka URI) for each message sequence to ensure message ordering and no duplication of messages. It also supports message acknowledgement. However, it leaves message persistence to the responsibility of the design implementation. Several implementations are available in both .NET and Java platforms, for example, Microsoft WSE version 3.0 (http://msdn.microsoft.com/webservices/webservices/building/wse/def ault.aspx?pull=/library/en-us/dnwse/html/newwse3.asp) and Apache Sandesha (http://ws.apache.org/sandesha/).

Reliability by Integration Strategies

Table 14-2 summarizes the reliability features by comparing synchronous integration, asynchronous integration, and bridge integration strategies. The reliability features are also discussed in Chapter 11.

Reliable delivery is often a feature provided by asynchronous integration and bridge integration strategies. The synchronous integration strategy does not provide reliable delivery of messages. It also does not have a message ordering mechanism.

Receipt acknowledgement is a mechanism used in asynchronous integration strategy to ensure that messages or service requests are sent to the recipient reliably. Synchronous integration strategy does not use receipt acknowledgement (because the service requester communicates with the service provider in a "block" mode and exits from the interaction when a return value is received). Some bridge integration implementations also support receipt acknowledgement.

Exception handling (such as mapping Java exceptions to .NET exceptions), data type mapping (such as converting an unsigned integer from .NET to an integer in Java), and shared logging (such as centrally storing the log messages for both Java and .NET applications) usually require customization by all integration strategies. Bridge integration implementation usually provides a shared logging mechanism for both Java and .NET applications.

Application security is always a complex design issue for interoperable solutions. Web services security (www.oasis-open.org/committees/tc_home.php?wg_abbrev=wss) provides a standard mechanism for Java EE .NET interoperability using Web services. This applies to all integration strategies. To achieve single sign-on, the recent Web Services Metadata

Exchange (WS-MEX) specification addresses specific Java EE .NET interoperability requirements. Please refer to Chapter 13, "Java EE .NET Security Interoperability" for details.

Table 14-2
Reliability Features by Different Integration Strategies

Reliability Features	Synchronous Integration	Asynchronous Integration	Bridge Integration
Reliable delivery—data transport	N/A	Supported by the messaging technologies such as MSMQ or JMS	Supported by the bridge technology
Receipt acknowledgement	N/A	Supported by the messaging implementation	Supported by the bridge technology
Message delivered once to the recipient, not multiple deliveries	Yes**	A feature of publish-subscribe or queue-based messaging model	Yes**
Message delivered in order	N/A	Yes*	Yes*
Message routing	N/A	Java Business Integration (JBI), BPEL (Business Process Execution Language)	Yes*
Exceptions converted to local platform	Yes**	Yes**	Yes**
Accuracy of data types/values	Yes**	Yes**	Yes**
Shared logging	Yes**	Yes**	Bridge can provide shared logging
Supported by security	Web services security, WS-MEX	Web services security, WS-MEX	Web services security, WS-MEX

Implementation-dependent.

**Need to customize.*

Availability

To ensure the service provider is highly available to provide the business system functionality, developers can usually consider the following availability design options:

- **Configure clustering for both the Java and .NET applications**   The objective of clustering technology is to enable multiple instances of the business applications to serve incoming service requests so that when one instance dies, another instance is still available. Another objective is to enable session failover, which means that if a business application (or a hardware node) fails, the session information (or session state) can be made available after the business application instance is recovered from failure. Details of Java EE application server and .NET support clustering are discussed in the next section.

- **Create a shared session state database to store session information**   A customized database schema can be created to store shared session information or session state for both Java and .NET applications (acting as an integration point). Figure 14-1 depicts the sequence of how the shared session state database works. In this sample scenario, a .NET client is issuing a service request to access the URL, www.javadotnet-interop.com/index.aspx in Step 1. The HttpModule in the ASP.NET server redirects the service request to a registration page written in JSP (first-time registration only) in Step 2. Then the Java application associates the ASP.NET session id and the current Java session id and creates an entry in the shared session state database in Step 3. Upon successful registration, the Java application redirects the client request to the target URL, which is currently served by the ASP.NET server (Step 4). Guest discusses in detail an example of a shared session state database in [GuestKit], pages 430 through 445. This sample scenario assumes that the shared session state database, the Java application, and the .NET application are highly available and resilient and that there may be multiple instances of the business application available to enable high availability.

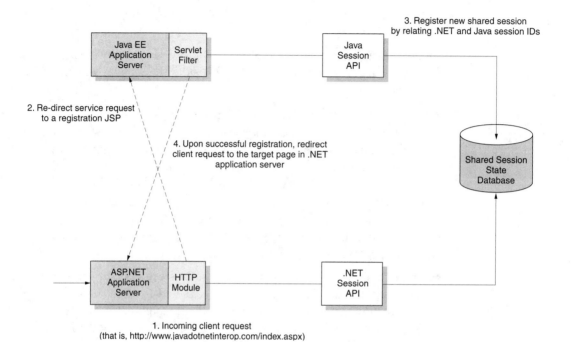

Figure 14-1
Shared session state database

- **Use the bridge infrastructure to store shared application and session information** This is similar to storing the shared application and session information in a shared session state database. As long as the Java EE .NET bridge middleware is highly available, either the Java or .NET client can be customized to retrieve the session information after the service failure. However, there is no standard mechanism in the container level (for example, a Java EE application server) to handle recovering the session information from the bridge after service failure.

- **Utilize Web SSO for managing session information** If the purpose of maintaining session information is to achieve single sign-on for both Java and .NET applications, it may be more sensible to utilize the session management features of vendor products that support Web SSO. Identity management products (such as Sun Java System Access Manager) that support Web SSO usually have the capability to persist session information and make the security service highly available.

Java EE Application Server Cluster

The Java EE application server supports clustering of application server instances and can allow session information (such as HttpSession) to be persisted and failed over in case of a service failure.

Figure 14-2 depicts a logical architecture using Sun Java System Application Server Enterprise Edition version 8.1 as an example. A cluster of three application server instances is created and is administered by an administration server (Domain Administration Server). A Java EE application can be deployed to all application server instances under the same cluster via the Domain Administration Server, without the need to deploy the business application individually to each server instance.

A service request from either a .NET client or a Java EE client is routed to different application server instances via a load balancer (or using a Web server load balancer plug-in). An application cluster provides the benefit of session failover. Although each Java EE application server vendor implements the cluster and the session failover slightly differently, they all achieve the same result.

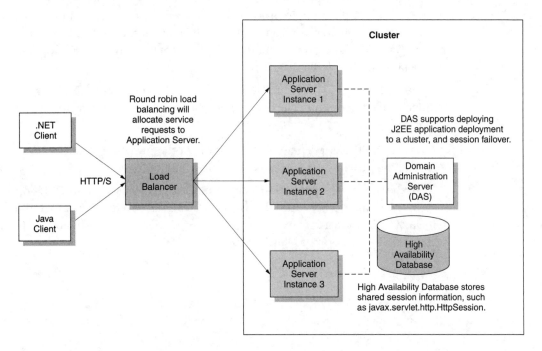

Figure 14-2

Sample Java EE application server cluster logical architecture

.NET Session Failover

Compared to Java EE application clustering, .NET application has a different approach (also known as a database-centric approach) to handle session failover. Developers can create session information and session states and store them in SQL Server. The SQL Server is deployed as a highly available relational database and is shared by multiple machines running Windows 2003 Server cluster. It is possible to create shared session states in the SQL Server so that the shared session between .NET and Java applications can be available. Refer to [NETStateManagement] and [NETSessionFailover] for details.

End-to-End Availability

Although developers can utilize the clustering and session failover in both Java and .NET platforms, this does not necessarily mean that end-to-end availability can be achieved. For example, consider a scenario of a clustered Java EE application server, clustered ASP.NET server, and a highly available SQL Server. A .NET application issues a service request (say, purchase order) for the Java EE application to process. The Java EE application supports high availability in a cluster environment, which denotes that if an application instance fails, the session information can be recovered by another application instance in the same cluster.

The end-to-end availability design needs to be considered for multiple architectural components. The design complexity may exist for the following scenarios:

- If the .NET client crashes in the middle of the purchase order creation, will the purchase order be recoverable from the session?

- If the Java EE application server instance crashes and the session failover takes place, does the .NET application have to reconnect to the Java EE application explicitly in order to recover the session state regarding the purchase order?

There is also an operating overhead associated with high availability (for example, additional system overhead to synchronize the session data between the application server instances). What's more, if the Java EE application does not persist session information, it seems that there is no obvious benefit of using Java EE application server clustering for high availability and session failover.

Availability of Integration Strategies

Table 14-3 summarizes the availability features by comparing synchronous integration, asynchronous integration, and bridge integration strategies. The availability features are also discussed in Chapter 11.

It is noted that both synchronous and asynchronous integration strategies share similar availability features because they both utilize the underlying infrastructures (such as the clustering capability from the Java EE application server container). Typically, messaging technologies (such as JMS or MSMQ) and bridge middleware support high availability. Business transactions can also be persisted using messaging technologies or bridge middleware so that they can be recovered after service failure.

With the availability of WS-Management technology (refer to Chapter 15, "Managing Java EE .NET Interoperability Applications," for more details), the capability to detect availability status has become more important in proactive service management. The detection of availability status allows design of some preventive actions to facilitate availability of the business applications (for example, restart the server instance when certain exception is met). WS-Management can support both synchronous and asynchronous integration strategies. For bridge integration, the detection of availability status and any remedial action to ensure availability depends on the vendor implementation.

Table 14-3
Availability Features by Different Integration Strategies

Availability Features	Synchronous Integration	Asynchronous Integration	Bridge Integration
Detection of availability status	WS-Management	WS-Management	Depending on the bridge implementation
Persistence	Need to customize	Uses JMS or MSMQ	Depending on the bridge implementation
End-to-end availability	Hardware system level clustering	Hardware/system level clustering	Depending on the bridge implementation
	Java EE Application Server cluster	Java EE Application Server cluster	
	ASP.NET stores session states in SQL Server to ensure availability.	ASP.NET stores session states in SQL Server to ensure availability.	
Up-time	N/A	N/A	N/A
Middleware	N/A	N/A	N/A

Scalability

The scalability of the interoperable solutions implies that the solution can be deployed on large configurations. It is important to remember that deploying business applications on faster CPUs or adding more CPUs and physical memory *does not necessarily* make the interoperable solution scalable. Moreover, because Java and .NET applications are likely to run on different hardware machines, there needs to be a consistent system performance measurement methodology (for example, measuring the performance of a round-trip from a .NET client to a Java application) to consider several performance enhancement design options. This puts the benchmarking and performance statistics into the proper context instead of using an apple-to-orange metric. The following section introduces some options to measure Java and .NET application performance.

Measuring Performance

There are a few options to measure the performance of a Java and .NET application. These timing functions are provided by the Java and .NET platforms. To measure the end-to-end performance throughout, developers need to aggregate the timing statistics from these basic timing functions for measurement.

- Adding a timer function in the business application (for example, a client application that invokes the business functions) before and after your function calls. This timer function can be used to measure the total response time required to run an interoperability operation. Refer to Figures 14-3 and 14-4 for Java and .NET program excerpts.

- Using a testing software package (for example, a stress test package) to measure the end-to-end, total response time and performance. Empirix (www.empirix.com/default.asp?action=category&ID=40) and Mercury LoadRunner (www.mercury.com/us/products/perform-ance-center/) are possible choices.

- Employing an external testing company to measure the end-to-end performance in a dedicated network or public Internet.

Listing 14-1 shows an example of how to add a timer function in Java applications. This approach applies to all integration strategies but requires a central place to store the time statistics.

Listing 14-1

Java Program Excerpt to Measure System Performance

```
package com.interop.performance;

public class Foo {

...
   public static void main(String args[]) {
      long time = System.nanoTime();
      // call your remote method or functions
      System.out.println("Foo took " + (System.currentTimeMillis()-
time) + "mill-seconds to run");
   }

}
```

Listing 14-2 shows a .NET sample program excerpt that performs a timer function to measure system performance.

Listing 14-2
.NET Program Excerpt to Measure System Performance

```
. . .
Counter q = new Counter();
. . .
long startCounting = q.Value;
long stopCounting = q.Value;
float totalTime = q.TimeElapsed(startCounting, stopCounting);
. . .
```

Listing 14-3 shows an alternative .NET sample program excerpt that performs a timer function to measure system performance. The difference is that Listing 14-2 uses the `Counter()` function, while Listing 14-3 uses the `Environment.TickCount` package to achieve similar objectives.

Listing 14-3
Another .NET Program Excerpt to Measure System Performance

```
. . .
int startTicks = Environment.TickCount;

//
// insert your function here
DoSomething();

int stopTicks = Environment.TickCount;
Console.WriteLine("Elapsed time = {0} milliseconds",
   stopTicks - startTicks);
. . .
```

When measuring the performance of a Java EE .NET interoperable solution, it is not helpful to take a measurement of individual Java or .NET application alone. The end-to-end application performance (such as round trip from the .NET client to the Java EE application server) needs to be measured. For example, in a scenario where a .NET application creates a purchase order and submits to a Java EE application server, a timer function can be customized to measure from the creation of a purchase order (from the .NET client) to the completion of processing the purchase order (return the processing result from the Java EE application server).

When benchmarking the performance of a Java EE .NET interoperable solution, one should compare different integration strategies for the same set of business requirements and environment constraints. This gives a better assessment of the interoperable solution. It is also useful to measure the resource utilization such as CPU and network. In the sample Supply Chain scenario discussed earlier in the chapter, performance architects may consider benchmarking the application performance of using different integration strategies. It is plausible that asynchronous integration strategy is optimal for Java applications running on a slow entry-level hardware platform—when compared to using a synchronous integration strategy.

Micro-Tuning

The performance of an application can be tuned and enhanced in two general directions: (1) a top-down approach; (2) a bottom-up approach. In the top-down tuning approach, performance engineers can scale the solution on a high-end machine with more CPUs, more physical memory, and larger data storage without examining each technical component in detail. If the interoperable solution does not scale as expected, performance analysis architects can drill down and identify bottlenecks. In analyzing the performance of a Java EE .NET interoperable solution, performance architects should also consider changing the integration strategy (say, from a synchronous to asynchronous strategy) based on the application.

In the bottom-up tuning approach, performance architects perform a fine-grained analysis of the application and make changes to a specific technical component. For example, they increase the hardware depending on the application requirements for resources (such as CPU and memory). They are referred to as *micro-tuning* strategies here.

[HansenLai] makes a few generalizations regarding micro-tuning strategies for XML Web services based on a vendor-specific JMS benchmarking. These generalizations can serve as general guidelines for tuning Java applications.

- Adding more CPUs to synchronous Web services has a non-linear scalability in improving system performance. For example, a specific customer benchmarking exercise shows that RPC-based Web service applications improve performance by adding up to eight CPUs (these quantities are specific customer scenarios and should be interpreted as references, not specific business rules).

- Adding more physical memory to synchronous Web services has a linear scalability in improving system performance.

- Adding more CPUs to asynchronous Web services has a slightly linear scalability in improving system performance.

- Adding more physical memory to asynchronous Web services appears to improve system performance until a certain number of physical memory is reached. After the ceiling is reached, the system performance remains constant.

- Adding more CPUs to achieve slightly linear scalability for business applications that require intensive XML parsing and XML encryption/decryption.

Rammer and Turner in [RammerTurner] provide an interesting discussion on improving .NET application performance by changing the underlying integration strategies. Rammer and Turner's summary is also a good guideline for choosing the appropriate .NET integration strategies.

- ASMX (ASP.NET version 2.0) has more than adequate system performance for business transactions and is a preferred choice of .NET technology due to its benefit of better interoperability.

- Enterprise Services/COM+ components are appropriate for performance-critical applications and are well integrated with Microsoft Windows Communication Foundation (WCF) or formerly Indigo technology.

- .NET Remoting performs well when using binary serialization over TCP. However, its performance diminishes when remoting components are hosted on Internet Information Server (IIS) and/or when sending and receiving SOAP messages.

Scalability by Integration Strategies

Table 14-4 summarizes the scalability features by comparing synchronous integration, asynchronous integration, and bridge integration strategies. The memory and CPU factors are relatively more prominent than other factors in enhancing the system performance of an interoperable solution. The scalability features are also discussed in Chapter 11.

Table 14-4
Scalability Features by Different Integration Strategies

Scalability Features	Synchronous Integration	Asynchronous Integration	Bridge Integration
Memory factor	Potentially slight linear scalability	Potentially slight linear scalability	Depending on the bridge implementation
CPU factor	XML parsing and encryption will be usually accelerated by faster CPU	XML parsing and encryption will be usually accelerated by faster CPU	Depending on the bridge implementation
Interface factor	N/A	N/A	N/A
Multi-threading factor	Java supports multi-threading	Java supports multi-threading	Depending on the bridge implementation
Distributed architecture factor	Depends on the distributed architecture design	Asynchronous messaging facilitates distributed architecture design	Bridge becomes a hub-centric or bus-centric architecture model

Best Practices and Pitfalls

The following identifies some best practices and pitfalls that are relevant to designing reliability, availability, and scalability features of a Java EE .NET interoperability solution.

Best Practices

- Always do a sanity check for end-to-end availability during the design review of a Java EE .NET interoperable solution. Examine each technical component to see how the application or service is recovered.

- Accuracy in measuring .NET application performance. The system packages `System.DateTime` and `System.TimeSpan` are accurate only within about 10 milliseconds for most applications. However, if XML object serialization is used, use the `QueryPerformanceCounter` API to obtain a more accurate representation of how much time is elapsed.

- Use MTOM rather than SwaRef (SOAP with Attachment) because MTOM should have better performance, and the use of XOP encoding (processing overhead) is expensive.

- Secure MTOM (using message encryption for MTOM messages) has overhead. Do not try to use message encryption for all types of data or business transactions unless required.

Pitfalls

- Do not compare Java and .NET application performance directly. This is like an apple-to-orange comparison. When comparing application performance in the context of Java EE .NET interoperability solutions, always compare the performance between integration strategies using the same set of business requirements, constraints, and hardware environment.

- Do not attempt to cluster every application and machine by default. Always consider the objectives for the clustering because clustering introduces considerable overhead and may not actually meet the overall technical objectives.

- Logging is a useful feature to track business transactions and system events. Some transaction logging can also help to recover transactions in case of service failure. However, turning on the highest level of logging by default does not necessarily make the application available. It will deteriorate system performance considerably.

- When exchanging data types between Java and .NET applications, there is a general lack of error control or exception handling to catch invalid data types during XML serialization or data transmission between Java and .NET clients.

Summary

Reliability, availability, and scalability (RAS) are three critical attributes of managing the Quality of Services in a Java EE .NET interoperable solution. Managing RAS is a complex subject area that requires many micro-tuning exercises and iterative, trial-and-error changes. This chapter has identified some major design factors for RAS and related them to different integration strategies. The text has also reviewed the current states of existing RAS technologies and explored what they can do today.

The reliability requirements for an interoperable solution basically assumes that the service requests (or messages) and the business data should be reliable and accurate. Asynchronous and bridge integration strategies are more flexible and appropriate in supporting messaging reliability.

The availability requirements for an interoperable solution are usually implemented by clustering in the container level. Clustering supports session failover. Shared session data is another strategy that can support availability requirements.

The scalability requirements for an interoperable solution are supported by either upgrading the infrastructure or by micro-tuning each technical component. Sometimes changing the underlying integration strategy may be more appropriate to enhance the end-to-end system performance.

References

[DotNetMQ] Bill O'Brien Weblog. "NET and MQSeries." March 16, 2005.
http://blogs.msdn.com/dotnetinterop/archive/2004/11/08/254113.aspx

[GuestKit] Simon Guest. *Microsoft .NET and J2EE Interoperability Toolkit*. Redmond, WA: Microsoft Press, 2004.

[HansenLai] Jon E. Hansen and Ray Lai. "Capacity Planning and Performance Management in a Web Services World." Sun Customer Engineering Conference. March 12–15, 2004.

[LuefPichler] Gottfried Luef and Michael Pichler. "Construct a Reliable Web Service." IBM DeveloperWorks. October 5, 2004.
http://www-128.ibm.com/developerworks/webservices/library/wsconstruct/index.html

[NETStateManagement] "INFO: ASP.NET State Management Overview." Microsoft Help and Support. January 21, 2004.
http://support.microsoft.com/kb/307598/

[NETSessionFailover] "How to Use ASP.NET Session State SQL Server Mode in a Failover Cluster." Microsoft Help and Support, November 16, 2004.
http://support.microsoft.com/default.aspx?scid=kb;en-us;323262

[RammerTurner] Ingo Rammer and Richard Turner. "Performance of ASP.NET Web Services, Enterprise Services, and .NET Remoting." Microsoft Developer Network, August 2005.

http://msdn.microsoft.com/webservices/default.aspx?pull=/library/enus/dnweb srv/html/asmxremotesperf.asp.

Managing Java EE .NET Interoperability Applications

15

Have you ever heard of the term "CNN moment?" Those in the software business may have heard of it, while others may have experienced it. It is often caused by a service interruption that became worldwide news. The always reachable Google site went down for 15 minutes on May 7, 2005, from 6:45 to 7pm EST. Not only did this become world news; what's worse is that some online users were rationalizing it as the beginning of the end of the world. I wouldn't consider Google a mission-critical service, and yet it created a panic for many people.

Monitoring the Quality of Service across a large-scale, distributed, heterogeneous enterprise landscape is a difficult task, as software and hardware components are prone to errors. Nevertheless, establishing this infrastructure is critical to reduce and possibly prevent system downtime. Imagine troubleshooting a glitch on a production system in which a problem is not easily reproducible. Sounds familiar? What if the service is made up of components from Java EE, .NET, and legacy applications commonly deployed in various businesses or is composed of a set of federated services distributed over the Internet? Hours of service interruptions often translate into millions of dollars in lost revenue. Without a management infrastructure in place, the troubleshooting process can consume days or weeks before the problem is identified and fixed, degrading overall service levels.

Deploying, configuring, monitoring, detecting, notifying, and in some cases self-healing a problem constitutes system management. The ultimate goal of system management is to ensure that the quality of service and operating requirements of all business applications are satisfied. In the ISO Network Management model that is referenced throughout this chapter, the key elements of this complex task are fault management, configuration management, accounting, performance management, and security management. Achieving these goals in a mixed Java EE .NET platform environment presents many management challenges that are discussed in this chapter. An implementation of the Simple Network Management Protocol (SNMP), designed for network management, is available for Windows and various UNIX platforms and can be leveraged to monitor platforms hosting Java EE and .NET applications. SNMP is often used as the lowest common denominator to monitor nodes on an IP network and to provide detailed networking statistics. SNMP, however, produces a large amount of information that has to be filtered. Telemetry is another way of addressing management and allows remote measurements to be transmitted to a centralized system for analysis. See [NetworkMgmtOverview] and [NetworkMgmtBasics] for overview of network management.

Managing Mixed Java EE and .NET Environments

IT managers regularly use distributed management systems to address Quality of Service requirements. Typical management systems can be agent-based, using standards such as SNMP or higher-level standards such as CIM (please refer to [DMTF] and [CIM]). Higher-level functionality at the system and application level requires platform-dependent management. The next sections explore management support offered by Java EE and .NET platforms.

Management of Java Applications

The Java Management Extensions (JMX) APIs (see [JMXIntro] and [JMX_WP]) enable instrumentation of Java applications [JMAN] and facilitate management of devices, services, or business applications referred to as

JMX resources. The JMX component model introduces the notion of a managed bean, **MBean**, which represents managed resources. Resources instrumented with MBeans represent the key component of the JMX architecture. These MBeans are registered and deployed within an MBean container that is part of a JMX agent. An agent also includes services for controlling MBeans and consolidating information gathered by MBeans into a remote management console. Finally, the JMX Agent is accessible to a remote management console by means of protocol adapters or connectors.

JMX is available for download, [JMX_Download], and accessible in the form of javax.management libraries. The diagram in Figure 15-1 outlines some of the core JMX components.

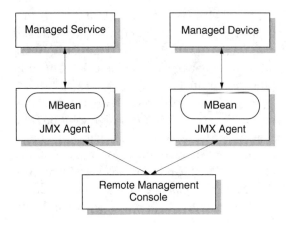

Figure 15-1
JMX overview

The JMX 1.2 specification consists of three layers: the Instrumentation layer, the Agent layer, and a Distributed layer. The Instrumentation layer encompasses resources such as applications, devices, or services instrumented using MBeans. The Agent layer contains an MBean Server along with additional services such as monitoring. A Distributed layer contains adapters and connectors to remotely access JMX agents [JMXIntro].

JMX represents a key management capability in Java. It is used for management of Java EE application servers, JSR-77, and compliant Java EE applications, JSR-88. Java Virtual Machine Profiling API, implemented in Java 5 improves a virtual machine profiling interface, [Java5Mgmt], and a way to enhance the JVM control. Java SE 5 is shipped with a console application, jconsole, aimed for basic troubleshooting purposes.

Aside from JMX, the Operations Support Systems (OSS) through Java Initiative (OSS/J), defines a standard set of Java APIs to enable compatibility across OSS systems. See [OSSJ] for more details. OSS/J includes the Service Quality Management API, Quality of Service API, and others that mitigate manageability risks of an enterprise system. The OSS/J initiative, which is part of the Java Community process, embraces multiple industry vendors and provides Java APIs to allow a consistent method for managing services.

Management of .NET Environment

Microsoft Windows provides the Windows Management Instrumentation (WMI) framework for instrumentation and monitoring of the operating system, frameworks, and applications [WMI], [WMIGuide]. Using WMI in a .NET application can be accomplished through `System.Management` and `System.Management.Instrumentation` namespaces. Both .NET managed applications and native code can be managed using these APIs. In addition to the WMI framework, the Microsoft Operations Manager (MOM) solution offers IT managers a way to administer OS-level services and Windows applications, including .NET. Another administrative solution from Microsoft called Microsoft Management Console (MMC) enables management of the Windows-based environment. An open source MMC .NET library is available from sourceforge.net [MMC_.NET] and provides MMC snap support for C# development. Another Microsoft management solution, Systems Management Server (SMS), assists users with patch management and software updates, [SMS].

Interoperability Technology Gap

Java EE .NET management interoperability embraces a number of interesting challenges. Java Management Extensions (JMX) is not interoperable with WMI, and OSS/J does not span across .NET platform. Microsoft Management Console cannot control JMX Agents.

To determine application-level crashes during development with .NET-based technologies, Microsoft leverages AVIcode Intercept Studio to extend MOM with application manageability. See [Avicode]. There are a number of commercial solutions to monitor Java EE such as Nastel's AutoPilot/IT that is actually based on JMX technology. See [AutoPilot] for more details. A gap that still needs to be filled is a commercial solution to monitor both Java and .NET applications.

WS-Management is gaining momentum and will eventually provide cohesive means to manage devices, systems, and applications; however, Java

EE and .NET developers cannot leverage WS-Management today for inter-operable application management.

At the systems level, Microsoft Operations Manager does not support the Java EE platform. Microsoft Operations Manager has commercial extensions, such as Vintela System Monitoring, that provide heterogeneous management of Windows, Solaris, Linux and Mac OS X environment. See [VSM]. Similarly, heterogeneous OS level management can be achieved with commercial extensions, such as Vintela Management Extensions, which enables Microsoft Systems Management Server (SMS) 2003 with the capability to support Solaris, Linux, and Mac OS X. See [VMX] and [VINT] for more details.

With an SNMP-based management solution, low-level networking information has to be interpreted into meaningful business messages. An intermediate solution is required for aggregating and filtering the QoS notification.

Agent and Proxy Management Deployment Architectures

Two prevalent architectures deployed for managing enterprise systems are agent-based or proxy-based. With an agent-based architecture, proprietary management software agents have to be deployed across managed systems. This requires additional installation, synchronous updates, and is not as transparent as a proxy-based architecture. The latter relies on a proxy acting as a broker between a centralized management console and distributed managed systems. With agentless proxy architecture, the main drawback is that the proxy often becomes a single point of failure for the entire management chain, as the proxy is the only link between managed resources and the management console. Figure 15-2 outlines agent and proxy-based architectures.

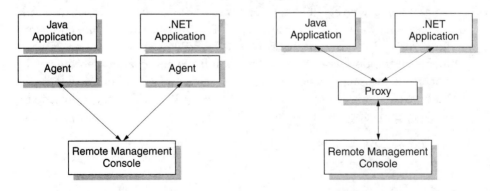

Figure 15-2

Agent and proxy-based management architectures

ISO Management Elements in Java EE .NET Platforms

In a heterogeneous application and platform environment, IT managers are faced with different and often incompatible management frameworks. IT organizations often partition the heterogeneous platforms into groups of application "silos"—subsystems with a common management infrastructure. Third-party products such as HP OpenView or CA Unicenter provide management consoles that consolidate the platform-specific management information and provide a common view of managed components. As for SOA, custom solutions from companies such as Infravio facilitate SLA compliance of deployed Web services. Computer Associates, AmberPoint, Actional, and Service Integrity developed a Web services extension to Microsoft's MOM solution to address management of .NET and Java EE Web services via a proprietary management solution. Java EE and .NET implementations that address individual ISO management elements are fundamentally different, as discussed in the following sections.

Fault Management

The goal of fault management systems is to discover faults in the application or in the system infrastructure and report and log the fault event. Where possible, the fault management system can take corrective action to correct the fault and automatically restore service. The Java EE platform and .NET platform have different models for logging and event handling. Java EE applications widely use Java Logging APIs, such as `java.util.logging`, which supports configurable application logging. Under JSR-77, application servers and modules can be queried for information and can provide event notifications. .NET applications use the `System.Diagnostics` namespace to log application events to the Windows event log. The Windows event log provides system-wide event logging and monitoring at the system, security, and application level but is a windows-specific infrastructure. In a mixed system, the error and logging messages reflect the different programming environments and underlying systems that complicate aggregation and interpretation of the messages. Failover is another characteristic of fault management. Both Java EE application servers and .NET on Windows Server provide for clustering to support failover.

Configuration Management

The goal of distributed configuration management is to deploy and monitor application and component assets and their configuration information. This task is made more complex in heterogeneous systems, where version changes and updates can create incompatibilities that may be difficult to anticipate. The Java EE and .NET deployment models are different. The Java EE deployment process supports the "develop once—deploy anywhere" model, with separation of responsibilities between the module development team and the deployment team. The programmatic management of the deployment process is specified in JSR-88 (Java EE Application Deployment Specification). Java EE does not provide support for module version control. .NET assemblies support a different model. Assemblies are self-describing deployment units that support .NET version management. In addition to the application configuration management issues, IT organizations must manage security and operating system patches on all the different systems.

Accounting

The goal of accounting management is to measure system and application usage. This allows the IT organization to understand the true cost of providing an IT service and to keep IT services aligned with the business requirements. At the platform level, most operating systems allow for monitoring and management of resources usage by users or groups. Typical system-level resources are CPU and disk space. This allows for integration with billing systems and enforcement of usage policies and the compliance with service level agreements (SLAs). At the application server level, Java EE does not provide an accounting framework, but account management systems are provided on top of the Java EE infrastructure. .NET-based systems rely on the Windows metering infrastructure for accounting.

Performance Management

The goal of performance management is to measure and maintain adequate system and application performance. Examples of performance metrics are user response times, application throughput, and resource utilization. Java EE and .NET provide facilities for measuring performance data at the component level. Java EE application servers provide facilities through JSR 77 for collection of statistics at the application server and module object levels. Both Java EE and .NET provide caching models that can be tuned for improved throughput. ASP.NET provides caching in the page-processing and data levels. Java EE provides extensive object caching for EJBs in the Business tier, and servlet containers cache JSPs and can be extended to support tunable caching of JSP fragments.

Security Management

Security management entails management of users, roles, credentials, and rights and is a key task of IT organization in ensuring secure operations. The goal of security management in mixed platform environments is to meet all of these security requirements while maintaining synchronized security schema on all platforms. Management of multiple user accounts and sets of credentials adds overhead for the IT organization and increases the potential for security holes. .NET relies heavily on IIS for implementation of authentication, which leverages the Windows infrastructure, [MSDN1] and [MSDN2]. Java EE has defined several interfaces for application server integration with user management. These systems typically support integration with directory services using JNDI (including Active Directory) and integration with the underlying operating system user management. Most recently, the JSR-196 specification describes the integration with JAAS, which is a more powerful and flexible model [JSR196]. From a management viewpoint, unifying the user repository on LDAP does not solve the different underlying schema and security models. Java EE application server vendors offer proprietary support for Windows Domain authentication; however, this model is not supported in a standard fashion across application servers and requires user management only through the Windows Domain, [BEA1] and [IBM1]. Some organizations have addressed this problem through single-sign-on solutions and cross-domain security solutions such as Kerberos, [KERB].

The support for security policy at the VM level differs between .NET and Java EE and is managed with different tools. .NET has a more sophisticated policy structure, but Java allows greater flexibility for overriding default policies. Java EE RMI supports the use of SSL for secure communications; whereas, there is no similar built-in solution for .NET Remoting. WS-Security implementation is available for .NET and Java for secure remote invocation of Web services [PILIPCHUK1], and Sun implements WS-Security as part of the Java Web Services Developer Pack. Apache WSS4J is another implementation of the OASIS Web Services Security (WS-Security) for Java. See [JWSDP] and [WSS4J] for more details.

For the code demonstration, this chapter continues to use WS-I Supply Chain Management application described in the following sections.

Management Scenario

These management requirements are illustrated through the Web Service Interoperability (WS-I) Supply Chain Management (SCM) Retailer System as an example, specifically the Purchase Goods Use Case. Figure 15-3 shows an overview of the features of this system. In this model, the SCM system represents an interoperable SOA-based application, where a specific subsystem, the Retailer System, operates within its own organization context.

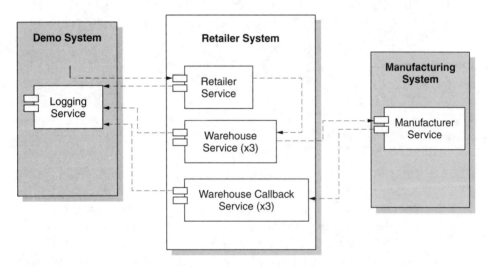

Figure 15-3
WS-I system deployment diagram

To illustrate the challenges of interoperability management, the Retailer system is implemented where the web front end is implemented on the .NET platform and the Retailer service is on the Java EE platform. For purposes of illustration, the UC1 Purchase Goods use case is used, as described in the Supply Chain Management Use Case Model document [WSI1]. The use case begins with the .NET front end retrieving the catalog from the Retailer service and the customer being presented the .NET Shopping Cart page. The customer interacts with the Shopping Cart page, selecting products and setting the quantity of each ordered item. At some point, the customer is satisfied with the order and submits the order to the Retailer Service. The Retailer

Service validates the order and determines which Warehouse Service will fulfill the order items. Order Validation verifies the order information is correct. If not, Order Validation sends an error message to the customer. The Retailer service then requests the products from the Warehouses. If a Warehouse is out of any of the products, it rejects the entire order and sends a response to the customer. However, when the Warehouse can fulfill the order, Order Summary sends a completion response to the customer.

It is assumed that there is a common IT organization that is managing the Retailer systems and is responsible for the operation of all of its components. The SCM system follows a loosely coupled SOA architecture, where the Retailer system exists within its own organizational context and may be implemented as a tightly-coupled subsystem. The interactions between the front end and the Retailer system components is described as a `request-response` sequence, both for the catalog requests and for the submit order requests [WSI2].

Applying ISO Management to the Application Architecture

The reference system should meet requirements for the management functionality that has just been described.

- **Fault Management**   There should also be a common logging system across the Retailer system. The error messages provided by the Warehouse system should be useable by the .NET front end error summary in order to provide coherent error messages to the end user. Additionally, failures in the warehouse service—such as a database failure, should be logged and alerted using the same interface and infrastructure as the back-end system.

- **Configuration Management**   There should be a common method for managing the configuration of the front end and back end. They must each maintain consistent programming interfaces across all version changes.

- **Accounting Management**   The system should provide metering to ensure that the warehouse systems fulfill the requirement for uptime, and to record the usage of the system per end-user.

- **Performance Management**   The system should deliver acceptable response time for the user experience in the use case described here. This includes the flow of order request including the response time for Order Validation.

- **Security Management**   The system should provide an authentication system that allows the front-end system to authenticate the user at login and allows the back-end system to trust the front-end authentication. There should be a single system for management of users, credentials, and their roles.

The next sections outline a few management strategies that can be successfully applied across Java EE and .NET-based systems. Web services management strategy will be the starting point to demonstrate how Web services can be leveraged to manage Java EE and .NET environments. This is often referred to as Management Using Web services. The subject of Web services management is also discussed. Following the Web services discussion, the chapter explores the Platform Unification strategy and at the end compares various management techniques available in the Java EE .NET interoperability space.

Web Services Management Strategy

The flexibility of Web services is now spreading across data center environments to simplify management of heterogeneous IT landscapes. Two management specifications, the Web Services Management (WS-Management) [WS-Management] and Web Services Distributed Management (WSDM), are similar in nature. Both of them share the common goal of uniquely identifying managed resources and monitoring resource status and can be leveraged to accomplish interoperability across Java EE and .NET applications. On the Java side the Web services Connector for Java Management Extensions (JMX) Agents, defined by JSR 262, intends to define a JMX Remote API to use Web services to transmit management information [JSR262]. This JSR may support WSDM and WS-Management. The chapter discusses how to apply each of these standards to realize management of Java EE and .NET applications.

Web Services Distributed Management (WSDM)

The OASIS WSDM standard consists of two specifications—Management Using Web Services (MUWS) and Management of Web Services (MOWS). WSDM defines a management capability, which is a composable set of operations, events, metadata, properties, and other semantics. The rationale behind composability is to be able to scale up or scale down the management task.

In a nutshell, the first specification, WSDM MUWS, outlines details of representing and accessing resources across heterogeneous IT environments. With WSDM MUWS, every resource has a unique Identity capability, Metrics capability, and a few more. For discovering and advertising resources, WSDM supports an Advertisement capability, used for notifying availability of a new manageable resource. To discover additional resources, WSDM supports Relationships among resources; whereas, for querying a resource registry, WSDM supports Registration events. MUWS defines an Operational Status capability retuning an Available, Unavailable, or Unknown status of a resource and also defines a State capability for managing the resource lifecycle.

The second specification, WSDM MOWS, extends MUWS with details on how to manage a resource represented in the form of a Web service. A service that is managed has Identification. MOWS defines numerous metrics such as ServiceTime, NumberOfSuccessfulRequests, and NumberOfFailedRequests to gather statistics of individual services. An Operational State of the managed service can be Up, with either Idle or Busy sub-states, or Down with Stopped, Crashed, or Saturated sub-states. If all services are Up, the OperationalState capability defined by MUWS, returns status Available; if all services are Down, the state indicates Unavailable. A Request Processing State defines what events to be taken when a request state changes.

To accomplish the management capabilities, WSDM relies on various Web services specifications including WS-I Basic Profile, WS-Resource Framework (WS-RF) Resource Properties (WSRP) for properties, WS-Notification (WSN) Base Notifications (WSBN) for management event transport, and WS-Addressing (WSA) for Web services references. Refer to [WSDM] for more details.

How does WSDM relate to Java and .NET application management? WSDM MUWS supports SOAP over HTTP, XML schema for data type definition, and WSDL for interface definition. JMX and WMI APIs can be used to instrument a business application, whereas MUWS can be used as a communication mechanism between business applications and management systems. This strategy can be accomplished by using custom, or a third-party adapter that would perform the mappings between WSDM and corresponding APIs, such as JMX or WMI. This strategy is demonstrated in Figure 15-4.

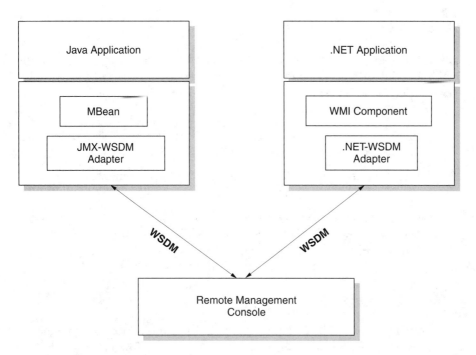

Figure 15-4
WSDM-based strategy

To learn more details about this approach and specifically on how to integrate JMX with WSDM, please refer to [JMX_WSDM]. MUWS can also be used in conjunction with SNMP, CIM, and other management frameworks. Because WSDM supports an agentless architecture, both proxy and agents can be used when deploying a WSDM-based solution.

Benefits and Limitations

The fact that WSDM became an OASIS standard, regardless of dependencies on various evolving specifications such as WS-Resource, WS-Addressing, and WS-Notification, is one of its biggest drawbacks. As of now there are no commercial implementations of this specification.

Despite its ability to integrate WSDM standards with Java and .NET, this strategy presents some difficulties. One-to-one mapping between MBeans and WSDM Manageability endpoints may result in an overwhelming amount of information to be processed. Another constraint pertains to the data type mismatch between Java and WSDM defined data types as well as C# or other .NET languages and WSDM types.

WSDM Implementations

HP has donated code for three Web Services Distributed Management (WSDM) 1.0 specifications to the Apache Foundation to eventually provide developers with an open source Java implementation of the WSDM standard. The three specifications include

- Management Using Web Services to represent a management interface or a resource in the form of Web services, see [Muse_Apache].

- Web Services Notification describing how to send management information, see [WSN_Apache].

- Web Services Resource Framework defining a way of exposing and representing managed resources such as CPU consumption and memory utilization, see [WSRF_Apache].

WS-Management

WS-Management is rapidly gaining popularity and is expected to have wide support from industry leaders such as Sun, Microsoft, and Intel. WS-Management (WSMAN) identifies a core set of Web service specifications and usage requirements to expose a common set of operations that are central to all systems management. The goal of WSMAN is to allow interoperability across managed applications and resources, which is in essence very similar to WSDM. WSMAN is designed to be applicable to small, memory-constrained devices; hence, compared to WSDM, WSMAN is a simpler way to implement a management solution and requires a minimal set of components to implement to comply with the specification. Any WSMAN-compliant device such as a baseboard management controller (BMC) can be managed via WS-Management. WSMAN also can be applied to manage Web services as well as applications. There are five core operations highlighted by the WS-Management specification:

1. Discover managed resources and navigate among them.
2. Get, put, create, rename, and delete resources.
3. Enumerate the content of containers and collections including large tables and logs.
4. Subscribe to events emitted by managed resources.
5. Execute a management method with strongly typed input and output parameters.

To discover management resources, the WSMAN uses the WS-Management Catalog specification, which defines metadata for managed resources. The WS-Management Catalog contains details on how a managed hardware or software resource is to be accessed via a WS-Addressing endpoint reference that includes a URL of the resource, the resource type identifier, and name/key value pairs identifying a resource. Managed *resources* are grouped into *Systems*; one or more *Systems* comprise a *Service*. Management services expose Web service APIs defined by the specification to the client application that consolidates management information. Event notifications can be delivered to endpoints via multiple delivery modes including batched and pull. Aside from WS-Addressing, the WS-Management specification also references WS-Eventing, WS-Enumeration, and WS-Transfer.

At the time of writing this chapter, there is no direct mapping between WS-Management and WMI or JMX APIs available in industry, although some work has been initiated by Sun. The initial set of implementations extends the WS-Management specification with mapping to the Common Information Model (CIM) schema. CIM specifies a common definition of management information for systems, networks, applications, and services to allow heterogeneous environments to adhere to a consistent management standard. A common way to represent CIM classes is by using the Managed Object Format (MOF). On Windows, the MOF compiler adds corresponding classes to the WMI repository. The Microsoft WMI Administrative Tool includes WMI CIM Studio component to create and manage classes, properties, and instances. The tool also facilitates generation and compilation of MOF files. See [WMISolutions] and [WMITools] for more details. With JMX, a managed client application can access MBeans using CIM/WS-Management, where CIM defines semantics of the data (what) being transferred and WS-Management outlines semantics of the communication (how) protocol between the client application and distributed resources. Figure 15-5 outlines a potential strategy to utilize WS-Management specification in a heterogeneous Java EE .NET domain.

JMX is a natural back-end technology for incrementing WSMAN resources in Java. Sun is in the process of prototyping a WSMAN adaptor that makes it possible to implement WSMAN resources using JMX MBeans.

Co-developers of the WS-Management specification have announced their intention to present the specification to the Distributed Management Task Force (DMTF).

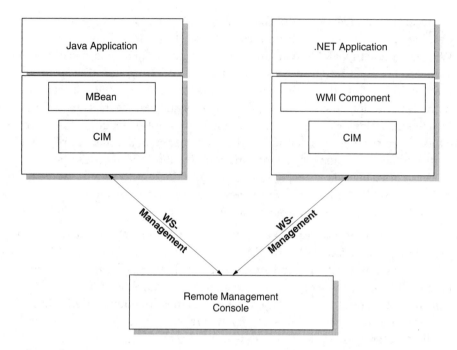

Figure 15-5
Java EE .NET Application Management with WS-Management

Benefits and Limitations

There is a clear desire among various industry players for WSDM and WS-Management to converge into a single specification. WS-Management is gaining popularity among various vendors, and it is simply a matter of time before it gets widely adopted by various hardware and software vendors. Benefits of cross-industry adoption would help to enable heterogeneous devices and applications to communicate their status using universal language defined by WS-Management.

In terms of interoperability, the main limitation is the lack of WSMAN adapters for JMX, which should be solved in the near future.

Example

Sun has published an open source implementation of the WSMAN specification (see [WISEMAN]).

In the WS-I Supply Chain Management application, a .NET application exchanges a PO message with a Java application. Should the physical machine on which the Java application is deployed fail, this failure could typically be manifested at the application level via a SOAP Fault received by a .NET component. With WS-Management, a Microsoft Management Console or a SharePoint Service would receive detailed information regarding the hardware failure and required remedial actions. In this scenario, management of interoperable environment can be easily addressed by repairing the hardware problem without a need to troubleshoot the problem at the application level.

Commercial Solutions

Microsoft Windows 2003 R2 includes the WS-Management Service for hardware-level support. WBEM Solutions plans to support WSMAN in both the J WBEM Server and C WBEM Server products later this year. See [WBEMSolutions] and [Win2003_WSMan] for details.

Management of Web Services

Both WS-Management and WSDM define a way to manage resources by using Web services as well as a way to manage Web services. For the latter, there are number of Custom Off The Shelf (COTS) solutions available to monitor Web services deployed in a distributed environment. See [WSMgmt] and [WSMgmtStandards] for an overview of various elements involved in Web services lifecycle management. Most of the commercial solutions address not only monitoring of the system performance, availability, and throughput, but also provide auditing and reporting functionality. Web services deployment and dynamic problem troubleshooting are often key features offered by commercial management solutions. Various products support both agents and proxy based deployments depending on the requirements. These products are available from Actional, AmberPoint (which provides both Java and .NET implementation of the SOA management solution), Flamenco Networks, and Systinet. AmberPoint Service Level Manager can track SLAs and send events to MOM in case monitored Web services experience performance or availability problems. AmberPoint also offers integration with enterprise monitoring solutions such as HP OpenView. See [ActionalSoapStation], [Systinet], [AmberPoint], [FlamencoNetworks] for detailed solution features. Among Web services management solutions, CA Unicenter WSDM (CA WSDM) Management Pack provides Microsoft Operations Manager 2000 with the ability to monitor Web services across Java EE and .NET applications. Refer to [CA_WSDM]and [CA_WSDM_MOM] for more information.

ISO Characteristics in the Web Services Management Scope

This section discusses ISO characteristics in the context of Web services management.

- **Fault Management**   The MOWS and WS-Management requirements address functionality for problem detection, root cause failure diagnosis. Web service standards do not guarantee Java EE-.NET encoding coherence both for complex data types as well as for several primitive data types, which can lead to hard-to-track failures [IBM2].

- **Configuration Management**   The WSDM functionality supports notification of service changes. The MOWS requirements specifically address service deployment and life cycle management.

- **Accounting Management**   The MOWS requirements address the functionality of service metering and auditing and integration with billing and SLA management.

- **Performance Management**   The overhead of XML processing and SOAP/HTTP is considerable, especially as compared with binary wire formats such as used in the bridging solutions described previously. SOAP messages are relatively large, often requiring a great deal of metadata, and parsing and validation effect through put and performance [BIJ1]. Performance metering is addressed in the MOWS requirements.

- **Security Management**   Because WS-Security supports different styles of authentication and encryption protocols, it is possible for endpoints to be WS-Security-compliant but still not have a common protocol between them. WS-Security is a more robust model than HTTPS transport-level security but can significantly impact performance and response time [IBM3].

Because SOAP is a multi-hop protocol, user credentials need to be managed and synchronized across all the Web service platforms in the application. PKI-based approaches can use SAML for a more robust solution but introduce the complexity of PKI management for all of the systems. Implementation of the WS-Trust and WS-Federation specification provide a Web services standard for propagation of trust and federated identity management. However, management problems such as role and attribute mapping between systems for authorization remain unsolved. It is possible for attributes assigned to a user in one system to have a different meaning in an interoperating system [GFMP].

Web services is not the only means to mitigate system management risks across Java EE and .NET environments. The Unification strategy, discussed next, is another way companies address management challenges. With this strategy the underlying platform is unified for both .NET and Java EE applications using Mono platform. See [Mono] for more details.

Platform Unification Strategy

The goal of interoperability solutions is to enable point-to-point integration between components on both platforms, while preserving the object calling syntax of each platform and without introducing additional performance or management overhead. Solutions such as bridging can to some degree preserve the native object calling semantics used by the .NET and Java EE developers. Web services provide a well-supported and standards-based interface. However, interfacing using Web services changes the object calling semantics and introduces significant performance and management issues.

These solutions do not address the management complexities of a mixed-system. .NET and Java EE have fundamentally different models for management and security that are not resolved by point-to-point solutions. This requires not only preserving .NET and Java EE calling semantics for component developers, but deployment of all of the components on a homogenous platform with a single management and security model. Managing interoperability solution incorporates two elements: a solution for development time—requiring multi-language support, and a solution for runtime and deployment—requiring the hosting of multiple environments on a single platform. In the case of this reference application, it would require seamless development of the front end in the .NET environment in C# or VB.NET and deployment of both the front end and the back end on Java EE.

Before delving into details of Java and .NET manageability, it is important to understand the fundamentals of the Unification strategy.

Platform Unification Overview

In the Platform Unification approach, the code and runtime environment run on one platform, for instance .NET, that is fully hosted on the interoperating system such as Java EE. This approach preserves the integrity of the .NET application and enables .NET developers to continue to develop their code, while providing deployment on a single, homogenous platform. Mainsoft's implementation of this approach in their Visual MainWin for the Java EE

Platform product provides the infrastructure to use Java EE as a cross-language platform—supporting .NET languages and Java on a common Java EE platform. This allows for a unified runtime deployment environment.

The Mainsoft implementation provides platform unification through cross-compilation, a Mono-based .NET environment implemented on Java EE, and integration with the development environment.

Cross Compilation

For .NET code to execute in the Java EE environment, the code must be executable as compliant Java bytecode that can execute in a Java virtual machine. The Mainsoft binary compiler converts Microsoft Intermediate Language code into pure Java bytecode. The conversion must bridge the difference in .NET and Java semantics, while producing efficient and compliant code. The key elements of the conversion are

Direct Mapping—The compiler directly maps object structure, classes, interfaces and types, and the flow of control semantics from .NET to the equivalent Java semantics.

.NET Semantics—The compiler handles .NET semantics not present in Java. These semantic gaps include

- **.NET unsigned type** Unsigned type variables and fields are represented by their signed equivalent (that is, a `uint` parameter will be an `int` parameter in the Java method). Unsigned semantics are provided by handling the unsigned opcodes of .NET and implementing them on top of Java.

- **.NET value types** `Struct` is supported by creating a class for the `struct`, by implementing copy on assignment semantics, and by specially initializing structs (fields and local variables) before their first use.

- **.NET Delegates** The delegate type is implemented by a class that defines an `Invoke` method with the `delegate` parameters and `return` value. Each creation of specific delegates (that is, `new MyDel(this.MyFunc)`) is implemented by creating a class for each case that inherits from the class of the delegate type and that implements `Invoke` to call the function passed to the delegate constructor. (in the case of *new* `MyDel(this.MyFunc)`, the created class `Invoke` simply calls `MyFunc`).

- **.NET basic type mapping to Java Native Types** The compilation maps the most basic .NET types to their native Java equivalents. This maintains the Java VM's special handling of the basic object types. `System.Object` is mapped to `java.lang.Object`, `System.Exception` to `java.langThrowable`, and `System.String` to `java.lang.String`—and arrays are mapped to Java arrays. This is essential for conversion to generate efficient code.

Implementing this approach requires use of a cross compiler as shown in Figure 15-6. The cross compiler resolves differences in the .NET and Java platforms and produces Java bytecode output from the .NET code that is part of the application. The output of the cross compiler is Java class files that are packaged as a Java Archive File (JAR).

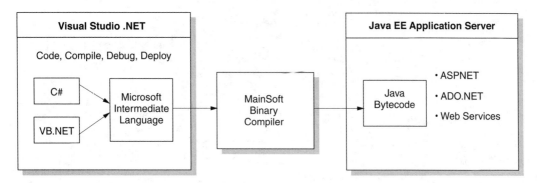

Figure 15-6
Visual MainWin Compiler

.NET Runtime Environment on Java EE

.NET code is hosted in a .NET environment running on Java EE. The Mainsoft implementation of the .NET environment is based on the open source Mono project.

The Mainsoft .NET runtime environment hosts the Mono libraries by cross-compiling these libraries to Java bytecode. Mainsoft classes provide the connection between the .NET namespace provided through Mono and the underlying Java SE and Java EE runtime. The Mainsoft integration of the Mono classes includes

- Support for .NET-based namespaces, such as `System`, `System.IO`, `System.Reflection`, and `System.Serialization`. These namespaces are implemented in libraries such as mscorlib, which provide integration with Java SE JDK classes.

- Support for connecting the .NET System.Web assembly, which is responsible for browser-server applications, with the Java EE Servlet API. The Mainsoft implementation provides a thin layer of classes that provide the connection and allow hosting the Mono implementation of the System.Web namespace.
- Support for OleDB and SqlClient the .NET data provider (part of System.Data assembly) implemented on top of the JDBC API, which enables components to access data from multiple data sources.

The structure of the runtime stack is shown in Figure 15-7.

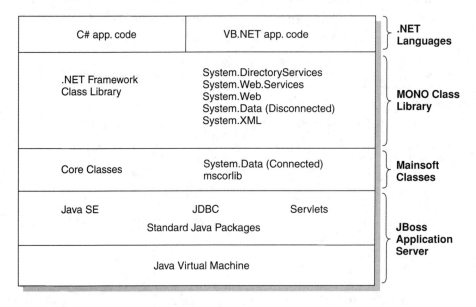

Figure 15-7
Visual MainWin technology stack

Interoperability of .NET and Java Code

Interoperability of Java code from .NET is supported natively. Because the runtime environment for all code, .NET and Java, remains the Java VM, all compliant Java code will run. The .NET programmer can access Java classes and namespaces transparently as from the .NET environment as if these classes were .NET classes. The JDK and Java EE classes are made available to the .NET developer as well.

.NET classes can be called by Java code as well, provided that the .NET classes expose interfaces that can be directly mapped to Java.

In a distributed environment, .NET code can reference Java components deployed either as EJBs or as Web services. Because the runtime environment is Java, point-to-point integration with EJBs is available over RMI. The .NET programmer sees the EJB as a .NET class with a .NET namespace. Additional tools in the provided development environment extensions generate wrapper code, which implements a service location pattern to map the EJB semantics of JNDI lookup and invocation of the home interface methods .NET class semantics [CORE]. .NET code can invoke Web services and implement Web service endpoints through the supported Mono implementation of the .NET `System.Web.Services` namespace.

The Visual MainWin environment provides an API for allowing .NET programmers to access the Java EE server context. This is necessary for programmatic security and for manipulating JNDI objects such as Data Sources. Additionally conversion routines are provided to allow conversion between Java types, such as `java.math.BigInteger` and functionally equivalent .NET types, such as `Decimal` and `DateTime`.

With this background on platform unification, the next sections elaborate on how to achieve management of .NET and Java EE applications.

Interoperability Management Solution

The Platform Unification approach enables .NET and Java EE code to interoperate by deploying all of the application components on a homogeneous Java EE environment. This achieves a cross-language/cross-environment platform with a uniform Java EE management model. Thus the challenges posed by the mixed management models described here are significantly reduced. In this model, the inter-component communications are based on native protocols—either Java method calls or RMI, and there are no additional marshaling or protocol interpretations. The platform unification model does not impose an architectural model on the components. It allows the components to be tightly or loosely coupled through .NET and Java EE Web services implementations deployed on Java EE. This architectural flexibility allows a .NET Java EE system to be designed to meet the organization structure, rather than be constrained by the interoperability technology. Additionally, the .NET semantics are preserved for the developer, but the manager has a coherent Java EE management view of the system. The management functionality leverages the Java EE platform and is not limited to the cross-platform implementation of Mono.

Platform Unification ISO Management Characteristics

There are significant benefits in meeting the management requirements just defined.

- **Fault Management**   Monitoring, event handling, and logging are implemented through the underlying Java EE mechanisms. The .NET System.Diagnostics APIs for logging can be implemented through Java logging APIs, `java.util.logging`, and those provided by the application server. The JMX and logging APIs are also available to the .NET environment.

- **Configuration Management**   System management is greatly simplified by deployment of a homogeneous Java EE platform. Tuning, updates, and patch management can be performed for a homogenous system configuration. As described here, all components are deployed as Java EE modules. This simplifies application management and update deployment as well. Application management is typically done through the Java EE administration console across the platform, including for the .NET components. This is more efficient than a mixed-platform system, which requires multiple consoles. Resources, such as DataSources and Enterprise services, are managed uniformly through the Java EE console.

  The Mainsoft Visual MainWin tool set is tightly integrated with the Visual Studio IDE, allowing .NET developers the full cycle of development and deployment on Java EE application servers.

- **Accounting Management**   Application deployment on a unified platform is managed through a single accounting management system running on Java EE. This reduces the complexity in managing SLAs across different accounting systems on different platforms.

- **Performance Management**   A key benefit of the Platform Unification approach is that inter-component communications do not incur the additional overhead of wire protocol conversions such as bridging or the overhead of SOAP/HTTP as in Web services. The performance of applications deployed on the unified platform should approach the expected performance of a native Java EE application. Statistics can be collected across the application through the Java EE metering facilities.

- **Security Management**   Under the Platform Unification model, the security model is provided through Java EE. The homogenous Java EE security model across the application, using either JAAS or Java EE security, allows for management of users and authorizations in a single domain. This greatly simplifies the management of security and eliminates the need for IT managers to synchronize users and authorizations across multiple domains.

This model allows the .NET components to benefit from the Java EE security model, allowing the use of Java EE declarative security. The access to the Java EE APIs also allows the use of programmatic security.

Benefits and Limitations

The Platform Unification approach, by design, assumes that the target deployment platform for both the Java EE and .NET components is Java EE. This strategy does not explicitly facilitate management of Java and .NET applications deployed on the Java EE platform. There is no added management functionality such as service lifecycle monitoring or metering provided with this solution. The Java EE application server typically provides management facilities that can be used along with commonly deployed enterprise management solutions such as CA Unicenter.

The Platform Unification approach is not appropriate where Microsoft-specific applications, such as Exchange or BizTalk-based applications, are necessary. Integrations with other applications that require native Windows functionality are also not suitable for this approach. The integrated development process requires access to the .NET source, in order to support the develop/compile/cross-compile/debug cycle. Thus this approach would not be applicable where the .NET source is not available to be recompiled.

The Co-Development Experience

The diversity of expertise of developers in a mixed platform development contributes to the productivity of the IT organization. However, the divergence of the development environment, such as the .NET and Java EE environments, presents a challenge for organizations with both .NET and Java EE development teams. The Visual MainWin tool set for platform unification provides the .NET development team with full integration for the Visual Studio .NET development environment. This preserves the development experience for each team and allows the .NET developer to continue to develop .NET code while deploying components on Java EE.

The developer builds a .NET project configured for Java EE servers and the complete build process from C# or VB.NET compilation through binary compilation to Java bytecode validation of Java references, as well as the packaging as Java EE JAR and WAR files, is performed within Visual Studio. Application deployment on Java EE servers is managed, again, from within Visual Studio .NET. The Visual MainWin integrated debugger enables C# or VB.NET programmers to debug applications running in the Java EE application server at the .NET source code level. The Visual MainWin environment simplifies the integration of Java and EJB components into the .NET code, as just described. This model allows the .NET team on-going integrated development with the Java EE team.

Related Patterns

There are several common integration patterns that can be applied using the Platform Unification strategy.

Front Controller

Front Controller implemented with ASP.NET front end and EJB back end is one pattern, see [MS_FrontController] and [J2EE_FrontController]. In the WS-I example application, the .NET Front Controller represents MVC-II type presentation layer and the Java EE component implements a Session Façade and Data Transfer object business layer patterns. This pattern addresses systems where the presentation layer exists or is most efficiently developed using ASP.NET, and the back-end enterprise requirements are best met using the Java EE infrastructure.

COM+ Adapter Component

.NET-serviced components that require enterprise services, such as transaction management and declarative security, can be deployed in the Platform Unification approach as an EJB. The EJB framework provides a COM+ component with Java EE enterprise services. This is implemented by wrapping the serviced component as an EJB that exposes a home and remote (or local home and local) interface.

Example

The challenges of interoperability management are illustrated in the Service Interoperability (WS-1) Supply Chain Management (SCM) Retailer System. As described earlier, this article considers an implementation of the Retailer system where the front-end components are implemented in .NET and the back-end components in Java EE as EJBs. The Retailer system is a subsystem of the SOA-based SCM application. This configuration would be typical of organizations where the front-end Web development team is proficient in ASP.NET and the integrated Visual Studio .NET development environment and the back-end development team is proficient in Java EE. The IT management team is faced with the challenges of system and application management across a mixed platform.

The front-end/back-end interoperability can be addressed by several of the interoperability technologies described previously:

- **Bridging Solutions** Both proprietary and CORBA-based solutions can provide point-to-point connectivity between the .NET front end and the back-end EJBs. The application is deployed on a mixed .NET/Java EE platform.

- **Web services** The back-end components provide a Web services interface to clients such as the .NET front end. This is the configuration that is implemented in the WS-I reference implementations. Using application server support for EJB 2.1, Web service endpoints are easily implemented using EJBs. The .NET front end uses these Web services, provided that the Web service interface types are interoperable with .NET supported types. The application is deployed on a mixed .NET/Java EE platform.

- **Mono** Mono enables the ASP.NET front end to be migrated to a non-Windows platform. This would allow the front and back ends to both run on a Unix or Linux platform but would not solve the interoperability management issues as described.

- **Platform Unification** The platform unification approach enables the .NET front end to access the back-end EJB components as .NET objects. The application is deployed on a unified Java EE platform.

The choice of interoperability technology should address the architectural and organizational requirements. If one assumes that the Retailer subsystem is contained within a common organizational boundary, the subsystem may be best implemented using a tight-coupling approach. Platform Unification provides the most complete management functionality for a tightly-coupled system and simplifies the complexity of mixed platform management.

The Platform Unification Solution

Using the Platform Unification approach, the Retailer sub-system is implemented using the .NET web front end and an EJB implementation of the Retailer functionality. Both the .NET front end and the EJB are deployed on a common Java EE platform. This delivers a tightly coupled solution for the subsystem. The Web service interfaces of the other subsystems can be deployed as .NET Web services on Java EE using Platform Unification or as Java EE or .NET platforms on other systems. Figure 15-8 outlines the deployment architecture of this example.

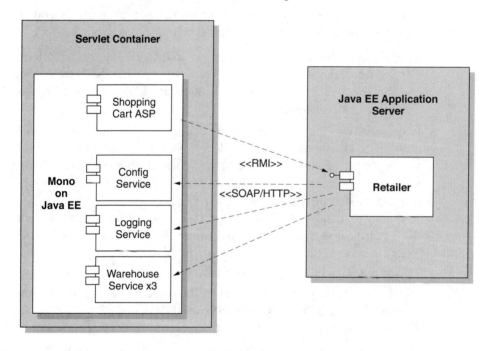

Figure 15-8
.NET Components deployed in a Java EE Servlet Container and EJB Components on a Java EE Server

The components described in the deployment diagram in Figure 15-8 are deployed on a unified Java EE platform. The Shopping Cart component in the Web front end is implemented in .NET using ASP, and the Configuration Service, the Logging Service, and the three Warehouse Services are implemented as .NET Web services. Through Platform Unification, all of the .NET components are deployed on a Java EE servlet container. The Retailer component is implemented as an EJB, and its functionality is exposed through its remote interface and accessed using RMI.

In the following discussion, the tightly coupled interface between the .NET front end and the Retailer EJB are detailed.

Listing 15-1
Retailer EJB Remote Interface

```
public interface Warehouse extends javax.ejb.EJBObject {

public interface Retailer extends javax.ejb.EJBObject {

    public Collection getCatalog() throws java.rmi.RemoteException;
    public SubmitOrderResponse SubmitOrder(
        String configURL,
        String userId,
        SubmitOrderRequest submitOrderIn)
        throws java.rmi.RemoteException;
};
}
```

The Mainsoft Visual MainWin development environment exposes the semantics of EJB use, such as JNDI lookup of the home interface and EJB remote interface invocation through a .NET proxy class.

Listing 15-2
Generated .NET C# Proxy for the Retailer EJB

```
public class Retailer : object, IDisposable, ISerializable {

    private static org.ws_i.www.retailer.RetailerHome home;

    private org.ws_i.www.retailer.Retailer ejbObj;

    static Retailer() {
        Context context;
        context = vmw.j2ee.Java EEUtils.CreateContext(null, null);
        object homeObj;
        homeObj = context.lookup(
            "java:comp/env/ejb/org/ws_i/www/retailer/RetailerHome");
        home = ((org.ws_i.www.retailer.RetailerHome)
            (javax.rmi.PortableRemoteObject.narrow(homeObj,
            java.lang.Class.forName(
            "org.ws_i.www.retailer.RetailerHome"))));
    }
```

continues

Listing 15-2 (continued)

```
    public Retailer(org.ws_i.www.retailer.Retailer ejbObj) {
        this.ejbObj = ejbObj;
    }

    public Retailer(SerializationInfo info, StreamingContext ctx) {
        home = ((org.ws_i.www.retailer.RetailerHome)
          (info.GetValue("home",
           typeof(org.ws_i.www.retailer.RetailerHome))));
        ejbObj = ((org.ws_i.www.retailer.Retailer)
          (info.GetValue("ejbObj",
           typeof(org.ws_i.www.retailer.Retailer))));
    }

    public Retailer() {
        this.ejbObj = home.create();
    }

    public virtual java.util.Collection Catalog {
        get {
          return this.ejbObj.getCatalog();
        }
    }

    public virtual void GetObjectData(SerializationInfo info,
        StreamingContext ctx) {

        info.AddValue("home", home);
        info.AddValue("ejbObj", ejbObj);
    }

    public virtual void Dispose() {
        ejbObj = null;
    }

    public virtual org.ws_i.www.retailer.SubmitOrderResponse
        SubmitOrder(string arg_0, string arg_1,
        org.ws_i.www.retailer.SubmitOrderRequest arg_2) {
        return this.ejbObj.SubmitOrder
(arg_0, arg_1, arg_2);
    }
}
```

Calling remote interface methods is done from the .NET code by invoking methods of the proxy class. The flow of the UC1 Purchase Goods use case in this implementation has the ShoppingCart ASP page calling the getCatalog method of the Retailer EJB to retrieve the catalog and then present it to the user. This is seen in Listing 15-3, which shows the .NET ShoppingCart ASP C# code behind creating an EJB proxy instance and calling the getCatalog Retailer EJB remote interface method.

Listing 15-3
.NET Code Accessing the Retailer EJB and Calling the *getCatalog* Method

```
WebClient.localhost.Retailer retailer =
   new WebClient.localhost.Retailer();
if(retailer == null){
   this.Session["OrderStatusMsg"] = "retailer unavailable ";
   Response.Redirect("OrderStatus.aspx");
   Response.End();
}
else{
   try {
      java.util.logging.ConsoleHandler handler =
         new java.util.logging.ConsoleHandler();
      java.util.logging.Logger logger =
      java.util.logging.Logger.getLogger("WebClient");
      logger.addHandler(handler);
      logger.info("calling Retailer EJB getCatalog");
//get product catalog
      java.util.Collection catCollection =retailer.Catalog;
      logger.info("after call to Retailer EJB getCatalog");
```

The catalog contents are returned to the .NET caller as a `java.util.Collection` of `CatalogItem` instances. This collection is manipulated in .NET as C# data structures, as shown in Listing 15-4. The mapping of `java.math.BigDecimal` to .NET `System.Decimal` is also shown in Listing 15-4.

Listing 15-4
C# .NET Code Manipulating Native Java Data Types Returned by the EJB

```
ArrayList cat=new ArrayList();
TableRow row=null;
java.util.Iterator iter = catCollection.iterator();
while(iter.hasNext()){
   org.ws_i.www.retailer.CatalogItem ciwsi =
      (org.ws_i.www.retailer.CatalogItem)iter.next();
   CatalogItem ci = new CatalogItem();
   ci.brand = ciwsi.getBrand();
   ci.category = ciwsi.getCategory();
   ci.description = ciwsi.getDescription();
   ci.name = ciwsi.getName();
   ci.price = Decimal.Parse(
   vmw.common.PrimitiveTypeUtils.BigDecimalToDecimal(
   ciwsi.getPrice()).ToString());
   ci.productNumber = ciwsi.getProductNumber();
   cat.Add(ci);
   row=AddProductRow(ci);
```

The `ShoppingCart` ASP page `btnPlaceOrder_Click` method is invoked on the user selection of the shopping cart. This method collects the selection data and prepares the Java parameters, as shown in Listing 15-5.

Listing 15-5
C# .NET Code Manipulating Native Java Parameters

```
java.util.ArrayList partsOrderList = new
    java.util.ArrayList(orderList.Count);
foreach(PartsOrderItem poi in orderList) {
    java.lang.Integer iQuantity =
        java.lang.Integer.valueOf(poi.quantity.ToString());
    java.math.BigDecimal bPrice =
        vmw.common.PrimitiveTypeUtils.
            DecimalToBigDecimal(poi.price);
    org.ws_i.www.retailer.PartsOrderItem item =
        new org.ws_i.www.retailer.PartsOrderItem(
        bPrice,poi.productNumber,iQuantity);
    partsOrderList.add(item);
}
```

The next logical step is to collect customer information such as Name, Street, City, State, and Country in order to submit the order. Logging is performed prior to submitting the purchase order. The most important operation here is the EJB `SubmitOrder` method invoked through the EJB proxy:

```
retailer.SubmitOrder(configuratorUrl,
(String)config["UserID"],order);
```

Listing 15-6 demonstrates customer data collection, logging, and the `SubmitOrder` method, along with retrieving an order response.

Listing 15-6
C# .NET Code Calling the Retailer EJB *SubmitOrder* Method

```
order.setPartsOrder(partsOrderList);
cust.setName((String)config["CustomerName"]);
cust.setCustnbr((String)config["CustomerNumber"]);
cust.setStreet1((String)config["CustomerStreet"]);
cust.setCity((String)config["CustomerCity"]);
cust.setState((String)config["CustomerState"]);
cust.setCountry((String)config["CustomerCountry"]);
order.setCustDetails(cust);

// Logging
java.util.logging.ConsoleHandler handler = new
```

```
   java.util.logging.ConsoleHandler();
java.util.logging.Logger logger =
java.util.logging.Logger.getLogger("WebClient");
logger.addHandler(handler);
logger.info("calling Retailer EJB SubmitOrder");

// Submitting Order
org.ws_i.www.retailer.SubmitOrderResponse
responseEJB = retailer.SubmitOrder(configuratorUrl,
   (String)config["UserID"],order);
logger.info("after Retailer EJB SubmitOrder");
submitOrderResponse response = new submitOrderResponse();
java.util.Collection responseCol = responseEJB.getOrderResponse();
```

Meeting Management Requirements

The implementation of the Retailer subsystem using Platform Unification is able to meet the management requirements detailed previously.

- **Fault Management**   In the examples shown, one can see integrated logging through the Java Logging Facility. Through the use of the `java.util.Logging` API in both the .NET and the Java EE code, all logging is integrated across the components on a common Java EE logging facility. Remote exceptions are delivered to the front end and caught as .NET exceptions.

- **Configuration Management**   The .NET front end is deployed on the Java EE platform as a fully-compliant WAR file, complete with `web.xml` and server-specific deployment descriptors. The WAR file contains all of the ASP pages and cross-compiled .NET code for the application. The WAR file is deployed and managed in the same way as any compliant servlet WAR file.

- **Accounting Management**   Metering of the .NET front end is provided by the Java EE application server through the standard statistics facilities provided to all Java EE modules by the Java EE Management Model (JSR-77). The .NET front end is a managed object represented in the model as a standard WebModule. The statistics facilities in the `javax.management.j2ee.statistics` API allow for collection of all of the invocation timing. These management objects (MEJBs) are accessed by administration tools such as JMX MBeans.

- **Performance Management**   The tight coupling of the .NET Web front end and Retailer EJB enables higher performance and improved user response time as compared with the Web services SOAP-based model.

The RMI transport and marshaling is more efficient than SOAP/HTTP. The platform unification approach enables the use of native Java data types in the .NET code, facilitating the use of RMI.

- **Security Management**   Using the Java EE declarative security model, authentication, access control, and transport-level security can be defined without changing the .NET code. Web Form authentication can be enabled by adding the appropriate declaration in the `web.xml` deployment description for the .NET front end. The authenticated security context is propagated through RMI calls to the EJBs. Access control declarations for the Shopping Cart page are declared. Additional security requirements, such as requiring SSL for the login page, can be specified declaratively. The Java EE application server provides facilities for management of user credentials, such as through JAAS.

Impact of Interoperability on Management

There are many ways by which companies can integrate Java EE and .NET applications. Some of them use technologies discussed in the book such as Java implementation of .NET Remoting and Web services. Additionally, there are strategies like CORBA discussed later in this chapter. There are cross-platform strategies that involve deployment of the application on a different platform. A .NET application can be deployed on a Unix platform using the Mono open source project, which provides an implementation of the .NET Framework for development and deployment of applications on a Unix-based environment. See [Mono]. Each of the solutions impacts the management infrastructure differently. It is important to note that these solutions do not solve underlying differences in platform security and management architecture.

Bridging/.NET Remoting

Bringing solutions allow tightly coupled point-to-point connectivity between .NET and Java EE components, while largely preserving the native calling semantics of each system. These solutions provide a runtime component to handle the wire protocol and marshaling and use tools to generate proxy classes that hide the details of the communications. This allows developers to call remote objects on other platforms with functionality that includes pass-by reference, object statefulness, and singleton objects.

In the case of this reference system, a bridging solution enables the front-end components to access the back-end warehouse components with the semantics of .NET Remoting. The bridging solution would introduce a runtime component that would translate .NET Remoting semantics to a wire protocol, such as CORBA and IIOP or a proprietary protocol over TCP or HTTP/SOAP. The runtime component would then invoke the Java EE components on the back end. The .NET developer would access the back-end EJB classes using .NET proxy classes that would be generated using the development tools.

Bridging/.NET Remoting and ISO Management Characteristics

Bridging solutions such as those described do not address key management elements, although they enable point-to-point interoperability.

- **Fault Management**   Bridging solutions do not offer resolution or integration of the underlying management APIs, and so they do not offer integration with .NET or JMX -based metering or event logging.

- **Configuration Management**   Commercial bridging solutions based on .NET Remoting such as Ja.NET or JNBridge require runtime configuration through specific configuration files. Components need to be deployed both on the .NET and on the Java EE sides of the application, and stub/proxy pairs may need to be regenerated when deploying version updates.

- **Accounting Management**   Bridging solutions do not offer resolution or integration of the underlying management APIs and so do not offer a unified accounting framework.

- **Performance Management**   Bridging solutions introduce an additional component and communication channel into the system. The runtime marshaling and unmarshaling and object mapping, along with the proxy code, introduce overhead and can reduce end-to-end performance, particularly in fine-grained access and call by value scenarios. As stated previously, because there is no resolution of the management APIs, there is no coherent metering framework.

- **Security Management** The propagation of the security context does not provide the functionality of the .NET channel nor of Java EE RMI. These runtime components may offer clustering, failover, and enterprise level resource management that are provided by enterprise class application servers, see [MSDL1], [INTRDL1], and [JNB].

The next sections explore management semantics of CORBA-based integration strategy.

CORBA

CORBA-based bridging solutions, such as Borland's Janeva, provide .NET Remoting semantics for CORBA-IIOP-based communications. By relying on the wide support for RMI—IIOP across Java EE application servers, these solutions provide a standards-based bridge [JRMI]. This functionality includes propagation of security, transaction, and QOS context to back-end Java EE servers [OMG]. The solution includes a runtime component that translates .NET Remoting to IIOP at the wire level and handles marshaling and type mapping. Development tools are provided to generate the necessary stubs. To leverage the propagation of the calling context, the .NET programmer needs to use a proprietary API. There is no automatic mapping of the .NET channel context to the CORBA calling context. Janeva supports load balancing and failover through its QOS facility and interceptors [BORJAN].

From the viewpoint of the key management elements, CORBA-based bridging solutions can leverage context propagation for security and transaction management. This allows for the propagation of user credentials, such as for ASP.NET front-end authentication to propagate security identities to Java EE servers. However, the underlying problem of the different .NET and Java EE security models is not addressed. Performance management in the CORBA-based solution is impacted by the CORBA runtime, as well as marshaling of data types and .NET type mapping, which introduces significant overhead. Configuration management has the additional complexity of the CORBA configuration.

Mono

Mono provides .NET developers targeting Linux or other Unix environments with an implementation of the standard CLI runtime, a C# compiler, and implementations of the .NET APIs including System classes, ASP.NET classes, and ADO.NET classes. Mono can be used to deploy a .NET application on Linux, Solaris, or MacOS X. A recent project by the city of Munich used Mono to migrate their ASP.NET and Web services applications to a deployment on 300 Linux servers [MCMILL].

From a management viewpoint, Mono provides management functionality through the implementation of the .NET APIs. Mono does not provide an integrated management framework across platforms or integrate the management APIs with the native management functionality, such as that provided by the underlying Unix or Linux platform. Mono provides partial implementations of the System.Diagnostics namespace. It does not currently provide support for instrumentation or WMI in the Mono runtime. The implementation of key management elements under Mono such as fault management, configuration management, accounting management, and performance management is incomplete with respect to the full .NET functionality. Mono provides an implementation of the ASP.NET security framework. This implementation is not integrated with security functionality in the system, such as user management.

Benefits and Limitations

Walking through common integration strategies allows side-by-side comparison. Table 15-1 outlines advantages and shortcomings of individual integration technologies.

Table 15-1
Benefits and Limitations of Integration Technologies

Interoperability

Technology	Implementations	Benefits	Limitations
Web services	Standards based implementations for .NET (Microsoft) and for Java EE (Java EE 1.4)	Web services enable loosely coupled applications to interoperate using standards (WS-I). They are firewall friendly, and it's easy to extend the protocol using SOAP. Web services also enjoy broad developer and infrastructure support.	Web services add the overhead of SOAP XML processing to each method invocation, as well as the overhead of the underlying HTTP transport. Web services security implementation and other Web services standards are not yet uniform across platforms. [WAGNER].
Bridging	Commercial products such as Ja.NET, JNBridge	Bridging solutions provide a more tightly coupled application interoperability solution than Web services. They offer the performance advantages of binary streams when compared to Web services. In addition, bridging solutions offer simplicity for the .NET programmer and preserve the .NET remoting syntax. This technology can offer pass-by reference, which means the developer works with the actual object, rather than an object copy.	Bridging solutions add overhead for marshaling protocol translation, and the bridging runtime engine may introduce scalability limitations. Bridging solutions do not uniformly support distributed security models or distributed transactions.

CORBA RMI/IIOP channel	Commercial products such as Janeva Several open source implementations	CORBA RMI/IIOP channel offers the performance advantages of binary streams. In addition, this technology is transparent to the Java EE application. These solutions support context propagation for security and transactions over IIOP. The developer typically applies this model to a .NET front-end Java EE back-end architecture.	CORBA—RMI channels add overhead for the protocol translation, and may introduce scalability limitations. The solution can require use of a proprietary API by the .NET programmer and extensive configuration.
Mono	Open source framework, adopted by Novell	Mono enables .NET applications to execute on other platforms, such as Linux. Mono supports a wide set of the .NET namespaces, such as ASP.NET and ADO.NET.	Mono does not yet support enterprise services. Mono does not integrate development into the standard .NET development tools.

The next section takes a look at best practices and limitations pertaining to the Java EE .NET management task.

Best Practices and Pitfalls

The best way to approach management is to use early planning and design applications with management in mind. The application design phase is typically the best time to determine, using logging instrumentation, how to disable, enable, minimize or maximize information output. Another key component to successful management is to ensure that systems can be managed accordingly at all stages of the development cycle including QA and production. Production-level management is essential for monitoring the overall IT environment. Remote monitoring and alert notification systems can be utilized to enhance control of the distributed heterogeneous applications. Additionally, individual management techniques should be utilized to monitor the hardware, operating system, infrastructure, and finally application layer. Being able to monitor systems' uptime and quickly troubleshoot management problems by drilling down to the corresponding layer to determine the failing module is an important factor for success. Implementing comprehensive management as discussed by the ISO characteristics has to be adequately addressed. Monitoring alone would not be sufficient if the fault management is not addressed. As an example, a failing instance of an application server needs to be transparently replaced by a working instance.

Common pitfalls in the management space include excessive logging of applications deployed in a production environment, causing performance degradation. Oppositely, lack of application instrumentation can affect the amount of time the problem takes to troubleshoot. Lack of discrete layer separation across various managed layers also degrades quality of management. Situations where an application flaw, an infrastructure component such as application server, or an OS unknowingly causes a problem require diverse skill sets and are typically time consuming. Therefore for successful IT management, it is critical to address management at individual layers.

Summary

Depending on your integration strategy, you may have to augment management components that are not available with an integration solution. Table 15-2 lists individual ISO management characteristics across different technologies and integration strategies.

Table 15-2
ISO Management Characteristics Across Interoperability Strategies

	Bridging Solution	CORBA-based Bridging	Web services	Mono	Platform Unification
Fault Management	No Integrated solution	No integrated solution	Integrated through WSDM/MOWS	No integrated solution	Integrated through Java EE
Configuration Management	No integrated solution	No integrated solution	Integrated through WSDM/MOWS	No integration between Mono and native deployment	Java EE deployment model
Accounting Management	No integrated solution	No integrated solution	Integrated through WSDM/MOWS	No integrated solution	Supports solutions running on Java EE
Performance Management	Network component and marshaling impacts performance	CORBA impacts performance	SOAP/HTTP impacts performance, Integrated through WSDM/MOWS	Inferior to .NET and Java [VOGELS]	Near Java EE performance, Java EE metering
Security Management	Limited integration context to Java	Propagation of .NET security WS-Trust EE, no integrated user management	WS-Security, WS Federation, Cryptographic support	Cross platform ASP.NET Security,	Java EE Security model, Java EE user management
When to use	Fine-grained interoperability; Intra-firewall applications; Binary application interoperability	Fine-grained interoperability; Intra-firewall applications; Binary application interoperability	SOA Environments; Loosely coupled business architecture; B2B integration	Platform migration key issue; .NET environment key issue	Performance key issue; Deployment on Java EE; Development Productivity key issue; Contain interoperability issues at development time

References

[ActionalSoapStation] Actional SOAPstation.
www.actional.com/products/web_services/soapstation/index.asp

[AmberPoint] AmberPoint.
www.amberpoint.com/

[AutoPilot] Nastel AutoPilot/IT.
www.nastel.com/products/ap_it.shtml

[Avicode] Avicode Intercept Studio Features.
www.avicode.com/content/products/InterceptStudio.asp

[BEA1] Overview of the WebLogic Security Service.
http://e-docs.bea.com/wls/docs90/secintro/model.html

[BIJ1] David Hicks and Andrew Yang: "Performance Anxiety: XML Web Services in Production," *Business Integration Journal*, 2004.
www.bijonline.com/Article.asp?ArticleID=951&DepartmentId=9

[BORJAN] Borland Janeva 6.0 Developer's Guide.
http://info.borland.com/techpubs/janeva/1_0/english/pdf/JanevaDevGuide.pdf

[CA_WSDM] Darina Stoyanova. How to Successfully Manage Web Services, 2005.
www3.ca.com/Solutions/Collateral.asp?CID=54520&ID=4714

[CA_WSDM_MOM] Operations Managers Visibility into .NET and J2EE Web Services. March 17, 2004. DMReview.com
www.dmreview.com/article_sub.cfm?articleId=1000110

[CIM] Common Information Model (CIM) Standards.
www.dmtf.org/standards/cim/

[CORE] Deepack Alur, John Crupi, Dan Malks: *Core J2EE Patterns*, page 367. Boston: Prentice Hall, 2002.

[DMTF] Distributed Management Task Force, Inc.
www.dmtf.org

[FlamencoNetworks] Flamenco Networks.
www.flamenconetworks.com/

[GFMP] Carlos Gutierrez, Eduardo Fenandez-Medina, Mario Piattini: Web Services Security is the Problem Solved? Auerbach Publications, 2005

[IBM1] IBM WebSphere Security Documentation
http://publib.boulder.ibm.com/infocenter/ws51help/index.jsp?topic=/com.ibm.websphere.nd.doc/info/ae/ae/welc_security.html

[IBM2] Wangming Ye: Web Services programming tips and tricks: Improve the interoperability between J2EE and .NET, 2005.
www-128.ibm.com/developerworks/webservices/library/ws-tip-j2eenet2.html

[IBM3] Hold Adams: Best Practices for Web Service: Web Services Security, IBM, 2004.

[INTRDL1] Intrinsyc Download Center: J-Integra for .NET.
http://j-integra.intrinsyc.com/download/default.aspx?
ProductId=net

[J2EE_FrontController] Core 2EE Pattern Catalog. Core J2EE Patterns—Front Controller
http://java.sun.com/blueprints/corej2eepatterns/Patterns/
FrontController.html

[Java5Mgmt] Calvin Austin. Java SE 5.0 in a Nutshell—Monitoring and Manageability. May 2004.
http://java.sun.com/developer/technicalArticles/releases/j2se15/#mnm

[JMAN] Java Management Extensions Documentation
http://java.sun.com/products/JavaManagement/

[JMX_Download] JMX Download
http://java.sun.com/products/JavaManagement/download.html

[JMXIntro] Quasay H. Mahmoud. Getting Started with JMX. Sun Microsystems, January 6, 2004.
http://java.sun.com/developer/technicalArticles/J2SE/jmx.html

[JMX_WP] Java Management Extensions White Paper. Sun Microsystems.
June 1999.
http://java.sun.com/products/JavaManagement/wp/

[JMX_WSDM] Pankaj Kumar and Chris Peltz. JMX and WSDM: Overlapping Technologies. November 2004.
http://devresource.hp.com/drc/resources/dc0411/dc0411.jsp

[JNB] JNBridge Documentation.
www.jnbridge.com/docs.htm

[JRMI] Java RMI over IIOP Documentation.
http://java.sun.com/j2se/1.4.2/docs/guide/rmi-iiop/index.html

[JSR196] JSR 196: Java Authentication Service Provider Interface for Containers.
www.jcp.org/en/jsr/detail?id=196

[JSR262] Web Services Connector for Java™ Management Extensions (JMXTM) Agents. JSR 262

www.jcp.org/en/jsr/detail?id=262

[JWSDP] Java Web Services Developer Pack

http://java.sun.com/webservices/jwsdp/index.jsp

[KERB] John Brezak, Presentation on Windows 2000 Kerberos Interoperability, 2000.

http://web.mit.edu/pismere/MSR-Summer-2000/DAY1_Finished/
KerberosWorkshop_Interoperability/default.htm

[MCMILL] Robert McMillan: Novell Releases First Mono Beta, Linux World 2004.

www.linuxworld.com.au/index.php/id;2103806279;fp;2;fpid;1

[MMC_.NET] MMC .NET Library.

http://sourceforge.net/projects/mmclibrary/

[Mono] The Mono Project.

www.Mono-project.com/Main_Page

[MSDL1] Microsoft Download Center: Application Interoperability White Paper.

www.microsoft.com/downloads/details.aspx?FamilyId=5FBA8E7A-B896-4E5F-
B3C0-FCF7FF1B9D29&displaylang=en

[MSDN1] Windows Authentication Provider documentation from MSDN.

http://msdn.microsoft.com/library/default.asp?url=/library/en-
us/cpguide/html/cpconthewindowsauthenticationprovider.asp

[MSDN2] ASP.NET Authentication documentation from MSDN.

http://msdn.microsoft.com/library/default.asp?url=/library/en-
us/cpguide/html/cpconaspnetauthentication.asp

[MS_FrontController] Microsoft Patterns & Practices.

http://msdn.microsoft.com/architecture/patterns/default.aspx?pull=/library/en-
us/dnpatterns/html/DesFrontController.asp

[Muse_Apache] Apache WebServices. *Muse*, May 25, 2005.

http://incubator.apache.org/muse/

[NetworkMgmtBasics] Network Management Basics, Cisco Systems, Inc.,
February 20, 2002.

www.cisco.com/univercd/cc/td/doc/cisintwk/ito_doc/
nmbasics.htm

[NetworkMgmtOverview] Network Management—an Overview. Carnegie
Mellon University, 2004.

www.sei.cmu.edu/str/descriptions/network_body.html

[OMG] Common Object Request Broker Architecture: Core Specification, Object Management Group, 2004.
www.omg.org/docs/formal/04-03-12.pdf

[OSSJ] OSS Through Java Initiative. www.ossj.org.

[PILIPCHUK1] Denis Pilipchuk, Java vs .NET Security, 2004.
www.oreilly.com/catalog/059600821X/index.html

[SMS] Systems Management Server (SMS) 2003 Solution Accelerators.
www.microsoft.com/smserver/evaluation/solutions.asp

[Systinet] Systinet.
www.systenet.com

[VINT] Vintela Corporate Web site.
www.vintela.com/

[VOGELS] Werner Vogels, "Comparing CLR, Mono, SSCLI and Java Performance", All Things Distributed Weblog, 2003.
http://weblogs.cs.cornell.edu/AllThingsDistributed/archives/000052.html

[VMX] SMS for Unix, Linux, and Mac OS X Systems.
www.vintela.com/products/vmx/

[VSM] Vintela Systems Monitor (VSM), Integrated Systems Monitoring.
www.vintela.com/products/vsm/

[WAGNER] Ray Wagner. "New WS-Security Extensions may be too much, too soon," Gartner, 2002.
www4.gartner.com/resources/112200/112263/112263.pdf

[WBEMSolutions] WBEM Solutions. Web Services for System Management (WS-Management).
www.wbemsolutions.com/ws_management.html

[Win2003_WSMan] Hardware Management in Microsoft Windows Server 2003 "R2" Beta 2.
www.microsoft.com/whdc/system/pnppwr/wsm.mspx

[WISEMAN] A Java implementation of WS-Management. Java.net. Copyright 2004 CollabNet.
https://wiseman.dev.java.net/

[WMI] Matthew Lavy, Ashley Meggitt. *Windows Management Instrumentation (WMI)*, first edition. Indianapolis: Sams, 2002.

[WMIGuide] A simple guide to WMI providers. Cohen Shwartz Oren. October 13, 2003.
www.thecodeproject.com/csharp/WMIproviderGuide.asp

[WMISolutions] Craig Tunstall and Gwyn Cole. *Developing WMI Solutions: A Guide to Windows Management Instrumentation*. Boston: Addison-Wesley: 2003.

[WMITools] WMI Administrative Tools.
www.microsoft.com/downloads/details.aspx?FamilyID=6430f853-1120-48db-8cc5-f2abdc3ed314&DisplayLang=en

[WS-Management] Web Services Specifications for Systems Management. developers.sun.com.
http://developers.sun.com/techtopics/webservices/management/

[WSDM] OASIS Web Services Distributed Management .
www.oasis-open.org/committees/tc_home.php?wg_abbrev=wsdm

[WSI1] WSI Supply Chain Management Use Case Model.
www.ws-i.org/SampleApplications/SupplyChainManagement/200312/SCMUseCases1.0.doc

[WSI2] WSI Supply Chain Management Sample Application Architecture.
www.ws-i.org/SampleApplications/SupplyChainManagement/2003-12/SCMArchitecture1.01.doc

[WSMgmt] Ray Lai. "Web Services Life Cycle: Managing Enterprise Web Services," www.sun.com. October 2003.
www.sun.com/software/whitepapers/webservices/wp_mngwebsvcs.pdf

[WSMgmtStandards] Heather Kreger and James Philips "Towards Web Services Management Standards," *Web Services Journal.*
www.sys-con.com/webservices/articleprint.cfm?id=665

[WSN_Apache] Apache WebServices – Hermes.
http://incubator.apache.org/hermes/

[WSRF_Apache] Web Services Resource Framework Implementation.
http://incubator.apache.org/apollo/

[WSS4J] Apache Web Services Security for Java.
http://ws.apache.org/ws-fx/wss4j/

Implementation

Migrating .NET Applications to Java

16

Introduction

While there are a number of technology choices that can be used when implementing applications, the market has consolidated into two major families of technology. These are the Microsoft .NET family and the Java 2 Enterprise Edition (Java EE) family. The latter of these, Java EE, is considered by many to be superior based on its security, scalability, and manageability merits, as well as the fact that much of the logic required to make applications highly available, reliable, and performant is already developed as part of Java EE Application Servers, preventing the need to develop this functionality individually. For this reason, among others, many development groups are looking into Java EE as a viable alternative to .NET and want to size and price what it would take to migrate their existing .NET applications to Java EE.

As such, the focus of this chapter is to look at how to port existing .NET applications to Java, and to assist in determining the best strategy for doing so.

Why Java EE?

Java EE Applications are flexible and work on most hardware and operating system configurations. Because they are based on Java, they work on any system that has a supported Java Virtual Machine. As the Java EE standards are open and implemented by many vendors, there are many alternatives to meet every budget, from free application servers such as Tomcat and JBoss, to fully-featured license-based ones such as BEA WebLogic and the Sun Application Server. The reliability and availability of Java EE applications are well known and well published, and the scalability of the platform is not a problem. Indeed, one of the main points of the Java EE specification is that the application server that is built on the platform handles much of the Enterprise "plumbing," such as object pooling or application clustering, without the developer having to write and support thousands of lines of code to do this for himself.

The driving factors for migration to the Java EE platform vary from company to company, but the main ones are

- **Security** The Microsoft Operating System platform and Internet Information Services Web Server have been frequent victims of successful security attacks. Many companies have been scared off by this and don't want to absorb the expense of almost daily patching, updating, and regression testing.

- **Rapid development using off-the-shelf components** While the Microsoft Visual Studio tools empower developers to quickly produce quality software, an Enterprise application requires functionality that allows it to scale well, scale securely, and be inherently manageable. For example, high availability applications require such functionality as object pooling. The cost of developing this functionality is extremely high, and when it can be purchased off the shelf (in the form of a Java EE Application Server) for a license fee that is orders of magnitude lower than the cost of developing it, Java EE becomes an attractive prospect.

- **Linux and Solaris**   More and more enterprises are factoring the use of Linux into their overall strategy for cost and security reasons. To allow for interoperability and maximization on skill sets and license expenditure, the cross-platform Java is more attractive. Solaris is free and has advantages over Linux with features such as Dtrace, zones, and more, [Solaris1].

Therefore another advantage of using Java EE is that not only does it provide the best available application platform, but it also has the flexibility for adopting Linux, Unix, or Solaris, potentially providing a cheaper and more secure operating system solution than many of the alternatives.

As has been made clear, there are many reasons why the Java and the Java EE platform in particular are compelling if one wants to deploy, run, and maintain mission critical, highly available, scalable, and performant applications. As such, if there are application assets presently built in .NET and the desire is to move toward the Java platform, there are many benefits to be obtained.

This chapter looks at the considerations to take into account when porting .NET applications to Java; it evaluates some strategies to make it as straightforward as possible and goes into detail on how to port an example based on the WS-I Supply Chain Management application [WSI-1]. It looks into what it takes to manually translate source code from C# to Java, as well as the innovative Visual MainWin for Java EE from Mainsoft and how it allows the use of existing .NET source code to build and deploy Java EE applications.

Porting Guidelines

High-Level Considerations

On the surface C# has many similarities to Java, and it would appear that a code-based port, where you take the C# code and translate it into Java, would be relatively straightforward, with only a few minor differences in semantics. It isn't. This is because in most cases, the code is written to use a specific class library. In the case of .NET, this library is defined by the .NET framework and any custom add-ons that are used. In the case of Java, this library is the Java SE, Java EE SDKs and any other custom add-ons used. While the language syntax is pretty similar between the two, the frameworks are going to be different in many ways, making a straight translation difficult.

As such, it is more accurate to think about translating an application from one that runs on the .NET Framework to one that runs on a Java SE/Java EE environment. When thinking about the translation in this way, it becomes easier (and more accurate) to isolate the potential issues that are faced in migration.

A number of these issues are

- **Optimization**   While Java and C# are syntactically similar, the underlying class libraries that do the bulk of the work in any application are vastly different. For example if a dynamic array is needed and coding were natively done in Java, a java.util.Vector could be used, whereas in C# there would be an array type.

- **Suitability**   There may be a way of doing things in .NET that isn't suitable for the Java Platform. For example, a session-based Web service may require lots of custom code using `ViewState` when developed in C# for .NET but could be implemented as a session bean in EJB, where there is no direct translation of code between the two. In addition, recoding an element in this way also breaks the direct translation of modules that depend on this one, leading to cascading amounts of poor suitability for translation.

- **Introduction of runtime errors**   There may be a number of cases where at runtime a .NET class may allow for specific bounds, but the equivalent Java one may have different bounds—and in a straight line for line translation you could potentially introduce new run-time errors. One example is the concept of a connection string for a database. In both .NET and Java, the data type is the same (String), but the JDBC syntax for a connection string differs hugely from ADO.NET syntax.

- **Dependencies**   In many cases a .NET application may have dependencies that cannot be directly translated into Java or would require additional license cost to purchase Java-specific versions. For example, if there is a dependency on a .NET specific third-party control, an equivalent control for Java would have to be found and the code translated to match the API of that control.

- **Application lifecycle**   While there may be tools and technologies deployed on one platform to develop, test, deploy, and execute enterprise applications, porting an application to a different platform may require a different set of tools and technologies to achieve the same tasks. For example, Web application request processing in Java is commonly accomplished by using Struts framework that won't transparently get deployed during the migration process. It is important that the migration process starts with the architectural discussion of most optimal transition.

- **Systemic qualities**   While porting a .NET application to Java, is it critical to assess various systemic qualities that are employed by the existing application architecture. Should it be a pessimistic locking for higher degree of reliability or configurable access control policies for security, the migration team has to scrutinize individual application requirements to adequately translate them to Java EE.

- **Understanding deployment**   One of the areas to address when moving applications from .NET to Java pertains to deployment. Microsoft Visual Studio.NET simplifies the application deployment process. When using it on the same machine that the application is to be run on, the deployment is implicit. When it needs to be moved to staging or production machines, tools that come with the IDE allow one to generate an installation script. One of the advantages of the Java EE platform, its diversity; it yields different deployment tasks for individual Web and application servers such as Tomcat, WebLogic, or Sun Application Server. Therefore when translating code from the .NET environment to a Java-based one, the developer will have to understand deployment specifics in the target environment. Deployment tasks are typically automated by the Web-based tools bundled with Java EE application server or `ant` scripts that can be easily configured for the target environment. The coming example works with deployment into Tomcat 5.0. The `ant` script demonstrated in this chapter can be used to build and deploy the application.

Strategies for Porting Enterprise Applications

There are many strategies and patterns that could be followed for porting Enterprise Applications, but the overarching desire behind all of them is to do it at minimum cost and with minimal disruption to the systems. One very useful strategy to enable this is to migrate in small steps and to use Web services at every application boundary. As Web services are based on known standards at the interface, namely Simple Object Access Protocol (SOAP), it doesn't matter how they are physically implemented. A Web service is in fact an abstract entity, accessed via HTTP using SOAP documents. If .NET applications are not currently implemented using Web services, a good first step would be to implement them as Web services. One can then take the interface to these Web services, which is defined using a standard language (Web Services Definition Language or WSDL), and create new Java-based Web services from this interface description. The systems that interface to this won't know the difference that providing the WSDL for the Java Web service is the same as that for the .NET. This gives a step-by-step migration which will help minimize disruption to operational systems.

The example that will be used for porting is based on the Web Services Interoperability Organization (WS-I), Supply Chain Management application [WSI-1], used throughout this book. The Web services-based distributed

Supply Chain Management application manages the request for a product through the consumer making an online purchase, a number of warehouses that may stock the required item, and the manufacturers of the cataloged items. It is a good example for an application that shows a number of different organizations with potentially different IT infrastructures operating together. This chapter looks at the relationship between the Retailer that sells the goods and its warehouse and the services that implement this relationship.

Figure 16-1 provides a high-level diagram of .NET Retailer system services that will be ported to Java EE.

Figure 16-1
.NET Retailer Service consuming .NET Warehouse service

The first thing to look at is how these services are built in C# and running on the .NET platform and then migrating them to Java EE in two ways: using Mainsoft's Visual MainWin and by manually rewriting the code from C# to Java. This provides a nice hands-on use case for a migration, as initially one ports the Warehouse service and leaves the Retailer one as-is—yet the application still works across the technology boundaries with a .NET-based Retailer service and a Java-based Warehouse service. This is shown in Figure 16-2.

Figure 16-2
.NET Retailer service consuming Java EE Warehouse service

Finally, the Retailer is ported in the same manner. This also shows an additional benefit of Service Oriented Architecture (SOA) and how it can reduce the costs and risks of incrementally porting projects due to their loosely coupled nature. The final set of components are shown in Figure 16-3.

This isn't the only strategy of course; there are many ways to achieve migration with minimal fuss, but this is a very useful one and is the basis of many of the examples in this chapter.

Figure 16-3
Java EE Retailer service consuming Java EE Warehouse *ShipGoods* service

The Porting Scenario

This example looks at a simple implementation of the Retailer-Warehouse interaction from the WS-I SCM example and builds them in C#. The Retailer can be considered the client of the Warehouse for an asynchronous call to the `ShipGoods` Web method. The sequence diagram for this interaction can be seen in Figure 16-4.

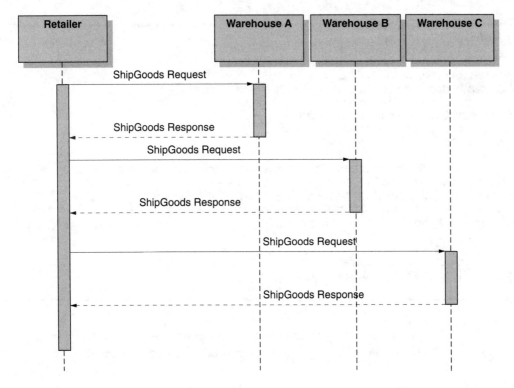

Figure 16-4
Sequence diagram for Retailer/Warehouse interaction

The contract between the Retailer and each Warehouse is identical, so for simplicity it just codes a single Warehouse service and consumes it.

Building the Scenario Using Microsoft.NET

This scenario simulates using Microsoft.NET by building the Warehouse as a Web service and the Retailer as a Web application that consumes this service. In the full SCM example, the Retailer is also a Web service, but as it isn't being consumed in this simulation, it is just built as a Web application that exposes a Graphical User Interface (GUI) to make testing easier.

WSDL for the Warehouse Service

The WSI published a WSDL document [WSI2] that outlines the interface that they would expect to see for the Warehouse service. A snippet of this document can be seen in Listing 16-1.

Listing 16-1
Warehouse Service WSDL

```
<wsdl:message name="ShipGoodsRequest">
  <wsdl:part name="ItemList" type="wh:ItemList"/>
  <wsdl:part name="Customer"
    type="wh:CustomerReferenceType"/>
  <wsdl:part name="ConfigurationHeader"
    element="ct:Configuration"/>
</wsdl:message>
<wsdl:message name="ShipGoodsResponse">
  <wsdl:documentation>
    A response of true indicates the goods have been
    shipped. A response of false indicates the warehouse
    either does not carry that part or does not have enough
    stock to fill the requested quantity.
  </wsdl:documentation>
  <wsdl:part name="Response"
    type="wh:ItemShippingStatusList"/>
</wsdl:message>
```

This snippet defines the contract for submitting an order asynchronously and how the ShipGoods request and response should be handled.

SOAP for the Warehouse Service

A snippet of an example SOAP document, also published by the WSI [WSI2] that conforms to this contract for a request, is shown in Listing 16-2:

Listing 16-2
Warehouse Service SOAP

```
<s:Body>
 <ns1:ShipGoods xmlns:ns1="<path to>/Warehouse.wsdl"
                xmlns:ns2="<path to>/Warehouse.xsd">
    <ItemList>
      <ns2:Item>
        <ns2:ProductNumber>605006</ns2:ProductNumber>
        <ns2:Quantity>23</ns2:Quantity>
      </ns2:Item>
      <ns2:Item>
        <ns2:ProductNumber>605007</ns2:ProductNumber>
        <ns2:Quantity>22</ns2:Quantity>
      </ns2:Item>
    </ItemList>
    <Customer>D22845-W8N349Y-tky</Customer>
 </ns1:ShipGoods>
</s:Body>
```

And the SOAP document for the response is below:

```
<Response>
  <ns2:ItemStatus>
    <ns2:ProductNumber>605006</ns2:ProductNumber>
    <ns2:Status>false</ns2:Status>
  </ns2:ItemStatus>
  <ns2:ItemStatus>
    <ns2:ProductNumber>605007</ns2:ProductNumber>
    <ns2:Status>true</ns2:Status>
  </ns2:ItemStatus>
</Response>
```

The important thing to note in building a service that implements this is the data types that are being passed to and from the service. The request message contains a number of items of type Item that is a structure containing a product number and a quantity, and the response message contains a number of items of type ItemStatus, which contain a product number and a status. The Request message is passed to the service containing the list of requested items based on their product number and the desired quantity. Taking a look at the preceding snippets, the request is for 23 items of type 605006, and the response to that is false, as sufficient quantity isn't available.

Defining the Data Classes in C#

The first step in implementing this service is to define classes in C# to handle these data structures.

Listing 16-3 presents the class representing the Item used for the request:

Listing 16-3
C# *Item* Class

```
public class Item
{
  private string _productNumber;
  private int _quantity;
  public string ProductNumber
  {
    get
    {
      return this._productNumber;
    }
    set
    {
      this._productNumber = value;
    }
  }
  public int Quantity
  {
    get
    {
      return this._quantity;
    }
    set
    {
      this._quantity = value;
    }
  }
}
```

The ItemStatus class is very similar to this, except that it has a property for Status instead of quantity. The Web service sets this property to true if there is sufficient quantity of the desired product available. The full source code is available in the download.

The C# Web Service

The Warehouse Web service has to expose a method called ShipGoods, which, upon receiving a request containing an array of type Item, checks through the list to see if there is sufficient quantity on hand of the desired item. It creates an array of `ItemStatus` objects that it uses to return the status of the ordered items. Should there be sufficient quantity of the desired item, it flags the shipping status for that product as `true`; otherwise, it flags it as `false`. The current quantities are stored in an SQL Server database. Listing 16-4 shows this `WebMethod`:

Listing 16-4
C# Web Service

```csharp
[WebMethod]
public ItemStatus[] ShipGoods(Item[] ItemList)
{
  // Intialize Data Connection
  string connectionString = "Data Source=(local);"
  connectionString+="uid=sa;pwd=welcome;
  connectionString+="database=Warehouse";
  SqlConnection con =
    new SqlConnection(connectionString);
  String sql = "";
  // Create return structure
  ItemStatus[] collRtn =
    new ItemStatus[ItemList.Length];
  // Open the Database connection
  con.Open();
  // Loop through the incoming list
  for(int lp=0;lp<ItemList.Length;lp++)
  {
    // Create a new ItemStatus for this item
    collRtn[lp] = new ItemStatus();
    // And give it the product number for the item
    collRtn[lp].ProductNumber =
        ItemList[lp].ProductNumber;
    // Look in the DB for this product
    sql = "Select QuantityOnHand from WarehouseStock"
    sql+="where ProductID='";
    sql+=ItemList[lp].ProductNumber;
    sql+="'";
    SqlCommand com = new SqlCommand(sql,con);
    SqlDataReader r = com.ExecuteReader();
    r.Read();
    // If the query returned something, check if there
    //is sufficient quantity and set the status
    if (r.HasRows)
    {
      int nQuantityonHand = (int) r.GetValue(0);
      if(nQuantityonHand>ItemList[lp].Quantity)
        collRtn[lp].Status=true;
      else
        collRtn[lp].Status=false;
    }
```

continues

Listing 16-4 (continued)

```
        else
        {
          // If the DB has nothing for this product, then
          // set the status as false
          collRtn[lp].Status=false;
        }
      }
      // Close the connection and free it up
      con.Close();
      // Return the Status array
      return collRtn;
    }
  }
}
```

Consuming the Web Service Using C#

Finally, following is some example C# code that consumes this Web service. This code requires a Web reference, called `Warehouse`, to be added to the project in Visual Studio.NET.

To call this service, asynchronously, using callbacks, the `AsyncCallback` class is used like this

```
AsyncCallback cb = new AsyncCallback(ServiceCallback);
theService.BeginShipGoods(itemsList, cb, theService);
```

This creates a callback, cb, which maps to a function called `ServiceCallback`. This should be implemented as a `public void` that takes an `IAsyncResult` as a parameter as shown below in Listing 16-5.

Listing 16-5
C# Web Service Callback

```
public void ServiceCallback(IAsyncResult ar)
{
  Warehouse.WarehouseService theService = new
              Warehouse.WarehouseService();
  Warehouse.ItemStatus[] itemsOut = theService.EndShipGoods(ar);
}
```

When the Web service completes processing, it calls back to this function, where the `EndShipGoods` function is called to complete the transaction.

Porting by Rewriting the Code in Java

General Steps to Follow when Converting C# to Java

Despite their syntactical similarities, building applications in C# and Java involve radically different processes, and the process of hand conversion is a complex one. Some best practices to consider in doing such a translation are as follows. (You will be translating the scenario using these best practices in the rest of this section.)

1. Examine the data types that you are using and make sure you have analogous data types in Java. When you don't have them, you'll need to figure out which data type best matches the problem that you are trying to solve. Remember that this can have a knock on effect throughout your code. If you have any custom data classes that you use in your application, you should consider changing them early on in the process too.

2. Examine the class libraries that you are using. Their namespaces are imported at the top of every module, so you can get a good grip on the family of class libraries that your application will use. You should find the equivalent namespace or namespaces in Java that support the same functionality and then look, reference by reference, for a class within each library that is analogous to the one that is used in the original. You should then plan for how you intend to translate from one to the other. Sometimes it makes sense to 'wrap' the properties, methods and events in the Java class with ones analogous to the .NET class so that you can minimize the changes to your application logic. You would then import your "wrapped" classes instead of the "base" Java ones.

3. Examine the dependencies that your application relies on. If you do not have access to the source code of these dependencies, you will need to find equivalent ones that your Java applications can use, or you will need to find a technology bridge that allows you to use these dependencies within your Java application should they exist. This includes access to databases. So if for example, your entire system is moving to Linux and your .NET application uses SQL Server, you will have to find an alternative database system and understand which parts of your code will only work with SQL Server and replace them with code that will work with your new database. The process of abstracting this code behind helper classes will assist in this.

4. Your application has probably grown and evolved over time into what it is now. As such, it might have a lot of spaghetti code and patched functions to meet late requirements, which aren't optimal for its current task. It might include kludges for quick fixes such as goto statements (though not in C#). You should evaluate your code against the requirements that it meets and see what can be streamlined and improved before translating any unnecessary parts.

5. Understand the nonfunctional requirements such as security and reliability. When translating, you may need to interface to different systems for these. For example, there is no concept of EJB in .NET, but for you to meet your reliability requirements it may be better to throw out a lot of .NET code that gives you the object pooling that EJB gives you by implementing your code as an EJB.

Translating the Data Classes

The previous sections described Item and ItemStatus classes, which were pretty simple, straightforward classes used to represent the Item as ordered and as shipped for the input and output to the Web service, respectively. On the surface, as they are pretty simple one might think that the C# code would probably work in Java without any change. But that would take another look. The .NET way of accessing properties uses get and set accessors. These keywords don't exist in Java, and to get and set a property, there is a private member variable that stores the property value and public functions that are used to get and set that value. Listing 16-6 provides an example of the translation of the Item class into Java.

Listing 16-6
Java *Item* Class

```
public class Item
{
  private String _productNumber;
  private int _Quantity;
  public String getProductNumber()
  {
    return _productNumber;
  }
  public void setProductNumber(String strIn)
  {
    _productNumber = strIn;
  }
  public int getQuantity()
  {
```

```
    return _Quantity;
}
public void setQuantity(int nQuantity)
{
    _Quantity = nQuantity;
}
}
```

The changes necessary to translate the ItemStatus classes are very similar.

When developing Web services, a top-down approach is recommended, and XSD files are the starting point for the generation of data structures. This example has already shown the .NET classes to represent these data structures and how to port these classes by translating their source code. However, if one prefers to take an XSD based approach, he or she can use ant and JAXB to generate what he/she needs. Listing 16-7 provides a snippet of an ant script that achieves this.

Listing 16-7
ant Script to Create Classes

```
<!-- Create stub classes from XSD-->
<target name="createJavaClassesFromSchema">
<echo message="--- creating java file of given schema-"/>
    <mkdir dir="${xsdclasses}"/>
    <exec executable="${wsdp.home}/jaxb/bin/xjc.bat">
    <arg value="-d"/>
    <arg value="${xsdclasses}"/>
    <arg value="${schema.dir}/PurchaseOrder.xsd"/>
    <arg value="${schema.dir}/ShippingNotice.xsd"/>
    </exec>
</target>
```

Translating the Web Service

The front door into a Web service in .NET is the ASMX file. When this file is accessed over HTTP, the .NET Framework looks for the underlying assembly, and if it doesn't exist, it compiles the source code and deploys the assembly to the correct location. It then acts as a proxy to the underlying class, specified in the Class= parameter.

```
<%@ WebService Language="c#"

Codebehind="WarehouseService.asmx.cs"
Class="CSharpWarehouse.WarehouseService" %>
```

In Java, Web services operate differently. However they still need a proxy developed. In this case the proxy is an interface that extends `java.rmi.remote` and is implemented by the underlying class. The code for that defines this interface to the `WarehouseCallback` service, as in Listing 16-8.

Listing 16-8
WarehouseCallback Interface

```
import java.rmi.RemoteException;
import java.rmi.Remote;
public interface WarehouseCallback extends Remote
{
public ItemStatus[] ShipGoods(Item[] ItemList)
throws RemoteException;
}
```

It is clear that there is no direct analogue, so when porting to Java an interface like this must be developed to each of your Web service classes, and the Web methods (in this case `ShipGoods`) must be prototyped in this interface.

Using Java Web Services Annotations

The JAX-RPC 2.0 early access [JAXRPC1] offers Web service annotations that are very similar to the C# annotations in the Java community. Along with JAX-RPC 2.0 Web services, the metadata that is submitted as part of the JSR181 will be available in Java EE5.0 [JSR181]. Listing 16-9 gives a brief example of how Java Web services can use these annotations:

Listing 16-9
JAX-RPC 2.0 Annotations

```
import javax.jws.WebService;
import javax.jws.WebMethod;
@WebService
public class WarehouseCallbackService
{
 @WebMethod
 public String getPOStatus(String poID)
 {
  // execute business logic here  return "Status";
 }
}
```

Translating the Underlying Web Service Class

Defining the Web Service Class

In C# the Web service class is one that derives from the `System.Web.Services.WebService` class. In Java there is no equivalent, so it's best to design a class to implement the interface class and `ServiceLifeCycle`, which enables the JAX-RPC runtime to manage the lifecycle of the objects built from this class and connect the application to external resources such as the database. The class can then be defined with

```
public class WarehouseCallbackImpl implements WarehouseCallback,
ServiceLifecycle
{
...
}
```

Importing the Required Libraries

The `ShipGoods` `Webmethod` was developed for the C#-based Web service connected to an SQL Server database to check the quantities of goods that were available to determine if they could be shipped or not. To do this, the following libraries had to be imported. In C# this is done with the `using` statement as shown here:

```
using System.Data;
using System.Data.SqlClient;
```

When accessing SQL Server from Java, the JDBC drivers for SQL Server first need to be obtained, which are available for download from Microsoft [MSDN1], and the JAR files containing the necessary classes placed into the `Classpath`. Remember also that these JARs need to be installed on the application server to get the application to run correctly. To use the SQL Server functionality in Java, import the libraries to the project as shown in Listing 16-10:

Listing 16-10

Java Class Library Imports

```
import com.microsoft.jdbc.*;
import com.microsoft.jdbcx.*;
import com.microsoft.util.*;
import java.sql.*;
```

Connecting to the Database

The C# code uses an object of type `SqlConnection` to manage the connection to the database. It is initialized with a connection string as shown here:

```
string connectionString = "Data
Source=(local);uid=sa;pwd=welcome;database=Warehouse";
SqlConnection con = new SqlConnection(connectionString);
```

The Java equivalent is quite similar. When using Java, the class that is used as the driver for SQL Server using the `Class.forName` command first must be registered. A Connection object (which is analogous to the .NET `SqlConnection` object) is then initialized by passing this `connection-string` to the `DriverManager` object.

Listing 16-11

JDBC Connection Setup

```
Class.forName
        ("com.microsoft.jdbc.sqlserver.SQLServerDriver");
String connectionString -
        "jdbc:microsoft:sqlserver://NYCMLMORO-
DEV2:1433;User=sa;Password=welcome;DatabaseName=Warehouse";
Connection conn =
        DriverManager.getConnection(connectionString);
```

Getting Data from the Database

In C# to execute a query against an SQL server database, a string is used that contains the desired SQL, and an `SqlCommand` object is created, passing this query and the current connection to its constructor. To read the results of the query, use an `SqlDataReader` object, to which is passed the results of the `ExecuteReader()` method of this command. The next step is then to iterate through the rows of results using the `SqlDataReader`.

```
SqlCommand com = new SqlCommand(sql,con);
SqlDataReader r = com.ExecuteReader();
```

Java is similar, but instead of an `SqlCommand`, a `Statement` object is used, which is quite comparable. The `Statement` is created on a specific connection. You use the `Statement` object to execute SQL and return a `ResultSet` using code like the following:

```
Statement com = conn.createStatement();
ResultSet r = com.executeQuery(sql);
```

Iteration through the `resultset` is done in a similar way to how it's done with `SqlDataReader` in C#. Do take note, however, that if porting a database, then the business logic residing within the database also needs to be ported. For example, if porting from a Microsoft SQL Server to another database, the database would need to be rearchitected on the new platform, moving all views, relationships, diagrams, stored procedures, and other necessary artifacts. This may not be a trivial task.

Putting It All Together

The full implementation class for the Web service in Java is shown in Listing 16-12. This can be compared to the C# listing earlier in this chapter. While it isn't drastically different and not too difficult to derive if one has a good understanding of both languages, it is certainly not a trivial task to derive this from the original C# code.

Listing 16-12
Java Web Service Source

```
import java.rmi.RemoteException;
import com.microsoft.jdbc.*;
import com.microsoft.jdbcx.*;
import com.microsoft.util.*;
import java.sql.*;

public class WarehouseCallbackImpl implements WarehouseCallback,
ServiceLifeCycle
{
  public ItemStatus[] ShipGoods(Item[] ItemList)
       throws RemoteException
  {
    ItemStatus[] collRtn = new ItemStatus[ItemList.length];
    try
    {
      Class.forName
```

continues

Listing 16-12 (continued)

```java
            ("com.microsoft.jdbc.sqlserver.SQLServerDriver");
      String connectionString = "jdbc:microsoft:sqlserver:";
      connectionString+="//SQLSERVER:1433;User=sa; ";
      connectionString+="Password=welcome; ";
      connectionString+="DatabaseName=Warehouse";
      Connection conn =
            DriverManager.getConnection(connectionString);
      String sql="";
      for(int lp=0;lp<ItemList.length;lp++)
      {
       collRtn[lp] = new ItemStatus();
       collRtn[lp].setProductNumber
                  (ItemList[lp].getProductNumber());
       sql="Select QuantityOnHand from WarehouseStock where";
       sql+= " ProductID='" +
            ItemList[lp].getProductNumber() + "'";
       Statement com = conn.createStatement();
       ResultSet r = com.executeQuery(sql);
       if(r.next())
       {
         int nQuantityonHand = r.getInt("QuantityOnHand");
         if(nQuantityonHand>ItemList[lp].getQuantity())
           collRtn[lp].setStatus(true);
         else
           collRtn[lp].setStatus(false);
       }
       else
       {
         collRtn[lp].setStatus(false);
       }
      }
    }
    catch(Exception e)
    {
      e.printStackTrace();
    }
    finally{
      try {
        com.close();
        r.close();
      } catch (Exception exe){}
    }
   return collRtn;
   }
   // Need to be overridden
   public void init(Object context)
   {
   }
   public void destroy()
   {
   }
}
```

Deploying the Web Service

The next logical step in porting a .NET to Java EE is deploying the application under a designated environment.

In Listing 16-13 are definitions of ant tasks for deploying and undeploying applications under Tomcat:

Listing 16-13
ant Script for Tomcat Deployment

```
<!-- Tomcat tasks, for deploy and undeploy targets" -->
<taskdef name="deploy"
    classname="org.apache.catalina.ant.DeployTask">
  <classpath refid="compile.classpath"/>
</taskdef>

<taskdef name="undeploy"
    classname="org.apache.catalina.ant.UndeployTask">
  <classpath refid="compile.classpath"/>
</taskdef>
```

The tasks in Listing 16-14 are used to deploy and undeploy a Web application under Tomcat:

Listing 16-14
ant Script for Tomcat Undeployment

```
<target name="deploy" depends="process-war"
  description="Deploys the processed WAR file">
  <deploy url="${tomcat.manager.url}"
      username="${tomcat.username}"
      password="${tomcat.password}"
      path="${tomcat.path}"
      war="file:${buildhome}/WarehouseService.war"/>
</target>

<target name="undeploy"
  description="Undeploys a Web application">
  <undeploy url="${tomcat.manager.url}"
      username="${tomcat.username}"
      password="${tomcat.password}"
      path="${tomcat.path}"/>
</target>
```

Tomcat doesn't provide a test harness for a Web service, but many other application servers do. Figure 16-5 shows the Web service from this section running on an Oracle Application Server.

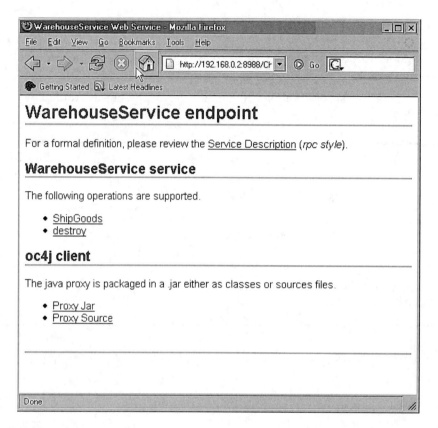

Figure 16-5
Warehouse service running on Java EE

Consuming the Web Service

When the C# Web service was consumed, Visual Studio.NET was used to create a proxy class that could then be used within a client application, be it an ASP.NET page or a Windows Form to consume the Web service. Most Java IDEs offer the same functionality—to create a Java Proxy class to the Web service based on its WSDL. Alternatively the WSDL2Java tool [Axis1] from Apache Axis can be used to create this from the command line. This proxy class can then become the basis for communications with the Web service on a servlet, a JSP, or an applet. The .NET client is then ported to the appropriate Java Client (Windows Form to Applet or Application, Web Form to JSP, and so on).

Next Steps

While porting of applications from .NET to Java EE has many advantages, it is a lot of work to go through the source code and translate it line by line to the appropriate Java equivalents. Despite the similarities between the two languages on the surface, this example has demonstrated that a relatively simple set of routines such as the ones used here to query a database and populate an array based on the results of that query still require extensive translation. More complicated routines and methods likely require more extensive changes—or indeed complete rewrites. In addition, when coming from a .NET environment, where there is no concept of Java EE, there is no direct translation to allow a build of EJBs that are managed by the container, helping to maximize investment in that container. To take advantage of these, the system might need to be rearchitected, negatively impacting the amount of source code that requires a straight translation. In addition deployment is more of a challenge and requires a thorough understanding if the goal is to do any porting of C# code to Java. Ultimately, it's important to weigh all these factors to adequately scope out the porting effort. While the work to do so is considerable, the advantages that the platform offers are generally worth the investment.

Porting Using Mainsoft's Visual MainWin for Java EE

Mainsoft has a solution for porting applications from C# to Java EE called Visual MainWin for Java EE. It is a cross compiler plug-in for Visual Studio.NET that allows the user to take C# code and compile it into Java bytecode for deployment on a Java platform. To understand how it does this, one must first understand, from a high level, the similarities between the .NET architecture and the Java EE architecture.

Whenever an application is built in .NET using C#, VB.NET, or any of the other languages that .NET supports, the compilation process generates a language called Microsoft Intermediate Language (MSIL), which normalizes the high-level language. In other words, if the same functionality is developed in C# or VB.NET and compiled, the MSIL for the two will be the same. MSIL is a CPU-independent language, which is converted into CPU-specific language at runtime by the .NET runtime using Just-in-Time (JIT) compilation. This is very similar to the Java concept of generating Java bytecode from source code, which in turn is executed by the Java Virtual Machine.

Visual MainWin for Java EE, at compile time in Visual Studio.NET, translates the MSIL into Java Bytecode. This bytecode can then be JAR'ed or WAR'ed up and deployed on an application server. When Visual MainWin for Java EE is installed, the desired application server must be specified (it presently supports WebLogic 8.1, WebSphere 5.1, JBoss, and Tomcat), and the process of compilation and cross compilation will deploy the application to its destination.

To support the .NET Framework, Mainsoft has provided a number of the .NET class libraries, based on the Mono project, as Java implementations, and the supporting JAR files can be installed on the application server. These namespaces are

- System.Web
- System.Web.Services
- System.Data
- System.XML
- System
- Mscorlib
- Microsoft.VisualBasic

This creates a unifed architecture for running .NET and Java EE applications within the same virtual machine. For more on this unifed architecture, see Chapter 15, "Managing Java EE .NET Interoperability Applications."

Translating the WS-I Scenario

If an application uses only these class libraries, it's not necessary to install any further dependencies. In following along with the application that was built in this chapter, porting to Java didn't present a challenge, based on the WSI SCM sample application.

Indeed, when using Visual MainWin for Java EE, an option is available upon right-clicking the solution in the Visual Studio.NET solution explorer to "Generate Java EE Project." This invokes the Java EE Project Wizard (Figure 16-6).

This wizard creates a Visual Studio workspace for containing the Java references to the converted .NET namespaces and sets up the properties for deployment to the application server, which is specified on the next step of the Wizard (refer to Figure 16-7). Note that this Figure shows that only Tomcat is available as an option. If the machine being used has BEA WebLogic or IBM WebSphere installed, they will show up also.

Figure 16-6
Visual MainWin Java EE Wizard

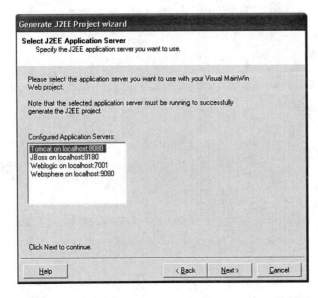

Figure 16-7
Java EE Application Server selection

Once the Wizard is complete, a new Visual Studio workspace is opened that contains the existing C# code; only now it is rebounded at compile time to the application server that was specified. In many cases the code can even be debugged as it runs on the application server using the Visual Studio debugger.

If the example code from this chapter is used and the wizard used step by step to create a Java EE application from it, it will execute without warning, without error, and most importantly without *modification*! Figure 16-8 shows the resulting Web service running on its test interface.

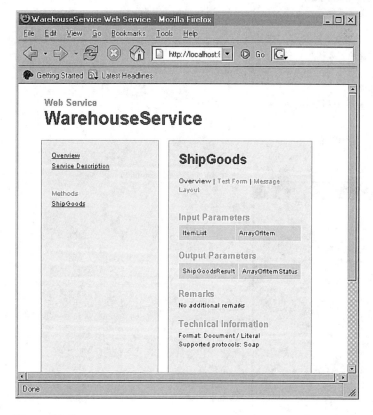

Figure 16-8
Warehouse Service running on Java EE with Visual MainWin test harness

Going Beyond the WS-I Scenario

Of course, not all scenarios are as straightforward as this one is to port. However, the tool is a full extension to Visual Studio.NET so a full debugging facility as well as the ability to manage references to Java Libraries and EJBs is provided.

As an example, consider the Retailer aspect of this scenario.

A simple Web application to consume the Warehouse Web service can be built in Visual Studio.NET as a Java EE project using Visual Mainwin for Java EE. Figure 16-9 shows this in the Visual Studio page designer. If the developer is familiar with Visual Studio.NET, he or she will notice that nothing has changed, and he or she can design the app without any changes to the methods of work even though it's going to run on Java EE.

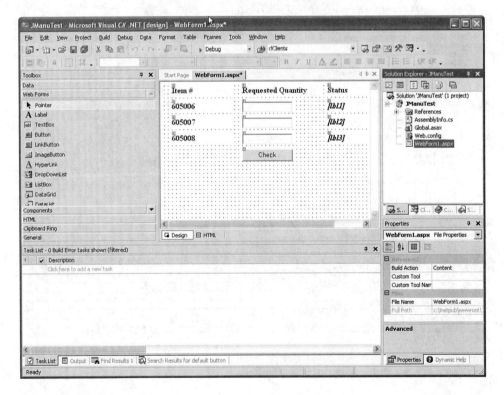

Figure 16-9
Visual MainWin for Java EE in Visual Studio

This application has a Web reference to the Web service that was built earlier, which is running on the Java EE platform. Visual Studio.NET generates the proxy to the Web service and automatically generates asynchronous stubs, used by the Web service consumer.

Figure 16-10 shows the application running on Java EE using the Visual Studio.NET debugger to capture the asynchronous callback from the Web service.

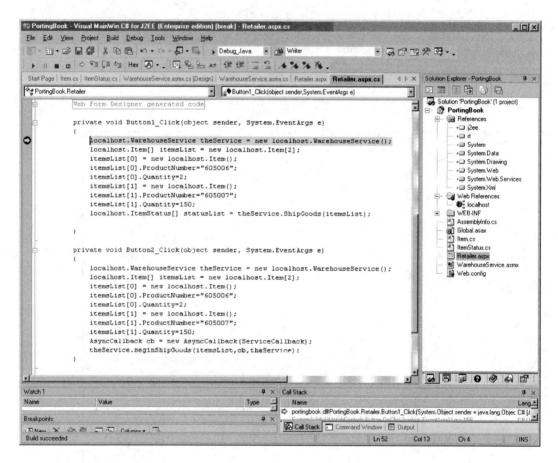

Figure 16-10
Using Visual MainWin to debug a Web application running on Tomcat

This provides a useful alternative to straight porting because many of the .NET-specific features can be kept on the source-level of the application (such as `ViewState` and Asynchronous Web services callbacks), and yet run and debug them on Java EE. In addition to this, the namespaces that it supports, as outlined earlier, reduce the need to port a number of dependencies.

For example, consider the `System.Data` namespace. The implication of this is that the ADO.NET class libraries for accessing SQL Server and Oracle are already available, and no extra JDBC drivers are required when something is cross-compiled. If any of the other databases are used, then a number of options are available. Should the database driver for ADO.NET be open source (as is the case with MySQL), this can simply be cross-compiled with the rest of the code. For dependencies that do no have .NET source code available, the environment allows the developer to import Java or EJB references and code to them—and the code will be ported. In this case, deployment needs to be able to talk to those references too, and one would use the administrative tools on the application server to set that up.

Finally, if there are already assets deployed on Java, such as JARs of class libraries or Enterprise Java Beans, references can be added to them to consume them from the Visual Studio.NET-developed Java applications, [MORO1].

If the goal is migrating applications from .NET to Java, the Visual MainWin significantly simplifies the migration process.

Summary

There are a number of good reasons to consider porting from a .NET-based environment to a Java EE-based one, particularly in the light of the growth of Linux and service-oriented applications. These reasons include cost drivers, thanks to Linux as well as open source application platforms such as JBoss; security considerations for applications on IIS and Windows; and scalability and reliability considerations—factors that Java EE can give "off the shelf" without requiring manual coding. This chapter looked at an example module from the WS-I SCM example and at the implications of porting it from a C#/.NET to a Java/Java EE implementation. This example covered a broad area of technologies, including XML, databases and Web services. The likely issues to be faced when porting code were explored, and the specific issues when porting the example code were outlined. In addition, the alternative, a post-compile harmonization by translating the .NET MSIL to Java Bytecode using a commercial tool, Visual MainWin for Java EE, was also explored.

The conclusions that can be drawn from this are many. Despite the similarity of their language syntax, Java and C# (the most widely used .NET language) are dissimilar enough to make porting a project from one to the other a difficult task. This is because language is only the surface layer. The class libraries that a framework supports and the underlying architecture that runs applications built on that framework are more important factors to consider when translating from one to the other. In this case, the frameworks are drastically different, and as a result, the underlying architecture is also fundamentally different, leading to complexities when porting. It is up to the architects and owners of the application to decide whether these costs are worth it and to factor those costs into the overall effort of moving platforms.

In addition, there are a number of challenges that development management faces when building on dual platforms, not the least of which is having an acceptable pool of development skills that will allow both platforms to be sufficiently covered. The solution where a single skill set can be spread across both platforms to ease migration and support is a very desirable one, and it is in this case that the Visual MainWin for Java EE toolkit can really assist one's efforts. As it manages the porting of code in the post-compile stage, it means that your developers can concentrate on developing with one technology (in this case C# on .NET), and deployment can be on either platform without worrying about difficult migration factors. In a survey of their customer base, Mainsoft (producers of Visual MainWin) found that the average amount of code changes necessary to get the average C#/.NET application to run on Java EE was around 1 percent of the overall code.

On the whole, it can be understood that porting from a .NET to a Java EE environment can be a very valuable exercise, depending on the needs of the company and the architecture, but it isn't without its inherent expense. The decision comes down to the architects and the technologists, if there is porting across platforms, and whether to do it by rewriting the source code or by trusting in a cross compiler that handles it alone. Each has its own intrinsic costs, and it is worth thoroughly investigating the impact of both before a decision is made.

References

[AXIS1] WSDL2Java: Building stubs, skeletons and data types from WSDL. http://ws.apache.org/axis/java/userguide.html#WSDL2JavaBuildingStubsSkeletonsAndDataTypesFromWSDL

[JAXRPC1] JAX-RPC Early Access Users Guide. https://jax-rpc.dev.java.net/jaxrpc20-ea/docs/UsersGuide.html

[JSR181] Java Community Process JSR181. http://jcp.org/en/jsr/detail?id=181

[MORO1] Laurence Moroney: EJB's For Everyone.
http://www.devx.com/dotnet/Article/20866/0

[MSDN1] Microsoft SQL Server 2000 Support for JDBC.
http://www.microsoft.com/downloads/details.aspx?FamilyID=9f1874b6-f8e1
4bd6-947c-0fc5bf05bf71&displaylang=en

[SOLARIS1] What's inside Solaris 10.
http://www.sun.com/software/solaris/inside.jsp

[WSI-1] WS-I Deliverables.
http://www.ws-i.org/deliverables/workinggroup.aspx?wg=sampleapps

[WSI2] WS-I WSDL File for Warehouse.
http://www.ws-i.org/SampleApplications/SupplyChainManagement/2002-
08/Warehouse.wsdl

Index

Java™

BLAZE the TRAIL to
BE THE FIRST

Check out Sun Microsystems Press Special offers and take advantage of Sun product, technology, training, and service discounts today!

To see the latest promotions for Java™ technology developers, go to *sun.com/javadev_bookpromo* and check back as new offers will be updated frequently.

Offers available to qualified customers in the USA and Canada